Computer and Network Professional's Certification Guide

J. Scott Christianson
Ava Fajen

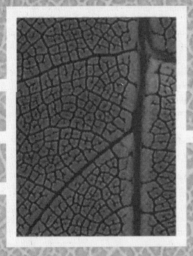

San Francisco • Paris • Düsseldorf • Soest • London

Associate Publisher: Guy Hart-Davis
Contracts and Licensing Manager: Kristine O'Callaghan
Acquisitions & Developmental Editor: Neil Edde
Editor: Linda Stephenson
Project Editor: Rebecca Rider
Book Designer: Bill Gibson
Electronic Publishing Specialist: Adrian Woolhouse
Project Team Leader: Teresa Trego
Proofreader(s): Laurie Stewart, Theresa Mori
Indexer: Matthew Spence
Cover Designer: Archer Design
Cover Illustrator/Photographer: The Image Bank

Library of Congress Card Number: 99-62999
ISBN: 0-7821-2545-X

Manufactured in the United States of America

10 9 8 7 6 5 4 3 2 1

Acknowledgments

Sybex did an excellent job of guiding us through the process of writing this book. Special thanks go to Rebecca Rider and Linda Stephenson for their advice and patience. We would also like to thank Guy Hart-Davis, Neil Edde, and Kristine O'Callaghan, and our production team of Teresa Trego and Adrian Woolhouse for helping to make this book a reality.

We would not have been able to complete this book without the help of numerous individuals and companies who provided and verified information about their certification programs, including:

Laura Adams (IBM), Doug Bastianelli (CompTIA), Kim Beahen (Cognos Incorporated), Jay Bender (Disaster Recovery Institute International), Judi Bernstein (Banyan), Anita Booker (Silicon Graphics), Norma Brown (Silicon Graphics), Kathy Buxton (Novell), Jennifer Cress (Help Desk 2000), Jean Caldwell (BICSI), Peter Childers (Red Hat Software), Tammy Christensen (Baan), Toby Cobrin (Xplor International), Sadonna Cody (Silicon Graphics), Stan Daneman (SAP), Bill Davies (Newbridge Networks Corporation), Robi Detwiler (CyberTech Institute, Inc.), Guy Di Bianca (Xylan), Scott Edwards (Software Publisher's Association), John Epeneter (Vinca), Colin Evans (International Function Point Users Group), John Forsythe (PCDOCS/Fulcrum), Denise Foth (Quality Assurance Institute), Alan Frost (CyberTech Institute, Inc.), Frances Garcia (3Com), Ana Rada George (Cisco Systems, Inc.), Rosemary Good (Sybase), Chris Greenslade (The Open Group), Carol Guzzo (Citrix), Melanie Harper (Compaq Computer Corporation), Sally Harthun (American Society for Quality), Greg Hartle (Microsoft), Angela Heitmeyer (IBM Netfinity/TechConnect), Ginny Hines (Lotus), Joanne Hodge (SAP), Linda Kennedy (Lotus), Bob Kile (National Association of Communication System Engineers), Mark Klingensmith (Hewlett-Packard Company), Richard Koenig (International Information Systems Security Certification Consortium), Tina Koyama (Microsoft), Jennifer Kress (Help Desk 2000), Judith Lauter (The Chauncey Group), Jeffrey Little (CyberTech Institute, Inc.), Kirsten Ludwig (AutoDesk), Tammy McBride (SCO), Jennifer Mastropoalo (Oracle), Stephanie Meek

(Checkpoint), Uday Om Pabrai (Prosofttraining.com), Stevie Ritch (Quality Assurance Institute), Tim Rondeau (Nortel Networks), Stan Rosen (CNX Consortium), Barbara Sandro (Compaq), Allan Scher (IBM Netfinity/TechConnect), Mike Serpe (Informix), Martin Shih (Inprise), Merris Sinha (Sybase), Nancy Smith (Compaq Computer Corporation), Bill Sodeman (Prosofttraining.com), Susie Spencer (Novell), Brant Stevens (Sybase), Charles Stevenson (Centura Software Corporation), Lisa Taylor (Vinca), Terry Trsar (Information Systems Audit and Control Association), Michelle Vahlkamp (CompTIA), Fiaaz Walji (Corel), Conery Wilbanks (Quality Assurance Institute), Steve Willett (Microsoft), Ginny Williams (Pine Mountain Group), and Jay Wilson (Callware Technologies, Inc.)

Table of Contents

Introduction

In the computer and networking fields, certification programs have become the roadmaps that many people use to chart their careers. The widespread popularity of professional certification in the computer industry began with Novell and Microsoft in the late 1980s and early 1990s. Today, nearly every major hardware and software manufacturer offers, or shortly will offer, a certification program. The sheer number of certification programs available has left both computer professionals and employers confused about the significance and value of these various certifications. Although there are literally hundreds of books on the market to help you study for specific vendor-based certification exams, this book is the only up-to-date, comprehensive guide that presents information on all the most important computing and networking certifications.

Your Comprehensive Certification Resource

This book provides the latest information on over 300 computer and networking certification titles authored by more than 60 companies and organizations. Our first goal in writing this book is to provide a much-needed guide to certification for professionals in the computing and networking fields, as well as for those wishing to enter these fields. At the same time, this book is intended to help employers and personnel departments understand the meaning and value of particular certifications. Finally, this book provides career planning and placement centers with an up-to-date resource on certification programs that can help them advise their clients on computer and networking career paths.

As you may already know, getting reliable, understandable information about current certification programs is not always easy. Often a company's Web site only lists partial or out-of-date information on their certification programs. In preparing this book, we have researched the current computer and networking certification programs—on the Web, in the literature, by phone, and by fax—to make sure that our information is complete and up-to-date. Some of the information included in this guide cannot be found on the Web or even in company literature.

This book makes the world of certification programs easy to understand. Instead of clustering all the programs offered by a particular vendor or organization together, we have classified the programs into logical groupings, such as "Network Management Certifications" (Chapter 10) and "Internet Certifications" (Chapter 13). As a result, programs that address similar topics are presented together so you can easily compare and contrast them. We provide information on the different programs in a standard organizational format so you can easily understand what is available and decide which certifications may be right for you.

We have provided information on the most relevant and credible certification programs available today. If a certification has been omitted, it may have been left out for one of several reasons. Some certification programs are only designed to be used internally within a company. For example, Motorola has several certification programs for its employees that are not available to the general public. You may find several certification programs advertised on the Web whose exams are not actually available yet. We included only those programs that are actually up and running. Finally, some programs may not really certify an individual's ability or training. For example, a certification may simply "certify" that you attended a conference or paid membership to an organization. Such a certification is not an assessment of knowledge or abilities; these have been omitted as well.

Why Become Certified?

The primary reason for the popularity of professional certification is that it provides an up-to-date, performance-based assessment of a person's knowledge and skills in a particular area. Traditional credentials, such as a university degree, offer a measure of the number of hours spent sitting in a classroom, but may provide little indication of an individual's current job-related skills. In addition, because of its targeted instruction and frequent updating of content, certification is the only credentialing method that can begin to keep pace with the rapid changes in the computing and networking industry. Certification offers job-related benefits to both employer and employee: the employer knows what a person can do, and an employee can demonstrate his or her computer and networking knowledge and skills without investing the money and time it takes to gain a university degree.

Computer and networking professionals are in demand across the employment spectrum, from business and industry to government and education. And the current high level of demand for information technology professionals—whether highly experienced or newly certified—is expected to continue and even accelerate in the years to come. This introduction outlines some of the many benefits that certification can offer you as a computer or networking professional, including jobs, promotions, professional credibility, and financial rewards. A number of these benefits offer advantages for employers and customers as well.

Open Information Technology Job Market

The present shortage of information technology workers in the United States has been well documented. What's more, estimates of the extent of this shortage are quickly being revised upward. For example, in February 1997, the Information Technology Association of America (ITAA) had estimated that 190,000 such positions were unfilled; by January of 1998, ITAA's second annual workforce study reported a shortage of 346,000 individuals—including programmers, systems analysts, and computer engineers—in the U.S. information technology work force.

Similarly, estimates of the number of information technology personnel that will be needed in the future have recently been revised upward. In 1997, the federal Office of Technology Policy (OTP) warned that the United States was not keeping up with the demand for new information technology workers and predicted that an average of 95,000 new jobs would open in the field annually; by 1998 an updated OTP report already had been issued, projecting a need for almost 140,000 information technology workers each year until the year 2006.

Meanwhile, the number of college students graduating with bachelor's degrees in computer science dropped from a peak of 41,889 per year in 1986 to 24,200 per year in 1994, a decrease of 42 percent (*Digest of Education Statistics*, Department of Education, 1996). Universities are clearly not training the numbers of information technology workers that will be needed to meet the demands of the marketplace.

It is anticipated that the shortage of information technology workers will have broad-ranging effects, not just in the computer industry, but in business and industry in general, as well as in education and the government. The ITAA and OTP reports suggest that a competent workforce skilled in information technology is crucial to the nation's economy. The ITAA urges industry, education, government, and professional associations to undertake a collaborative effort to head off this shortage. More and more, the information industry is turning to certification programs to fill the gap.

Benefits for Individuals

Many people pursue computer and networking certifications because they expect to receive increased salaries, promotions, or job offers. Evidence does indicate that having the right certification at the right time can have excellent salary and promotion potential. Magazines are full of stories about newly certified individuals with little or no experience who have snagged high-paying jobs.

But certification offers other benefits as well. It provides a portable credential that validates your knowledge and abilities, and it shows others that you are willing to do what it takes to keep your knowledge and skills current. As a result, certification improves your marketability and increases your options, whether you seek regular employment or want to promote your skills and abilities as an independent contractor.

Although the effort and cost involved in attaining some certifications is considerable, it is generally much less than the time and expense involved in obtaining a college degree. And, in many situations, an employer will carry the financial burden for certification training and testing. In addition, a number of certification programs can help you accumulate college credit while you are earning a certification.

Increased Salary

A number of surveys have documented the financial benefits of certification. For example, average 1998 salaries were $77,700 for Microsoft Certified Trainers (MCTs) and $67,600 for Microsoft Certified Systems Engineers (MCSEs), according to Linda Briggs's third annual salary survey in *Microsoft Certified Professional Magazine* (1998). These salaries were for persons with an average total of five and a half years of experience in information technology (for more information on the MCP, MCSE, and MCT certification programs, see Chapters 5, 9, and 15, respectively). Survey results also indicated that 58 percent of Microsoft-certified respondents believed that their certifications had resulted in salary increases. Briggs estimated that earning an MCSE credential could add approximately $11,000 per year to a previously uncertified individual's salary.

Jobs and Promotions

Certification provides employers with objective evidence that you have a defined set of skills and abilities. Job-seekers and independent contractors alike find that having the right certification can get them preference in the hiring process. Certification can open doors for individuals who have the initiative to seek out new knowledge and skills, but have limited on-the-job experience. Certification can also help experienced computer and networking professionals move up within their current organizations or get good job offers elsewhere. In Linda Briggs's survey, 42 percent of Microsoft-certified respondents received a promotion as a result of attaining certification. Some businesses have actually incorporated vendor certification programs into their internal company certification programs.

Improved Professional Credibility

Potential employers or clients respond well when a computing or networking professional can offer clear evidence of having the skills needed to get the job done. Having relevant, current certifications on your resume gives you an important advantage in this regard; college degrees or years of experience on the resume may not tell an employer whether you have the specific abilities they seek.

A 1995 evaluation of the Microsoft Certified Systems Engineer credential found that more than 90 percent of MCSEs surveyed felt that obtaining certification was useful in helping them improve their professional credibility ("Evaluation of the Microsoft Systems Engineer Certification," a report by the Applied Experimental Psychology Group at SIU-Carbondale in conjunction with Applied Research Consultants, July 1995).

College Credit

Certification programs have increasingly incorporated more sophisticated assessment methods to measure and certify learning and competency. A number of certification programs have established a level of quality and reliability that has made them eligible to provide college credit to their participants. For example, it is possible to obtain college credit for Learning Tree International certifications or courses. The American Council of Education (ACE) in Washington, D.C., has determined college course equivalencies for Learning Tree International's courses and certifications. As a general rule, ACE will recommend two college credit hours for each four-day Learning Tree course. The ICCP Certified Computing Professional exams also have been approved by ACE for college credit. Approximately 1,500 colleges and universities in the United States will accept ACE recommendations for college credit.

Other opportunities for getting college credit exist as well. A number of community and technical colleges in the United States offer college credit for courses that are part of the Microsoft curriculum. Vendors have partnered with colleges and universities in some interesting ways. For example, at North Carolina's High Point University, computer information system majors can graduate with both a degree and certification in Visual Basic, Windows NT, and Microsoft Office. Lord Fairfax Community College in Virginia offers a popular 15-credit Network Engineer Certificate Program that gives students hands-on experience in installing and configuring servers and workstations, implementing network security, and planning for disaster recovery. At Seattle Pacific University in Washington, the Microsoft Certified Engineer curriculum implemented in 1996 attempts to ensure the quality of its graduates by incorporating an experience requirement—students must have either a degree or industry experience to be admitted to the program. If you are interested in college credit, look for similar opportunities in your area.

Benefits for Employers

In the world of computers and networking, both hardware and software change quickly. Technologies and programs that are cutting edge this year may be considered outdated by next year. In this environment of fast-paced change, traditional resume credentials may not provide an employer much information about whether an individual has up-to-date knowledge and skills. How can an employer know whether a prospective employee will be competent to use, implement, or support the most current technologies and programs? For many employers today, certification is the answer.

Hiring

Many employers and human resources managers don't have the information technology background needed to quickly assess an individual's abilities by reading a resume. In addition, many hiring managers find that a person's years of computer-related experience are not always an indication that an individual has the specific technical knowledge that is needed. For these reasons, employers may view certification as an objective measure for evaluating the abilities of applicants. If an employer needs someone to set up a system for secure, online commerce, for example, he or she needs to know that a potential hire or independent consultant has some pretty specific skills. A variety of certifications that provide evidence of these skills are now available (see Chapter 13, "Internet Certifications," and Chapter 14, "Computer and Network Security Certifications," for information on relevant certification programs).

While certification may not guarantee that an individual knows all there is to know about a certain piece of hardware or software, it does provide information that employers value. It indicates that a person has at least a basic knowledge of a product—a core level of knowledge that can be the foundation for additional learning. It indicates that an individual is interested in learning about new technologies or products and maintaining up-to-date skills. And it can—depending on the comprehensiveness and rigor of the certification program—indicate an advanced level of knowledge and skill with a particular system, or even indicate ability to manage complex, heterogeneous company networks.

On-the-Job Effectiveness

Certifications help employers identify individuals with proven knowledge and skill levels. As we have noted, this is certainly important in hiring. But many employers are also encouraging their current employees to get certified. Companies need to have individuals with specific skills on staff, and many have found that certification programs offer the verifiable skills and knowledge their employees need. In addition, employers who send staff for training want to see concrete results. Certification programs that involve performance-based testing give employers independently verified results that demonstrate the value of their training investments.

Research indicates that certification increases employee productivity and effectiveness. A 1995 study by Dataquest, Inc. reported that "managers feel that certified employees provide higher levels of service, learn new technologies faster, and are generally more productive" (Bob Filipczak, "Certification!" *Training* magazine, August 1995). Other studies confirm these results. A 1996 survey of managers who supervise individuals with the Microsoft Certified Solution Developer credential found that managers considered their certified employees to have a significantly higher level of competence on those tasks that were key to their job effectiveness than did non-certified employees under their supervision ("The Value of Certification for Solution Developers," a report by the Applied Experimental Psychology Group at SIU-Carbondale, August 1996).

In 1995, IDC Consulting, a Massachusetts research firm, surveyed managers on the benefits of certification. They found that managers felt certification gave their employees a reliable level of skill and expertise. Managers said that with certified information technology professionals on staff, a company could operate a more complex and decentralized information technology environment without hiring additional employees. Further, the IDC survey reported that managers found the average payback time for certification costs was only nine months. Having certified employees resulted in increased network availability and more effective technical support. These improvements were judged to be worth approximately $14,000 per year to the company per trained employee ("Benefits and Productivity Gains Realized Through IT Certification," IDC Report 1995).

Benefits to Customers and Clients

Hiring and supporting certified employees gives resellers and service firms a competitive advantage. In the current market, having a staff that holds respected certifications in a variety of relevant computing and networking technologies can be crucial to getting clients. When companies outsource their information technology management needs, they expect a service provider to have employees with in-depth knowledge and proven competency with a variety of systems. Service firms with certified employees can provide clients with high-quality, consistent services; many organizations know this and hire only contractors who offer certified staff.

Even companies that are not specifically in the business of providing information technology services to others are likely to find that they can provide higher quality service to their customers by having certified employees on staff. Certification improves user support, whether for internal or external purposes. Employees with certified technical skills can provide effective support for other employees and facilitate quick resolution of problems that impede customer service.

Employees Value Career Growth Opportunities

In today's volatile business environment, companies are unable to guarantee their employees lifetime job security and generous pension plans. Some companies that want to keep their employees happy have begun offering them meaningful career development opportunities instead. Some employers are fearful that paying for training and certification will help employees find better jobs outside their company. Such employers, however, may find themselves losing out anyway, as their employees move away to companies that do support their employees in maintaining up-to-date, marketable credentials.

At the same time that career growth increases employees' job capabilities and enhances their marketability, it can also lead to higher morale and job commitment. Employees appreciate the opportunity to maintain current job skills. As a result, employers that support their employees in obtaining certification may see improved employee morale and job satisfaction at the same time as the company benefits from improved productivity and customer service.

Criticisms of Certification

Certification is not without its detractors. Some critics assert that a single multiple-choice test can't tell you whether a person can handle real-world problems using a particular product. It is true that not all certification programs involve hands-on, performance-based testing. Many programs do, however, and the general trend is to move certification programs in that direction. Furthermore, the multiple-choice tests that vendors use are typically designed—by teams of practicing information technology professionals and skilled prometricians (professionals in testing and measurement)—to assess knowledge and abilities as they will be needed in real-world applications.

In addition, some critics have observed that there are certification programs available that do not actually require either any experience or any testing. Such programs are not covered in this book. It is true that certification programs vary widely in their level of difficulty. Some programs don't offer much challenge, while others—such as

Cisco's CCIE program or Sun's Java Developer certification—have gained notoriety for their difficulty. In addition, some of the more rigorous certification programs require documentation of a specified number of months or years of relevant on-the-job experience as a prerequisite to even entering the program.

Other critics of vendor-based certification assert that the vendors are the primary beneficiaries of certification programs because they generate vendor income, create product loyalty, and improve customer satisfaction (because the availability of certified personnel gives customers improved access to qualified product support). While some of this skepticism is undoubtedly justified, those who reject certification outright because it benefits vendors will miss out on the many benefits that certification offers to individuals, employers, and customers. Further, many of the criticisms leveled against vendor-based certification programs are not applicable to organization- or association-based programs, which tend to offer substantive, comprehensive, standards-based training at a reasonable cost.

Other detractors remind us that good customer service requires more than technical skill. There is an important lesson here as well. Without a doubt, the individuals who reap the most success in the information technology field are those who combine high levels of product-related skill and knowledge with strong interpersonal skills.

Managing Certification Programs: Vendor Cooperation Benefits Everyone

Mike Serpe, Chairman, CEdMA Certification Task Force

While the competition between computer and networking vendors can be intense, managers of computer-related education and certification programs do find it beneficial to communicate with each other. One vehicle for this communication is the Computer Education Management Association (CEdMA), a worldwide nonprofit organizationfor information technology education and certification managers. CEdMA holds a wide variety of meetings and conferences for its membership and provides a unique sharing environment

continued on the next page

for program managers to exchange insights and experiences. A large number of the world's most influential computer and information technology product companies are active members of CEdMA.

Within CEdMA, there are several task forces that emphasize specific areas of interest. One of these, the CEdMA Certification Task Force, is specifically designed around the needs of certification program and testing management. This task force promotes communication in several ways. First, it holds monthly conference calls. Each call is run as an open forum, but is focused on one particular topic or hot issue. An average of   20 managers and executives from prominent information technology product corporations around the world participate in each call. Participants receive discussion topics in advance and prepare to either ask questions or share insights on that particular topic with the rest of the Task Force. In addition, the task force meets twice annually at CEdMA conferences, and holds seminars at other information technology education conferences such as Tech Learn, ITTA, and others. The CEdMA Certification Task Force also hosts an electronic newsgroup that allows members to continue discussions from meetings or share information and findings relevant to certification.

CEdMA provides a unique, secure, confidential environment, free of vendor interests and competition. All information discussed in CEdMA forums is considered highly classified and is not available to outsiders. If you are interested in CEdMA, check out the Web site at (`www.cedma.org`).

You can also find out more by contacting Mike Serpe, CEdMA Certification Task Force Chairman, at `mserpe@informix.com`. Originally from New York City, Mike is now based in San Francisco as the Worldwide Manager of the Informix Software Certified Professional Program. Mike has wide experience in computer education, training, and certification programs, and also teaches high performance driving and racing with vintage Porsche racing cars.

How to Use This Book

The first part of this book, entitled "Preparing for and Taking Certification Tests," provides general information and ideas on resources and strategies to use when preparing to take certification tests. Chapter 1, "Instructor-Led Training," discusses the value of instructor-led courses for test preparation, while Chapter 2, "Self-Study for Certification," covers developing a self-study program. Chapter 3, "Taking Your Test," which is the final chapter in the first section, provides valuable information and tips for taking certification tests.

The second part of the book, "Certification Programs and Requirements," consists of 14 chapters that describe the certification programs, organized according to discipline. We have ordered these subject-based chapters in a progression that begins with the most basic aspects of computing (computing hardware and operating systems) and proceeds to the more abstract or higher levels of computing and networking (Internet/intranets and network management). The certification programs are organized into the following chapters:

- Chapter 4: Hardware Certifications

- Chapter 5: Operating Systems Certifications

- Chapter 6: Software Certifications

- Chapter 7: Programming Certifications

- Chapter 8: Networking Hardware Certifications

- Chapter 9: Network Operating Systems Certifications

- Chapter 10: Network Management Certifications

- Chapter 11: Telecommunications Certifications

- Chapter 12: Client/Server and Database System Certifications

- Chapter 13: Internet Certifications

- Chapter 14: Computer and Network Security Certifications

- Chapter 15: Instructor and Trainer Certifications

- Chapter 16: Other Vendor-Based Certifications

- Chapter 17: Organization-Based Certifications

Each chapter follows the same basic motif in presenting information on a set of certification programs. Within a chapter, certification programs are listed in alphabetical order by the name of the certifying entity—a vendor, organization, or consortium. Within each subsection of the chapter you will find general information about the certifying company or organization, details about the certification program's recertification or maintenance requirements, and the benefits provided to certified individuals. This will be followed by one or more sections that describe each of the certification programs offered by that vendor that are relevant to the chapter's topic. Each description of an individual certification program starts with an overview of the program, and then includes a standardized set of headings (as listed below) with information that will answer your questions on the details of that certification program.

Who Needs It

Is this certification relevant to you and your career goals?

Requirements for Certification

What do you have to do to attain this certification? What tests, courses, or other requirements must be met?

Administrator

Who is responsible for administering tests or giving courses? How do you contact them?

Fee

What are the costs associated with the required tests or courses?

Format

What is the length and format of any required tests?

Resources

How can you get more information on this certification program? What study guides, sample tests, or other preparatory materials are available?

Finally, the book provides two appendices. Appendix A provides a listing of retired and renamed certification programs for your reference, and Appendix B provides information on how to access the book's Certification Update Web site.

Keeping Updated

It can be difficult to keep up with the changes in various certification programs. Company mergers, changes in product lines and management, and a number of other variables cause some companies to rapidly change, add, or delete specific certifications within their certification programs. In order to make sure that you are apprised of the latest changes to these certification programs, we have set up the Certification Update Web site (http://www.certification-update.com) as a supplement to this book. This companion Web site provides information on new certifications and changes to existing certifications. You will find links to information on the certifications listed in this guide and a section on job-hunting resources for the computer and networking professional. Several vendors plan to contact us directly before the release of new certifications and tests; by accessing the Web site, you will have first access to this information.

NOTE   We have made every effort to ensure that the information in this book is complete and up-to-date at the time of release. Because of the dynamic nature of the certification field, however, the text may contain minor inaccuracies. Once you have selected a particular certification to pursue, we recommend you check the Certification Update Web site or contact the sponsoring vendor or organization to confirm details, particularly costs. Please note that unless otherwise indicated, telephone numbers and exam fees apply to the United States.

Importance of Recertification

An issue that will take on increasing importance over time is the need for recertification. Many certification programs are brand new, or less than a year or two old, while others have been revamped recently. But any certification will have a limited useful life.

Many certification programs are tied to specific versions of certain products. An individual who wants to have current credentials will need to obtain certification on new versions as they are released. Programs that do offer recertification options vary widely in the effort required for maintaining certification. Some require testing or extensive continuing education coursework; in other programs, the effort needed to maintain certification is minimal.

It's important to remember that, in the field of information technology, your need to seek new education opportunities will be ongoing. Because skills and knowledge can become outdated more quickly today than ever before, the most successful computer and networking professionals are those who commit themselves to lifelong learning. In addition, it will be important to periodically assess whether you want to adhere to the same certification path you have been following or whether it's time to target different technologies or product lines instead. An eagerness to learn new technologies and products as they emerge will keep you highly employable for many years to come.

Copyrights and Trademarks

3Com, U.S. Robotics, Master of Network Science, and 3Wizard are registered trademarks of 3Com Corporation.

Ascend, MAX, and Pipeline are trademarks of Ascend Communications.

Adobe, Portable Document Format, PDF, Adobe Certified Expert, Illustrator, Acrobat, AfterEffects, FrameMaker, PageMaker, PageMill, Photoshop, Premiere, and PostScript are registered trademarks or service marks of Adobe Systems Incorporated.

American Society for Quality, Certified Software Quality Engineer, Certified Quality Auditor, Certified Mechanical inspector, Certified Quality Engineer, and Certified Quality Manager are registered trademarks or service marks of the American Society for Quality.

Apple, AppleTalk, and Macintosh are registered trademarks of Apple Computer, Inc.

AutoDesk and AutoCAD are registered trademarks of AutoDesk Corporation.

Baan IV is a registered trademark of The Baan Company.

Banyan, VINES, StreetTalk, Certified Banyan Specialist, and Certified Banyan Expert are registered trademarks of Banyan Systems, Inc.

Callware, Certified Network Telephony Engineer, and Callegra, are registered trademarks of Callware Technologies.

CATGlobal is a registered trademark of Computer Adaptive Technologies, Inc.

Centura, SQLBase, SQLWindows, and Centura Team Developer are registered trademarks or service marks of Centura Software Corporation.

Certified Technical Trainer is a registered trademark of The Chauncey Group International Ltd.

Check Point, Certified Network Traffic Engineer, Certified Infrastructure Engineer, Certified Security Engineer, FireWall-1, Floodgate –1, Connect Control, and MetaIP are registered trademarks or service marks of Check Point Software, Inc.

Cisco Systems, Certified Cisco Network Associate, Certified Cisco Network Professional, Certified Cisco Design Associate, Certified Cisco Design Professional, and Cisco Certified Internetworking Expert are trademarks of Cisco Systems, Inc.

Citrix, WinFrame, and MetaFrame are registered trademarks or service marks of Citrix Systems, Inc.

Cognos, Impromptu, and PowerPlay are registered trademarks or service marks of Cognos Corporation.

Compaq, Compaq Accredited Systems Engineer (ASE), and Proliant Servers are registered trademarks of Compaq Corporation.

Computer Associates and Certified Unicenter Engineer are registered trademarks or service marks of Computer Associates, Inc.

Computer Telephony Institute is a registered trademark of the Computer Telephony Institute.

CompTIA, A+, Network +, and Certified Document Imaging Architect are registered trademarks or service marks of CompTIA.

Corel, CorelDRAW, Quattro Pro, WordPerfect, and Presentations are registered trademarks of Corel Corporation Limited.

Dialogic and Computer Telephony Professional are registered trademarks of Dialogic.

DRI International is a registered trademark of the Disaster Recovery Institute International.

FORE, PowerHub, and CellPath are registered trademarks or service marks of FORE Systems, Inc.

Help Desk 2000, Certified Help Desk Professional, Certified Help Desk Manager, and Certified Help Desk Director are registered trademarks or service marks of Help Desk 2000, Inc.

HP and OpenView are registered trademarks of Hewlett-Packard Company.

HyCurve is a registered trademark or service mark of Hycurve Corporation.

IBM Certified Specialist, Professional Server Specialist, Professional Server Expert, IBM Certified Networking Solutions Engineer, IBM Certified Instructor, OS/2 Warp Server Engineer, IBM

PART

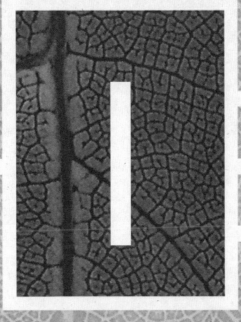

I

Preparing for and Taking
Certification Tests

CHAPTER

1

Instructor-Led Training

Instructor-led training can be a great way to learn the ins and outs of a product or technology and to prepare yourself for taking a certification exam. Typical courses last two to five days and involve both lecture and lab sessions. The instructor lectures on a topic or feature of the product and then provides an opportunity for hands-on practice with the technology. Labs provide a chance to work through a variety of tasks and scenarios yourself, with the help of an instructor readily available. This allows you to try things that you might not normally want to attempt with your company's server or network.

Another advantage to taking instructor-led courses is that if you take a course from a vendor, or a vendor's training partner, you may be able to take a course that corresponds directly to a certification test. These courses offer a curriculum that is designed by the vendor to provide content that corresponds to the test objectives on the certification exam.

A disadvantage, however, to taking instructor-led courses, is that they are usually fairly expensive. A typical two-day course may cost $500 to $1,500, while a five-day course may cost $1,000 to $2,500 or more. In many situations, however, employers foot the bill to send their employees to instructor-led courses. In a recent survey of Microsoft-certified professionals, 57 percent reported that their employers paid for their certification programs, 33 percent paid their own costs, and in 10 percent of cases, individuals and their employers split the cost ("Third Annual Salary Survey," Linda Briggs, *Microsoft Certified Professional Magazine*, February 1998). For independent contractors in the U.S., the situation is usually reversed. A survey by Kenda Systems found that 60 percent of independent contractors end up paying for their own training, and only 27 percent had their training paid for by the client company. The other 13 percent worked an arrangement to split the costs ("By the Numbers," *Contract Professional*, September/October 1998).

Whether you are paying out of your own pocket or your company is footing the bill, it is critical that you select your course provider carefully.

Selecting a Training Provider

A wide variety of course providers are available, and the market is growing rapidly. The different provider options—higher education training partners, authorized training providers, and independent training organizations—are outlined below. Regardless of the type of provider you select, there are several things to consider before you enroll in a course, including the provider's real-world experience and knowledge base, their teaching experience, and the design and level of the course.

Experience

Do the instructors have computer or networking experience outside the classroom? If so, is that experience current? A number of training organizations require their trainers to work as consultants in the field so they maintain current skills and have experience confronting and mastering unique problems and situations. University instructors may also have plenty of up-to-date experience; for example, night instructors may also be the daytime support staff for the campus network. If you make sure you take your course from an instructor who has current, real-world experience, you will be likely to get training that is practical and directly applicable to your work environment.

Certification

What training certifications does the instructor possess? If there is a training certification available for this specific product or technology, does the trainer have it? What other certifications does the instructor hold, including both training credentials and product-related certifications? An instructor with sound instructional skills and a wide range of product and technology knowledge is likely to offer high-quality instruction. In addition, such an instructor will be conversant with other technologies and products that are related to the topic at hand and will be equipped to provide you with a well-rounded learning experience.

Instructional Design

Does the course follow the vendor's official curriculum or one that has been approved by the vendor or organization? If not, how is the course structured?

Does the course provide only lectures or does it also involve lab components? A course that offers only lectures or has only minimal lab time won't prepare you to use a new product or technology on your own. Always look for a course that allows you plenty of hands-on time with the product or technology you want to learn to use—this is crucial to good learning.

What type of materials will you receive when you take the course? Will you take home a good text and/or lab books that you can use as a reference as you implement your new knowledge? Will you be able to receive a copy of the instructor's slides on CD-ROM?

Advisement

It may seem too obvious to mention, but the importance of enrolling in the appropriate course cannot be overemphasized. This is a key factor in maximizing your investment; a course that is too basic or too advanced will be a waste of your time and money. A good training organization will provide you with some means to determine which course is appropriate for you. This may involve an interview or completion of a questionnaire. Be sure to carefully read the brochure or description of the course in which you are interested. Most companies require that their instructors cover, at a minimum, all the points listed in the brochure for the course.

A variety of providers offer instructor-led courses that can lead to computer and networking certifications. The three main categories of organizations that provide this type of instruction are described below.

Colleges, Universities, and Vocational Schools

Many vocational schools, technical and community colleges, and four-year colleges and universities now offer good training opportunities at a reasonable price. We mention this option first because many people tend to overlook this alternative. Some high schools, colleges, and universities have become academic educational partners with vendors. A vocational school or college may offer the training you need as a short course; depending on the content, you might find a one- or two-day course, a weekend course, or a two- to four-week evening course that meets your needs.

It may be worth your while to seek out such opportunities in your local area, especially if you are interested in having the opportunity to get college credit as well as a certification. The section in the Introduction entitled "Benefits for Individuals" provides some specific examples of the different types of opportunities academic education partners provide.

Authorized Training Providers

An authorized training provider is a training center that has been authorized by a particular vendor to offer an approved curriculum covering that vendor's product line. Vendors are usually happy to provide you with a list of authorized training providers located in your area. There are literally thousands of authorized training provider locations across the United States and around the world (for links to authorized training providers for various vendors, see this book's Web site at http://www.certification-update.com/).

Independent Training Organizations

A number of independent training companies also provide courses throughout the United States and around the world. There are literally hundreds of such organizations to choose from. This book's Certification Update Web site provides links to the major independent training providers (http://www.certification-update.com/).

A number of certification programs offered by independent providers have established a level of quality and reliability that has made them eligible to provide college credit to their participants. For example, it is possible to obtain college credit for Learning Tree International certifications or courses and for ICCP Certified Computing Professional exams. The American Council of Education (ACE) in Washington, D.C. has determined college course equivalencies for these courses and certifications. Approximately 1,500 colleges and universities in the United States will accept ACE recommendations for college credit.

Certification "Boot Camps"

A new phenomenon in the IT training world is certification "boot camps." These are intensive, one- to two-week sessions that quickly bring you up to speed on the information you need to pass the required tests for a particular certification. Student typically work 12 to 16 hours each day, taking courses, working on labs, and studying in groups. There are several popular programs for obtaining the MCSE and CNE credentials. For those who can't work a self-study program or set of occasional courses into their schedule, attending such an intensive program can be just the ticket. The Certification Update Web site has current links to these programs.

CHAPTER

2

Self-Study for Certification

For most people, the process of obtaining certification will involve at least some amount of self-study. In some instances, self-study will be the only way to learn the information one needs to know to pass a certification test. In other cases, an individual may choose to combine some self-study with other study approaches as part of an overall plan for achieving their certification and career development goals.

Self-study has many advantages. One of the most important features of self-study is that it can be much less expensive than instructor-led study. While an instructor-led course might cost several thousand dollars, a comprehensive self-study book or video may cost less than a hundred dollars.

Even if cost isn't a big issue, however, you still may find that self-study has appealing advantages in some cases. Self-study allows you to select study times that fit well with your schedule. In addition, self-study lets you work at your own pace. You can select the topics you need to work hardest on and focus your energies on those areas. And, also in contrast to being in a class, you will not have to waste any time dealing with topics that you have already mastered. These advantages— flexible scheduling and working at your own pace—can be disadvantages for some people, of course. A successful self-study program requires a greater level of self-discipline than a program of instructor-led training.

A variety of resources can be used in a self-study program, including study guides and books, videotapes, computer-based training, online training, and practice tests.

NOTE One of the most effective techniques you can use to check your understanding and retention of new material is to try to teach it to someone else. Try telling a colleague at work what you have learned. If you are not able to clearly explain the concept or process, it is time to hit the books again.

Study Guides and Books

Most certification programs offer a basic study guide and preparation materials for their exams. These can be an excellent resource for self-study and may also inform you about other helpful learning resources. And, although you may want to explore additional learning resources, the information you get directly from the certifying entity will most accurately portray the knowledge and skills that will be evaluated on their tests.

A number of publishers, including Sybex, sell excellent books that provide entire self-study programs for specific certification tests. When selecting a text for self-study there are several things to consider:

Level of Presentation

Some books begin at a very basic level, while others assume that you already have a good understanding of the fundamentals. For some of the more popular certifications, a wide selection of books will be available. Take time to find a text that starts at the level that will work best for you.

Exercises

Does the text provide instructions for hands-on exercises that you can try out on your machine?

Sample Questions/ Sample Tests

Does the text provide questions to assess your comprehension at the end of each chapter? Does it offer a sample test that you can take to determine whether you are ready for the real test? Some books include a CD-ROM that contains multiple sample tests.

Pointers to Other Sources of Information

Does the book provide references to additional sources of useful information? Some texts suggest other resources on specific topics, including other books, product manuals, and online help files.

Endorsement

Some study guides have been endorsed or otherwise approved by the certification program they cover. This is a good indication that the book will cover the salient points of the certification you are pursuing.

Videotaped Study Programs

If you prefer the instructor-led training format, but time or money constraints prevent you from attending an instructor-led course, a videotaped course may be what you want. A videotape lacks the interaction of the classroom, but it may compensate for this with an increased use of graphics and special effects. Some videotape programs offer supplementary items that enhance your learning process. For example, a video package may include a student workbook with step-by-step instructions on setting up the program or process you are learning.

Computer-Based Training

Computer-based training, most often in a CD-ROM format, can offer a combination of video, text, and simulation exercises. One of the advantages of this type of training format is that you can jump from one topic to another in a way that best suits your learning needs

The cost of computer-based training can vary widely, depending on the type of certification program and the subject matter. Some of the more specialized computer-based training programs can be quite expensive. Depending on the type of software license associated with a training package, you may be able to sell or trade your software when you are done with it (several providers exclusively prohibit this practice, however, so check your licensing agreement carefully).

A large number of training providers offer computer-based training programs. Check this book's Certification Update Web site for links to some of the best-known providers (http://www.certification-update.com/).

Online Training

Online training for certification is very popular. One of the big advantages of online training is that you can network and share information with your classmates. This type of training varies widely in quality and cost, and can take several formats. Available offerings range from slick multimedia presentations that students download at their convenience, to a set of e-mail lectures that are sent to the student on a preset schedule.

There are many source for online training. Some of the best-known providers include Ziff-Davis University (http://www.zdu.com/) and Scholars.com (http://www.scholars.com/). There are hundreds of others as well; see the Certification Update Web site (http://www.certification-update.com/) for links to some of the best-known online training providers.

Practice Tests

Practice tests, if available, are an important component of your study program. They offer an excellent opportunity for you to test your knowledge before you fork over the bucks to take the real test. A practice test can help you zero in on the areas where you need extra study. In addition, practice tests help you become familiar with the format of the exam.

A number of certification programs offer free sample tests on their Web sites. Some of these don't offer a lot of questions, however. If you want more sample tests, you may be able to buy them. Several companies are in the business of making practice tests for use by certification candidates. These tests may allow you to take multiple practice exams that contain randomly selected questions drawn from a large pool of test items. These practice exams may also provide explanations of the questions and the correct (and incorrect) answers; this can be extremely useful in understanding the concepts that are giving you trouble. See the Certification Update Web site for links to some of the best-known providers of practice tests (http://www.certification-update.com/).

CHAPTER

3

Taking Your Test

After all the preparation comes the moment of truth: the certification exam. This chapter focuses on three topics: the types of tests you are most likely to encounter, tips on taking the tests, and an overview of the three major testing center networks.

Test Formats

Typically, tests for vendor certifications have two main assessment objectives: to measure your knowledge of the vendor's product or products, and to assess your competence in using those products to accomplish specific job tasks. Many certification programs now use some type of performance-based testing. The vendors and organizations who offer certification exams want their exams to measure an individual's performance on job-related tasks, not just that person's ability to memorize details. It is partly this performance-based aspect of certification testing that makes certifications so significant to employers and clients.

Certification tests are usually computer-based exams that are taken at commercial testing centers or at vendor-based education centers. Different organizations and different technologies often demand different testing procedures. You may encounter a variety of test formats, including multiple-choice tests, adaptive tests, hands-on lab tests, and live-application tests. Each of these formats will be described briefly below.

Some certification programs use more than one type of testing. For example, the candidate might first take a test that is in a scenario-based multiple-choice format. This test would assess the candidate's understanding of *when* to use a certain product or a feature of a product. This test might be followed by another type of test, such as a hands-on lab test or a live-application test. This test would assess whether the candidate knew *how* to use that product or feature of a product. In this case, depending on the nature and level of the certification sought, the candidate might be expected to perform a real task using a software program, or to plan, design, implement, maintain, troubleshoot, or upgrade a network, or to integrate a system with other systems.

Different vendors and organizations may have different names for their particular approaches to testing. You may also encounter testing that is categorized as one of the types below but is a little different from the descriptions given here. The descriptions below are intended to give you a general idea of what to expect. To be prepared for a particular certification test, it is always a good idea to take practice tests designed for that specific test.

Multiple-Choice Testing

The multiple-choice test is still the most commonly used exam format. Multiple-choice, computer-based exams are typically generated in a way that makes the test different for each test taker. The exam program consists of a large pool of several hundred or more questions. A certain number of those questions are selected for each candidate. Each candidate receives a different—but equivalent—exam.

Multiple-choice questions may be structured in different ways. You may encounter tests where more than one answer is correct. In this situation, you may be asked to select the one best correct answer; alternatively, you may be expected to select a specific number of correct answers. When you read the question, be sure to note how many responses you are being asked to select. Other questions may be of the true/false type.

At the end of a computer-based multiple-choice exam, the computer will display a score report that indicates your score, the required passing score, and a notification of whether you passed or failed the exam. Your score report will also include a breakdown of your score in the various categories of the test. For example, a typical Microsoft

Certified Professional exam will indicate your score in the following areas: planning, installation and configuration, connectivity, monitoring and optimization, and troubleshooting. The testing program will then print a copy of the score report for you to keep as evidence of your score. The testing center will emboss the score report to ensure authenticity. Your score is also automatically sent to the certifying vendor or organization.

A few organization-based certification programs use traditional paper-based multiple-choice exams. These exams are not usually administered by commercial testing centers, but rather by the organization itself.

Test Security: The Microsoft Story

Test security is a major concern for every certification program. Test security is a two-fold problem. First is the problem of making sure that no one cheats during the exams. Second, the content of the exams must remain secret. Most testing centers have these basic rules about cheating and test security:

- Unless the vendor specifically allows it, no notes can be brought into the testing room.

- You cannot attempt to write down test questions and take them with you.

- You cannot talk to other test takers.

- You cannot look at the monitors of other test takers.

Depending on the certification program, the consequences for violating these rules can be severe. For example, if you are caught violating the test rules during a Microsoft exam, you will lose credit for the exam you are taking, you will lose credit for ALL exams you have taken in the past, and you will lose all your current Microsoft certifications. In addition, you will not be allowed to take another Microsoft test for six months. And, if you are caught violating the testing rules again, you will be permanently ineligible for any Microsoft certification.

Continued

In addition to preventing cheating, Microsoft is also very concerned about keeping the exam questions secret. A couple of years ago, several companies emerged that sold practice exams that were too similar to the official Microsoft exams. Most people believed that these companies got their practice test questions by sending their employees to take the tests and memorize the test questions. Some of these practice exam products were, not surprisingly, very popular, because testing candidates found that by the time they were sitting for the real exam they had already seen a majority of the questions.

This type of unscrupulous behavior devalues the entire certification program. If all that is required to pass is to memorize the answers, what is the value of an MCSE? Hence the nickname attributed to those who pass exams this way—a "Paper MCSE." To combat this practice, Microsoft has made several changes to their exam security policy:

- All Microsoft exams are now considered a trade secret. When you take your test you are required to agree that you will not discuss the content of the exam with anyone else.

- Microsoft has implemented a mandatory wait period between test retakes. If you fail an exam on the second try, you must wait 14 days before you can retake it. This way, people who take the test several times in a row in hopes of learning all the questions, will come up against a new pool of questions every two weeks.

- Most Microsoft tests are being changed to an adaptive testing format. It is much harder to cheat or steal questions on an adaptive test. In addition, an adaptive test is often a better assessment of the candidate's abilities.

Adaptive Testing

This type of testing will be new to many people. The first large-scale use of this testing method was done in 1991 by Drake Prometric testing centers and Novell. This computer-based test "adapts" itself to the abilities of the test-taker. An adaptive test is designed to ask only the minimum number of questions necessary to determine your level of ability. As you go through the exam, the difficulty of the next question you receive is determined by your response to the previous question. In other words, if you answer a question correctly, the next question will be more difficult. If you answer incorrectly, the next question will be an easier question. The test is continually working to determine which questions are most appropriate for your level of ability.

As you respond to each question, the testing program continually calculates an estimate of your level of ability. As the test progresses, the statistical value of that estimate becomes more accurate. The test ends when one of three things occurs: your ability has been accurately estimated; the program is at least 95 percent confident that your ability lies above the passing score; or all the questions have been given. Novell's adaptive tests use a minimum of 15 questions and a maximum of 25 questions.

The scores for adaptive tests are not simply based on the number of questions you answer correctly. Instead, the score is based on the *difficulty* of the questions you answer correctly. In the case of Novell's adaptive tests, scores will have values between 200 and 800. You will pass if your score is greater than a pre-established cutoff score.

Those who use adaptive testing believe that it is a more efficient way of testing because it saves time. It is also believed to be less stressful for the test-taker because the questions generated will, for the most part, be at a level that the candidate finds moderately challenging. Novell's Web site offers a discussion of the testing theory behind their adaptive exams (`http://education.novell.com/testinfo/theory.htm`).

Hands-On Lab Testing

Several certification programs, such as Nortel and Cisco, require the candidate to attend a hands-on lab exam. In these situations, you will be given appropriate equipment and software, and then instructed to complete a series of lab exercises within a given time period. At the end of the time limit, the lab proctors will inspect your work to see if you successfully completed the exercise. In addition, they will check to see if you completed the task according to standard procedures and safety practices.

These exams can be expensive and difficult. Several of the vendors and organizations that require such exams will provide you with practice exercises so that you will have a better feel for the types of activities you will be asked to perform. Some vendors provide practice exercises by mail or on the Web, while others have made special arrangements to provide practice hands-on lab sessions at specially equipped designated facilities.

Live-Application Testing

The live-application test is becoming a popular way to assess the ability of a candidate to use an application to perform a series of tasks. For example, both the Microsoft Office User certification program and the Certified Lotus Professional program use live-application testing.

This type of test is similar the to hands-on lab exam, but is typically less complex and takes less time. In a typical live-application test, the candidate sits at a computer with the appropriate application loaded and a proctor tells the candidate what task or tasks to perform. At the end of the time period, the candidate submits the work to the proctor and the proctor either grades it on-site, according to set of standard criteria, or forwards it to the certifying entity for scoring.

Test Taking

Taking a test is a stressful situation for everyone. Not only do you have to complete your test within a given time limit, in a unfamiliar environment, but you may also feel stressed about wanting to pass so you haven't wasted the money you paid to take the test. There are a few steps you can take to make the testing a more enjoyable experience.

Prior to Taking a Test

1. Study well in advance. Don't schedule your exam until you are confident that you can pass it.

2. As a part of your study plan, schedule time for hands-on work with the application, operating system, or technology that you will be tested on.

3. Take advantage of any opportunity to take practice tests.

4. In the week before your exam date, spend time reviewing the test objectives, including the areas that you think you know—don't let overconfidence allow you to miss an easy question.

5. Get a good night's sleep the night before your exam.

While Taking Your Test

1. You will typically be given a paper and pencil for use during the exam. Some people find it valuable to jot down pertinent information from memory immediately, prior to starting to answer test questions. For example, prior to taking a TCP/IP exam you may want to memorize the formula for calculating the number of sub-networks for different sub-net masks and then jot it down from memory at the beginning of your exam.

2. Use the paper and pencil to diagram the word problems and the presented scenarios. There will often be subtle differences between one answer and another. Make sure that you have interpreted the question correctly.

3. If your test format allows, mark the questions that you do not immediately understand and return to them later. Answer the easiest questions first and then go back and answer the questions that you skipped. This strategy is not possible with adaptive tests, however, because the answer for each question determines which question is given next.

NOTE If you do fail your test, don't feel bad. Most people fail a couple of exams during their careers. Just chalk this one up to experience and determine what you need to do the next time to succeed.

Testing Centers

Because their tests are computer-based, testing centers typically offer certification tests on whatever day is convenient for the individual test-taker. In addition, test results are usually available on-site right after the test is completed, and they can then be sent electronically to universities or certifying agencies.

Vendor-authorized testing centers have their own policies and procedures for test registration and test taking. If you plan to take a test at a vendor's testing center, contact the vendor's education program to get more information. The addresses, phone numbers, and electronic contact information for the individual vendors are located throughout this book in the sections that describe the vendors' certification programs.

In many instances, the test you want to take will also be offered at one of the three major testing centers: CatGlobal, Sylvan Prometric, and VUE. Information on each of these types of centers is provided below. Sylvan has the longest history of offering certification exams for information technology professionals, and currently offers testing for a larger number of vendors than do CATGlobal and VUE. VUE and CATGlobal have offered testing services for some time, but have only recently gotten into the business of offering certification exams for information technology vendors.

NOTE   Another testing company is CertificationNet, which is a division of Merrimac, a business education company. CertificationNet offers testing for several different vendors' tests at certification centers and online. See `http://www.certification.net/` for more information.

CatGlobal

Computer Adaptive Technologies, Inc. (CAT), founded in 1984, is a high-technology firm that delivers all types of computer-based testing and assessment services worldwide. CAT launched the CATGlobal Testing Network in September 1997. This service allows certification candidates to schedule their own exams at CATGlobal's Web site (`http://www.catglobal.com`). CAT offers testing at over 200,000 corporate and private sites, and with the addition of the CATGlobal Testing Network, more than 750 public testing sites have been added.

CATGlobal testing centers offer Lotus exams and anticipate offering exams for other vendor-based certifications in the near future. For more information on taking an exam from CATGlobal, contact the company at:

Web	http://www.catglobal.com/
E-mail	cat@catinc.com
Mail	Computer Adaptive Technologies
	1007 Church Street
	Evanston, IL 60201
Phone	(800) 255-1312
Fax	(847) 866-2002

Sylvan Prometric

Sylvan Prometric, a division of Sylvan Learning Systems, Inc., operates the world's largest network of public testing centers. They administer testing programs for educational institutions, professional associations, corporations, and other organizations. Sylvan offers computer-based testing services at more than 2,000 locations in 80 countries. Sylvan operates two types of testing centers: Sylvan Technology Centers, which are operated by Sylvan or a franchisee, and Authorized Prometric Testing Centers, which are testing sites that are housed at training institutions, colleges, and universities. Sylvan claims that 80 percent of the population of the United States is within an hour's drive of a Sylvan testing center. Tens of thousands of certification exams are administered by Sylvan each month.

Sylvan Prometric administers testing for professional certification programs offered by a wide variety of information technology vendors and organizations. Sylvan has a different telephone number for each vendor's exams. The numbers that are specific to each vendor's exams are provided in the certification chapters in this book. To schedule an exam with Sylvan, call the vendor-specific Sylvan phone number or call one of the general telephone numbers listed below.

NOTE   Sylvan now offers online registration for a number of vendor exams. Visit http://www.sylvanprometric.com/ to register online for an exam.

If you are using phone registration, tell the customer service representative which test you are interested in taking and where you would like to take it. Sylvan will tell you the locations of the testing centers available in your area and will reserve your test for the date and time you prefer. Be prepared to supply the following information when you call:

- Your name

- Your Sylvan Personal Identification Number (this is usually your social security number)

- Phone numbers (home and work)

- Your mailing address

- Test title or Test ID number

- Method of payment (voucher number or credit card)

You may schedule a test with Sylvan up to six weeks in advance, and no less than 24 hours in advance. In most cases, you may cancel or reschedule your test with no penalty if you do so at least 24 hours prior to your scheduled test time. If you schedule a test but don't take it, and don't call in time to reschedule it, you will forfeit the test fee. If you pay by credit card you can schedule your test at the time you call Sylvan; if you pay by check, you cannot schedule the actual test date until Sylvan receives your check. In some cases, tests are paid for with vouchers that have been issued by a vendor.

You should arrive at the test center at least 15 minutes before the test is scheduled to begin. Candidates are required to bring two forms of identification to the testing site. One must be a photo ID, such as a valid passport or a driver's license. The other must have a signature. You will be asked to sign a logbook. Unless your exam specifies it, no materials will be permitted inside the test center. You will be given a pencil and some paper to use during the test; the paper must be left at the testing center when you complete your exam. Candidates are monitored by proctors during testing. For more information on taking a test from Sylvan, contact the company at:

Web   http://www.sylvanprometric.com

Mail	Sylvan Prometric
	1000 Lancaster Street
	Baltimore, MD 21202
Phone	(800) 627-4276

VUE

Virtual University Enterprises (VUE) is another provider of certification exams related to information technology. VUE, a division of National Computer Systems (NCS), is based in Minneapolis, Minnesota, and has operations in The Netherlands and Australia. VUE was established in 1994 and was acquired by NCS in April 1997.

Like CATGlobal and Sylvan, VUE offers real-time, Internet-based registration for testing. You can schedule, change, or cancel testing appointments and check your certification status from your own computer 24 hours a day. VUE began offering Novell certification exams at its testing centers in September 1997 and has since added testing for the following vendors: HyCurve, IBM, Microsoft, and Sybase. For more information on taking an exam from VUE, contact the company at:

Web	http://www.vue.com/
E-mail	info@vue.com
Mail	VUE, Inc.
	5001 W. 80th St., Suite 401
	Bloomington, MN 55437
Phone	(612) 897-7999
Fax	(612) 897-1015

PART

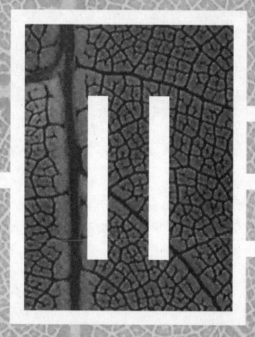

II

Certification Program and Requirements

CHAPTER

4

Hardware Certifications

FEATURING

- Compaq Certifications

- Disaster Recovery Institute (DRI) International Certifications

- IBM Certifications

- Intel Certifications

- Learning Tree International Certification

For the sheer amount of frustration and panic it can generate, working with hardware problems is probably unbeatable. Most of the truly critical problems with computers are hardware-related; if the hardware doesn't work, nothing else will. Advanced knowledge about a certain software package or programming language is moot if you're dead in the water because your computer's hard disk needs replacing, or you can't get your network card to work correctly.

A solid understanding of how to install and maintain hardware is invaluable to computer and networking professionals and to the organizations that employ them. And if you're into being the computer hero in your organization, just watch the accolades you'll receive after resurrecting your boss's computer from the dead, just in time for an important report to go out.

Unfortunately, because working with hardware is often seen as a mundane task, there are not a lot of certifications available in this field. Compaq and IBM have programs to certify professionals who have knowledge and experience with their product lines. Intel has recently introduced two certifications for professionals who implement systems and networks based on Intel's line of microprocessors. Learning Tree International, a training organization, has developed its own vendor-independent hardware certification program. The other certification program listed in this chapter—offered by the Disaster Recovery Institute (DRI) International—involves preparation to ensure that a company can survive a disaster or natural catastrophe; this obviously involves a lot of issues, but recovering a company's information infrastructure is a major concern.

Professionals seeking or holding the certifications covered in this chapter run the gamut from service technicians for computer dealers to chief information officers at major corporations. To be sure, the knowledge and skills learned by achieving any one of these certifications will be valuable in your career in information technology. Those who may be interested in pursuing these certifications include:

- Help-desk personnel

- Service technicians

- Field engineers

- System administrators

- Information specialists, information planners, and information officers

- Technology coordinators

NOTE If your expertise and interest lie in computer hardware, also check out the Computing Technology Industry Association (CompTIA) A+ certification program detailed in Chapter 17. This vendor-independent credential is probably the most widely recognized hardware certification.

Use Table 4.1 to compare the number of required tests, the test format, the approximate cost of taking the test(s), number of required courses, cost of any required courses, and the relative difficulty of the certification programs in this chapter. The cost information is a general guideline; since things change rapidly in the world of certification programs, once you have selected a specific course of action you may want to double-check the costs.

We classified the difficulty of these certifications into three categories—Moderate, Challenging, and Very Challenging—based on the number of required tests and courses, and the relative difficulty of those tests or lab exams. These ratings are approximate and are offered simply as a general guide to help the reader distinguish between entry-level programs and those that require more advanced skill and knowledge. (This rating scale assumes that one has experience with the product or technology and has studied the appropriate subject content before attempting the exams.)

TABLE 4.1: Hardware Certifications

Certification	# of Required Tests	Test Format(s)	Total Cost of Required Tests	# of Required Courses	Total Cost of Required Courses	Difficulty	Notes
Compaq Certifications							
Associate Accredited Systems Engineer (Associate ASE)	2–4	MC	$200–$400	—	—	◖	Number of tests depends on specialization. Specializations include: Intel/NetWare, Intel/Windows NT, Critical Problem Resolution, Workstation, Communication-LAN.
Accredited Systems Engineer (ASE)	2–4	MC	$200–$400	—	—	◖	All of the specializations for the associate level are available, plus Alpha/Tru64 UNIX, Alpha/Open VMS, alpha/Windows NT. Must also have an approved network operating system certification (CNE, MSCE, etc.) or recognized experience.
Master Accredited Systems Engineer (Master ASE)	1–4	MC	$100–$400	—	—	●	Must already be an ASE. Specializations include: BAAN, Enterprise Management, Enterprise Storage, High Availability and Clustering, Internet/Intranet, Messaging and Collaboration, Oracle, SAP, SQL Server.

TABLE 4.1: Hardware Certifications *(continued)*

Certification	# of Required Tests	Test Format(s)	Total Cost of Required Tests	# of Required Courses	Total Cost of Required Courses	Difficulty	Notes
Disaster Recovery Institute (DRI) International Certifications							
Associate Business Continuity Planner (ABCP)	1	MC	$250	—	—	○	
Certified Business Continuity Planner (CBCP)	—	—	—	—	—	◑	Must be an ABCP and have two years' experience in the field. $100 Application Fee.
Master Business Continuity Planner (MBCP)	—	—	—	—	—	●	Must be a CBCP, have five years' experience and complete a case study or independent research project. $200 Application Fee.
IBM Certifications							
Professional Server Specialist (PSS)	1	MC	CV	1	$750	○	
Professional Server Expert (PSE)	1	MC	CV	1	$600	●	Must have PSS certification and be a Certified Novell Engineer (CNE) or Microsoft Certified Systems Engineer (MCSE).
Intel Certifications							
Certified Solutions Consultant	3	MC	VF	1	None	◑	
Certified Integration Specialist	5–6	MC	VF	1	None	●	Specializations include: Desktop/ Server Integration and Networking.

TABLE 4.1: Hardware Certifications *(continued)*

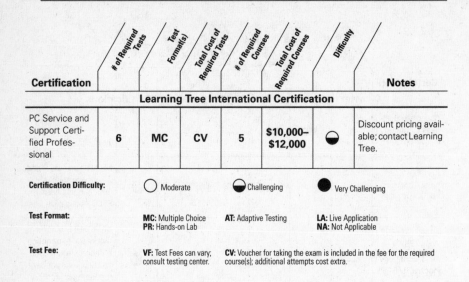

Certification	# of Required Tests	Test Format(s)	Total Cost of Required Tests	# of Required Courses	Total Cost of Required Courses	Difficulty	Notes
Learning Tree International Certification							
PC Service and Support Certified Professional	6	MC	CV	5	$10,000–$12,000	◖	Discount pricing available; contact Learning Tree.

Certification Difficulty: ○ Moderate ◖ Challenging ● Very Challenging

Test Format:
- **MC:** Multiple Choice **AT:** Adaptive Testing **LA:** Live Application
- **PR:** Hands-on Lab **NA:** Not Applicable

Test Fee:
- **VF:** Test Fees can vary; consult testing center. **CV:** Voucher for taking the exam is included in the fee for the required course(s); additional attempts cost extra.

Additional Hardware Certifications

There are a couple of hardware-related certification programs that deal specifically with the practice of making and repairing hardware components. The Institute for Interconnecting and Packaging Electronic Circuits specializes in supporting the designers and manufacturers of printed circuit boards, and offers a certification in this aspect of computer manufacture. The International Society of Certified Electronic Technicians offers a number of certifications for those involved with the repair and installation of electronic equipment, ranging from computers and electric motors to refrigeration equipment.

Continued on next page

Institute for Interconnecting and Packaging of Electronic Circuits Certification

The Institute for Interconnecting and Packaging Electronic Circuits (IPC) is a trade association comprised of over 2,300 companies that make circuit boards and interconnection components. IPC currently offers the Printed Wiring Board (PWB) Designer certification for technical professionals in this industry. IPC is planning to add additional designations to its certification program in the near future. Contact IPC at:

Web	http//www.ipc.org/
Mail	IPC
	2215 Sanders Road
	Northbrooks, IL 60062-6135
Phone	(847) 509-9700
Fax	(847) 509-9798

International Society of Certified Electronics Technicians Certification

The International Society of Certified Electronics Technicians (ISCET) was founded in 1965, in the absence of any governmental licensing program, to address the need for certification of electronic repair service personnel. The Certified Electronics Technician (CET) program has since expanded to include two levels of certification—Associate and Journeyman—with specialties at the Journeyman level in a variety of technologies. Currently over 38,000 individuals are certified as CETs.

For more information, contact ISCET at:

Web	http//www.iscet.org
Mail	ISCET
	2708 West Berry Street
	Fort Worth, TX 76109
Phone	(817) 921-9101
Fax	(817) 921-3741

Compaq Certifications

- Associate Accredited Systems Engineer (Associate ASE)

- Accredited Systems Engineer (ASE)

- Master Accredited Systems Engineer (Master ASE)

Compaq makes several lines of workstations, and was one of the first makers of a PC "clone" in the early 1980s. They earned a reputation for making a clone computer that was much better and cheaper than the original design. Today Compaq is a multi-billion-dollar business and a leading manufacturer of servers.

The Compaq Accredited Systems Engineer (ASE) program was originally developed in 1991 to evaluate and recognize expertise in installing and administering Compaq workstations and servers operating in Novell and Microsoft networking environments. There are now three levels to this program—the Associate ASE, the ASE, and the Master ASE—as well as numerous specializations in the areas of networking, server installation and integration, problem resolution, and communications, among others.

Because ASEs can obtain information from Compaq that has not yet been released for public consumption, all ASEs are required to submit a confidentiality and nondisclosure agreement and cannot be employed by a competitor of Compaq.

NOTE In addition to the ASE program, Compaq also offers the Accredited Compaq Technician Program, which trains technical personnel to deliver post-sales service and support for Compaq desktop and server products (for information on this program, see `http://www.compaq.com/training/2083.html`).

Recertification or Maintenance Requirements

ASEs at all levels must submit annual renewal applications. In addition, Compaq requires ASEs to participate in periodic training to maintain their certifications. The amount of training required in a given year is based on what new products Compaq releases, and whether Compaq feels that additional training is required for an ASE to successfully install and maintain these products. ASEs and Master ASEs must also maintain their outside operating system vendor certifications, as appropriate.

Benefits of Certification

ASEs can receive the following benefits which vary within the three certification levels.

- Internet access to the Compaq ASE Connection, which provides access to news, the purchase plan, and links to useful documents

- Toll-free priority access to Compaq technical support (varies with level and specialization of certification)

- Access to private training events on upcoming Compaq products and technologies

- Invitation to the annual Compaq Systems Engineering Conference

- Use of the ASE logo for stationery and business cards

- Special discounts on selected Compaq products and training sessions

- Free subscriptions to Compaq SmartStart, a CD-ROM resource that includes an intelligent program for integrating hardware configuration and software installation into a single automated process, Compaq Insight Manager, Compaq QuickFind, and software support CDs for desktops, workstations, and portables

- Free quarterly ASE Newsletter with information about upcoming events, promotions, and the ASE program

Associate Accredited Systems Engineer (Associate ASE)

To attain certification as an Associate ASE, one must pass two, three, or four tests, depending on the specialization desired. The specific exams required are listed below. Compaq offers a preparatory course for each of the exams, and strongly recommends that candidates take these courses prior to attempting the exams. For some of the specialization tracks, one has a choice of taking the courses individually or all at once in an accelerated four- or five-day course package. Compaq offers online self-assessment study guides for some of the exams (see http://www.compaq.com/training/ase-tsas.html).

Associate ASEs can select from the following certification areas:

- Intel/NetWare Specialist
- Intel/Windows NT Specialist
- Critical Problem Resolution Specialist
- Workstation Specialist
- Communications-LAN Specialist

Who Needs It

This Associate ASE certification is an excellent way to show potential employers that you can integrate and configure Compaq hardware. This credential can also be of value to systems engineers who do independent consulting and want to validate their expertise for clients.

Requirements for Certification

The certification process requires the following steps:

1. Pass the required tests for the specialization you seek (see Table 4.2).

2. Submit an application to Compaq.

T A B L E 4.2: Specializations and Required Tests for Associate ASE Certification

Specialization	Required Tests
Intel/NetWare	▪ Compaq Systems Technologies (ID:10-397) ▪ Compaq/NetWare Integration and Performance (ID:10-055) ▪ Compaq Systems Management (ID:10-293)
Intel/Windows NT	▪ Compaq Systems Technologies (ID:10-397) ▪ Compaq/Windows NT Integration and Performance (ID:10-057) ▪ Compaq Systems Management (ID:10-293)
Critical Problem Resolution	▪ Compaq Systems Technologies (ID:10-397) ▪ Either Compaq/NetWare Integration and Performance (ID:10-423) *OR* Compaq Windows NT Integration and Performance (ID:10-422) ▪ Compaq Systems Management (ID:10-293) ▪ Compaq Server Diagnostics (ID:10-201)
Workstation	▪ Compaq Workstation Technologies (ID:10-430) ▪ Compaq Workstation Integration (ID:10-428) ▪ Compaq Workstation Management (ID:10-429)
Communications-LAN	▪ Compaq Network Management Software (ID:10-375) ▪ Designing and Implementing Compaq Local Area Networks (ID:10-512)

Administrator

Compaq exams are administered by Sylvan Prometric. Call (800) 366-3926 to register for Compaq tests; if outside the U.S., use the online Sylvan Test Center Locator at www.sylvanprometric.com to find the nearest testing center. (See Chapter 3 for additional information on Sylvan Prometric.)

Fee

The cost is $100 per test.

Format

The tests are taken online at Sylvan Prometric testing centers. In some cases, a brand new test will be administered in a paper-based beta format. Test scores are available immediately after completion of the test, and are automatically forwarded to Compaq. Each of the tests consists of 50 questions. To pass, you must answer 30 questions correctly within the one-hour time limit. Most of the tests are closed-book.

Accredited Systems Engineer (ASE)

The Compaq ASE designation indicates that the holder has completed a set of required exams and also has completed an advanced certification appropriate for the specialty designation. The specific exams and certifications required are listed below. Compaq offers a preparatory course for each of the exams, and strongly recommends that candidates take these courses prior to attempting the exams. For some of the specialization tracks, one has a choice of taking the courses individually or all at once in an accelerated four- or five-day course package. Compaq offers online self-assessment study guides for some of the exams (see `http://www.compaq.com/training/ase-tsas.html`).

ASEs can select from the following certification areas:

- Intel/NetWare Specialist
- Intel/Windows NT Specialist
- Critical Problem Resolution Specialist
- Workstation Specialist
- Communications-LAN Specialist
- Alpha/Tru64 UNIX Specialist
- Alpha/Open VMS Specialist
- Alpha/Windows NT Specialist

Who Needs It

This ASE certification is an advanced accreditation that indicates that you have knowledge and expertise in the integration of Compaq hardware and a specific operating system. It is typically awarded to systems engineers, consultants or others who sell, support, integrate, plan, or optimize Compaq platforms. This credential can be a great way to get a higher-paying position within your current company or elsewhere.

Requirements for Certification

The certification process requires the following steps:

1. Pass the required tests for the specialization you seek. Note that in a few cases the required tests are Microsoft exams (see Table 4.3).

2. Attain the operating system certification required for your specialization (see Table 4.4).

3. Submit an application to Compaq.

TABLE 4.3: Required Tests for ASE Certification

Specialization	Required Tests
Intel/NetWare	▪ Compaq Systems Technologies (ID:10-397) ▪ Compaq/NetWare Integration and Performance (ID:10-055) ▪ Compaq Systems Management (ID:10-293) (These are the same three tests required of Associate ASE Intel/NetWare candidates.)
Intel/Windows NT	▪ Compaq Systems Technologies (ID:10-397) ▪ Compaq/Windows NT Integration and Performance (ID:10-057) ▪ Compaq Systems Management (ID:10-293) (These are the same three tests required of Associate ASE Intel/Windows NT candidates.)
Critical Problem Resolution	▪ Compaq Systems Technologies (ID:10-397) ▪ Either Compaq/NetWare Integration and Performance (ID:10-423) OR Compaq Windows NT Integration and Performance (ID:10-422)

T A B L E 4.3: Required Tests for ASE Certification *(continued)*

Specialization	Required Tests
Critical Problem Resolution (cont.)	• Compaq Systems Management (ID:10-293) • Compaq Server Diagnostics (ID:10-201) (These are the same four tests required of Associate ASE Critical Problem Resolution candidates.)
Workstation	• Compaq Workstation Technologies (ID:10-430) • Compaq Workstation Integration (ID:10-428) • Compaq Workstation Management (ID:10-429) (These are the same three tests required of Associate ASE Workstation candidates.)
Communications-LAN	• Compaq Network Management Software (ID:10-375) • Designing and Implementing Compaq Local Area Networks (ID:10-512) (These are the same two tests required of Associate ASE Communications-LAN candidates.)
Alpha/UNIX	• Compaq AlphaServer (ID:330-220) • Compaq UNIX v4.0 (ID:330-130)
Alpha/OVMS	• Compaq AlphaServer (ID:330-220) • Compaq OpenVMS (ID:330-140)
Alpha/Windows NT	• Compaq AlphaServer (ID:330-220) • Microsoft Implementing and Supporting Microsoft Windows NT Server V4.0 (Microsoft exam ID:70-067) • Microsoft Implementing and Supporting Microsoft Windows NT Workstation V4.0 (Microsoft exam ID:70-073)

T A B L E 4.4: Required Operating System Certifications for ASE Certification

Specialization	Required Certification
Intel/NetWare	CNE or Master CNE
Intel/Windows NT	MCSE
Critical Problem Resolution	If you take the Compaq/NetWare Integration and Performance exam, the CNE or MCNE is required. If you take the Compaq/Windows NT Integration and Performance exam, the MCSE is required.
Workstation	MCSE
Communications-LAN	MCSE, CNE, or Master CNE
Alpha/UNIX	A specific certification is not required, but the candidate must have intermediate-level experience with UNIX.
Alpha/OVMS	A specific certification is not required, but the candidate must have intermediate-level experience with OpenVMS v7.0 or above.
Alpha/Windows NT	A specific certification is not required, but the candidate must have intermediate-level experience with Windows NT.

Administrator

Compaq exams are administered by Sylvan Prometric. Call (800) 366-3926 to register for Compaq tests; if outside the U.S., use the online Sylvan Test Center Locator at `www.sylvanprometric.com` to find the nearest testing center. Microsoft tests are administered by both Sylvan Prometric and Virtual University Enterprises (VUE). To register for a test with VUE, visit the VUE Web site (`http://www.vue.com/student-services/`). Call Sylvan at (800) 755-3926 to register for Microsoft tests; if outside the U.S., use the online Sylvan Test

Center Locator at www.sylvanprometric.com to find the nearest testing center. (Chapter 3 contains detailed information on taking tests from Sylvan or VUE.)

Fee

The Compaq exams cost $100 each. Microsoft exams, if required, also cost $100 each.

Format

Compaq tests are taken online at Sylvan Prometric testing centers. In some cases, a brand new test will be administered in a paper-based beta format. Test scores are available immediately after completion of the test, and are automatically forwarded to Compaq. Each of the tests consists of 50 questions. To pass, you must answer 30 questions correctly within the one-hour time limit. Most of the tests are closed-book.

Master ASE

The Master ASE designation is the highest level of Compaq certification and indicates an advanced level of competence. To attain Master ASE status, the candidate must be a Compaq Associate ASE, hold the required outside vendor certifications, and pass one or more additional exams that demonstrate specific expertise. The exams and certifications required are listed below.

Compaq offers a preparatory course for each of the exams, and strongly recommends that candidates take these courses prior to attempting the exams. For some of the specialization tracks, one has a choice of taking the courses individually or all at once in an accelerated four- or five-day course package. Compaq offers online self-assessment study guides for some of the exams (http://www.compaq.com/training/ase-tsas.html).

Master ASEs can select from the following certification areas:

- BAAN Specialist
- Enterprise Management Specialist
- Enterprise Storage Specialist
- High Availability and Clustering Specialist
- Internet/Intranet Specialist
- Messaging and Collaboration Specialist
- Oracle Specialist
- SAP Specialist
- SQL Server Specialist

Who Needs It

The Master ASE certification is the highest credential awarded in the Compaq ASE program. It indicates that, in addition to hardware, operating system, and platform knowledge, you have the skills needed to integrate and manage enterprise applications and solutions. Master ASEs are typically systems engineers, consultants, and others who work for companies that sell, support, integrate, plan, or optimize Compaq platforms. This credential can be a great way to get a higher-paying position within your current company or elsewhere.

Requirements for Certification

The certification process requires the following steps:

1. Attain the appropriate Compaq ASE certification and additional required certification(s) for your specialization (see Table 4.5).

2. Pass the required test(s) for the specialization you seek. Note that in a few cases the required tests are Microsoft exams (see Table 4.6).

3. Submit an application to Compaq.

T A B L E 4.5: Required Certifications for Master ASE Certification

Specialization	Required Certifications
BAAN	• Microsoft MCSE • Compaq Intel/Windows NT ASE • BAAN IV Certified Installer
Enterprise Management	• Microsoft MCSE, Novell CNE, or Novell MCNE • Compaq Intel/Windows NT or Intel/NetWare ASE
Enterprise Storage	• Microsoft MCSE, Novell CNE, or Novell MCNE • Compaq Intel/Windows NT, Intel/NetWare, Alpha/UNIX, Alpha/OVMS, or Alpha/Windows NT ASE
High Availability and Clustering	• Microsoft MCSE, Novell CNE, or Novell MCNE • Compaq Intel/Windows NT or Intel/NetWare ASE
Internet/Intranet	• Microsoft MCSE • Compaq Intel/Windows NT ASE
Messaging and Collaboration	• Microsoft MCSE • Compaq Intel/Windows NT or Alpha/Windows NT ASE
Oracle	• Microsoft MCSE • Compaq Intel/Windows NT ASE
SAP	• Microsoft MCSE • Compaq Intel/Windows NT ASE • SAP Basis Consultant
SQL Server	• Microsoft MCSE • Compaq Intel/Windows NT ASE

T A B L E 4.6: Required Tests for Master ASE Certification

Specialization	Required Test(s)
BAAN	Compaq/BAAN Integration and Performance (ID:10-438)
Enterprise Management	Compaq Integrated Systems Management (ID:10-291)
Enterprise Storage	▪ Backup and Restore for Compaq Servers (ID:10-442) ▪ Designing and Implementing Fibre Channel Solutions (ID:10-370) ▪ Designing and Implementing Compaq StorageWorks Backup Solution (ID:10-440) ▪ Compaq StorageWorks Technical Training as implemented on Intel-based Windows NT platforms (ID:10-322)
High Availability and Clustering	▪ Designing and Implementing Fibre Channel Solutions (ID:10-370) ▪ Implementing Compaq ProLiant Clusters (ID:10-365)
Internet/Intranet	▪ Compaq/Internet Integration (ID:10-443) ▪ Internet Security Solutions (ID:10-415)
Messaging and Collaboration	▪ Compaq Messaging and Collaboration Solutions (ID:330-260) ▪ Implementing and Supporting Microsoft Exchange Server 5.5 (Microsoft exam ID:70-081)
Oracle	Compaq/Oracle Integration and Performance (ID:10-434)
SAP	Compaq/SAP R/3 Integration and Performance (ID:10-436)
SQL Server	Compaq/SQL Server Integration and Performance ID:10-432)

Administrator

Compaq exams are administered by Sylvan Prometric. Call (800) 366-3926 to register for Compaq tests; if outside the U.S., use the online Sylvan Test Center Locator at www.sylvanprometric.com to find the nearest testing center. Microsoft tests are administered by both Sylvan Prometric and Virtual University Enterprises (VUE). To register for a test with VUE visit the VUE Web site (http://www.vue .com/student-services/). Call Sylvan at (800) 755-3926 to register for Microsoft tests; if outside the U.S., use the online Sylvan Test Center Locator at www.sylvanprometric.com to find the nearest testing center. (Chapter 3 contains detailed information on taking tests from Sylvan or VUE.)

Fee

The Compaq exams cost $100 each. Microsoft exams, if required, also cost $100 each.

Format

Compaq tests are taken online at Sylvan Prometric testing centers. In some cases, a brand new test will be administered in a paper-based beta format. Test scores are available immediately after completion of the test, and are automatically forwarded to Compaq. Each of the tests consists of 50 questions. To pass, you must answer 30 questions correctly within the one-hour time limit. Most of the tests are closed-book.

Compaq Resources

Compaq offers several resources to help you prepare for their certification exams. Compaq ASE Self-Assessment Guides provide information about the topics covered on the exams. The Assessment Guides are free and can be downloaded from Compaq's Web site. Compaq offers a preparatory course for each of the exams, and strongly recommends that candidates take these courses prior to attempting the exams. For some of the specialization tracks, one has a choice of taking the courses individually or all at once in an accelerated four- or five-day course package. Course registration can be done online. For more information on this organization's certification program and courses, contact Compaq at:

Web	http://www.compaq.com/ase
E-mail	ASE.Program@compaq.com
Mail	ASE Program Manager
	Compaq Computer Corporation
	Mailstop 580505
	PO Box 692000
	Houston, TX 77269-2000
Phone	(800) 732-5741
	For information specific to the ASE program, call (281) 514-2266.
Fax	(281) 514-6039
Faxback	(800) 345-1518

Disaster Recovery Institute (DRI) International Certifications

- Associate Business Continuity Planner (ABCP)

- Certified Business Continuity Planner (CBCP)

- Master Business Continuity Planner (MBCP)

The Disaster Recovery Institute (DRI) International is an independent, nonprofit organization that was founded in 1988 to establish a base of common knowledge and professional practices in business continuity/disaster recovery planning. DRI International also certifies professionals in this field. This certification is not related exclusively to computer hardware; it involves preparation to ensure that a company can survive a disaster or natural catastrophe. Preserving and recovering a company's information infrastructure is clearly a major concern in this type of training. DRI International provides professionals with the knowledge and methodology to help ensure that critical data is not lost and downtime is minimized in the event of a major catastrophe.

DRI International offers three levels of certification: Associate Business Continuity Planner (ABCP), Certified Business Continuity Professional (CBCP), and Master Business Continuity Professional (MBCP). Professionals who have found it useful to obtain these certifications include independent consultants and information technology professionals in large corporations.

Recertification or Maintenance Requirements

Both CBCPs and MBCPs are required to maintain their certification by participating in 80 continuing education credits on related topics every two years. In addition, there is an annual recertification fee of $75 for CBCPs and $100 for MBCPs.

Benefits of Certification

While DRI International certification does not offer some of the incidental benefits provided with vendor-based certifications (logos, coffee cups, etc.), there can be a great benefit in job security and/or advancement for individuals obtaining any of these three certifications. As more companies invest their future in information infrastructures, having an employee on staff who can plan for and deal with any contingency becomes crucial.

Associate Business Continuity Planner (ABCP)

The one test required for this certification covers basic information on business continuity planning and disaster recovery. To help you prepare for this test, DRI International offers related course work and study guides (see the "DRI International Resources" section that follows for more information).

Who Needs It

This certification is great for individuals who have not yet acquired the necessary experience to become a CBCP. The ABCP is an important step in building your credentials as a continuity planner for your company's computing resources.

Requirements for Certification

The certification process requires only one step:

1. Pass the written qualifying exam with a score of 75 percent.

Administrator

Contact DRI International for the location nearest you.

Fee

The test costs $250; candidates who fail may retake the exam within one year for $50.

Format

The test consists of approximately 125 questions. Candidates for the ABCP and CBCP certifications must score a minimum of 75 percent, while those seeking the MBCP need to pass with an 85 percent score.

Certified Business Continuity Planner (CBCP)

This is the second level of certification for business continuity planners. It uses the same test as the ABCP certification, but also requires related work experience and board certification.

Who Needs It

This certification targets individuals who have or desire a high degree of responsibility for business continuity planning and have at least two years of experience in a related field. The CBCP can be an excellent way to prove that you are ready to move up in responsibility within your company or elsewhere.

Requirements for Certification

The certification process requires the following steps:

1. Pass the written qualifying exam (described for the ABCP above) with a score of 75 percent.

2. Have at least two years of experience in three of the following areas: project initiation and management, risk evaluation and control, business impact analysis, developing business continuity strategies, emergency response and operations, developing and implementing

business continuity plans, awareness and training programs, maintaining and exercising business continuity plans, public relations and crisis communication, and coordination with public authorities.

3. Submit the CBCP application and processing fee.

Administrator

Contact DRI International for the location nearest you.

Fee

In addition to the cost of the test (see the ABCP section above) there is a $100 fee for processing the CBCP application.

Master Business Continuity Planner (MBCP)

This is the highest level of certification for business continuity planners. It uses the same test as the ABCP certification, but requires a higher score. To qualify for the MBCP you must have recently (within the past 10 years) had five years of significant experience in business continuity or disaster recovery planning. In addition, the MBCP requires board certification and a case study exam or an independent research effort in the field.

Who Needs It

The MBCP is the top-of-the-line certification for business continuity planners. It is an excellent credential for independent consultants in the field.

Requirements for Certification

The certification process requires the following steps:

1. Meet the prescribed experience requirement.

2. Pass the written qualifying exam (described for the ABCP above) with a score of 85 or higher.

3. Complete either a case study project or directed research paper.

4. Submit the MBCP application and processing fee.

Contact DRI International for more information about the criteria for the case study project or directed research paper.

Administrator

Contact DRI International for the location nearest you.

Fee

In addition to the cost of the test (see the ABCP section above) there is a $200 fee for processing the MBCP application.

DRI International Resources

DRI International offers a number of basic, advanced, and specialty courses in business continuity planning and disaster recovery. They also provide a free study guide for the basic continuity-planning test. For more information on this organization's courses and certification programs, or to request a study guide, contact DRI International at:

Web	`http://www.dr.org`
E-mail	`drii@dr.org`
Mail	Disaster Recovery Institute International
	1810 Craig Road, Suite 125
	St. Louis, MO 63146
Phone	(314) 434-2272
Fax	(314) 434-1260

IBM Certifications

- IBM Certified Professional Server Specialist (PSS)

- IBM Certified Professional Server Expert (PSE)

IBM makes all types of computers, from mainframes to PCs. IBM offers two certifications that are relevant for professionals dealing with PC server hardware issues: the IBM Certified Professional Server Specialist (PSS) and the IBM Certified Professional Server Expert (PSE). The PSE certification offers two options for server specialization.

NOTE IBM offers a large number of certification program tracks (see `http://www.ibm.com/Education/certify/certs`).

Recertification or Maintenance Requirements

After initial certification, IBM requires annual update tests for all IBM Certified Professional Server Experts and Professional Server Specialists. These tests can be taken online through the TechConnect Web site (see `http://www.ibm.com/pc/techconnect/`). The update test consists of 25 multiple-choice questions. Test takers have 50 minutes to complete the online test and may attempt the test up to three times.

Benefits of Certification

IBM offers several valuable support features to those who complete its hardware certification programs. (Some of these features are even offered to those at the novice level; see the information Tip about the TechConnect Member, that follows.)

TechConnect Certified Members, including Professional Server Specialists (PSSs), receive the following benefits:

- A subscription to the TechConnect CD, which offers the latest product updates, reference materials, and industry news

- Access to current drivers and fixes

- Access to the online TechConnect Forum

- A subscription to *TechConnect Priority,* a mailing with up-to-date technical information

- Certification kit with personalized, framed certificate

IBM Certified PSEs receive the TechConnect CD, the latest drivers and fixes, and access to the TechConnect Forum, plus the following benefits:

- *PSE Priority,* a large collection of technical materials that includes an additional IBM gift (the nature of this gift changes periodically)

- Certification kit with personalized, framed certificate

- Priority access to the IBM HelpCenter with a personal identification code

- Special electronic access to IBM support

- Access to interactive forums on the IBM PC Company Bulletin Board System

- Opportunity to attend IBM's annual PSE recognition event, referred to as IMPACT

TIP   IBM also offers the designation TechConnect Member—which is not a certification, but provides some very nice benefits—to anyone who registers online (see `http://www.ibm.com/pc/techconnect`). TechConnect Members receive a subscription to the TechConnect CD, which offers the latest product updates, reference materials, industry news, and the latest drivers and fixes, and access to the online TechConnect Forum.

IBM Certified Professional Server Specialist (PSS)

This is the introductory level of IBM hardware certification. The IBM Certified PSS certification program involves taking one required course and passing the test given at the end of that course. The test assesses knowledge of IBM Netfinity architecture, design, installation, and configuration. If you fail the test at the end of a training course, you can retake the test at a later date.

You must also sign an IBM certification agreement that spells out the terms under which you are authorized to use the IBM certification logos and titles.

Who Needs It

The IBM Certified Professional Server Specialist is a key initial certification for computer professionals who will be installing, maintaining, and administering IBM Netfinity Server.

Requirements for Certification

The certification process requires the following steps:

1. Take the three-day IBM Course V5051 (IBM Netfinity Technical Training) and pass the test at the end of the course.

2. Submit a signed IBM Certification Agreement.

Administrator

The test is administered at the completion of the required course. IBM courses are offered throughout the world by IBM TechConnect Training Partners. See the "IBM Resources" section that follows for more information.

Fee

The course costs $750. There is no additional cost for the test.

Format

The one-hour test consists of approximately 46 multiple-choice questions.

IBM Certified Professional Server Expert (PSE)

The PSE certification builds on the PSS program and offers specialization in a particular network operating system. This certification program involves achieving IBM Certified PSS status, attaining the appropriate operating system credential required for the desired specialization, and then taking one additional required two-day IBM course and passing the test at the end of that course. The required IBM course and test cover knowledge of the installation process for the desired operating system using IBM Server Guide, and tuning the software and hardware for optimal performance. If you fail the test at the end of a training course, you can retake the test at a later date. You must also sign an IBM certification agreement that spells out the terms under which you are authorized to use the IBM certification logos and titles. See the Tip that follows this section for another option for getting your PSE certification. PSEs can specialize in the following areas:

- Novell NetWare
- Windows NT

Who Needs It

This certification provides proof of your expertise in installing, administering, and troubleshooting Novell NetWare or Windows NT server software running on IBM Netfinity Server. The PSE certification is especially valuable to field engineers or independent contractors who are responsible for servers at multiple locations.

Requirements for Certification

The certification process requires the following steps:

1. Attain PSS certification (see the previous section for details).

2. Take the two-day IBM Course required for the desired specialization and pass the test at the end of the course (see Table 4.7).

3. Submit proof of the operating system certification required for the specialization you seek (see Table 4.8).

4. Submit a signed IBM Certification Agreement.

T A B L E 4.7: Required IBM Courses and Exams for PSE Certification

Specialization	Required IBM Course and Exam
Novell NetWare	V5052 (IBM Netfinity and Server/NetWare Installation and Performance)
Windows NT	V5055 (IBM Netfinity and PC Server/Windows NT Installation and Performance)

T A B L E 4.8: Required Operating System Certifications for PSE Certification

Specialization	Required Certification
Novell NetWare	Novell NetWare CNE
Windows NT	Microsoft Certified Systems Engineer (MCSE)

NOTE See Chapter 9 for details on the certifications referenced in Table 4.8.

Administrator

In each case, the test is administered at the completion of the required course. IBM courses are offered throughout the world by IBM Tech-Connect Training Partners. See the "IBM Resources" section that follows for more information.

Fee

Each PSE course costs $600. There is no additional cost for the test.

Format

Each PSE test consists of approximately 35 multiple-choice questions and lasts 45 minutes.

TIP If you want to become an IBM Certified PSE specializing in either Novell or Windows NT, there is an alternative route to certification. IBM PC Institute, the U.S. TechConnect Training Partner, offers four-day courses that combine the PSS and PSE courses for these two specializations. Course V5072 (IBM Netfinity Technical/IntranetWare) leads to the PSE certification in Novell, and course V5075 (IBM Netfinity Technical/Windows NT) leads to the PSE certification in Windows NT. Each course costs $1,200 (for more information check out `http://www.pc.ibm.com/training/us_info_certification.html`).

IBM Resources

The required IBM courses and tests are offered by the following IBM TechConnect Training Partners: the IBM PC Institute (U.S.), Computer-2000 (Germany), and TechData. The IBM Web site offers links to each of these organizations. Test objectives and sample tests are available online or from IBM's faxback service. For more information on these courses and certification programs, contact IBM at:

Web `http://www.ibm.com/pc/techconnect/`

E-mail	Techconn@us.ibm.com
Mail	Professional Certification Program
	IBM Corporation, Mail Stop 3013
	11400 Burnet Rd.
	Austin, TX 78758
Phone	(800) 235-4746
Fax	(512) 838-7961
Faxback	(800) 426-4329, request item 3211

Intel Certifications

- Certified Solutions Consultant

- Certified Integration Specialist

Intel's microprocessors have driven the microcomputer industry since the early development of the PC. In addition to manufacturing most of the processors found in servers and workstations today, Intel now offers a line of networking products, including intelligent hubs, routers, and other essential network devices.

Intel's two certification tracks—Certified Solutions Consultant and Certified Integration Specialist—are primarily for those people involved in the sale and support of computers based on Intel's microprocessors. The Certified Solution Consultant is tailored to those responsible for pre-sale design and consulting, while the Certified Integration Specialist title is best for those providing post-sales technical support. The Certified Integration Specialist track features two specializations: Desktop/Server Integration and Networking.

Recertification or Maintenance Requirements

Intel certification is valid for 12 months. In order to maintain your certified status, you must complete update exam(s) as specified by Intel. Intel notifies all certified individuals about the recertification requirements prior to their certification expiration date.

Benefits of Certification

Intel Certified Solutions Consultants and Integration Specialists receive the following benefits:

- Priority support and tools for use in assisting your clients
- Notification about new releases and developments
- Plaque
- Intel Certified lapel pin
- Use of Intel Certified logo on business cards and stationery

Certified Solutions Consultant

The Intel Certified Solutions Consultant track is designed for professionals who are primarily involved in the design, analysis, and management of projects involving Intel's products. Obtaining this certification involves first taking one Web-based test and then taking three exams administered by Sylvan Prometric. Intel offers training courses and online pre-tests to help you prepare for their tests. See the "Intel Resources" section below for more information.

Who Needs It

The Certified Solutions Consultant is an ideal certification for the "pre-sales" engineer who is focused on recommending technologies and designing solutions for customers. This certification is an excellent way to demonstrate your ability to design solutions based on Intel microprocessors and can help you move into a position of higher responsibility.

Requirements for Certification

The certification process requires the following steps:

1. Complete and submit the Intel Certification Agreement.

2. Take Intel's Web-based course titled "The New Computer Industry and Intel" and pass the associated Web-based test.

3. Pass the DS300 Desktop/Server Design test (administered by Sylvan).

4. Pass the AN300 Networking Design test (administered by Sylvan).

5. Pass the S400 Intel Business Solutions test (administered by Sylvan).

Administrator

Call Sylvan Prometric at (800) 930-3926 to register for an Intel exam; if outside the U.S., use the online Sylvan Test Center Locator at www.sylvanprometric.com to find the nearest testing center. (See Chapter 3 for detailed information on taking tests from Sylvan.)

Fee

There is no fee for the Web-based "New Computer Industry and Intel" test. Fees for Intel tests administered by Sylvan vary based on test length and format; call Sylvan Prometric at (800) 930-3926 for pricing.

Format

The tests administered by Sylvan Prometric are computer-based, multiple-choice tests. Call Sylvan Prometric at (800) 930-3926 for current information on the number of questions, time limit, and passing score.

Certified Integration Specialist

Intel Certified Integration Specialist track is designed for those involved in the post-sale support and configuration of Intel technology. This track requires individuals to specialize in either desktop/server integration or networking. Regardless of the specialty selected, Certified Integration Specialists will be able to install, configure, maintain and troubleshoot Intel components in a wide variety of situations. Attaining this certification involves taking one Web-based test and either five or six tests administered by Sylvan Prometric. Intel offers training courses and online pre-tests to help you prepare for their tests. See the "Intel Resources" section below for more information. Certified Integration Specialists can specialize in the following areas:

- Desktop/Server Integration
- Networking

Who Needs It

The Intel Certified Integration Specialist certification is an excellent way to showcase your ability to go beyond the basics in designing systems based on Intel products; it proves your ability to handle complex implementations and real-world problems. The desktop/server integration specialty is of most value to those interested in server design and performance testing. The network infrastructure specialty is most appropriate for those involved with designing optimal network systems.

Requirements for Certification

The certification process requires the following steps:

1. Complete and submit the Intel Certification Agreement.

2. Take Intel's Web-based course titled "The New Computer Industry and Intel" and pass the associated Web-based test.

3. Pass the DS100 Desktop/Server Integration test (administered by Sylvan).

4. Pass the AN100 Networking Implementation test (administered by Sylvan).

5. Pass the AM100 Client/Server Management Technologies test (administered by Sylvan).

6. Pass the additional required tests for the specialization you seek (see Table 4.9).

T A B L E 4.9: Additional Required Tests for Certified Integration Specialists

Specialization	Additional Required Tests
Desktop/Server Integration Specialty	DS200 Advanced Desktop/Server Integration DS300 Desktop/Server Design
Networking Infrastructure Specialty	AN200 Networking Router Implementation AN250 Networking Advanced Implementation AN300 Networking Design

NOTE   All of the exams in Table 4.9 above are administered by Sylvan.

Administrator

Call Sylvan Prometric at (800) 930-3926 to register for an Intel exam; if outside the U.S., use the online Sylvan Test Center Locator at www.sylvanprometric.com to find the nearest testing center. (See Chapter 3 for detailed information on taking tests from Sylvan.)

Fee

There is no fee for the Web-based "New Computer Industry and Intel" test. Fees for Intel tests administered by Sylvan vary based on test length and format; call Sylvan Prometric at (800) 930-3926 for pricing.

Format

The tests administered by Sylvan Prometric are computer-based, multiple-choice tests. Call Sylvan Prometric at (800) 930-3926 for current information on the number of questions, time limit, and passing score.

Intel Resources

Intel offers a number of training courses to help prepare you for the required tests; consult the online Intel Certification Course Catalog at the Web address listed below. In addition, Intel offers a number of online pre-tests for candidates to use to determine if they are ready for the real test. For more information on this organization's certification program and courses, contact Intel at:

Web	http://channel.intel.com/training/ certification/
Mail	Intel Corporation
	c/o D. Spinden
	MS JF3-315
	5200 NE Elam Young Pkwy
	Hillsboro OR 97124
Phone	(800) 978-8897
Fax	(612) 897-1015

Learning Tree International Certification

- PC Service and Support Certified Professional

Learning Tree International is a worldwide training organization that currently offers over 150 computer and networking courses in the United States, Europe, and Asia. As part of their curriculum in information technology, Learning Tree International offers 26 different vendor-independent professional certification programs, one of which is oriented toward PC hardware. (See Chapters 5, 7, 8, 13, and 14 for additional Learning Tree International Certification programs.)

The Learning Tree International PC Service and Support Certified Professional credential may be useful to PC support staff, service technicians, engineers, system and network administrators, and anyone else involved with the configuration, operation, maintenance, and support of PC hardware. This certification involves the mastery of a series of hardware service and support courses. These courses offer extensive hands-on training with PC hardware, operating systems, and networks.

Recertification or Maintenance Requirements

There is no recertification requirement for any of Learning Tree International's certification programs.

Benefits of Certification

Learning Tree International PC Service and Support Certified Professionals receive the following benefits:

- Framed diploma
- An official record of the courses that you have completed
- Option to obtain college credit

NOTE It is possible to obtain college credit for Learning Tree International certifications or courses. The American Council of Education (ACE) in Washington, D.C. has worked in cooperation with Learning Tree International to determine college course equivalencies for these courses and certifications. Approximately 1,500 colleges and universities in the United States will accept ACE recommendations for college credit. As a general rule, ACE will recommend two college credit hours for each four-day course. Learning Tree International will pay to have your Learning Tree International credentials registered with ACE and you can then request that your transcript be sent from ACE to any college or university. (Check with your college or university registrar to make sure that your institution accepts ACE recommendations for credit.)

PC Service and Support Certified Professional

This certification program consists of taking four core courses and one elective course and passing the tests given at the end of each course. The courses and exams are designed to teach and test the candidate's ability to disassemble and reassemble a complete PC system; diagnose and fix PC hardware and software problems; install and configure motherboards, adapter cards, and disk drives; recover lost files and directories; solve memory management conflicts; install, configure, optimize, and troubleshoot Windows 95/98; work with NetWare, Windows NT Server, and Windows 95/98; and optimize PC network performance.

Who Needs It

This certification is a good vendor-independent credential for those who want to get a position working with hardware and software from multiple vendors and manufacturers (a situation typical of many organizations). Since the certification program requires comprehensive training classes, Learning Tree International certifications offer a means for those just beginning their computing careers to gain hands-on experience and training that may not currently be available on the job.

Requirements for Certification

The certification process requires the following steps:

1. Complete the three core courses listed below and pass the test given at the end of each course.

2. Complete one of the two optional core courses and pass the test given at the end of the course.

3. Complete one of the elective courses and pass the test given at the end of the course. See Table 4.10 for details.

T A B L E 4.10: Course Requirements for PC Service and Support Certified Professional

Three Core Requirements		
Course	**Course Number**	**Length**
Hands-On PC Configuration and Troubleshooting	145	4 days
Advanced PC Configuration, Trouble-shooting and Data Recovery: Hands-On	150	4 days
Hands-On PC Networking	253	4 days
Fourth Core Requirement Options		
Course	**Course Number**	**Length**
Windows 95 Support and Networking: Hands-On	153	5 days
Managing Windows 98 Systems and Networks: Hands-On	553	5 days

T A B L E 4.10: Course Requirements for PC Service and Support Certified Professional *(continued)*

Electives		
Course	**Course Number**	**Length**
Integrating Microsoft Office 97	208	4 days
LAN Troubleshooting	254	4 days
UNIX Introduction	336	4 days
Windows NT 4	455	5 days
NetWare 4.x Administration	264	5 days
Windows NT and UNIX Integration	158	4 days
Notes and Domino Introduction	179	4 days
Introduction to Internetworking	364	4 days

Administrator

Contact Learning Tree International. Call (800) THE-TREE.

Fee

At this writing, the prices for Learning Tree International courses are $1,295 for a two-day course, $1,745 for a three-day course, $2,195 for a four-day course, and $2,495 for a five-day course. Learning Tree International offers some significant discounts for those taking more than one course and for government employees. There is no additional charge for the tests.

Format

Each exam consists of 40 to 60 questions. If you fail to pass on the first try, Learning Tree International will arrange for you to take a proctored exam at your place of work.

Learning Tree International Resources

For more information on this organization's courses and certification programs, contact Learning Tree International at:

Web	http://www.learningtree.com
E-mail	uscourses@learningtree.com
Mail	Learning Tree International
	1805 Library Street
	Reston, VA 20190-5630
Phone	(800) THE-TREE or (800) 843-8733
Fax	(800) 709-6405

CHAPTER

5

Operating Systems
Certifications

FEATURING

- IBM AIX Certifications

- IBM AS/400 Certifications

- IBM OS/2 Certification

- Learning Tree International Certification

- Microsoft Certification

- Red Hat Certification

- Santa Cruz Operation (SCO) Certifications

- Silicon Graphics Certifications

- Sun Certifications

An operating system brings life to a computer's chips and electrons. It's the basic code that controls access to a computer's resources and manages all the programs running on that computer. Because of its central importance, an incorrectly configured operating system can suck the speed and productivity right out of the fastest processor.

Desktop computers usually have one of three types of operating systems:

- Apple's Macintosh operating system
- A version of UNIX
- Microsoft's DOS or Windows operating system

There are also several vendor-specific operating systems designed for use only on certain machines.

Certifications offered by several makers of UNIX-based operating systems are covered in this chapter—IBM, Red Hat, Santa Cruz Organization, Silicon Graphics, and Sun—as well as Learning Tree International's vendor-independent UNIX certification. Microsoft offers the Microsoft Certified Professional credential for technical professionals who are proficient in either Windows 95 or Windows NT. In addition, IBM offers certifications related to its AS/400 operating system and two certification programs on OS/2, IBM's PC-based operating system.

NOTE   UNIX is used both as a workstation operating system and a network operating system. We chose to list UNIX-based certifications in this chapter because UNIX can be considered—at its most basic level—a computer operating system.

Since problems with networking and software operation are often related to a computer's operating system, many technical professionals will benefit from the knowledge and skills gained from operating system certification programs. An operating system certification may be valuable to:

- Help desk personnel
- Technical staff
- System administrators
- Network administrators
- Field personnel

Use Table 5.1 to compare the number of required tests, the test format, the approximate cost of taking the test(s), number of required courses, cost of any required courses, and the relative difficulty of the certification programs in this chapter. The cost information is a general guideline; since things change rapidly in the world of certification programs, once you have selected a specific course of action you may want to double-check the costs.

We classified the difficulty of these certifications into three categories—Moderate, Challenging, and Very Challenging—based on the number of required tests and courses, and the relative difficulty of those tests or lab exams. These ratings are approximate and are offered simply as a general guide to help the reader distinguish between entry-level programs and those that require more advanced skill and knowledge. (This rating scale assumes that one has experience with the product or technology and has studied the appropriate subject content before attempting the exams.)

TABLE 5.1: Operating Systems Certifications

Certification	# of Required Tests	Test Format(s)	Total Cost of Required Tests	# of Required Courses	Total Cost of Required Courses	Difficulty	Notes
IBM AIX Certifications							
IBM Certified AIX User Version 4	1	MC	VF	—	—	○	Designed for AIX users rather than technical specialists.

T A B L E 5.1: Operating Systems Certifications *(continued)*

Certification	# of Required Tests	Test Format(s)	Total Cost of Required Tests	# of Required Courses	Total Cost of Required Courses	Difficulty	Notes
IBM AIX Certifications							
IBM Certified Specialist	1 or 2	MC	VF	—	—	◐	IBM Certified Specialist credentials are available in these areas: AIX System Administration, AIX System Support, and AIX HACMP.
IBM Certified Advanced Technical Expert—RS/6000 AIX	3	MC	VF	—	—	●	You must first be an IBM Certified Specialist in AIX System Administration or Support.
IBM AS/400 Certifications							
IBM Certified Specialist	1	MC	VF	—	—	◐	IBM Certified Specialist credentials are available in these areas: AS/400 Associate System Operator, AS/400 Professional System Operator, AS/400 Associate System Administrator, AS/400 client Access.
IBM OS/2 Certification							
IBM Certified Systems Expert—OS/2 Warp 4	3–4	MC	VF	—	—	◐	
Learning Tree International Certification							
UNIX Systems Certified Professional	5	MC	CV	5	$10,000–$12,000	◐	Discount pricing available; contact Learning Tree.

T A B L E 5.1: Operating Systems Certifications *(continued)*

Certification	# of Required Tests	Test Format(s)	Total Cost of Required Tests	# of Required Courses	Total Cost of Required Courses	Difficulty	Notes
Microsoft Certification							
Microsoft Certified Professional (MCP)	1	MC	$100	—	—	○	MCP status can be obtained by passing an operating system exam or a specific product exam.
Red Hat Certification							
Red Hat Certified Engineer (RHCE)	1	PR	CV	1	$2,498	◐	
Santa Cruz Operation, Inc. (SCO) Certifications							
Certified UNIX System Administrator (CUSA)	1	MC	VF ($125–$180)	—	—	○	Specializations include: SCO OpenServer Release 5, and SCO UnixWare 7.
Advanced Certified Engineer (ACE)	3	MC	VF ($375–$540)	—	—	◐	Specializations include: SCO OpenServer Release 5, and SCO UnixWare 7.
Silicon Graphics, Inc. (SGI) Certifications							
Certified IRIX 6.*x* Systems Administrator	2	MC	VF	—	—	◐	
Certified IRIX 6.*x* Network Administrator	1	MC	VF	—	—	●	You must first be a Silicon Graphics Certified IRIX 6.*x* Systems Administrator.
SUN Certifications							
Certified System Administrator	2	MC	$300	—	—	◐	You can be certified on either Solaris version 2.5 or 2.6.

T A B L E 5.1: Operating Systems Certifications *(continued)*

Certification	# of Required Tests	Test Format(s)	Total Cost of Required Tests	# of Required Courses	Total Cost of Required Courses	Difficulty	Notes
SUN Certifications							
Certified Network Administrator	1	MC	$150	—	—	●	You must first be a Sun Certified System Administrator. Specialize in either Solaris version 2.5 or 2.6.

Certification Difficulty: ○ Moderate   ◐ Challenging   ● Very Challenging

Test Format: **MC:** Multiple Choice   **AT:** Adaptive Testing   **LA:** Live Application
PR: Hands-on Lab   **NA:** Not Applicable

Test Fee: **VF:** Test Fees can vary; consult testing center.   **CV:** Voucher for taking the exam is included in the fee for the required course(s); additional attempts cost extra.

IBM AIX Certifications

- IBM Certified AIX User Version 4

- IBM Certified Specialist AIX Certifications

- IBM Certified Advanced Technical Expert—RS/6000 AIX

The AIX operating system is the IBM version of UNIX designed for the RS/6000 series of computers. IBM offers three important certifications related to the AIX operating system at the IBM Certified Specialist level—the IBM Certified Specialist—AIX System Administration, the IBM Certified Specialist—AIX System Support, and the IBM Certified Specialist—AIX High Availability Cluster Multi-Processing (HACMP). A more advanced level of AIX ability is validated by the IBM Certified Advanced Technical Expert designation. The relevant credential in this case is the IBM Certified Advanced Technical Expert—RS/6000 AIX. An introductory-level certification—IBM Certified AIX User—is also available.

Recertification or Maintenance Requirements

The IBM Certified AIX User Version 4, IBM Certified Specialist, and IBM Certified Advanced Technical Expert designations apply to specific version numbers of the AIX operating system, so there is no requirement for recertification on a particular version. Since your certification is tied to a certain version of a product, however, you will want to become certified on the newer versions, when they become available, if you want to continue to have the most current credential in this area.

Benefits of Certification

IBM Certified Specialists receive these benefits:

- Certification logo for use on business cards or stationery
- Certificate
- Wallet-size certificate
- Lapel pin

TIP   IBM offers a large number of certification program tracks. For a complete listing, check out http://www.ibm.com/certify. Click the certification logo to display the site map and then select "Roadmaps."

IBM Certified AIX User Version 4

This certification is the most basic certification related to the AIX operating system. It certifies a candidate's understanding of AIX fundamentals and ability to apply AIX concepts to the effective use and operation of an AIX system. The exam for this certification covers basic file management, using the screen editor, setting up login sessions, controlling print jobs, and using windows.

IBM recommends that those who seek this certification have six months' experience using the AIX operating system prior to attempting the test. IBM's Web site provides a list of objectives for this test, as well as sample test questions (see `http://www.ibm.com/certify`).

Who Needs It

This certification can help you get your foot in the door at a company that uses AIX. It lets employers know that you have fundamental knowledge and skill in using the AIX operating system.

Requirements for Certification

The certification process requires only one step:

1. Pass the IBM AIX V4 User test (Test ID: 000-160).

Administrator

IBM exams are administered by Sylvan Prometric. Call (800) 959-3926 to register for IBM tests; if outside the U.S., use the online Sylvan Test Center Locator at `http://www.sylvanprometric.com` to find the nearest testing center. (See Chapter 3 for detailed information on taking tests from Sylvan.)

Fee

Fees for IBM tests vary based on test length and format; call Sylvan Prometric at (800) 959-3926 for current pricing.

Format

The exam is a one-hour, computer-based test with 60 multiple-choice questions. Call Sylvan Prometric at (800) 959-3926 for the most current information on the number of questions, time limit, and passing score.

IBM Certified Specialist AIX Certifications

This certification is designed for technical professionals who will be working with AIX systems on a daily basis, either in administering a system or in providing technical support.

The following IBM Certified Specialist designations are relevant for those who work with AIX systems:

- IBM Certified Specialist—AIX System Administration
- IBM Certified Specialist—AIX System Support
- IBM Certified Specialist—AIX HACMP

The test for the AIX System Administration designation assesses the candidate's ability to install AIX and to perform a broad range of general system administration tasks. The test for the AIX System Support designation covers the administration and networking of AIX systems, with an emphasis on the skills needed for problem determination and resolution. IBM recommends that prior to taking either test, candidates have one year of general AIX or UNIX experience, at least six months of experience with an AIX system, and substantial training or experience in AIX system administration. Those attempting the AIX system support test should also have training or experience in TCP/IP and AIX Performance Tuning.

The AIX HACMP designation indicates that one has the skills needed to plan, install, configure, troubleshoot, and support AIX High Availability Cluster Multi-Processing (HACMP) systems. To attain the AIX HACMP credential, one must pass either the AIX System Administration test or the AIX System Support test, plus one additional test. IBM also recommends that the candidate have a minimum of six months to one year of experience in installing, configuring, and supporting HACMP for AIX.

IBM's Web site provides a list of objectives for each of these tests, as well as sample test questions (see http://www.ibm.com/certify).

Who Needs It

The IBM Certified Specialist AIX designations are great credentials for getting a job in AIX support or administration. The AIX System Administration designation lets employers know that you have the knowledge and skills needed to install and administrate AIX systems, while the AIX System Support credential shows that you know how to troubleshoot and maintain AIX systems. The AIX HACMP credential certifies your ability to plan, install, and configure AIX High Availability Cluster Multi-Processing (HACMP) systems, and to perform the diagnostic tasks needed for their support.

Requirements for Certification

The certification process requires one or two steps, depending on the credential selected:

1. Pass the required exam(s) for the specialization you seek (See Table 5.2).

T A B L E 5.2:   Required Exams for IBM Certified Specialist (AIX) Certifications

IBM Certified Specialist Designation	Required Exam(s)
AIX System Administration	IBM AIX V4.3 System Administration (Test ID: 000-181)
AIX System Support	IBM AIX V4.3 Support (Test ID: 000-189)
AIX HACMP	EITHER IBM AIX V4.3 System Administration (Test ID: 000-181) OR IBM AIX V4.3 Support (Test ID: 000-189), AND HACMP for AIX V4.2 (Test ID: 000-167)

Administrator

IBM exams are administered by Sylvan Prometric. Call (800) 959-3926 to register for IBM tests; if outside the U.S., use the online Sylvan Test Center Locator at http://www.sylvanprometric.com to find the nearest testing center. (See Chapter 3 for detailed information on taking tests from Sylvan.)

Fee

Fees for IBM tests vary based on test length and format; call Sylvan Prometric at (800) 959-3926 for current pricing.

Format

The AIX System Administration and Support exams are computer-based tests with approximately 60 multiple-choice questions. They range in length from 60 to 90 minutes. The AIX HACMP exam has 50 multiple-choice questions and lasts 135 minutes. Call Sylvan Prometric at (800) 959-3926 for the most current information on the number of questions, time limit, and passing score.

IBM Certified Advanced Technical Expert— RS/6000 AIX

This is the most prestigious certification associated with the AIX operating system, and it builds on the IBM Certified Specialist designations discussed previously. An individual with this certification has the ability to perform in-depth analyses, apply complex AIX concepts, and provide resolution to critical problems. The three additional exams for this certification delve into considerable detail on troubleshooting, networking, and optimizing performance. IBM's Web site provides a list of objectives for each of these tests, as well as sample test questions (see `http://www.ibm.com/ certify`).

Who Needs It

The IBM Certified Advanced Technical Expert—RS/6000 AIX designation is a great credential for getting a high-level job in AIX support and administration. It lets employers know that you have an advanced level of knowledge and skills in all aspects of AIX.

Requirements for Certification

The certification process requires the following steps:

1. Attain certification as an IBM Certified Specialist in AIX System Administration or AIX System Support (described previously).

2. Pass three of the seven exams listed in Table 5.3 (do not select both exam 168 and exam 178).

T A B L E 5.3: Exam Options for IBM Certified Advanced Technical
Expert—RS/6000 AIX

Exam	Test ID
IBM AIX V4.2 Installation and System Recovery	000-163
IBM AIX V4.2 Performance and System Tuning	000-164
IBM AIX V4.2 Problem Determination Tools and Techniques	000-165
IBM AIX V4.2 Communications	000-166
IBM HACMP for AIX V4.2	000-167
IBM RS/6000 SP* and PSSP** V2.2	000-168
IBM RS/6000 SP* and PSSP** V2.4	000-178

* Scalable POWERparallel
** Parallel System Support Program

Administrator

IBM exams are administered by Sylvan Prometric. Call (800) 959-3926 to register for IBM tests; if outside the U.S., use the online Sylvan Test Center Locator at http://www.sylvanprometric.com to find the nearest testing center. (See Chapter 3 for detailed information on taking tests from Sylvan.)

Fee

Fees for IBM tests vary based on test length and format; call Sylvan Prometric at (800) 959-3926 for pricing.

Format

These exams are computer-based tests with approximately 50 to 70 multiple-choice questions. They range in length from 75 to 135 minutes. Call Sylvan Prometric at (800) 959-3926 for the most current information on the number of questions, time limit, and passing score.

IBM AIX Resources

IBM's Web site offers a number of excellent resources for AIX certification candidates, including recommended courses, test objectives, study guides, and sample tests. For more information on these certification programs and related courses, contact IBM at:

Web	http://www.ibm.com/certify
E-mail	certify@us.ibm.com
Mail	Professional Certification Program from IBM
	IBM Corporation, Int. Zip 3013
	11400 Burnet Road
	Austin, TX 78758
Phone	(800) 426-8322
Fax	(512) 838-7961

IBM AS/400 Certifications

- IBM Certified Specialist Certifications

IBM's mid-range AS/400 computers are used by many businesses, organizations, and government agencies. We describe five key IBM credentials related to the AS/400 operating system: IBM Certified Specialist—AS/400 Associate System Operator, IBM Certified Specialist—AS/400 Professional System Operator, IBM Certified Specialist—AS/400 Associate System Administrator, IBM Certified Specialist—AS/400 Professional System Administrator, and IBM Certified Specialist—AS/400 Client Access.

TIP   IBM offers several other AS/400 certifications that are not covered in this book. Check out http://www.ibm.com/certify for a complete listing.

Recertification or Maintenance Requirements

The IBM AS/400 certifications apply to specific versions of the AS/400 operating system, so there is no requirement for recertification on a particular version. Since your certification is tied to a certain version of a product, however, you will want to become certified on the newest versions, when they become available, if you want to continue to have the most current credential in this area.

Benefits of Certification

IBM Certified Specialists receive these benefits:

- Certification logo for use on business cards or stationery
- Certificate
- Wallet-size certificate
- Lapel pin

IBM Certified Specialist Certifications for AS/400

To attain an IBM Certified Specialist credential related to the AS/400 operating system a candidate must pass one exam. The tests for the associate level credentials assume an intermediate level of experience and skill in working with AS/400 systems, while the professional level credentials target those who have a more advanced level of experience and skill. The following IBM Certified Specialist designations are relevant for those who work with AS/400 systems:

- IBM Certified Specialist—AS/400 Associate System Operator
- IBM Certified Specialist—AS/400 Professional System Operator
- IBM Certified Specialist—AS/400 Associate System Administrator
- IBM Certified Specialist—AS/400 Professional System Administrator
- IBM Certified Specialist—AS/400 Client Access

The system operator exams cover basic AS/400 operational concepts related to object management, saving and restoring files, managing the system, managing devices, controlling printer output, and controlling jobs. The professional system operator exam also covers problem management, starting and stopping the system, and security issues. The system administrator exams cover AS/400 administration concepts related to hardware, system software, operations, and security. The professional-level exam also addresses planning issues, such as capacity planning, backup and recovery, and disaster management. The AS/400 Client Access test assesses one's ability to install and support client access by adjusting both the AS/400 and PC environments. IBM's Web site provides a list of objectives for each of these tests, as well as sample test questions (see http://www.ibm.com/certify).

Please note that, at the time of publication, these exams test OS/400 version 4 Release 1 (V4R1) features, so you should read and respond to the questions from an OS/400 V4R1 perspective. At some point these tests will be updated to test a later version/release of OS/400.

Who Needs It

The IBM Certified Specialist AS/400 designations are great credentials to help you get your foot in the door at a company that uses an AS/400 system. The associate-level specializations let employers know that you have fundamental knowledge and skill on AS/400 systems, while the professional-level specializations indicate that you have the knowledge and skills needed to provide an advanced level of administration or technical support for AS/400 systems. The AS/400 Client Access specialization indicates that you can plan, assess, and implement client access solutions, and have the ability to optimize both AS/400 and PC environments.

Requirements for Certification

The certification process requires only one step:

1. Pass the exam required for the desired specialization (See Table 5.4).

TABLE 5.4: Required Exams for IBM Certified Specialist (AS/400) Certifications

Specialization	Required Exam
AS/400 Associate System Operator	IBM AS/400 Associate System Operator (Test ID: 000-052)
AS/400 Professional System Operator	IBM AS/400 Professional System Operator (Test ID: 000-053)
AS/400 Associate System Administrator	IBM AS/400 Associate System Administrator (Test ID: 000-054)
AS/400 Professional System Administrator	IBM AS/400 Professional System Administrator (Test ID: 000-055)
AS/400 Client Access	IBM AS/400 Client Access (Test ID: 000-058)

Administrator

IBM exams are administered by Sylvan Prometric. Call (800) 959-3926 to register for IBM tests; if outside the U.S., use the online Sylvan Test Center Locator at http://www.sylvanprometric.com to find the nearest testing center. (See Chapter 3 for detailed information on taking tests from Sylvan.)

Fee

Fees for IBM tests vary based on test length and format; call Sylvan Prometric at (800) 959-3926 for pricing.

Format

The associate and professional system operator and administrator exams are one-hour computer-based tests with approximately 60 multiple-choice questions. The client access test has 56 questions and lasts 75 minutes. Call Sylvan Prometric at (800) 959-3926 for current information on the number of questions, time limit, and passing score.

IBM AS/400 Resources

IBM's Web site offers a number of excellent resources for certification candidates, including recommended courses, test objectives, study guides, and sample tests. For more information on these courses and certification programs, contact IBM at:

Web	http://www.ibm.com/certify
E-mail	certify@us.ibm.com
Mail	Professional Certification Program from IBM
	IBM Corporation, Int. Zip 3013
	11400 Burnet Road
	Austin, TX 78758
Phone	(800) 426-8322
Fax	(512) 838-7961

IBM OS/2 Certification

- IBM Certified Systems Expert—OS/2 Warp 4

During the 1980s, IBM and Microsoft worked together to develop the OS/2 operating system as a graphical interface for the PC. After a much-publicized breakup of the partnership, IBM continued to develop OS/2 while Microsoft took off in its own direction with Windows.

IBM offers the IBM Certified Systems Expert—OS/2 Warp 4 credential for those who use its OS/2 operating system. If you are already certified as an IBM Certified OS/2 Engineer (OS/2 2.1) or an IBM Certified Systems Expert—OS/2 Warp (V3), you can quickly update your certification to OS/2 Warp 4 by taking the OS/2 Warp 4 Update exam (Test ID: 000-203).

Recertification or Maintenance Requirements

IBM OS/2 certification applies to a specific version of this operating system, so there is no requirement for recertification on a particular version. Since your certification is tied to a certain version of a product, however, you will want to become certified on the newest versions, when they become available, if you want to continue to have the most current credential in this area.

Benefits of Certification

IBM Certified OS/2 Systems Experts receive these benefits:

- Certification logo for use on business cards or stationery
- Certificate
- Wallet-size certificate
- Lapel pin

IBM Certified Systems Expert—OS/2 Warp 4

Attaining OS/2 Warp 4 certification requires passing three tests. It is recommended that all candidates have fundamental knowledge of DOS as well as experience in installing, configuring, and supporting OS/2 Warp 4.

The OS/2 Warp 4 Fundamentals test covers the basic concepts of planning and installation, customization and usage, and problem determination. The OS/2 Warp 4 Connectivity exam covers TCP/IP and the Internet, network operating system connectivity, remote access and host connectivity, and remote installation. The OS/2 Warp 4 Advanced Concepts and Support exam covers advanced topics, including speech and multimedia, troubleshooting and support services, performance optimization, application support, and system extensions.

Who Needs It

This certification can help you get your foot in the door at a company that uses OS/2 systems. This credential lets employers know that you have the necessary knowledge and skill to maintain OS/2 systems and support OS/2 users.

Requirements for Certification

The certification process requires the following step:

1. Pass the three tests listed in Table 5.5. It is recommended that the tests be taken in the order in which they are listed.

T A B L E 5.5:   Required Exams for IBM Certified Systems Expert—OS/2 Warp 4 Certification

Required Exams
IBM OS/2 Warp 4 Fundamentals (Test ID: 000-200)
IBM OS/2 Warp 4 Connectivity (Test ID: 000-201)
IBM OS/2 Warp 4 Advanced Concepts and Support (Test ID: 000-202)

Administrator

IBM exams are administered by Sylvan Prometric. Call (800) 959-3926 to register for IBM tests; if outside the U.S., use the online Sylvan Test Center Locator at http://www.sylvanprometric.com to find the nearest testing center. (See Chapter 3 for detailed information on taking tests from Sylvan.)

Fee

Fees for IBM tests vary based on test length and format; call Sylvan Prometric at (800) 959-3926 for pricing.

Format

The exams are computer-based tests with approximately 60 to 90 multiple-choice questions. Some of the exams have a 60-minute time limit and others last 75 minutes. Call Sylvan Prometric at (800) 959-3926 for current information on the number of questions, time limit, and passing score.

IBM OS/2 Resources

IBM's Web site offers a number of excellent resources for certification candidates, including test objectives, study guides, and sample tests. Several computer-based training courses and instructor-led training courses are also offered. Another excellent resource, the *OS/2 Warp 4 Certification Handbook*, is available for $60 from the IBM Direct publications catalog Web site (`http://www.elink.ibmlink.ibm.com/pbl/pbl`). Request publication number SG24-4869-00. For more information on these courses and certification programs, contact IBM at:

Web	`http://www.ibm.com/certify`
E-mail	`certify@us.ibm.com`
Mail	Professional Certification Program from IBM
	IBM Corporation, Int. Zip 3013
	11400 Burnet Road
	Austin, TX 78758
Phone	(800) 426-8322
Fax	(512) 838-7961

Learning Tree International Certification

- UNIX Systems Certified Professional

Learning Tree International currently offers over 150 computer and networking courses throughout the United States, Europe, and Asia. As part of their curriculum in information technology, Learning Tree International offers 26 different professional certification programs, one of which is a vendor-independent certification program on UNIX operating systems. (See Chapters 4, 7, 8, 13, and 14 for other Learning Tree International certification programs.)

The Learning Tree International UNIX Systems Certified Professional credential will prove useful to UNIX users, system administrators, network managers, system analysts, and anyone else involved in operating a UNIX-based system. Learning Tree International also offers a UNIX programming certification; see Chapter 7 for more information on this certification.

Recertification or Maintenance Requirements

There is no maintenance requirement for any of Learning Tree International's certification programs.

Benefits of Certification

Learning Tree International UNIX Systems Certified Professionals receive these benefits:

- A framed diploma of Professional Certification

- An official record of the courses that you have completed

- Option of obtaining college credit

NOTE It is possible to obtain college credit for earning your certification or for taking Learning Tree International courses. The American Council of Education (ACE) in Washington, D.C. has worked in cooperation with Learning Tree International to determine college course equivalencies for these courses and certifications. Approximately 1,500 colleges and universities in the United States will accept ACE recommendations for college credit. As a general rule, ACE will recommend two college credit hours for each four-day course. Learning Tree International will pay to have your Learning Tree International credentials registered with ACE and you can then request that your transcript be sent from ACE to any college or university. (Check with your college or university registrar to make sure that your institution accepts ACE recommendations for credit.)

UNIX Systems Certified Professional

Attainment of this certification requires taking four core courses and one elective course, and passing a test given at the end of each course. The required introductory course covers user services and utilities, use of the X Window system, common desktop environment and applications, and maintenance functions. The workstation administration course covers menu-driven and command-line workstation management, installation and configuration of system and application software, and shared network resources. The server administration course covers all aspects of implementing TCP/IP network services on UNIX platforms. The final required course covers the knowledge and skills you need in order to establish and maintain security for UNIX platforms. Detailed descriptions of the elective courses are available on "Learning Tree International's" Web site (see the "Learning Tree International Resources" section that follows).

After completing this program, certified professionals will be able to install and configure UNIX on a workstation; manage and provide local system resources; create, edit, find, manage, and protect files in the UNIX directory hierarchy; use the UNIX shells, useful commands, scripts, and shortcuts; centralize and distribute UNIX resources among appropriate servers; optimize UNIX server and network performance; secure UNIX systems from internal and external threats; and configure tools and utilities to minimize exposure and detect intrusions.

Who Needs It

This certification is a good vendor-independent credential for those who want to get a position working with UNIX operating systems from multiple vendors. Since their certification programs require comprehensive training classes, Learning Tree International certifications offer a way for you to gain hands-on experience and training that may not currently be available to you on the job.

Requirements for Certification

The certification process requires the following steps:

1. Complete four core courses listed in Table 5.6 and pass the test given at the end of each course.

2. Complete one elective course from those listed in Table 5.7 and pass the test given at the end of that course.

T A B L E 5.6:   Core Courses for Learning Tree International UNIX Systems Certified Professional Certification

Course Number	Course	Length
336	UNIX: A Hands-On Introduction	4 days
435	UNIX Workstation Administration: Hands-On	4 days
436	UNIX Server Administration: Hands-on	4 days
433	UNIX System and Network Security: Hands-On	4 days

T A B L E 5.7:   Elective Options for UNIX Systems Certified Professional Certification

Course Number	Course	Length
434	KornShell Programming	4 days
330	Linux Installation, Configuration and Support	4 days
467	Internetworking with TCP/IP	4 days
158	UNIX and Windows NT Integration	4 days
468	Internet and System Security: A Comprehensive Introduction	4 days
396	UNIX Tools and Utilities	4 days
488	Deploying Internet and Intranet Firewalls	4 days
333	UNIX Programming	4 days
363	TCP/IP Programming	4 days
Course 338	C Programming	4 days

Administrator

"Learning Tree International" (see the "Learning Tree International Resources" section for contact information).

Fee

At this writing, the prices for Learning Tree International courses are $1,295 for a two-day course, $1,745 for a three-day course, $2,195 for a four-day course, and $2,495 for a five-day course. Learning Tree International offers some significant discounts for those taking more than one course and for government employees. There is no additional charge for the tests.

Format

Each exam consists of 40 to 60 questions. If you fail a test on the first try, Learning Tree International will arrange for you to take a proctored exam at your place of work.

Learning Tree International Resources

For more information on this organization's courses and certification programs, contact Learning Tree International at:

Web	http://www.learningtree.com
E-mail	uscourses@learningtree.com
Mail	1805 Library Street
	Reston, VA 20190-5630
Phone	(800) THE-TREE
Fax	(800) 709-6405

Microsoft Certification

- Microsoft Certified Professional (MCP)

The Microsoft Certified Professional designation is an entry-level certification. The MCP credential typically denotes expertise with at least one Microsoft Windows operating system. It has recently become possible, however, to obtain MCP status by passing a product test (for example, on Microsoft FrontPage). We have chosen to include the MCP in this chapter because it is best designed for new administrators who want to demonstrate their proficiency with Microsoft Windows 95/98, Windows NT, or Windows NT Server.

The Microsoft Certified Professional certification is intended as a stepping-stone to one of Microsoft's premium certifications: the Microsoft Certified Solution Developer (MCSD), Microsoft Certified Systems Engineer (MCSE), Microsoft Certified Database Adminis-trator, (MCDBA) or MCSE + Internet. See Chapters 7, 9, 12, and 13, respectively, for more information on these certifications.

Recertification or Maintenance Requirements

As Microsoft introduces new products and new versions of its oper-ating systems, it retires the tests for previous versions. If your certifi-cation is based on a test that Microsoft is retiring, you will be informed by certified mail of the need to take a current test to maintain your certification. You will have at least six months to complete this new test; if you do not take and pass the test your status as an MCP will no longer be valid.

Benefits of Certification

Microsoft Certified Professionals receive the following benefits:

- An MCP certificate
- Access to technical information through a secured MCP-only Web site
- Use of MCP logos on stationery and business cards
- Invitations to Microsoft-sponsored conferences and technical briefings
- A free subscription to *Microsoft Certified Professional* magazine

Microsoft Certified Professional (MCP)

Attaining this certification requires passing one exam. Candidates have the choice of specializing in Microsoft Windows 95, Windows NT, Windows NT Server, or a specific Microsoft product. Each test covers the basic concepts and skills involved with installing, using, and troubleshooting a particular operating system or product.

The candidate is expected to have hands-on experience with the product prior to attempting the exam. Microsoft's Web site provides exam guidelines, sample tests, and links to authorized training providers (see the "Microsoft Resources" section that follows).

NOTE You can obtain MCP status by passing any Microsoft test, with only one exception. You cannot become an MCP by passing Exam 70-058: Networking Essentials.

Who Needs It

The MCP certification is an excellent entry point for technical professionals getting into network and system administration of Microsoft operating systems. This certification is also valuable to support and help-desk personnel.

Requirements for Certification

The certification process requires only one step:

1. Pass one of the exams listed in Table 5.8.

T A B L E 5.8: Exam Options for Microsoft Certified Professional (MCP)

Exam	Test ID
Designing and Implementing Distributed Applications with Microsoft Visual C++ 6.0	70-015
Designing and Implementing Desktop Applications with Microsoft Visual C++ 6.0	70-016

T A B L E 5.8: Exam Options for Microsoft Certified Professional (MCP) *(continued)*

Exam	Test ID
Designing and Implementing Data Warehouses with Microsoft SQL Server 7.0	70-019
Developing Applications with C++ Using the Microsoft Foundation Class Library	70-024
Implementing OLE in Microsoft Foundation Class Applications	70-025
Administering Microsoft SQL Server 6.5	70-026
Implementing a Database Design on Microsoft SQL Server 6.5	70-027
Administering Microsoft SQL Server 7.0	70-028
Designing and Implementing Databases with Microsoft SQL Server 7.0	70-029
Designing and Implementing Web Sites with Microsoft FrontPage 98	70-055
Implementing and Supporting Web Sites Using Microsoft Site Server 3.0	70-056
Designing and Implementing Commerce Solutions with Microsoft Site Server 3.0, Commerce Edition	70-057
Internetworking Microsoft TCP/IP on Microsoft Windows NT 4.0	70-059
Implementing and Supporting Microsoft Windows 95	70-063
Implementing and Supporting Microsoft Windows NT Server 4.0	70-067
Implementing and Supporting Microsoft Windows NT Server 4.0 in the Enterprise	70-068
Application Development with Microsoft Access for Windows 95 and the Microsoft Access Developer's Toolkit	70-069

T A B L E 5.8: Exam Options for Microsoft Certified Professional (MCP) *(continued)*

Exam	Test ID
Implementing and Supporting Microsoft Windows NT Workstation 4.0	70-073
Implementing and Supporting Microsoft Exchange Server 5	70-076
Implementing and Supporting Microsoft Internet Information Server 3.0 and Microsoft Index Server 1.1	70-077
Implementing and Supporting Microsoft Proxy Server 1.0	70-078
Implementing and Supporting Microsoft Internet Explorer 4.0 by Using the Internet Explorer Administration Kit	70-079
Implementing and Supporting Microsoft Exchange Server 5.5	70-081
Implementing and Supporting Microsoft SNA Server 4.0	70-085
Implementing and Supporting Microsoft Internet Information Server 4.0	70-087
Implementing and Supporting Microsoft Proxy Server 2.0	70-088
Designing and Implementing Solutions with Microsoft Office 2000 and Microsoft Visual Basic for Applications	70-091
Implementing and Supporting Microsoft Windows 98	70-098
Analyzing Requirements and Defining Solution Architectures Elective Exams	70-100
Designing and Implementing Web Solutions with Microsoft Visual InterDev 6.0	70-152
Developing Applications with Microsoft Visual Basic 5.0	70-165
Designing and Implementing Distributed Applications with Microsoft Visual Basic 6.0	70-175
Designing and Implementing Desktop Applications with Microsoft Visual Basic 6.0	70-176

Administrator

Microsoft tests are administered by Sylvan Prometric and Virtual University Enterprises (VUE). To register for a test with VUE visit the VUE Web site (`http://www.vue.com/student-services/`). Call Sylvan at (800) 755-3926 to register for Microsoft tests; if outside the U.S., use the online Sylvan Test Center Locator at `www.sylvanprometric.com` to find the nearest testing center. Chapter 3 contains detailed information on taking tests from Sylvan or VUE.

Fee

Test fee is $100.

Format

These are multiple-choice, closed-book tests. The number of questions and time limit depend on the test selected.

TIP Microsoft offers the MCP + Internet certification to MCPs who pass the Implementing and Supporting Microsoft Windows NT Server 4.0 exam and two additional tests. If you think this is a certification you may want in the future, be sure to take the NT Server 4.0 exam as your operating system exam for the MCP certification. (See Chapter 13 for more information on the MCP + Internet certification.) Microsoft also offers the MCP + Site Builder certification for those involved in Web site design (see Chapter 13 for details).

Microsoft Resources

For more information on this certification program, contact Microsoft at:

Web	`http://www.microsoft.com/mcp/`
E-mail	`Mcp@msprograms.com`
Mail	Microsoft Corporation
	One Microsoft Way
	Redmond, WA 98052-6399
Phone	(800) 636-7544
Fax	(425) 936-7329

Red Hat Certification

- Red Hat Certified Engineer

Red Hat Software is one of several companies that develop and distribute the Linux operating system, a public domain version of UNIX developed by Linus Torvalds in 1991. Linux is distributed as Open Source Software (OSS) under the terms of the GNU Public License (GPL). Many people use Linux not only for its features, but also to prove that they have an alternative to Microsoft's Windows line of operating systems. Red Hat Linux is very popular in the United States because it is a stable, reliable, useable, well-documented, and well-supported operating system.

Red Hat currently offers one level of certification: the Red Hat Certified Engineer (RHCE) certificate. The Red Hat Certified Engineer program is the first piece of a comprehensive training and certification program being developed at Red Hat Software in 1999. A complete suite of skills courses leading up to the RHCE certificate is planned. When ready, these skills courses will be available from Red Hat and through authorized training centers.

Recertification or Maintenance Requirements

This Red Hat certification applies to version 5.2 of Red Hat Linux, so there is no requirement for recertification on this particular version. Since your certification is tied to a certain version of Red Hat, however, you will want to become certified on the newest version when it becomes available if you want to continue to have the most current credential in this area. Certification will remain "current" for several months after any major new release of Red Hat Linux. Participants who want or need certification on the most recent release can be recertified by retaking the RHCE certification lab exam.

Benefits of Certification

Red Hat Certified Engineers receive the following benefit:

- Red Hat Certified Engineer (RHCE) certificate

Red Hat Certified Engineer (RHCE)

The Red Hat Certified Engineer certification program is designed for UNIX and Linux administrators and networking specialists who want to certify their skills with Red Hat. An individual who holds the RHCE certificate has demonstrated the knowledge and skills needed by a system administrator who will work with Red Hat Linux in the following capacities: installation and configuration; configuration of X Windowing systems; setup of basic networking and security; and performance of basic systems administration, diagnostics, and troubleshooting.

Obtaining this certification involves passing the RHCE Certification Lab Exam, which can be taken on its own (one day), or at the end of the Red Hat Certified Engineer course, a four-day intensive lab-based course aimed at rapid training of persons who are already experienced with systems administration, network operations, or other advanced roles in a UNIX or Linux environment. The course provides two content units and two hands-on labs per day. The test is given the day after completion of the four days of training, and takes another full day.

It is assumed that the candidate already has significant systems administration experience or knowledge in a UNIX or Linux environment. Red Hat strongly recommends that those planning to enroll in the Certified Engineer course have experience in the following areas: UNIX systems administration experience, networking concepts and technology, Intel X86 architecture computers, UNIX file systems, UNIX/Linux shell programming and configuration, basic kernel configuration, basic TCP/IP networking, IP routing, standard networking services, and basic security concepts and network security. Red Hat's Web site offers a detailed list of the recommended prerequisite knowledge and experience, and warns that those who come to the course unprepared are not likely to pass the test.

Who Needs It

The Red Hat Certified Engineer title is valuable to those working in a Linux environment (Internet Service Providers, Web hosting services, or any number of specialized applications) who want to certify their skills. The RHCE certificate is also useful for those who are working in a UNIX environment and want to shift to Linux systems administration or networking. This credential can also be of value to independent consultants who want to validate their expertise to their clients.

Requirements for Certification

The certification process requires the following steps:

1. Complete the four-day Red Hat Certified Engineer course or obtain equivalent preparation.

2. Pass the seven-hour certification lab exam given on the day after the course is completed.

Administrator

Red Hat administers both the course and the lab exam. Both are offered exclusively at Red Hat's training center in Durham, North Carolina. See Red Hat's Web site (http://www.redhat.com) for a current listing of course dates or to register.

Fee

If you sign up for the course and the test at the same time the total cost is $2,498 ($2,099 for the training and $399 for the lab exam). If you fail the certification exam, or decide to take it at a later date, the cost for the exam alone is $749.

Format

The certification lab exam has three components: a written test (1–2 hours); an installation and configuration lab (2 hours); and a diagnostics and troubleshooting lab (3 hours). The lab exam presents realistic problems that require planning, diagnosis, and solution development.

Red Hat Resources

Red Hat offers detailed online information about the course prerequisites, as well as a detailed outline of the Red Hat Certified Engineer course. For more information on this organization's certification program and courses, contact Red Hat at:

Web	http://www.redhat.com/
E-mail	Training@redhat.com
Mail	Red Hat Software
	P.O. Box 13588
	Research Triangle Park, NC 27709
Phone	(919) 547-0012 ext. 258
Fax	(919) 547-0024

Santa Cruz Operation, Inc. (SCO) Certifications

- Certified UNIX System Administrator (CUSA)

- Advanced Certified Engineer (ACE)

The Santa Cruz Operation, Inc. (SCO), founded in 1979, is a well-known maker of business system software for network computing. The SCO Advanced Certified Engineer (ACE) certification program is for technical professionals who use SCO's system software. Two levels of certification and two program tracks are offered: The SCO Certified UNIX System Administrator (CUSA) certification is an entry-level certification, while the SCO Advanced Certified Engineer (ACE) program certifies a high level of proficiency with SCO UNIX. Each level offers specializations in either SCO OpenServer Release 5 or UnixWare 7.

Recertification or Maintenance Requirements

SCO's current policy on recertification is that you can retain your certification indefinitely, although SCO reserves the right to change its recertification policy in the future. So, technically, there is no recertification requirement. If you want to continue to receive the "benefits" given to SCO ACEs, however, you must take a recertification test every year.

SCO ACE recertification exams are comprehensive two-hour tests that consist of approximately 80 multiple-choice questions. Currently, recertification involves passing either the SCO OpenServer Release 5 ACE Recertification exam (Test ID: 090-153) or the SCO UnixWare 7 ACE Recertification exam (Test ID: 090-077).

NOTE If you have one SCO ACE certification, you can become certified in the other track by taking the recertification exam for that track.

Benefits of Certification

SCO CUSAs receive the following benefits:

- Congratulations letter
- Certificate
- Desk trophy
- Logo diskette

SCO ACEs receive the CUSA benefits, plus the following:

- Lapel pin
- Stickers
- A copy of the SCO Support Library on CD-ROM
- Invitation to SCO's Annual Forum held in August at the University of California at Santa Cruz

SCO Certified UNIX System Administrator (CUSA)

Attaining either of the SCO CUSA certifications involves passing one test. SCO offers preparation courses for each exam. These courses are not required, but the content of the courses is closely aligned with the corresponding exam. The recommended courses for the OpenServer Release 5 test are #241 (SCO OpenServer Release 5 System Administration I: User Services) and # 242/243 (SCO OpenServer Release 5

System Administration II: Installation, Configuration & Maintenance). The recommended courses for the UnixWare 7 test are #245 (UnixWare 7 System Administration I: User Services) and #255 (UnixWare 7 System Administration II: Installation, Configuration and Maintenance). See the "SCO Resources" section that follows for more information about taking these courses.

In preparing for the test, remember that the exams are open book: It is not important to memorize specific details. Instead, practice using the system and resolving problems. Sample exam questions can be found on SCO's Web site. Certified UNIX Systems Administrators can choose from the following certification options:

- SCO OpenServer Release 5

- UnixWare 7

Who Needs It

The SCO CUSA certification is designed for system administrators who will be supporting UNIX-based servers. This designation can help you get a job administering UNIX servers and networks, whether they are SCO-based or not.

Requirements for Certification

The certification process requires one step:

1. Pass the SCO Administration test for the specialization you seek (see Table 5.9).

T A B L E 5.9:   Required Exams for CUSA Certifications

Specialization	Required Exams
SCO OpenServer Release 5	SCO OpenServer Release 5 Administration (Test ID: 090-052)
UnixWare 7	UnixWare 7 Administration (Test ID: 090-076)

Administrator

SCO exams are administered by Sylvan Prometric. Call (800) 775-3926 to register for SCO tests; if outside the U.S., use the online Sylvan Test Center Locator at `http://www.sylvanprometric.com` to find the nearest testing center. (See Chapter 3 for detailed information on taking tests from Sylvan.)

Fee

One-hour exams cost $125; two-hour exams cost $180.

Format

The exams are multiple choice. They consist of 40 or 80 questions, and last one or two hours. Passing score on each exam is 80 percent. SCO exams are open book. SCO allows candidates to take any written materials to the exam, including SCO documentation, notes, and third-party books and documentation. The candidate is prohibited, however, from bringing a laptop computer or removing any notes taken during the exam.

SCO Advanced Certified Engineer (ACE)

Attaining either of the SCO ACE certifications involves passing three tests. SCO offers preparation courses for these exams. These courses are not required, but the content of the courses is closely aligned with the corresponding exams.

Advanced Certified Engineers can choose from the following certification options:

- SCO OpenServer Release 5
- UnixWare 7

The recommended preparation courses for the SCO OpenServer Release 5 tests are #241 (SCO OpenServer Release 5 System Administration I: User Services), #242/243 (SCO OpenServer Release 5 System Administration II: Installation, Configuration and Maintenance), #325 (SCO OpenServer Network Administration), and #610 (Shell Programming for System Administrators). The recommended preparation courses for the UnixWare 7 tests are #245 (UnixWare 7

System Administration I: User Services), #255 (UnixWare 7 System Administration II: Installation, Configuration and Maintenance), #355 (UnixWare 7 Network Administration), and #610 (Shell Programming for System Administrators). See the "SCO Resources" section that follows for more information about taking these courses.

In preparing for the exams, remember that the exams are open book: It is not important to memorize specific details. Instead, practice using the system and resolving problems. Sample exam questions can be found on SCO's Web site.

Who Needs It

The SCO ACE certification is an expert-level designation for system administrators responsible for installing, managing, and supervising SCO based servers. This certification can help you get a high-level job administering and troubleshooting SCO UNIX servers and networks.

Requirements for Certification

The certification process requires the following step:

1. Pass the three steps that are required for the specialization that you seek (see Table 5.10).

TABLE 5.10: Required Tests for Advanced Certified Engineers

Specialization	Required Tests
SCO OpenServer Release 5	SCO OpenServer Rel 5 Administration (Test ID: 090-052) Shell Programming for System Administrators (Test ID: 090-056) SCO OpenServer Rel 5 Network Administration (Test ID: 090-054)
UnixWare 7	UnixWare 7 Administration (Test ID: 090-076) Shell Programming for System Administrators (Test ID: 090-056) UnixWare 7 Network Administration (Test ID: 090-055)

From the time the first exam is taken, a candidate has one year to successfully complete the remaining SCO ACE requirements.

Administrator

SCO exams are administered by Sylvan Prometric. Call (800) 775-3926 to register for SCO tests; if outside the U.S., use the online Sylvan Test Center Locator at http://www.sylvanprometric.com to find the nearest testing center. (See Chapter 3 for detailed information on taking tests from Sylvan.)

Fee

One-hour exams cost $125; two-hour exams cost $180.

Format

The exams are multiple choice. They consist of 40 or 80 questions, and last one or two hours. Passing score on each exam is 80 percent. SCO exams are open book. SCO allows candidates to take any written materials to the exam, including SCO documentation, notes, and third-party books and documentation. The candidate is prohibited, however, from bringing a laptop computer or removing any notes taken during the exam.

SCO Resources

SCO exam preparation courses—which are two to five days long—are available at SCO Authorized Education Centers (AECs). SCO's Web site offers sample test questions, test objectives, and a listing of AECs and training courses. Self-study materials are available. For more information on this organization's courses and certification program, contact SCO at:

Web	http://www.sco.com/Training/ace/aceguide.html
E-mail	info@sco.com
Mail	Santa Cruz Operation, Inc.
	400 Encinal Street
	P.O. Box 1900
	Santa Cruz, CA 95061-1900
Phone	(800) 726-8649
Fax	(408) 458-4227

Silicon Graphics, Inc. (SGI) Certifications

- Certified IRIX 6.x System Administrator

- Certified IRIX Network Administrator

Silicon Graphics, founded in 1982, offers a wide range of computing systems and related products. Their computers—from desktop workstations to Cray supercomputers—are used in manufacturing, government, science, telecommunications, and entertainment.

Silicon Graphics's UNIX operating system is called IRIX. The Certified IRIX System Administrator program became available in October 1997. This certification can be augmented with a specialization in network administration.

Recertification or Maintenance Requirements

The IRIX system and network administration designations apply to specific version numbers of the operating system, so there is no requirement for recertification on a particular version. Since your certification is tied to a certain version of a product, however, you will want to become certified on the newest versions, when they become available, if you want to continue to have the most current credential in this area.

Benefits of Certification

Certified IRIX System and Network Administrators receive these benefits:

- Use of certification logo
- Certificate

Certified IRIX 6.*x* System Administrator

Attaining this certification involves passing two exams. Silicon Graphics recommends taking three courses in preparation for the exams: Introduction to IRIX; either the System Administration course or the IRIX Specific System Administration course; and Advanced System Administration. The objectives and prerequisites for the courses can be found on SGI's Web site (see "SGI Resources" section).

Who Needs It

This certification lets employers know that you are proficient in administrating and maintaining Silicon Graphics IRIX systems. It can be valuable for getting a job as a system administrator in a company that uses Silicon Graphics workstations.

Requirements for Certification

The certification process requires the following steps:

1. Pass the Silicon Graphics IRIX System Administration test (Test ID: 002).

2. Pass the Silicon Graphics IRIX Advanced System Administration test (Test ID: 003).

Administrator

Silicon Graphics exams are administered by Sylvan Prometric. Call (800) 815-3926 to register for Silicon Graphics tests; if outside the U.S., use the online Sylvan Test Center Locator at http://www.sylvanprometric.com to find the nearest testing center. (See Chapter 3 for detailed information on taking tests from Sylvan.)

Fee

$100 per exam.

Format

This is a computer-based, multiple-choice test. Call Sylvan Prometric at (800) 815-3926 for current information on the number of questions, time limit, and passing score.

Certified IRIX Network Administrator

This certification builds on the Silicon Graphics Certified IRIX 6.*x* System Administrator certification program described above. To achieve the network administrator certification, a candidate must pass one additional exam. Silicon Graphics recommends taking their Network Administration course in preparation for this exam. The objectives and prerequisites for the course can be found on SGI's Web site (see "SGI Resources" section).

Who Needs It

This certification lets employers know that you are proficient in networking and administrating Silicon Graphics IRIX systems. It can be valuable for getting a job as a network administrator in a company that uses Silicon Graphics workstations.

Requirements for Certification

The certification process requires the following steps:

1. Achieve certification as a Silicon Graphics Certified IRIX System Administrator (see previous section).

2. Pass the Silicon Graphics IRIX Network Administration exam (Test ID: 001).

Administrator

Silicon Graphics exams are administered by Sylvan Prometric. Call (800) 815-3926 to register for Compaq tests; if outside the U.S., use the online Sylvan Test Center Locator at http://www.sylvanprometric.com to find the nearest testing center. (See Chapter 3 for detailed information on taking tests from Sylvan.)

Fee

The test costs $100.

Format

This is a computer-based, multiple-choice test. Call Sylvan Prometric at (800) 815-3926 for current information on the number of questions, time limit, and passing score.

SGI Resources

For more information on this organization's courses and certification programs, contact Silicon Graphics at:

Web	`http://www.sgi.com/support/custeducation/` `us/certified.html`
Mail	Silicon Graphics, Inc, M/S 171
	2011 N. Shoreline Blvd.
	Mountain View, CA 94043
Phone	(800) 800-4744
Fax	(650) 932-0309

Sun Certifications

- Certified System Administrator

- Certified Network Administrator

Sun Microsystems, Inc., the originator of the Java programming language, is well known for its high performance computer systems. The Solaris operating system is Sun's version of UNIX. Sun's Certified System Administrator certification program, formerly known as the Certified Solaris Administrator program, validates technical expertise in using and administering Solaris-based systems. It is available for Solaris 2.5 or Solaris 2.6. Like other UNIX vendors, Sun also offers a Certified Network Administrator credential that builds on the System Administrator designation. The network certification is also available for either Solaris 2.5 or 2.6. System administration and network administration certification exams for Solaris 7 are also scheduled to be available by the time this book is released.

Recertification or Maintenance Requirements

The Solaris system and network administration designations apply to specific version numbers of the operating system, so there is no requirement for recertification on a particular version. Since your certification is tied to a certain version of a product, however, you will want to become certified on the newest versions, when they become available, if you want to continue to have the most current credential in this area.

Benefits of Certification

Sun Certified Solaris Administrators receive a logo for use on business cards and materials.

Certified System Administrator

Attaining the Certified System Administrator certification involves passing two exams. With the release of the new exams for Solaris 2.6, Sun has changed the name of their system administrator certification from Certified Solaris Administrator to Certified System Administrator. Candidates can choose from the following two certification options:

- Solaris 2.5

- Solaris 2.6

The exams for these certifications cover the basic installation and operation of the Solaris 2.5 or 2.6 operating system.

Sun recommends these two five-day instructor-led courses as preparation for the Solaris 2.5 System Administrator exam: Course SA-135: Solaris 2.5 System Administration Essentials ($2,195), and Course SA-285B: Solaris 2.5 System Administration ($2,195). Another option for exam preparation is to take Sun's self-paced courses. The self-paced courses recommended for Solaris V2.5 are JTL-SA280 (JavaTutor: Solaris 2.5 System Admin I Library) and JTL-SA286 (JavaTutor: Solaris 2.6 System Admin II Library).

The new exams for Solaris 2.6 have a format that is a little different from the exams used on earlier versions of Solaris; they incorporate multiple-choice questions with multiple correct answers as well as short answer questions. Sun recommends these two five-day instructor-led courses as preparation for the Solaris 2.6 System Administrator exams: Course SA-235: Solaris 2.x System Administration I ($2,195), and Course SA-286: Solaris 2.*x* System Administration II ($2,195). Another option for exam preparation is to take Sun's self-paced courses. The self-paced courses recommended for Solaris V2.6 are JTL-SA235 (JavaTutor: Solaris 2.6 System Admin I Library) and JTL-SA286 (JavaTutor: Solaris 2.6 System Admin II Library).

By the time this book is released, certification exams and courses for Solaris 7 should also be available.

Who Needs It

This certification lets employers know that you are proficient in administrating and maintaining Sun Solaris systems. It can be valuable for getting a job as a system administrator in a company that uses Sun workstations.

Requirements for Certification

The certification process requires the following step:

1. Pass the two exams listed for the specialization desired, shown in Table 5.11.

T A B L E 5.11: Required Exams for Sun Certified System Administrator Certifications

Specialization	Required Exams
Solaris 2.5	Solaris 2.5 System Administrator Exam: Part I (Test ID: 310-005) Solaris 2.5 System Administrator Exam: Part II (Test ID: 310-006)
Solaris 2.6	Sun Certified System Administrator for Solaris 2.6 Exam: Part I (Test ID: 310-007) Sun Certified System Administrator for Solaris 2.6 Exam: Part II (Test ID: 310-008)

Administrator

Call Sun Educational Services at (800) 422-8020 to purchase an exam voucher. You will receive the voucher by mail, as well as information on how and when to take the exam. The exams are taken through Sylvan Prometric.

Fee

The fee is $150 per test.

Format

The Solaris 2.5 System Administrator Exam: Part I has 108 multiple-choice questions and must be completed in 90 minutes; the passing score is 63 percent. The Solaris 2.5 System Administrator Exam: Part II consists of 83 multiple-choice questions, which must be completed in 90 minutes; the passing score is 67 percent.

Each of the Solaris 2.6 exams has 72 multiple-choice/multiple correct answer and short answer/fill-in questions. Each test must be completed in 90 minutes. The passing score for the part I exam is 75 percent, while the passing score for the part II exam is 70 percent.

Certified Network Administrator

This certification builds on the Solaris System Administrator certification. Attaining this certification involves passing one additional exam. Candidates can choose from the following two certification options:

- Solaris 2.5
- Solaris 2.6

The Network Administrator test covers networking and security aspects of Solaris 2.5 or 2.6. Sun recommends that those who are preparing to take either of the Sun Certified Network Administrator exams take Course SA-380B: Solaris 2.*x* Network Administration ($2,495). If the candidate prefers, a self-paced course (JTL-SA380; JavaTutor: Solaris 2.6 Network Admin Library) is also available.

By the time this book is released, certification exams and courses for Solaris 7 should also be available.

Who Needs It

This certification lets employers know that you are proficient in networking and administrating Sun Solaris systems. It can be valuable for getting a job as a network administrator in a company that uses Sun workstations.

Requirements for Certification

The certification process requires the following steps:

1. Become a Solaris System Administrator certified on any release of Solaris.

2. Pass either the Sun Certified Network Administrator Exam for Solaris 2.5 (Test ID: 310-040) or the Sun Certified Network Administrator Exam for Solaris 2.6 (Test ID: 310-041).

Administrator

Call Sun Educational Services at (800) 422-8020 to purchase an exam voucher. You will receive the voucher by mail, as well as information on how and when to take the exam. The exam is taken through Sylvan Prometric.

Fee

Test fee is $150.

Format

The Sun Certified Network Administrator exams have 77 questions and must be completed in 90 minutes; the passing score is 70 percent. Sun's exams are available in both English and Japanese.

Sun Resources

Sun Educational Services offers instructor-led courses for those who are preparing for Solaris certification tests. Each course involves both classroom instruction and lab work. Self-paced courses are also available. The instructor-led courses range in cost from $2,195 to $2,495; the self-paced courses cost $995 each. Sun's exams are available in both English and Japanese. For more information on this organization's courses and certification programs, contact Sun at:

Web	`http://suned.sun.com/suned/`
E-mail	`who2contact@chocolate.ebay.sun.com`
Mail	Sun Microsystems
	901 San Antonio Road
	Palo Alto, CA 94303
Phone	(800) 422-8020
Faxback	(800) 564-4341 (code #250)

CHAPTER

6

Software Certifications

FEATURING

- Adobe Certification

- AutoDesk Certification

- Baan Certifications

- Cognos Certifications

- Corel Certifications

- Lotus Certifications

- Microsoft Certifications

- SAP Certifications

- Solomon Software Certifications

This chapter contains a number of certifications that are of interest to all computer users, and not targeted exclusively to the technical professional. The certifications described in this chapter range from those for widely-used word processing and spreadsheet programs—such as the Microsoft Office or the Corel WordPerfect suites of products—to very specialized business applications. These credentials can be invaluable to proficient software users who want to have evidence of their true abilities.

Employers will also want to be aware of these certifications. Too many employers have been burned by hiring a person who claimed to know how to use a certain software product, only to find out later that the new employee had no idea how to start the program, let alone use it! Another benefit for employers and employees is that the programs for these software certifications offer well-defined curricula for in-house training programs, and the certification tests provide benchmarks for successful training.

Professionals seeking software certifications might include:

- Office support personnel
- Graphic designers
- Desktop publishing experts
- Electronic imaging professionals
- Web designers
- Financial clerks
- Help-desk personnel
- Architects
- Engineers and mechanical designers

A wide array of software certifications is currently available. Adobe offers the Adobe Certified Expert certification for a number of its products. AutoDesk, makers of AutoCAD, offers the AutoCAD Certified Professional credential for architects, draftsmen, and designers that use AutoCAD. Baan, a maker of business intelligence software, offers certifications on its products. Corel's certification program includes two levels of certification on its WordPerfect, Quattro Pro, Presentations, CorelDRAW, and Photo-Paint programs. Lotus offers a wide variety of certifications on its software. In addition, Microsoft offers several levels of certification on its Microsoft Office products. SAP offers two certifications related to its R/3 business intelligence software product. Solomon Software offers a two-part certification program in support of its Solomon IV financial software for the Windows operating system.

Use Table 6.1 to compare the number of required tests, the test format, the approximate cost of taking the test(s), number of required courses, cost of any required courses, and the relative difficulty of the certification programs in this chapter. The cost information is a general guideline; since things change rapidly in the world of certification programs, once you have selected a specific course of action you may want to double-check the costs.

We classified the difficulty of these certifications into three categories—Moderate, Challenging, and Very Challenging—based on the number of required tests and courses, and the relative difficulty of those tests or lab exams. These ratings are approximate and are offered simply as a general guide to help the reader distinguish between entry-level programs and those that require more advanced skill and knowledge. (This rating scale assumes that one has experience with the product or technology and has studied the appropriate subject content before attempting the exams.) (See Table 6.1.)

T A B L E 6.1: Software Certifications

Certification	# of Required Tests	Test Format(s)	Total Cost of Required Tests	# of Required Courses	Total Cost of Required Courses	Difficulty	Notes
Adobe Certification							
Adobe Certified Expert	1	MC	$150	—	—	○	Available on: Illustrator 8, Acrobat 3, AfterEffects 3.1, FrameMaker 5.5, FrameMaker + SGML 5.5, PageMaker 6.5, PageMill 2, Photoshop 5, and Premiere 5
AutoDesk Certification							
AutoCAD Certified Professional	1–2	MC, LA	$185–$370	—	—	●	The Level I test is not required, but is recommended as preparation for the Level II exam.
Baan Certifications							
Baan Basic Certification	1	MC	VF	—	—	○	
Baan Advanced Certification	1	MC	VF	—	—	◐	Specializations include: Finance, Sale/Distribution, Manufacturing, and System Administration
Cognos Certifications							
Cognos Certified Impromptu Professional	1	MC	VF	—	—	○	
Cognos Certified PowerPlay Professional	1	MC	VF	—	—	○	
Cognos Certified Business Intelligence Professional	2	MC	VF	1	VF	◐	

T A B L E 6.1: Software Certifications *(continued)*

Certification	# of Required Tests	Test Format(s)	Total Cost of Required Tests	# of Required Courses	Total Cost of Required Courses	Difficulty	Notes
Corel Certifications							
Corel Certified Proficient User	1	LA	$50	—	—	◯	Specializations: WordPerfect 8, WordPerfect 9, Quattro Pro 9, Presentations 9, CorelDRAW 9, or Photo-Paint 9
Corel Certified Expert User	1	LA	$50	—	—	◯	Specializations: WordPerfect 8, WordPerfect 9, Quattro Pro 9, Presentations 9, CorelDRAW 9, or Photo-Paint 9
Lotus Certifications							
Certified Lotus Specialist	1	MC or LA	$100	—	—	◯	
Certified Lotus Professional (CLP) Application Developer	3	MC or LA	$300	—	—	◖	
CLP Principal Application Developer	1	MC or LA	$100	—	—	●	You must first be a CLP Application Developer.
CLP System Administrator	3	MC or LA	$300	—	—	◖	
CLP Principal System Administrator	1	MC or LA	$100	—	—	●	You must first be a CLP System Administrator.
CLP cc:Mail System Administrator	2	MC or LA	$200	—	—	◖	

T A B L E 6.1: Software Certifications *(continued)*

Certification	# of Required Tests	Test Format(s)	Total Cost of Required Tests	# of Required Courses	Total Cost of Required Courses	Difficulty	Notes
Microsoft Office User Specialist (MOUS) Certifications							
MOUS: Core or Proficient (entry-level)	1	LA	**VF (suggested fee is $50)**	—	—	○	Available for Word, Excel, Access or Outlook.
MOUS: Expert	1	LA	**VF (suggested fee is $50)**	—	—	◒	Available for Word, Excel, Access or Outlook.
MOUS: Master	4 or 5	LA	**VF (Approxim ately $200–$250)**	—	—	●	Options: Office 97 or Office 2000
SAP Certifications							
SAP R/3 Certified Application Consultant	1	MC	VF	—	—	◒	Choose from 11 version and content options
SAP R/3 Technical Consultant Certification	1	MC	VF	—	—	◒	Test has three components: R/3 Basis, operating system, and database
Solomon Certifications							
Solomon IV Certified Systems Engineer (SCSE)	1	MC	VF	—	—	◒	
Solomon IV Certified Financial Specialist (SCFS)	1	MC	VF	—	—	◒	

Certification Difficulty: ○ Moderate ◒ Challenging ● Very Challenging

Test Format: **MC:** Multiple Choice **AT:** Adaptive Testing **LA:** Live Application
PR: Hands-on Lab **NA:** Not Applicable

Test Fee: **VF:** Test Fees can vary: consult testing center **CV:** Voucher for taking the exam is included in the fee for the required course(s) additional attempts cost extra.

Adobe Certification

- Adobe Certified Expert

Adobe produces a number of excellent page layout and imaging programs used in desktop publishing and for producing Web pages. Adobe's Photoshop has become the *de facto* standard for creating and manipulating images. Adobe also developed the Portable Document Format (PDF), which is a platform-independent file format for preserving page layout information—including graphics—that is widely used on the Web.

The Adobe Certified Expert program allows users to document their expertise with a number of Adobe products, including Illustrator 8, Acrobat 3, After Effects 3.1, FrameMaker 5.5, FrameMaker + SGML 5.5, PageMaker 6.5, PageMill 2, Photoshop 5, and Premiere 5.

NOTE   Adobe also offers the Adobe Certified Training Program (ACTP) for individual instructors, training businesses, and academic institutions that teach Adobe products; see Chapter 15, "Instructor and Trainer Certifications," for more information on the ACTP program.

Recertification or Maintenance Requirements

Adobe requires Adobe Certified Experts (ACEs) to update their certifications within 90 days of the release of a new version of the product for which they are certified. Adobe notifies ACEs of new product releases and related exam information by e-mail. As an ACE, you will be eligible for a 25 percent discount when taking a test to update your certification (be sure to use the code "RETEST" when registering for your recertification test to get the discount).

Benefits of Certification

Adobe Certified Experts receive these benefits:

- Logo for use on business cards and stationery
- Product-specific certificate

Adobe Certified Expert

Attaining Adobe Certified Expert (ACE) status involves passing one exam on a specific Adobe software product. An individual can become an ACE on any one or more of the following software products:

- Acrobat 3
- After Effects 3.1
- Adobe FrameMaker 5.5
- FrameMaker + SGML 5.5
- Illustrator 8
- PageMaker 6.5
- PageMill 2
- Photoshop 5
- Premiere 5

Acrobat 3 is a program for creating and publishing documents in the Portable Document Format (PDF). This format allows users to view, print, and annotate documents—independent of any one operating system or page-layout program—while retaining all the page layout information, including graphics and images. The exam for this certification tests the candidate's knowledge of Acrobat concepts and program operation, including the creation and viewing of PDF files.

After Effects 3.1 is a program for creating digital compositions, 2D animations, and special effects for multimedia programs, the Web, TV, and film. The exam for this certification tests the candidate's knowledge of After Effects concepts and program operation, including animation, motion controls, and advanced special effects.

Adobe FrameMaker 5.5 is a document authoring and publishing package that includes tools for writing and distributing long, structured, content-rich documents across all major computing platforms. The exam for this certification tests the candidate's knowledge of FrameMaker concepts and program operation, including character and paragraph formatting, tables, document design, and hypertext links.

FrameMaker + SGML 5.5 is an enhancement to Adobe FrameMaker 5.5 that allows the user to create and publish Standard Generalized Markup Language (SGML) documents. A candidate for this certification can select either an authoring exam or a development exam.

Illustrator 8 is the latest version of Adobe's sophisticated illustration and drawing program. The exam for this certification tests the candidate's knowledge of Illustrator concepts and program operation. You will need to know basic Illustrator terms and concepts; how to use filters, pens, and other tools; how to manipulate color; and how to import and export files.

PageMaker 6.5 is Adobe's popular desktop publishing program. The exam for this certification tests the candidate's knowledge of Page-Maker concepts and program operation, including working with color, graphics, typestyles, plug-ins, table editors, and book features. Adobe is the only company that currently offers a certification program in desktop publishing.

PageMill 2 is a graphical program for creating and editing HTML (Hypertext Markup Language), the language in which Web documents are created. The program allows the user to create Web pages, import images, and publish Web sites without having to learn how to write in HTML. The exam for this certification tests the candidate's knowledge of PageMill concepts and program operation, creating and editing links, creating tables and frames, and publishing Web documents.

Photoshop 5 is a popular program for manipulating, creating, and formatting images. It is used in both electronic and traditional publishing. The Photoshop exam tests the user's ability to apply color correction, use Photoshop tools, import and export files, and deal with pre-press and publishing issues.

Premiere 5 is a program for editing broadcast-quality movies for video, multimedia, or the Web. The test for this exam covers system requirements; windows and palettes; assembly tools and commands; title creation; motion controls; working with time; filters and transitions; audio, video, and images; composing, transparency, and superimposing; input/output; and working with other applications.

See the online Adobe exam bulletins for more information about all of the above exams. Adobe also offers instructor-led courses and the Adobe *Classroom in a Book* lessons to help candidates prepare for exams. See the "Adobe Resources" section for contact information.

Who Needs It

The ACE designation indicates that you are a skilled user of a specific Adobe software product. An Adobe Certified Expert certification can help you advance your career in graphic design, Web design, desktop publishing, electronic document management, and other related fields. This certification may also be valuable to freelance artists, Web page designers, or desktop publishers.

Requirements for Certification

The certification process requires only one step:

1. Pass the Adobe test for the specific software product on which you seek certification (see Table 6.2).

T A B L E 6.2: Adobe Certified Expert Exams

Specialization	Required Tests	Test ID
Acrobat 3	Acrobat 3 Exam	9A0-007
After Effects 3.1	After Effects 3.1 Exam	9A0-010

T A B L E 6.2: Adobe Certified Expert Exams *(continued)*

Specialization	Required Tests	Test ID
FrameMaker 5.5	FrameMaker 5.5 Exam	9A0-004
FrameMaker + SGML 5.5	FrameMaker + SGML 5.5 Authoring Exam OR	9A0-012
	FrameMaker + SGML 5.5 Developer Exam	9A0-013
Illustrator 8	Illustrator 8 Exam	9A0-005
PageMaker 6.5	PageMaker 6.5 Exam	9A0-008
PageMill 2	PageMill 2 Exam	9A0-009
Photoshop 5	Photoshop 5. Exam	9A0-006
Premiere 5	Premiere 5 Exam	9A0-014

Administrator

Adobe exams are administered by Sylvan Prometric. Call (800) 356-3926 to register for Adobe tests; if outside the U.S., use the online Sylvan Test Center Locator at http://www.sylvanprometric.com to find the nearest testing center. (See Chapter 3 for additional information on Sylvan Prometric.)

Fee

Each exam costs $150.

Format

Adobe tests are closed-book, computer-based exams. Each test consists of 60–90 multiple-choice questions and must be completed in one to two hours. Exams are available worldwide in English, and a number are being translated into additional languages this year.

Adobe Resources

The Adobe Web site offers exam bulletins that detail the objectives of each exam, as well as information about instructor-led and self-paced training. Adobe's Web site also provides information about the Adobe Certified Training Providers program. For more information on this organization's certifications and courses, contact Adobe at:

Web	http://partners.adobe.com/asn/training aceprogram.html
E-mail	certification@adobe.com
Mail	Certification Coordinator
	Adobe Systems Incorporated
	Mailstop W07-123
	345 Park Avenue
	San Jose, CA 95110-2704
Phone	(800) 685-4172
Fax	(408) 537-4033

AutoDesk Certification

- AutoCAD Certified Professional (ACP)

AutoDesk makes software for graphic design and Computer Aided Design (CAD). AutoDesk's AutoCAD product is the most popular CAD program and is used by architects, engineers, and design professionals worldwide. AutoDesk offers a certification program for AutoCAD, which leads to the AutoCAD Certified Professional credential. Currently, exams for this certification test knowledge and experience with AutoCAD Release 14. Certification on AutoCAD 2000 should be available soon (check the AutoDesk Web site for updates at http://www.autodesk.com/).

Recertification or Maintenance Requirements

AutoDesk certifications apply to specific version numbers of AutoCAD software, so there is no requirement for recertification on a particular version. Since your certification is tied to a certain version of a product, however, you will want to become certified on the newer versions, when they become available, if you want to continue to have the most current credential in this area.

Benefits of Certification

AutoDesk certified professionals receive:

- A certificate

- Use of logo

- AutoDesk will include your name in their directories of Certified Professionals.

AutoCAD Certified Professional (ACP)

There are currently two tests involved in obtaining this certification, the AutoCAD Level I and AutoCAD Level II tests. Both exams consist of 100 questions that test your general knowledge and skill with the current release of AutoCAD (You will be required to use AutoCAD during your test). The Level I exam is not required. Upon successful completion of the Level II exam you will be recognized as an AutoCAD Certified Professional (ACP).

Candidates will need a comprehensive knowledge of AutoCAD. AutoDesk recommends that candidates take an AutoCAD course at an official AutoDesk Training Center. Hands-on experience with the product is also strongly recommended. For more information about the exams, visit AutoDesk's Testing and Certification site (`http://www.autodesk.com/support/resource/exams/exams.htm`).

Who Needs It

This certification is an excellent way for graphic design professionals, draftsmen, and architects to enhance their careers in organizations that use AutoCAD. This credential can also be of value to independent designers and draftsmen who do independent consulting and want to validate their expertise for clients.

Requirements for Certification

The certification process requires the following steps:

1. Pass the AutoCAD Level I Exam. (Note: this exam is not required, but it is recommended as a first step for those not yet ready for the Level II exam.)

2. Pass the AutoCAD Level I Exam.

Administrator

AutoDesk certification exams are administered via the Web at CertificationNet Authorized Proctor Centers. Locate testing centers and register for your test at the AutoDesk Web site (http://www.autodesk.com/exams).

Fee

AutoDesk exams cost $185 each.

Format

The test consists of 100 questions, most of them multiple-choice, that must be completed within 180 minutes. Approximately 25 percent of the questions will require you to use AutoCAD; a digitizing pad is provided at the testing center.

AutoDesk Resources

AutoDesk offers a number of courses in AutoCAD. For more information on this organization's certification program and courses, contact AutoDesk at:

Web   http://www.autodesk.com/

Mail   AutoDesk, Inc.
            Attn: Testing & Certification Program Coordinator
            Learning & Training
            111 McInnis Parkway
            San Rafael, CA 94903
            Phone(800) 964-6432

Baan Certifications

- Baan Basic Certification

- Baan Advanced Certification

The Baan Company makes enterprise and inter-enterprise business software used by major corporations around the world. These software products are used for managing manufacturing, distribution, finance, transportation, services, projects, and organizational structure data. Essentially, Baan does for large companies like General Motors what QuickBooks does for a local "mom and pop" store.

The current set of business programs are referred to as the Baan IV suite of programs. Baan offers both basic and advanced levels of certification in Baan IV applications. After completing basic certification, advanced certification can be obtained in one of four specialties: Enterprise Logistics, Enterprise Finance, Enterprise Tools, and Enterprise Modeler. Any company that wants to become a Baan consulting or business partner—a company working closely with Baan to design custom applications and installations—must have at least one person on staff who is Baan-certified in at least one specialty.

Recertification or Maintenance Requirements

The Baan certifications apply to a specific release of Baan products—currently, the Baan IV suite of programs—so there is no requirement for recertification on that release. Since your certification is tied to a certain version of the product, however, you will want become certified on the newer versions when they become available if you want to continue to have the most current Baan credential.

NOTE Baan is working on the development of additional role-based certification programs on other Baan products. (A white paper on this topic can be downloaded from the Baan Web site at `http://www.baan.com/`).

Baan Basic Certification

Baan Basic Certification is a prerequisite to any Baan Advanced Certification. The exam for this certification covers the basic use and operation of the programs in the Baan IV suite. Baan offers an overview multimedia-based training product to help candidates gain an overall understanding of these programs (see the "Baan Resources" section that follows for information on how to contact Baan).

Who Needs It

This certification is valuable to anyone who needs to demonstrate basic proficiency with entering data, developing reports, and tracking data using Baan IV products.

Requirements for Certification

The certification process requires only one step:

1. Pass the Baan Basic Certification for Baan IV test (Test ID: 1AO-160).

Administrator

Baan exams are administered by Sylvan Prometric. Call (800) 304-2226 to register for Baan tests; if outside the U.S., use the online Sylvan Test Center Locator at www.sylvanprometric.com to find the nearest testing center. (See Chapter 3 for additional information on Sylvan Prometric.)

Fee

Contact Sylvan Prometric for current pricing information.

Format

Baan exams contain 50 questions and have a 90-minute time limit. The exams are computer-based and contain true/false, multiple-choice, and multiple-correct questions. The passing score is 75 percent.

Baan Advanced Certification

This certification builds on the Basic Baan Certification. After passing the Baan Basic exam described above, the current Baan certification program allows an individual to attain an advanced certification in one or more of four tracks:

- Finance

- Sales/Distribution

- Manufacturing

- System Administration

Attaining Baan Advanced Certification in Finance involves passing three additional exams. The exams for this certification test the candidate's ability to use the finance modules in Baan IV, including General Ledger, Financial Budgets, Financial Statements, Accounts Receivable, Accounts Payable, Cash Management, Fixed Assets, and Cost Allocation. The first exam covers introductory finance topics. The second exam covers accounts payable and accounts receivable, while the final exam in the Finance track covers general ledger and budgets, financial statements, cost allocation, and fixed assets.

Attaining Baan Advanced Certification in Sales/Distribution involves passing three additional exams. The first exam covers introductory logistics topics. The second exam covers sales and commissions. The final exam in this track covers purchasing, prices and discounts, replenishment orders, distribution requirements planning, and warehouse inventory management.

Attaining Baan Advanced Certification in Manufacturing involves passing three additional exams. The first exam covers introductory logistics topics. The second exam covers cost accounting, and project control and budgets. The final exam in this track covers master production scheduling, materials and capacity planning, and discrete production control.

Attaining Baan Advanced Certification in System Administration involves passing two additional exams. The exams for this certification test the candidate's ability to administrate and operate the Baan Tools application. The information covered includes the following topics: configuring the system; system security; initial setup; submitting jobs; and setting up users, menus, jobs, devices, and databases. The first exam covers introductory topics, while the final exam in this track covers the more advanced system administration topics.

Baan offers a set of multimedia tools to help you prepare for their exams (see the "Baan Resources" section that follows for more information).

Who Needs It

These certifications are valuable to professionals in large corporations that use Baan products.

Requirements for Certification

The certification process requires the following steps:

1. Attain Baan Basic Certification (see previous section).

2. Pass the Baan exams for the certification track you are pursuing (see Table 6.3).

TABLE 6.3: Baan Specializations

Specialization	Required Tests
Finance	Foundation Finance
	Finance Electives I
	Finance Electives II
Sales/Distribution	Foundation Logistics
	Sales/Distribution Electives I

T A B L E 6.3: Baan Specializations *(continued)*

Specialization	Required Tests
	Sales/Distribution Electives II
Manufacturing	Foundation Logistics
	Manufacturing Electives I
	Manufacturing Electives II
System Administration	Foundation Tools
	System Administration Electives I

NOTE If you are already Baan IV certified, you can obtain a BaanERP Upgrade Certification. The upgrade process involves taking a 5-hour course on the Baan Virtual Campus, attending a 5- to 10-day training and case study workshop course, and passing an upgrade exam. For more information see the Baan Web site (`http://www. baan.com/`).

Administrator

Baan exams are administered by Sylvan Prometric. Call (800) 304-2226 to register for Baan tests; if outside the U.S., use the online Sylvan Test Center Locator at `www.sylvanprometric.com` to find the nearest testing center. (See Chapter 3 for additional information on Sylvan Prometric.)

Fee

Contact Sylvan Prometric for current pricing information.

Format

Baan exams contain 50 questions and have a 90-minute time limit. The exams are computer-based and contain true/false, multiple-choice, and multiple-correct questions. The passing score is 75 percent.

Baan Resources

Baan offers a number of CDs that can help you learn about their products. For more information on this organization's certification program and other resources, contact Baan at:

Web	http://www.baan.com/
E-mail	certification@baan.com
Mail	Baan USA Inc.
	11911 Freedom Drive
	Reston, VA 20910-5602
Phone	(888) 597-2700

Cognos Certifications

- Cognos Certified Impromptu Professional

- Cognos Certified PowerPlay Professional

- Cognos Certified Business Intelligence Professional

Cognos, founded in 1969 and headquartered in Ottawa, Canada, makes business intelligence software to help companies increase their productivity and streamline their business processes. Cognos software allows users to explore summary-level company information to identify and understand trends, and to perform analyses necessary in the development of business models and forecasts. Cognos also makes software tools for application development.

Cognos offers certification programs on their main products: Impromptu and PowerPlay. A third certification, the Cognos Certified Business Intelligence Professional, tests a candidate's abilities to use both products and is also useful for those who sell Cognos products.

Recertification or Maintenance Requirements

All Cognos certifications apply to specific version numbers of Cognos products, so there is no requirement for recertification on a particular version. Since your certification is tied to a certain version of a product, however, you will want to become certified on the newer versions, when they become available, if you want to continue to have the most current credential in this area. You can update your certification to a new product version by taking a one-hour exam.

Benefits of Certification

Cognos Certified Impromptu and PowerPlay Professionals receive the following benefits:

- A certificate
- A free one-year subscription to *Supportlink*, the Cognos technical newsletter

Cognos Certified Business Intelligence Professionals receive the following benefits:

- Lapel pin
- Business Intelligence Professional logo for use on business cards

Cognos Certified Impromptu Professional

The Cognos Certified Impromptu Professional certification documents the knowledge and skills of report builders, analysts, and system administrators who customize, support, administer, and maintain both user and administration versions of Impromptu. The exam tests both basic and advanced knowledge of the Impromptu product. Cognos recommends, but does not require, that the candidate attend the following courses: Report Building with Impromptu 5.x, Impromptu 5.x Advanced Reporting, Impromptu 5.x Administration, and Impromptu Automation.

Who Needs It

This certification is a great way to demonstrate your abilities to use and support Impromptu. This credential can also be of value to those who do independent consulting and want to validate their Impromptu expertise for clients.

Requirements for Certification

The certification process requires one step:

1. Pass the Certified Impromptu Administration Version 5 exam (Test ID: 9B0-102).

Administrator

Cognos tests are administered by Sylvan Prometric. Call Sylvan at (800) 343-3926 to register for Cognos tests; if outside the US, use the online Sylvan Test Center Locator at http://www.sylvanprometric.com to find the nearest testing center. Chapter 3 contains detailed information on taking tests from Sylvan.

Fee

The exam fee is $175.

Format

The exam has 120 multiple-choice questions and must be completed in two hours.

Cognos Certified PowerPlay Professional

The Cognos Certified PowerPlay Professional certification documents the skills and knowledge of report builders, analysts, and system administrators who customize, support, administer, and maintain both user and administration versions of PowerPlay. The exam tests both basic and advanced knowledge of the PowerPlay product. Cognos recommends, but does not require, that the candidate attend the following courses: PowerPlay Explorer; PowerPlay Report Builder; PowerPlay Administration (Part 1); PowerPlay Administration (Part 2); and PowerPlay Automation.

Who Needs It

This certification is an great way to demonstrate your abilities to use and support PowerPlay. This credential can also be of value to those who do independent consulting and want to validate their PowerPlay expertise for clients.

Requirements for Certification

The certification process requires one step:

1. Pass the Certified PowerPlay Administration Version 6 exam (Test ID: 9B0-103).

Administrator

Cognos tests are administered by Sylvan Prometric. Call Sylvan at (800) 343-3926 to register for Cognos tests; if outside the US, use the online Sylvan Test Center Locator at http://www.sylvanprometric.com to find the nearest testing center. Chapter 3 contains detailed information on taking tests from Sylvan.

Fee

The exam fee is $175.

Format

The exam has 120 multiple-choice questions and must be completed in two hours.

Cognos Certified Business Intelligence Professional

The Cognos Certified Business Intelligence Professional credential is targeted toward those with advanced skills in both PowerPlay and Impromptu. This certification is most useful for Cognos dealers and business partners. Obtaining the certification involves passing the two tests described in the two Cognos sections above and attending a business intelligence workshop: the Cognos Business Intelligence Hothouse.

The Cognos Business Intelligence Hothouse is a five-day training course that takes participants through a business intelligence implementation life cycle in which they interact with application users, build prototypes, and present the results to other course participants.

Who Needs It

This certification is an excellent way for salespeople to demonstrate their technical abilities and their understanding of the business intelligence software market.

Requirements for Certification

The certification process requires three steps:

1. Pass the Certified Impromptu Administration Version 5 exam (described in the "Cognos Certified Impromptu Professional" section).

2. Pass the Certified PowerPlay Administration Version 6 exam (described in the "Cognos Certified PowerPlay Professional" section).

3. Successfully complete the five-day Business Intelligence Hothouse training course.

Administrator

Cognos tests are administered by Sylvan Prometric. Call Sylvan at (800) 343-3926 to register for Cognos tests; if outside the US, use the online Sylvan Test Center Locator at http://www.sylvanprometric.com to find the nearest testing center. Chapter 3 contains detailed information on taking tests from Sylvan.

The Business Intelligence Hothouse training course is offered by Cognos in Australia, Canada, Holland, South America, the United Kingdom, and the United States. To register or obtain more information, contact Cognos at (800) 4COGNOS, extension 2263, or (http://www.cognos.com/partnerline/winter99/bihot.html).

Fee

Fees for Cognos tests vary; call Sylvan Prometric at (800) 343-3926 for current pricing.

Format

Each exam has 120 multiple-choice questions and must be completed in two hours. The Business Intelligence Hothouse training is a five-day course offered by Cognos.

Cognos Resources

Cognos offers a number of courses that cover the knowledge and skills tested on the exam. The Web site provides downloadable study guides with sample test questions for each exam. For more information on this organization's certification program and courses, contact Cognos at:

Web	Http://www.cognos.com/services/ccpp.html
E-mail	ccpp@cognos.com
Mail	Cognos Corporation
	67 South Bedford Street
	Burlington, MA 01803-5164
Phone	800-426-4667 or 781-229-6600
Fax	781-229-9844

Corel Certifications

- Corel Certified Proficient User

- Corel Certified Expert User

Corel Corporation produces excellent word processing, spreadsheet, presentation, and drafting programs used in offices around the world. Corel's Certified User program offers two levels of end user certification on Corel products. The Corel Certified Proficient User designation is for software users with a good basic understanding of the features and functions of one or more of the Corel WordPerfect Suite programs. The Corel Certified Expert User program is for those with more in-depth knowledge of program operation. Both Proficient User and Expert User certifications are available for the following Corel programs: WordPerfect, Quattro Pro, Presentations, CorelDRAW, and Corel Photo-Paint.

NOTE The Corel Certified Instructor (CCI) program offers credentials for those who want to teach Corel products. CCIs must obtain their Corel product certifications at the Expert User level. For more information on the CCI program, see Chapter 15.

Recertification or Maintenance Requirements

The Corel Certified Proficient User and Expert User designations apply to specific version numbers of Corel software products, so there is no requirement for recertification on a particular version. Since your certification is tied to a certain version of a product, you will want to become certified on the newest versions when they become available if you want to continue to have the most current Corel credential.

Benefits of Certification

Corel Certified Proficient Users and Certified Expert Users receive the following benefits:

- Letter of approval

- Certificate

- Logo for stationery and business cards

- Opportunity to purchase one copy of each academic Corel product for personal use at a significant discount

Corel Certified Proficient User

The Corel Certified Proficient User credential certifies that an individual has the skills to perform routine tasks on existing documents and can produce new documents using templates and the basic features of a specific Corel application. Attaining this certification involves passing one exam. The objectives for the Corel exams and information about instructor-led and self-study opportunities can be found on Corel's Web site (see the "Corel Resources" section).

The Corel Certified Proficient User designation can be obtained on the following applications:

- Corel WordPerfect 8
- Corel WordPerfect 9
- Corel Quattro Pro 9
- Corel Presentations 9
- CorelDRAW 9
- Corel Photo-Paint 9

WordPerfect is one of the two most popular word processing programs available. The exam for this certification covers the basic features of WordPerfect; it tests the candidate's ability to perform routine tasks on existing documents and to produce new documents using templates.

Quattro Pro is Corel's spreadsheet program. The exam for this certification covers the basic features of Quattro Pro; it tests the candidate's ability to perform routine tasks on existing spreadsheets and to produce new spreadsheets using templates.

Corel Presentations is a program for making and presenting computer-based slide shows or presentations. The exam for this certification covers the basic features of Presentations; it tests the candidate's ability to create and edit new presentations using templates.

CorelDRAW is a graphics program for professional illustration, page layout, photo editing, and raster/bitmap creation. The Proficient User exam tests the candidate's ability to use the basic features of the application to create and edit CorelDRAW documents using existing templates.

Corel Photo-Paint offers a set of tools for image and photo editing, painting, publishing Web graphics, making QuickTime movies, and font and media management. The exam for this application tests the user's ability to use the basic features of Photo-Paint.

Who Needs It

These certifications can help you get a position as an office professional by demonstrating your ability to use a specific Corel product effectively.

Requirements for Certification

The certification process requires only one step:

1. Pass the Corel exam on the appropriate product (see Table 6.4 for a list of available exams).

T A B L E 6.4: Corel Certified Proficient User Required Exams

Specialization	Required Test
WordPerfect 8	Corel WordPerfect 8 Proficient User
WordPerfect 9	Corel WordPerfect 9 Proficient User
Quattro Pro 9	Corel Quattro Pro 9 Proficient User
Presentations 9	Corel Presentations 9 Proficient User
CorelDRAW 9	CorelDRAW 9 Proficient User
Photo-Paint 9	Corel Photo-Paint 9 Proficient User

Administrator

Corel exams are administered by Sylvan Prometric. Call (800) 662-6735 to register for Corel tests; if outside the US, use the online Sylvan Test Center Locator at http://www.sylvanprometric.com to find the nearest testing center. (See Chapter 3 for additional information on Sylvan Prometric.)

Fee

Each exam costs $50 in North America.

Format

These new Corel exams for versions 8 and 9 are taken at a testing center, but are Web-delivered, live-application exams. You will be working within an application in a simulated real-world situation. Exams contain 40 to 60 questions and must be completed in 60 minutes.

Corel Certified Expert User

The Corel Certified Expert User credential certifies that an individual has the skills to produce complex, non-routine documents requiring features such as graphics, charts, formulas, and tables. The Corel Certified Expert User designation can be obtained on the following applications:

- Corel WordPerfect 8
- Corel WordPerfect 9
- Corel Quattro Pro 9
- Corel Presentations 9
- CorelDRAW 9
- Corel Photo-Paint 9

The above Corel applications are described in the Corel Certified Proficient User section, which precedes this section. The objectives for the Expert level exams are available on Corel's Web site (see the "Corel Resources" section for details).

Who Needs It

These certifications can help you get a position as an office professional by documenting your ability to use a specific Corel product at a high level of skill.

Requirements for Certification

The certification process requires only one step:

1. Pass the Corel exam on the appropriate product (see Table 6.5 for a list of available exams).

TABLE 6.5: Corel Expert User Required Exams

Specialization	Required Test
WordPerfect 8	Corel WordPerfect 8 Expert User
WordPerfect 9	Corel WordPerfect 9 Expert User
Quattro Pro 9	Corel Quattro Pro 9 Expert User
Presentations 9	Corel Presentations 9 Expert User
CorelDRAW 9	CorelDRAW 9 Expert User
Photo-Paint 9	Corel Photo-Paint 9 Expert User

Administrator

Corel exams are administered by Sylvan Prometric. Call (800) 662-6735 to register for Corel tests; if outside the U.S., use the online Sylvan Test Center Locator at http://www.sylvanprometric.com to find the nearest testing center. (See Chapter 3 for additional information on Sylvan Prometric.)

Fee

Each exam costs $50 in North America.

Format

These new Corel exams for versions 8 and 9 are taken at a testing center, but are Web-delivered, live application exams. You will be working within an application in a simulated real-world situation. Exams contain 40 to 60 questions and must be completed in 60 minutes.

Corel Resources

Exam guidelines are available from the Corel Web site. Instructor-led courses on Corel products are available through Corel Training Partners. Corel also offers self-study materials. For more information on this organization's certification programs, contact Corel at:

Web   http://www.corel.com/learning/training/

E-mail	custserv2@corel.com
Mail	Corel Corporation
	1600 Carling Avenue
	Ottawa, Ontario
	K1Z 8R7
Phone	(800) 772-6735
Fax	(613) 761-9176
Faxback	(613) 728-0826, ext. 3080

Lotus Certifications

- Certified Lotus Specialist

- Certified Lotus Professional (CLP) Application Developer

- Certified Lotus Professional (CLP) Principal Application Developer

- Certified Lotus Professional (CLP) System Administrator

- Certified Lotus Professional (CLP) Principal System Administrator

- Certified Lotus Professional (CLP) cc:Mail System Administrator

Lotus was launched in 1982 with the popular spreadsheet program, Lotus 1-2-3. In 1989, Lotus introduced its groupware products that facilitate business collaboration via the Internet: Lotus Notes and Domino. Lotus now offers certification programs related to Lotus Notes and Domino, and to the Lotus e-mail system, cc:Mail. These programs certify technical expertise in system administration or in developing applications that run on Lotus Notes.

There are three levels of certification: the Certified Lotus Specialist (CLS), which is designed for those who have basic technical knowledge of a product; and the Certified Lotus Professional (CLP) and Principal CLP, for those with more in-depth knowledge and experience. To become a Certified Lotus Specialist, an individual must pass one product-specific exam. The Certified Lotus Professional designation follows specific product-related tracks and requires passing several related exams. At the beginning of this section, CLP certification options are listed.

An additional certification, the Certified Lotus Professional (CLP) Domino Messaging Administration designation, is also available (see the Lotus Web site for more information).

Recertification or Maintenance Requirements

The Certified Lotus Specialist and Certified Lotus Professional designations apply to specific releases of Lotus software products, so there is no requirement for recertification on a particular release. Since your certification is tied to a certain version of a product, however, you will want to become certified on the newest releases when they become available if you want to continue to have the most current Certified Lotus Specialist or Certified Lotus Professional credential.

NOTE   R4 CLPs can upgrade their certification to Domino R5 by taking only one or two exams. This must be done within the first six months after the release of Domino R5. If the upgrade is not done within the six month limit, you will have to take the entire set of R5 exams to become an R5 CLP.

Benefits of Certification

As a Certified Lotus Specialist or a Certified Lotus Professional you will receive:

- Welcome kit with certificate, logo sheet, and usage guidelines

- Free subscription to Lotus' bimonthly certification newsletter

- Access to private Lotus Certification Web site, which includes special offers and discounts

NOTE Lotus also offers a Certified Lotus Instructor credential for those who want to deliver Lotus education training courses at Lotus Authorized Education Centers. See Chapter 15 for details.

Certified Lotus Specialist (CLS)

A Certified Lotus Specialist (CLS) specializes in one Lotus product and must pass an exam associated with that product. The product options for the CLS certification include: Lotus Domino (System Administration, Application and Web development); Lotus 1-2-3 (spreadsheet); Lotus Notes (collaborative business software); and cc:Mail (e-mail).

The Domino Web Development and Administration exam assesses the candidate's knowledge and skills in developing and deploying Web sites using Domino 4.5. The LotusScript exam tests advanced knowledge of coding and troubleshooting Lotus Script for 1-2-3 applications. The Notes R4 Application Development 1 test and the Notes R4 System Administration 1 tests are described in the "Certified Lotus Professional (CLP)—Application Developer" section that follows. The cc:Mail R6 Systems Administration test is described in the "Certified Lotus Professional (CLP)—cc:Mail System Administrator" section that follows. The Domino 4.6 Messaging Administration exam tests a candidate's ability to design and deploy Lotus messaging solutions. Some exams are offered in two different formats, as described below.

Who Needs It

The Certified Lotus Specialist credential demonstrates to employers that you can use a particular Lotus product effectively and can be a resource for others in the office. In addition, it is valuable to those in charge of developing Internet- and intranet-based solutions based on Lotus products.

Requirements for Certification

The certification process requires only one step:

1. Pass one of the tests listed in Table 6.6; select the test for the product in which you plan to specialize.

T A B L E 6.6: Certified Lotus Specialist Exams

Specialization	Required Tests	Test ID
Domino R5 Application Development	Domino R5 Designer Fundamentals	190-510
Domino R5 System Administration	Maintaining Domino R5 Servers and Users	190-520
Notes R4 Application Development	Notes R4 Application Development 1 (multiple choice) OR	190-271
	Notes R4 Application Development 1 (live application)	190-171
Domino Web Development and Administration	Domino Web Development and Administration	190-281
Developing Lotus Script Applications for SmartSuite	Developing Lotus Script Applications for SmartSuite using 1-2-3 '97	190-291
Notes R4 System Administration	Notes R4 System Administration 1 (multiple-choice) OR	190-274
	Notes R4 System Administration 1 (live application)	190-174
cc:Mail R6 System Administration	cc:Mail R6 Systems Administration 1	190-251
Domino Messaging Administration	Domino 4.6 Messaging Administration	190-311

Administrator

Lotus exams can be taken from Sylvan Prometric (call (800) 745-6887 to register for a Lotus exam) or from CATGlobal (see their Web site at http://www.catglobal.com/ for registration information). Chapter 3 contains detailed information on taking tests from both Sylvan and CATGlobal.

Fee

Cost is approximately $100 per test; fee can vary outside the U.S.

Format

Some Lotus tests are offered in two formats: a multiple-choice format or a "live application" format (a hands-on, performance-based exam in which the candidate performs tasks within the Notes environment). Live application exams are only offered by CATGlobal.

The Domino Web Development and Administration multiple-choice test consists of 39 questions. The passing score is 82 percent. The Notes Application Development 1 multiple-choice test consists of 37 questions. A score of 75 percent is required to pass. The Notes System Administration 1 multiple-choice test consists of 34 questions. A score of 64 percent is required to pass. The cc:Mail R6 Systems Administration 1 multiple-choice test consists of 36 questions. A score of 77 percent is required to pass.

All the multiple-choice tests are one hour long. Tests are revised periodically, so contact Lotus Education for the latest information.

Certified Lotus Professional (CLP) Application Developer

This certification denotes expertise in Notes application architecture, application development, application security, and application documentation. To become a CLP Application Developer, a candidate must pass three tests. A CLP Application Developer can specialize in either of the following:

- Notes/Domino R4

- Notes/Domino R5

For R4 candidates, the first test is the Notes R4 Application Development 1 test, which assesses the candidate's ability to build a Notes database application. The second exam, the Notes R4 System Administration 1 test assesses a candidate's ability to set up, operate, and maintain Notes and Domino servers and client workstations. Finally, the Notes R4 Application Development 2 test assesses the candidate's ability to create advanced Notes applications and troubleshoot problems.

For R5 candidates, the first exam is the Domino R5 Designer Fundamentals test, which assesses the candidate's ability to build a Notes database application. The second exam, the Domino R5 Application Security and Workflow test, assesses the candidate's ability to secure an application and add workflow. Finally, the Domino R5 Application Architecture exam assesses the candidate's ability to use the Notes object store to develop complex applications.

Who Needs It

Many employers are eager to hire technical professionals with the CLP designation. The CLP Application Developer certification demonstrates to employers that you have a high level of competence in developing and troubleshooting complex Lotus Notes applications, and that you can provide high quality support for other Lotus users.

Requirements for Certification

The certification process requires the following steps:

1. Pass the three required tests for the specialization you seek (see Table 6.7).

T A B L E 6.7: CLP Application Developer Required Exams

Specialization	Required Tests	Test ID
Notes/Domino R4	Notes R4 Application Development 1 (multiple-choice test) OR	190-271
	Notes R4 Application Development 1 (live application test)	190-171

TABLE 6.7: CLP Application Developer Required Exams *(continued)*

Specialization	Required Tests	Test ID
	Notes R4 System Administration 1 (multiple-choice) OR	190-274
	Notes R4 System Administration 1 (live application)	190-174
	Notes R4 Application Development 2 (multiple-choice test)	190-272
Domino R5	Domino R5 Designer Fundamentals	190-510
	Domino R5 Application Security and Workflow	190-511
	Domino R5 Application Architecture	190-512

Administrator

Lotus exams can be taken from Sylvan Prometric (call (800) 745-6887 to register for a Lotus exam) or from CATGlobal (see their Web site at http://www.catglobal.com/ for registration information). Chapter 3 contains detailed information on taking tests from both Sylvan and CATGlobal.

Fee

Cost is approximately $100 per test; fee can vary outside the U.S.

Format

Some of the R4 tests are offered in two formats: a multiple-choice format or a "live application" format (a hands-on, performance-based exam in which the candidate performs tasks within the Notes environment). Live application exams are only offered by CATGlobal.

The Notes Application Development 1 multiple-choice test consists of 37 questions. A score of 75 percent is required to pass. The Notes

System Administration 1 multiple-choice test consists of 34 questions. A score of 64 percent is required to pass. The Notes Application Development 2 multiple-choice test consists of 42 questions. A score of 76 percent is required to pass.

All the multiple-choice tests are one hour long. Tests are revised periodically, so contact Lotus Education for the latest information.

Certified Lotus Professional (CLP) Principal Application Developer

The CLP Principal Application Developer program builds on the CLP Application Developer certification, and denotes a high level of expertise and ability. The candidate for this level of certification must meet the requirements for the CLP Application Developer and pass an additional elective test in their selected area of specialization.

NOTE Principal Application Developer exams for Domino R5 are under development. Check the Lotus Web site or our Certification Update Web site for the latest information (see Appendix B for information on how to access the Certification Update Web site).

Who Needs It

Many employers are eager to hire technical professionals with the CLP designation. The CLP Principal Application Developer certification demonstrates to employers that you are capable of high-level management of expanding their business solutions by creating workflow and mail-enabled applications.

Requirements for Certification

The certification process requires the following steps:

1. Attain CLP Application Developer certification (described above).

2. Pass one of the elective exams listed in Table 6.8.

T A B L E 6.8: CLP Principal Application Developer Elective Exams

Elective Tests	Test ID
LotusScript in Notes for Advanced Developers	190-273
Developing Domino Applications for the Web	190-278
Developing LotusScript Applications for SmartSuite Using 1-2-3 '97	190-291
Domino Web Development and Administration	190-281
Supporting Domino and Notes	190-401

Administrator

Lotus exams can be taken from Sylvan Prometric (call (800) 745-6887 to register for a Lotus exam) or from CATGlobal (see their Web site at http://www.catglobal.com/ for registration information). Chapter 3 contains detailed information on taking tests from both Sylvan and CATGlobal.

Fee

Cost is approximately $100 per test; fee can vary outside the U.S.

Format

The LotusScript in Notes for Advanced Developers multiple-choice test consists of 39 questions, and must be completed in 60 minutes. A score of 71 percent is required to pass. The Developing Domino Applications for the Web multiple-choice test consists of 38 questions, and must be completed in 60 minutes. A score of 73 percent is required to pass. The Domino Web Development and Administration test has 39 multiple-choice questions and must be completed in 60 minutes. The passing score is 82 percent. The Developing LotusScript Applications for SmartSuite using 1-2-3 '97 test has 77 questions and must be completed in 90 minutes. The passing score is 60 percent. The Supporting Domino and Notes exam has 40 questions and must be completed in 60 minutes. The passing score is 67 percent.

Certified Lotus Professional (CLP) System Administrator

The CLP System Administrator certification program covers all aspects of working with Notes/Domino servers, managing multiple Notes/Domino domains, and controlling Notes/Domino communications. Attaining this certification involves passing three tests. This program parallels the CLP Application Developer program, described previously, and uses two of the same tests. For information on the Notes R4 Application Development 1 and System Administration 1 tests, see the "Certified Lotus Professional (CLP): Application Developer" section. The third required test for this certification—the Notes R4 System Administration 2 test—assesses the candidate's ability to administrate, operate, maintain, and troubleshoot Notes and Domino servers and client workstations. Two of the R4 exams are offered in two formats.

Who Needs It

Many employers are eager to hire technical professionals with the CLP designation. The CLP System Administrator certification demonstrates to employers that you have a high level of competence in the installation, configuration, maintenance, and operation of Notes servers, and that you can provide high quality support for other Lotus users.

Requirements for Certification

The certification process requires the following steps:

1. Pass the three required tests for the specialization you seek (see Table 6.9).

TABLE 6.9: CLP System Administrator Required Exams

Specialization	Required Tests	Test ID
Notes/ Domino R4	Notes R4 Application Development 1 (multiple-choice test) OR	190-271

T A B L E 6.9: CLP System Administrator Required Exams *(continued)*

Specialization	Required Tests	Test ID
	Notes R4 Application Development 1 (live application test)	190-171
	Notes R4 System Administration 1 (multiple-choice) OR	190-274
	Notes R4 System Administration 1 (live application)	190-174
	Notes R4 System Administration 2 (multiple-choice test)	190-275
Domino R5	Maintaining Domino R5 Servers and Users	190-520
	Implementing a Domino R5 Infrastructure	190-521
	Deploying Domino R5 Applications	190-522

Administrator

Lotus exams can be taken from Sylvan Prometric (call (800) 745-6887 to register for a Lotus exam) or from CATGlobal (see their Web site at http://www.catglobal.com/ for registration information). Chapter 3 contains detailed information on taking tests from both Sylvan and CATGlobal.

Fee

The fee is approximately $100 per test; fee can vary outside the U.S.

Format

Two of the R4 tests are offered in two formats: a multiple-choice format or a "live application" format (a hands-on, performance-based exam in which the candidate performs tasks within the Notes environment). Live application exams are only offered by CATGlobal.

The Notes Application Development 1 multiple-choice test consists of 37 questions, and must be completed in 60 minutes. A score of 75 percent is required to pass. The Notes System Administration 1 multiple-choice test consists of 34 questions, and must be completed in 60 minutes. A score of 64 percent is required to pass. The Notes System Administration 2 multiple-choice test consists of 38 questions, and must be completed in 60 minutes. A score of 76 percent is required to pass.

Certified Lotus Professional (CLP) Principal System Administrator

The CLP Principal System Administrator program builds on the CLP System Administrator certification, and denotes a high level of expertise and ability. The candidate for this level of certification must meet the requirements for the CLP System Administrator and pass an additional elective test in their selected area of specialization.

NOTE Principal System Administrator exams for Domino R5 are under development. Check the Lotus Web site or our Certification Update Web site for the latest information (see Appendix B for information on how to access the Certification Update Web site).

Who Needs It

Many employers are eager to hire technical professionals with the CLP designation. The CLP Principal System Administrator certification demonstrates to employers that you are capable of high level management of Lotus Notes, e.g., you can integrate additional technologies into the Lotus Notes environment, and that you can provide high-quality support for other Lotus users.

Requirements for Certification

The certification process requires the following steps:

1. Attain CLP System Administrator certification (described previously).

2. Pass one of the following elective exams:

- Administrating Specialized Tasks for Domino 4.5 (Test ID: 190-276)

- cc:Mail R6 System Administration (Test ID: 190-251)

- Domino Messaging: Migration and Coexistence Strategies (Test ID: 190-313)

Administrator

Lotus exams can be taken from Sylvan Prometric (call (800) 745-6887 to register for a Lotus exam) or from CATGlobal (see their Web site at http://www.catglobal.com/ for registration information). Chapter 3 contains detailed information on taking tests from both Sylvan and CATGlobal.

Fee

The fee is approximately $100 per test; fee can vary outside the U.S.

Format

The Administrating Specialized Tasks for Domino 4.5 multiple-choice test consists of 39 questions, and must be completed in 60 minutes. A score of 72 percent is required to pass. The cc:Mail R6 System Administration multiple-choice test consists of 36 questions, and must be completed in 60 minutes. A score of 77 percent is required to pass. The Domino Messaging exam consists of 36 questions and must be completed in 60 minutes. Passing score is 63 percent.

Certified Lotus Professional (CLP) cc:Mail System Administrator

The CLP cc:Mail System Administrator certification—the credential for those who work with cc:Mail—involves passing two exams. The cc:Mail System Administration 1 test assesses the candidate's ability to set up and operate cc:Mail servers. The cc:Mail System Administration 2 test assesses the candidate's ability to administrate, operate, maintain, and troubleshoot cc:Mail servers and clients. Both tests are available for either cc:Mail R2 or cc:Mail R6.

Who Needs It

Many employers are eager to hire technical professionals with the CLP designation. The CLP cc:Mail System Administrator certification demonstrates to employers that you have a high level of competence in the deployment, installation, and configuration of cc:Mail across multiple networks and platforms, and that you can provide high quality support for Lotus users.

Requirements for Certification

The certification process requires the following steps:

1. Pass the cc:Mail R2 System Administration 1 test (Test ID: 190-051), OR
   the cc:Mail R6 System Administration 1 test (Test ID: 190-251).

2. Pass the cc:Mail R2 System Administration 2 test (Test ID: 190-052), OR
   the cc:Mail R6 System Administration 2 test (Test ID: 190-252).

Administrator

Lotus exams can be taken from Sylvan Prometric (call (800) 745-6887 to register for a Lotus exam) or from CATGlobal (see their Web site at http://www.catglobal.com/ for registration information). Chapter 3 contains detailed information on taking tests from both Sylvan and CATGlobal.

Fee

The fee is approximately $100 per test; fee can vary outside the U.S.

Format

The cc:Mail R2 System Administration 1 multiple-choice test consists of 62 questions, and must be completed in 60 minutes. A score of 75 percent is required to pass. The 60-minute cc:Mail R6 System Administration 1 test has 36 multiple-choice questions. Passing score is 77 percent. The cc:Mail R2 System Administration 2 multiple-choice test consists of 50 questions, and must be completed in 60 minutes. A score of 72 percent is required to pass. The 60-minute cc:Mail R6 System Administration 2 test has 39 multiple-choice questions. Passing score is 77 percent.

Lotus Resources

Lotus's Web site offers exam guides and practice tests. Instructor-led Lotus courses are available at Lotus Authorized Education Centers. For more information on this organization's certification programs and training resources, contact Lotus at:

Web	http://www.lotus.com/certification
Mail	Lotus Education Programs
	One Charles Park
	Cambridge, MA 02142
Phone	(800) 346-6409 or (617) 693-4436

Microsoft Certifications

- Microsoft Office User Specialist (MOUS)

- Microsoft Office User Specialist (MOUS): Expert

- Microsoft Office User Specialist (MOUS): Master

The Microsoft Office suite of programs—Word, Excel, Access, Outlook, and PowerPoint—offers an excellent set of tools for business and personal productivity. Microsoft Word is one of the two most popular word processing programs, while the Microsoft Excel spreadsheet program is used by businesses around the world. Access is a database program also used by many small businesses. Outlook is an integrated e-mail and communication system. PowerPoint is Microsoft's presentation program.

The Microsoft Office User Specialist (MOUS) designation was introduced in 1997 as a way to certify the skills of users of one or more of the programs offered in the Microsoft Office suite. The MOUS program offers entry level, expert level, and master level certifications on the Microsoft Office 97 and Microsoft Office 2000 products. The entry and expert level certifications apply to individual Office applications, while the master level certification connotes mastery of the entire Office product suite.

Recertification or Maintenance Requirements

The Microsoft Office User Specialist designations apply to specific version numbers of Microsoft software products, so there is no requirement for recertification on a particular version. Since your certification is tied to a certain version of a product, you will want to become certified on the newest versions when they become available if you want to continue to have the most current Microsoft Office User Specialist credential.

Benefits of Certification

Microsoft Office User Specialists receive this benefit:

- A certificate of accomplishment

Microsoft Office User Specialist (MOUS)

The entry-level certification in the Microsoft Office User series covers the core features in a specific Microsoft Office application. This level of certification indicates that the holder can perform basic tasks—such as creating new documents, printing and saving documents, basic formatting, and data entry—using a particular Microsoft program. To achieve this certification, the candidate must pass one of the exams listed below. Candidates may want to take basic/beginner or intermediate level Microsoft courses in preparation for these exams.

The following entry-level Microsoft Office User Specialist credentials are available:

- Microsoft Office User Specialist: Microsoft Word 97 Proficient

- Microsoft Office User Specialist: Microsoft Excel 97 Proficient

- Microsoft Office User Specialist: Microsoft Word 2000*

- Microsoft Office User Specialist: Microsoft Excel 2000*

- Microsoft Office User Specialist: Microsoft PowerPoint 2000*

- Microsoft Office User Specialist: Microsoft Access 2000*

- Microsoft Office User Specialist: Microsoft Outlook 2000*

  *Be sure to check the availability of the Office 2000 exams (http://www.mous.net/).

Who Needs It

This certification is a great way for office professionals to demonstrate their skills with a specific Microsoft Office application. It can be especially valuable to those seeking entry-level office positions.

Requirements for Certification

The certification process requires only one step:

1. Pass one of the exams listed below; select the one for the program in which you plan to specialize:

    - Microsoft Word 97 Proficient

    - Microsoft Excel 97 Proficient

    - Microsoft Word 2000*

    - Microsoft Excel 2000*

    - Microsoft PowerPoint 2000*

    - Microsoft Access 2000*

    - Microsoft Outlook 2000*

  *Be sure to check the availability of these Office 2000 exams (http://www.mous.net/).

Administrator

MOUS tests are given at Microsoft Authorized Client Testing (ACT) Centers. Call (800) 933-4493 to register for a test or to locate an ACT center near you.

Fee

The suggested price is $50 per test; actual price may vary with location.

Format

Performance-based, hands-on test in which you are required to perform a set of basic tasks using the software program for which you are testing. The test takes approximately one hour.

Microsoft Office User Specialist (MOUS): Expert

The Expert Microsoft Office User designation denotes a higher level of proficiency with a particular Microsoft product than does the entry-level certification. This certification indicates that the holder can use the more advanced features—e.g., advanced formatting and macro creation—of the selected program. This certification also requires passing one exam, and it is not necessary to take the entry-level exam before taking the Expert exam. Candidates may want to take Microsoft advanced or intermediate level courses in preparation for the Expert exams.

The following expert level Microsoft Office User Specialist credentials are available:

- Microsoft Office User Specialist: Microsoft Word 97 Expert
- Microsoft Office User Specialist: Microsoft Excel 97 Expert
- Microsoft Office User Specialist: Microsoft PowerPoint 97 Expert
- Microsoft Office User Specialist: Microsoft Access 97 Expert
- Microsoft Office User Specialist: Microsoft Word 2000 Expert*
- Microsoft Office User Specialist: Microsoft Excel 2000 Expert*

    *Be sure to check the availability of the Office 2000 exams (http://www.mous.net/).

Who Needs It

This certification is a great way for office professionals to demonstrate to current or potential employers that they have an advanced level of competence with one or more of the Microsoft Office programs.

Requirements for Certification

The certification process requires only one step:

1. Pass one of the exams listed below; select the exam for the program in which you plan to specialize:
    - Microsoft Access 97 Expert
    - Microsoft Excel 97 Expert
    - Microsoft PowerPoint 97 Expert

- Microsoft Word 97 Expert

- Microsoft Word 2000 Expert*

- Microsoft Excel 2000 Expert*

*Be sure to check the availability of these Office 2000 exams and possible additional Office 2000 exams (http://www.mous.net/).

Administrator

MOUS tests are given at Microsoft Authorized Client Testing (ACT) Centers. Call (800) 933-4493 to register for a test or to locate an ACT center near you.

Fee

The suggested price is $50 per test; actual price may vary with location.

Format

Performance-based, hands-on test in which you are required to perform a set of basic tasks using the software program for which you are testing. The test takes approximately one hour.

Microsoft Office User Specialist (MOUS): Master

The Master designation is the highest level of certification in the Microsoft Office User Specialist series. This certification indicates that the holder is not only an expert in each of the individual Office products, but is also skilled in using these products in an integrated fashion. For example, a Master-level Microsoft Office User Specialist knows how to use the linking and cross-program abilities of the Microsoft Office Suite to produce Word documents that contain charts and data that are automatically updated when data in the linked Excel spreadsheets is changed. To attain this certification, you must pass four or five MOUS Expert exams, depending on whether you select the Office 97 suite or the Office 2000 suite. The following Master-level designations are available through the MOUS program:

- Microsoft Office User Specialist: Microsoft Office 97 Master

- Microsoft Office User Specialist: Microsoft Office 2000 Master*

*Be sure to check the availability of these Office 2000 exams (http://www.mous.net/).

Who Needs It

This certification is a great way for office professionals to demonstrate that they have an advanced level of knowledge and skill in using all of the Microsoft Office programs. It can be especially valuable to those seeking office positions with a high level of responsibility.

Requirements for Certification

The certification process requires the following steps:

1. Pass the required Expert-level exams for either Office 97 or Office 2000 (see Table 6.10).

TABLE 6.10: Microsoft Office User Specialist: Master Level Required Exams

Specialization	Required Tests
Microsoft Office 97 Master	Microsoft Word 97 Expert
	Microsoft Excel 97 Expert
	Microsoft PowerPoint 97 Expert
	Microsoft Access 97 Expert
Microsoft Office 2000 Master	Microsoft Word 2000 Expert*
	Microsoft Excel 2000 Expert*
	Microsoft PowerPoint 2000*
	Microsoft Access 2000*
	Microsoft Outlook 2000*

*Be sure to check the availability of these Office 2000 exams (http://www.mous.net/).

Administrator

MOUS tests are given at Microsoft Authorized Client Testing (ACT) Centers. Call (800) 933-4493 to register for a test or to locate an ACT Center near you.

Fee

The suggested price is $50 per test; actual price may vary with location.

Format

Performance-based, hands-on test in which you are required to perform a set of basic tasks using the software program for which you are testing. The test takes approximately one hour.

If you want more resources, tips, and suggestions about becoming a Microsoft Office User Specialist (affectionately known as a MOUS), check out *OfficeCert.com* magazine. This magazine is available online at www.OfficeCert.com.

OfficeCert.com provides the latest information on the certification program, tips for passing exams, ideas on how to get your boss to pay for certification, messages from successful candidates, and job listings. In addition, it offers links to training providers, sample tests, and reviews of self-study resources.

Microsoft Resources

Microsoft Office tests are administered at Microsoft Authorized Client Testing (ACT) Centers. To register for a test, call (800) 933-4493 or contact a local ACT Center directly. For more information on this organization's certifications, contact Microsoft at:

Web	http://www.microsoft.com/office/train_cert/
Mail	Microsoft Corporation
	One Microsoft Way
	Redmond, WA 98052-6399
Phone	(800) 933-4493
Fax	(425) 936-7329

SAP Certifications

- SAP R/3 Certified Application Consultant

- SAP R/3 Technical Consultant Certification

SAP is a leading maker of business intelligence software. SAP's main product, R/3, is a complete business software package that allows companies to integrate sales, materials planning, production planning, warehouse management, financial accounting, and human resources management into one system. SAP currently offers two certifications for R/3: the SAP R/3 Certified Application Consultant and the SAP R/3 Technical Consultant.

Recertification or Maintenance Requirements

SAP Certifications apply to specific version numbers of R/3 software (currently certification is offered on version 3 and version 4), so there is no requirement for recertification on a particular version. Since your certification is tied to a certain version of a product, however, you will want to become certified on the newer versions, when they become available, if you want to continue to have the most current credential in this area.

Benefits of Certification

SAP certified professionals receive:

- A certificate suitable for framing

- Listing in a directory of SAP certified professionals

SAP R/3 Certified Application Consultant

R/3 Certified Application Consultants know how to use and support the R/3 product. Candidates must pass a test in one of the following seven areas of R/3: Accounting; Controlling (Release 4 only); Materials Management; Production, and Production Scheduling; Sales

Order Processing; Human Resources: and Application Development in the ABAP Development Workbench. Candidates can become certified on the following R/3 versions:

- Release 3.*x*
- Release 4

NOTE Note: If you are currently certified on Release 3, you can take a one-hour upgrade test in your area of specialization to receive certification on Release 4.

Who Needs It

This certification is an excellent way to advance your career in a company that uses or implements R/3.

Requirements for Certification

The certification process requires the following step:

1. Pass the required test for the specialization and version on which you want to become certified (See Table 6.11).

TABLE 6.11: SAP Versions and Specializations

Version	Specializations Available
Release 3.*x*	Accounting and Controlling
	Materials Management
	Production and Production Planning
	Sales and Distribution
	Human Resources
	Application Development in ABAP/4

TABLE 6.11: SAP Versions and Specializations *(continued)*

Version	Specializations Available
Release 4	Financial Accounting
	Controlling
	Materials Management
	Production and Production Planning
	Sales and Distribution
	Human Resources
	Application Development in ABAP

Administrator

All tests are administered by SAP. Contact your SAP representative to register for the test (see the SAP Web site to find SAP representatives). You will receive the results of your test three to four weeks after taking the exam. If you fail the test, you can attempt it again after three months.

Fee

Fees for SAP tests vary; contact SAP for current pricing.

Format

Multiple-choice test with a three-hour time limit.

SAP R/3 Technical Consultant Certification

R/3 Technical Consultants have advanced knowledge of R/3 as well as detailed knowledge of an operating system (Windows NT or UNIX) and a database system (Oracle, Informix, Microsoft SQL Server, or IBM DB2). When you register to take the exam you will specify which operating system and database system you want to be tested on. Candidates can become certified on the following R/3 versions:

- Release 3.*x*

- Release 4

NOTE If you are currently certified on Release 3, you can take a 60 to 90 minute upgrade test in your specialization to receive certification in Release 4.

Who Needs It

This certification is an excellent way to advance your career in a company that uses or implements R/3.

Requirements for Certification

The certification process requires the following step:

1. Pass the technical certification test for the version on which you want to become certified (Release 3 or Release 4). The test is composed of three modules: (1) the R/3 Basic test, (2) the network operating system test, and (3) the database system test. You must choose the Operating System and Data System modules that are appropriate for you when you register for the test. Your certification will then be based on the combination of tests that you choose, for example, R/3 for UNIX/Oracle.

Administrator

All tests are administered by SAP. Contact your SAP representative to register for the test (see the SAP Web site to locate SAP representatives). You will receive the results of your test three to four weeks after taking the exam. If you fail the test, you can attempt it again after three months.

Fee

Fees for SAP tests vary; contact SAP for current pricing.

Format

Multiple-choice test with a four-hour time limit.

SAP Resources

SAP offers courses, a detailed certification requirements list and other resources for test preparation. For more information on this organization's certification program and courses, contact SAP at:

Web	Http://www.sap.com/
Mail	SAP America Inc.
	Strategic Planning & Support Office
	3999 West Chester Pike
	Newton Square, PA 19073
Phone	(610) 355-2500
Fax	(610) 355-2501

Solomon Software Certifications

- Solomon IV Certified Systems Engineer (SCSE)

- Solomon IV Certified Financial Specialist (SCFS)

Solomon offers a number of accounting and finance software products. The best known products are the Solomon IV versions for Windows NT and Microsoft BackOffice. The Solomon certification program documents a candidate's ability to implement and support Solomon IV for the Windows product line.

Recertification or Maintenance Requirements

Solomon Certifications apply to specific version numbers of Solomon software (currently Solomon IV), so there is no requirement for recertification on a particular version. Since your certification is tied to a certain version of a product, however, you will want to become certified on the newer versions, when they become available, if you want to continue to have the most current credential in this area.

If you are an authorized reseller for Solomon, you may be required to meet certain continuing education requirements.

Benefits of Certification

Solomon IV Certified System Engineers and Financial Specialists receive the following benefits:

- Certificate

- Eligibility to become an Authorized Solomon IV Reseller

Solomon IV Certified System Engineer (SCSE)

The Solomon IV Certified Systems Engineer (SCSE) certification process tests candidates' knowledge of the Solomon product and SQL in the following areas: Solomon IV architecture; installation; conventions and facilities; SQL; operating environment; and data security. Obtaining certification involves taking one test.

Who Needs It

This certification is an excellent way to document your knowledge about the implementation and management of Solomon IV.

Requirements for Certification

The certification process requires one step:

1. Pass the Solomon IV SCSE exam (Test ID: 370-001).

Administrator

Solomon tests are administered by Sylvan Prometric. Call Sylvan at (800) 307-3926 to register for a Solomon test; if outside the U.S., use the online Sylvan Test Center Locator at http://www.sylvanprometric.com to find the nearest testing center. Chapter 3 contains detailed information on taking tests from Sylvan.

Fee

Fees for Solomon tests vary; contact Sylvan for current pricing.

Format

Solomon exams consist of 75 multiple-choice questions and have a 75-minute time limit. Passing score is 68 percent.

Solomon IV Certified Financial Specialist (SCFS)

The one exam for the Solomon IV Certified Financial Specialist (SCFS) certification program tests candidates' knowledge of the Solomon IV product in the following areas: General Ledger, Accounts Payable, and Accounts Receivable.

Who Needs It

This certification is an excellent way to document your knowledge about the implementation and management of Solomon IV.

Requirements for Certification

The certification process requires one step:

1. Pass the Solomon IV SCFS exam (Test ID: 370-002).

Administrator

Solomon tests are administered by Sylvan Prometric. Call Sylvan at (800) 307-3926 to register for a Solomon test; if outside the US, use the online Sylvan Test Center Locator at http://www.sylvanprometric.com to find the nearest testing center. Chapter 3 contains detailed information on taking tests from Sylvan.

Fee

Fees for Solomon tests vary; contact Sylvan for current pricing.

Format

Solomon exams consist of 100 multiple-choice questions and have a 100-minute time limit. Passing score is 65 percent.

Solomon Resources

Solomon offers preparation courses for SCSE and SCFS candidates. Detailed information about the test content is available at the Solomon Web site. For more information on this organization's certification program and courses, contact Solomon at:

Web   http://www.solomon.com

Mail	200 East Hardin Street
	P.O. Box 414
	Findlay, OH 45840
Phone	(800) 476-5666
Fax	(419) 424-3400

CHAPTER

7

Programming Certifications

FEATURING

- American Society for Quality (ASQ) Certification

- International Function Point Users Group (IFPUG) Certification

- Learning Tree International Certifications

- Microsoft Certification

- Quality Assurance Institute Certification

- Software Publishers Association Certification

- Sun Certifications

A variety of excellent programming certifications are now available. This chapter includes certification programs for a number of programming languages, as well as certifications that focus on software development and software compliance issues.

American Society for Quality (ASQ) offers the Certified Software Quality Engineer for those involved with software design, inspection, testing, and verification. The International Function Point Users Group (IFPUG) is a membership-governed, nonprofit organization, which offers the Certified Function Point Specialist (CFPS) certification program to recognize expertise in Function Point Analysis.

Learning Tree International offers seven excellent vendor-independent programming certification programs: the C and C++ Programming Certified Professional, the C++ Object-Oriented Programming Certified Professional, the Java Programming Certified Professional, the Software Development Certified Professional, the Visual Basic Enterprise Development Certified Professional, the Windows Programming Certified Professional, and the UNIX Programming Certified Professional.

The Microsoft Certified Solution Developer certification program is designed for computer professionals who develop custom applications using Microsoft products and/or programming languages. The Software Publishers Association (SPA), which recently merged with the Information Industry Association (IIA) to form the Software Information Industry Association (SIIA), offers the Certified Software Manager (CSM) certification program, which addresses software protection and compliance issues.

Quality Assurance Institute has developed the Certified Software Test Engineer for those responsible for testing software products. Finally, the challenging Sun Certified Programmer, Sun Certified Developer, and Sun Certified Architect for Java Technologies are popular certifications offered by the inventors of the Java programming language.

Those who may be interested in pursuing programming certifications include:

- Help-desk personnel
- Programmers
- Consultants
- Network administrators

NOTE The International Programmers Guild (IPG), established in Switzerland in 1984, offers three levels of certification: Fellow Programmer, Senior Programmer, and Master Programmer. The certification process is unique, offering a much more involved and subjective evaluation process than is typical of other certification programs. For information about this organization and its certification program, see the IPG Web site (`http://www.ipgnet.com`).

Use Table 7.1 below to compare the number of required tests, the test format, the approximate cost of taking the test(s), number of required courses, cost of any required courses, and the relative difficulty of the certification programs in this chapter. The cost information is a general guideline; since things change rapidly in the world of certification programs, once you have selected a specific course of action you may want to double-check the costs.

We classified the difficulty of these certifications into three categories—Moderate, Challenging, and Very Challenging—based on the number of required tests and courses, and the relative difficulty of those tests or lab exams. These ratings are approximate and are offered simply as a general guide to help the reader distinguish between entry-level programs and those that require more advanced skill and knowledge. (This rating scale assumes that one has experience with the product or technology and has studied the appropriate subject content before attempting the exams.)

TABLE 7.1: Programming Certifications

Certification	# of Required Tests	Test Format(s)	Total Cost of Required Tests	# of Required Courses	Total Cost of Required Courses	Difficulty	Notes
American Society for Quality Certification							
Certified Software Quality Engineer	1	MC	$90–$120	—	—	●	You must also meet experience and professionalism requirements.
International Function Point Users Group (IFPUG) Certification							
Certified Function Point Specialist	1	MC	$200	—	—	○	Test fee is $100 for members.
Learning Tree International Certifications							
C and C++ Programming Certified Professional	5	MC	CV	5	$12,000–$14,000	◒	Discount pricing available; contact Learning Tree.
C++ Object-Oriented Programming Certified Professional	5	MC	CV	5	$12,000–$14,000	◒	Discount pricing available; contact Learning Tree.
Java Programming Certified Professional	5	MC	CV	5	$12,000–$14,000	◒	Discount pricing available; contact Learning Tree.
Software Development Certified Professional	5	MC	CV	5	$12,000–$14,000	◒	Discount pricing available; contact Learning Tree.
Visual Basic Enterprise Development Certified Professional	5	MC	CV	5	$12,000–$14,000	◒	Discount pricing available; contact Learning Tree.
Windows Programming Certified Professional	5	MC	CV	5	$12,000–$14,000	◒	Discount pricing available; contact Learning Tree.

TABLE 7.1: Programming Certifications *(continued)*

Certification	# of Required Tests	Test Format(s)	Total Cost of Required Tests	# of Required Courses	Total Cost of Required Courses	Difficulty	Notes
Learning Tree International Certifications							
UNIX Programming Certified Professional	5	MC	CV	5	$12,000–$14,000	◑	Discount pricing available; contact Learning Tree.
Microsoft Certification							
Microsoft Certified Solutions Developer (MCSD)	4	MC	$400	—	—	●	Exams have been updated since last year.
Quality Assurance Institute Certification							
Certified Software Test Engineer	1	MC	VF	—	—	◑	You must also meet education and experience requirements.
Software Publishers Association Certification							
Certified Software Manager (CSM)	1	MC	VF	1	$395	○	Course fee is reduced if organization sends more than one person.
Sun Certifications							
Sun Certified Programmer	1	MC	$150	—	—	◑	
Sun Certified Developer	1	PR (see note)	$150	—	—	●	Must be a Sun Certified Programmer. Test in essay format. Must complete a programming assignment ($250).
Sun Certified Architect for Java Technologies	1	MC	$150	—	—	●	

Certification Difficulty: ○ Moderate ◑ Challenging ● Very Challenging

T A B L E 7.1: Programming Certifications *(continued)*

Test Format:	**MC:** Multiple Choice **PR:** Hands-on Lab	**AT:** Adaptive Testing	**LA:** Live Application **NA:** Not Applicable
Test Fee:	**VF:** Test Fees can vary; consult testing center.	**CV:** Voucher for taking the exam is included in the fee for the required course(s) additional attempts cost extra.	

American Society for Quality Certification (ASQ)

- Certified Software Quality Engineer (CSQE)

The American Society for Quality (ASQ) certification program was created over 30 years ago to provide certifications in a number of fields. The Certified Software Quality Engineer (CSQE) credential validates the knowledge and skills needed by those involved in software quality development and implementation, as well as software inspection, testing, verification, and validation.

ASQ's list of certification programs also includes the following credentials: Certified Quality Auditor, Certified Mechanical Inspector, Certified Quality Engineer, and Certified Quality Manger; see the ASQ Web site (http://www.asq.org/) for more information on these certifications.

Recertification or Maintenance Requirements

ASQ requires all Certified Software Quality Engineers to participate in their Maintenance of Certification program to keep their certifications up-to-date.

Benefits of Certification

Certified Software Quality Engineers receive the following benefits:

- Letter of congratulations

- Wallet card and certificate

- Name published in the ASQ newsletter, *On Q*

Certified Software Quality Engineer (CSQE)

To obtain the Certified Software Quality Engineer (CSQE) credential, candidates must document their education and experience, provide proof of professionalism, and pass a test. The experience and the exam requirements are based on ASQ's "Body of Knowledge" in software development. This Body of Knowledge covers the following topics:

- General knowledge, conduct, and ethics

- Software quality management

- Software processes

- Software project management

- Software metrics, measurement, and analytical methods

- Software inspection, testing, verification, and validation

- Software audits

- Software configuration management

Who Needs It

The CSQE certification can help you move into a management or supervisory position in a software development group or company. This credential can also be of value to independent consultants who do contract work for software development companies.

Requirements for Certification

The certification process requires the following steps:

1. Meet the experience requirement of eight years of on-the-job experience in one or more of the areas of the Body of Knowledge listed above. A minimum of three years of this experience must be in a decision-making position. If you have completed a degree from an accredited school, fewer years of experience are required.

2. Provide proof of professionalism by one of the following means: membership in ASQ; registration as a professional engineer; or letters from two people who can testify to your abilities.

3. Submit an application to ASQ.

4. Pass the CSQE examination.

Administrator

The ASQ administers the CSQE exam. The exam is held twice a year in June and December at several locations throughout the world.

Fee

The test costs $90 for ASQ members, $120 for ASQ members outside the U.S., $195 for non-members in the U.S., and $225 for non-members outside the U.S. If you cancel, ASQ will retain $20 of the prepaid test fee.

Format

The exam is an open-book test with 160 questions. The exam must be completed in four hours.

American Society for Quality Resources

For more information on this organization's certification program and preparation courses, contact the American Society for Quality at:

Web	http://www.asq.org/
Mail	American Society for Quality
	P.O. Box 3066
	Milwaukee, WI 53201-3066
Phone	(800) 248-1946
Fax	(414) 272-1734

International Function Point Users Group (IFPUG) Certification

- Certified Function Point Specialist (CFPS)

The International Function Point Users Group (IFPUG) is a membership-governed, nonprofit organization that promotes and supports the use of Function Point Analysis and other software measurement techniques. The group endorses Function Points (FPs) as a standard software sizing metric. Approximately 550 companies are members of IFPUG.

Function Point Analysis (FPA) is a technique that quantifies the functions in a piece of software. This technique provides an objective, comparative measure that can be used in the evaluation, planning, management, and control of software production.

IFPUG created the Certified Function Point Specialist (CFPS) certification program to formally recognize expertise in Function Point Analysis.

Recertification or Maintenance Requirements

The Certified Function Point Specialist credential is valid for three years. It can be renewed by retaking the exam during the third year.

Benefits of Certification

Certified Function Point Specialists receive these benefits:

- Certificate
- Recognition at IFPUG Conference and in IFPUG newsletter

Certified Function Point Specialist (CFPS)

IFPUG recommends that candidates study the most recent version and release of the IFPUG Counting Practices Manual in preparation for the exam. At this time, the most recent version is Version 4.1. The manual can be obtained online at the IFPUG Web site. Candidates should also practice counting. Most successful CFPS candidates have counted at least 16,000 Function Points.

Who Needs It

This credential indicates that an individual knows how to perform consistent and accurate function point counts and understands current counting practices.

Requirements for Certification

The certification process requires the following steps:

1. Review the online CFPS brochure, which includes the application form and code of ethics; submit the application form and fee ($100 for members and $200 for non-members).

2. Pass the CFPS exam.

Administrator

The exam is offered twice each year in conjunction with the IFPUG Spring and Fall Conferences (see the "IFPUG Resources" section for contact information).

Fee

The test costs $100 for members and $200 for non-members. If you do not pass, you may retake the exam once within the next six months for a $25 fee.

Format

The open-book exam lasts three hours. It has three sections: definitions, implementation, and case studies. To pass the exam, candidates must score at least 90 percent in each of the three sections. IFPUG supplies copies of the current IFPUG Counting Practices Manual for use during the exam. Candidates may also bring to the test vendor-supplied reference cards or calculators.

The IFPUG Certification Committee reviews and grades exams. Candidates are notified of the test results in 4 to 6 weeks.

IFPUG Resources

For more information on this organization's certification program and courses, contact IFPUG at:

Web	`http://www.ifpug.org`
E-mail	`ifpug@ifpug.org`
Mail	IFPUG
	Blendonview Office Park
	5008-28 Pine Creek Drive
	Westerville, OH 43081-4899
Phone	(614) 895-7130
Fax	(614) 895-3466

Learning Tree International Certifications

- C and C++ Programming Certified Professional

- C++ Object-Oriented Programming Certified Professional

- Java Programming Certified Professional

- Software Development Certified Professional

- Visual Basic Enterprise Development Certified Professional

- Windows Programming Certified Professional

- UNIX Programming Certified Professional

Learning Tree International is a worldwide training organization that currently offers over 150 computer and networking courses in the United States, Europe, and Asia. As part of their curriculum in information technology, Learning Tree International offers 27 different vendor-independent professional certification programs, seven of which are programming certifications. (For information on additional Learning Tree International certification programs, see Chapters 4, 5, 8, 13, and 14.)

The Learning Tree International C and C++ Programming Certified Professional certification is based on the mastery of a comprehensive set of programming courses. This credential may be useful to software engineers, system and application programmers, systems analysts, technical managers, and others who want to apply advanced programming techniques in C and C++.

The Learning Tree International C++ Object-Oriented Programming Certified Professional certification is based on the mastery of a comprehensive set of programming courses. This credential may be useful to software engineers, system and application programmers, systems analysts, technical managers, and others who want to develop or maintain object-oriented applications with C++.

The Learning Tree International Java Programming Certified Professional certification is based on the mastery of a comprehensive set of Java and Web development courses. This credential may be useful to programmers and developers who want to use Java applets and applications, and develop or maintain Internet/intranet Web sites.

The Learning Tree International Software Development Certified Professional certification is based on the mastery of a comprehensive set of courses on software planning and development. This credential may be useful to software development staff and managers, programmers, system and business analysts, quality assurance professionals, and others involved in software development.

The Learning Tree International Visual Basic Enterprise Development Certified Professional certification is based on the mastery of a comprehensive set of courses on developing distributed database and Web applications. This credential may be useful to database and applications developers, analysts, technical mangers, and others who want to develop and maintain enterprise-wide applications.

The Learning Tree International Windows Programming Certified Professional certification is based on the mastery of a comprehensive set of courses on programming Windows applications. This credential may be useful to system and applications developers and programmers who want to build robust, user-friendly Windows-based applications.

The Learning Tree International UNIX Programming Certified Professional certification is based on the mastery of a comprehensive set of courses on developing and using applications in a UNIX environment. This credential may be useful to application and system programmers, system integrators, and technical personnel involved in developing and maintaining programs for UNIX-based systems.

Recertification or Maintenance Requirements

There is no recertification requirement for any of Learning Tree International's certification programs.

NOTE It is possible to obtain college credit for Learning Tree International certifications or courses. The American Council of Education (ACE) in Washington, D.C. has worked in cooperation with Learning Tree International to determine college course equivalencies for these courses and certifications. Approximately 1,500 colleges and universities in the United States will accept ACE recommendations for college credit. As a general rule, ACE will recommend two college credit hours for each four-day course. Learning Tree International will pay to have your Learning Tree International credentials registered with ACE and you can then request that your transcript be sent from ACE to any college or university. (Check with your college or university registrar to make sure that your institution accepts ACE recommendations for credit.)

Benefits of Certification

Learning Tree International Certified Professionals receive the following benefits:

- Framed diploma of Professional Certification

- An official record of the courses that you have completed
- Option of obtaining college credit

C and C++ Programming Certified Professional

C and C++ are powerful, general-purpose languages used to develop software for many purposes. This certification program involves taking four core courses and one elective course, and passing the tests given at the end of each course. The courses and exams are designed to teach and test the candidate's ability to write, compile, and execute ANSI C programs; use C's structured programming features; develop modular C programs and packaged data structures; use object-oriented analysis and design methods; adapt software designs for use with object-oriented and traditional languages; use C++ programming environments and tools; build software libraries in C++; and use advanced C++ development libraries and techniques.

Who Needs It

The Learning Tree International C and C++ Programming Certified Professional credential is a respected vendor-independent certification for software engineers, system and application programmers, systems analysts, technical managers, and others who apply advanced programming techniques in C and C++.

Since the certification program requires comprehensive training classes, Learning Tree International certifications offer a means for those just beginning their programming careers to gain hands-on experience and training that may not currently be available on the job.

Requirements for Certification

The certification process requires the following steps:

1. Complete the four core courses listed in Table 7.2, and pass the test given at the end of each course.

2. Complete one of the elective courses from Table 7.3, and pass the test given at the end of the course.

T A B L E 7.2:   Required Courses/Tests for C and C++ Programming Certified Professional

Course/Test	Course/ Test ID	Course Length
Hands-On C Programming	338	4 days
C++ for C Programmers: Hands-On	337	4 days
Hands-On C Advanced Programming: Techniques and Data Structures	339	4 days
Hands-On Advanced C++ Programming	397	4 days

T A B L E 7.3:   Elective Courses/Tests for C and C++ Programming Certified Professional

Course/Test	Course/ Test ID	Course Length
Introduction to Programming: Hands-On	325	4 days
Win32 GUI Programming: Hands-On	300	4 days
Win 32 Systems and Network Programming: Hands-On	302	4 days
Hands-On Visual C++: Windows Programming with MFC for C Programmers	301	5 days
Windows Programming with Visual C++ and MFC for C++ Programmers: Hands-On	403	4 days
Exploiting the Advanced Features of MFC: Hands-On	414	4 days
Hands-On Java Programming	471	4 days
Java for C++ Programmers: Hands-On	478	4 days
Object-Oriented Analysis and Design with UML	323	5 days
Hands-On UNIX Programming	333	4 days

Administrator

Courses and tests are administered by Learning Tree International (call (800) THE-TREE).

Fee

At this writing, the prices for Learning Tree International courses are $1,295 for a two-day course, $1,745 for a three-day course, $2,195 for a four-day course, and $2,495 for a five-day course. Learning Tree offers some significant discounts for those taking more than one course and for government employees. There is no additional charge for the tests.

Format

Each exam consists of 40 to 60 questions based on the course material. If you fail to pass on the first try, Learning Tree International will arrange for you to take a proctored exam at your place of work.

C++ Object-Oriented Programming Certified Professional

C++ is a powerful, general-purpose language used for large programming projects and software systems. This certification program involves taking three core courses and two elective courses, and passing the tests given at the end of each course. The courses and exams are designed to teach and test the candidate's ability to define and use C++ classes; write functions, decisions, and loops in C++; analyze requirements documents and identify key objects; convert an object-oriented design into a language implementation; exploit C++ to build adaptable object-oriented programs; use good programming style; use advanced C++ development libraries and techniques; and increase C++ program quality and efficiency with design patterns.

Who Needs It

The Learning Tree International C++ Object-Oriented Programming Certified Professional is a respected, vendor-independent credential for software engineers, system and application programmers, systems analysts, technical managers, and others who develop or maintain object-oriented applications with C++.

Since the certification program requires comprehensive training classes, Learning Tree International certifications offer a means for those just beginning their programming careers to gain hands-on experience and training that may not currently be available on the job.

Requirements for Certification

The certification process requires the following steps:

1. Complete the three core courses listed in Table 7.4, and pass the test given at the end of each course.

2. Complete two of the elective courses from Table 7.5, and pass the test given at the end of each course.

TABLE 7.4: Required Courses/Tests for C++ Object-Oriented Programming Certified Professional

Course/Test	Course/ Test ID	Course Length
C++ for Non-C Programmers OR	327	4 days
C++ for C Programmers: Hands-On	337	4 days
Object-Oriented Analysis and Design with UML	323	5 days
Hands-On Advanced C++ Programming	397	4 days

TABLE 7.5: Elective Courses/Tests for C++ Object-Oriented Programming Certified Professional

Course/Test	Course/ Test ID	Course Length
Introduction to Programming: Hands-On	325	4 days
Introduction to Object-Oriented Applications Development	215	4 days

TABLE 7.5: Elective Courses/Tests for C++ Object-Oriented Programming Certified Professional *(continued)*

Course/Test	Course/ Test ID	Course Length
Hands-On Java Programming	471	4 days
Java for C++ Programmers: Hands-On	478	4 days
Java for Enterprise Systems Development: Hands-On	472	5 days
Hands-On Visual C++: Windows Programming with MFC for C Programmers	301	5 days
Windows Programming with Visual C++ and MFC for C++ Programmers: Hands-On	403	4 days
Exploiting the Advanced Features of MFC: Hands-On	414	4 days
COM and ActiveX Programming with C++: Hands-On	406	4 days

Administrator

Courses and tests are administered by Learning Tree International (call (800) THE-TREE).

Fee

At this writing, the prices for Learning Tree International courses are $1,295 for a two-day course, $1,745 for a three-day course, $2,195 for a four-day course, and $2,495 for a five-day course. Learning Tree offers some significant discounts for those taking more than one course and for government employees. There is no additional charge for the tests.

Format

Each exam consists of 40 to 60 questions based on the course material. If you fail to pass on the first try, Learning Tree International will arrange for you to take a proctored exam at your place of work.

Java Programming Certified Professional

The Java programming language enables the creation of secure, architecture-neutral, object-oriented applications. This certification program involves taking three core courses and two elective courses, and passing the tests given at the end of each course. The courses and exams are designed to teach and test the candidate's ability to write, compile, and execute Java programs; create Web applets using Java run-time class libraries; develop flexible database applications using Java Database Connectivity (JDBC); use advanced Java programming to build cross-platform client/server applications; create secure Java applications with Digital Signatures and SSL; and configure application servers to support secure Java Commerce Messages (JCM).

Who Needs It

The Learning Tree International Java Programming Certified Professional certification is a respected, vendor-independent credential that documents the ability of programmers and developers to use Java applets and applications, and develop or maintain Internet/intranet Web sites.

Since the certification program requires comprehensive training classes, Learning Tree International certifications offer a means for those just beginning their programming careers to gain hands-on experience and training that may not currently be available on the job.

Requirements for Certification

The certification process requires the following steps:

1. Complete the three core courses listed in Table 7.6, and pass the test given at the end of each course.

2. Complete two of the elective courses from Table 7.7, and pass the test given at the end of each course.

TABLE 7.6: Required Courses/Tests for Java Programming Certified Professional

Course/Test	Course/Test ID	Course Length
Java Programming OR	471	4 days
Java for C++ Programmers	478	4 days
Java for Enterprise Systems Development	472	5 days
Developing Electronic Commerce Applications with Java: Hands-On	479	4 days

TABLE 7.7: Elective Courses/Tests for Java Programming Certified Professional

Course/Test	Course/Test ID	Course Length
Introduction to Programming: Hands-On	325	4 days
Object-Oriented Analysis and Design with UML	323	5 days
C++ for Non-C Programmers	327	4 days
C++ for C Programmers: Hands-On	337	4 days
Perl Programming: Hands-On	431	4 days
Developing a Web Site: Hands-On	470	4 days
Designing and Building Great Web Pages: Hands-On	487	4 days
Implementing Web Security: Hands-On	486	4 days

Administrator

Courses and tests are administered by Learning Tree International (call (800) THE-TREE).

Fee

At this writing, the prices for Learning Tree International courses are $1,295 for a two-day course, $1,745 for a three-day course, $2,195 for a four-day course, and $2,495 for a five-day course. Learning Tree offers some significant discounts for those taking more than one course and for government employees. There is no additional charge for the tests.

Format

Each exam consists of 40 to 60 questions based on the course material. If you fail to pass on the first try, Learning Tree International will arrange for you to take a proctored exam at your place of work.

Software Development Certified Professional

This program focuses on the knowledge and skills needed in software project planning, requirements analysis, quality assurance, and configuration management. This certification program involves taking four core courses and one elective course, and passing the tests given at the end of each course. The courses and exams in this program are designed to teach and test the candidate's ability to plan and manage software development projects; select and adapt development models; identify and confirm user requirements; define and implement effective quality assurance; organize and implement an effective configuration management process; and use effective processes, methodologies, and tools to ensure the development of quality software.

Who Needs It

The Learning Tree International Software Development Certified Professional certification is a respected, vendor-independent credential that is valuable to software development staff and managers, programmers, system and business analysts, quality assurance professionals, and others involved in software development.

Since the certification program requires comprehensive training classes, Learning Tree International certifications offer a means for those just beginning their programming careers to gain hands-on experience and training that may not currently be available on the job.

Requirements for Certification

The certification process requires the following steps:

1. Complete the four core courses listed in Table 7.8, and pass the test given at the end of each course.

2. Complete one of the elective courses from Table 7.9, and pass the test given at the end of the course.

T A B L E 7.8:   Required Courses/Tests for Software Development Certified Professional

Course/Test	Course/Test ID	Course Length
Software Project Planning and Management	340	4 days
Identifying and Confirming User Requirements	315	4 days
Software Quality Assurance	312	4 days
Software Configuration Management	342	4 days

T A B L E 7.9:   Elective Courses/Tests for Software Development Certified Professional

Course/Test	Course/Test ID	Course Length
Practical Software Testing Methods	316	4 days
Software Systems Analysis and Design	322	4 days
Introduction to Object-Oriented Applications Development	215	4 days

T A B L E 7.9: Elective Courses/Tests for Software Development Certified Professional *(continued)*

Course/Test	Course/Test ID	Course Length
Object-Oriented Analysis and Design with UML	323	5 days
Managing the Year 2000 Conversion: Hands-On	285	3 days
Business Process Re-engineering	381	4 days
Hands-On Project Management: Skills for Success	296	4 days
Management Skills for IT Professionals	290	4 days
Hands-On Microsoft Project	299	3 days

Administrator

Courses and tests are administered by Learning Tree International (call (800) THE-TREE).

Fee

At this writing, the prices for Learning Tree International courses are $1,295 for a two-day course, $1,745 for a three-day course, $2,195 for a four-day course, and $2,495 for a five-day course. Learning Tree offers some significant discounts for those taking more than one course and for government employees. There is no additional charge for the tests.

Format

Each exam consists of 40 to 60 questions based on the course material. If you fail to pass on the first try, Learning Tree International will arrange for you to take a proctored exam at your place of work.

Visual Basic Enterprise Development Certified Professional

Visual Basic is used as both a client/server and Web-based development tool in the development of enterprise applications. This certification program involves taking four core courses and one elective course, and passing the tests given at the end of each course. The courses and exams are designed to teach and test the candidate's ability to use Microsoft SQL Server and Visual Basic to develop client/server applications; develop advanced database applications using DAO, RDO, and ActiveX Data Objects; create ActiveX controls and code components in Visual Basic; design object-oriented software in Visual Basic; create Web-based applications with Visual InterDev; evaluate and use Visual Basic data access methods, including RDO and ODBCDirect; distribute applications with Microsoft Transaction Server (MTS); add MTS as an object broker; and leverage MTS database connection pooling capabilities.

Who Needs It

The Learning Tree International Visual Basic Enterprise Development Certified Professional certification is a respected, vendor-independent credential that affirms an individual's ability to develop distributed database and Web applications using Visual Basic, Visual InterDev, Microsoft SQL Server, and Microsoft Transaction Server.

Since the certification program requires comprehensive training classes, Learning Tree International certifications offer a means for those just beginning their programming careers to gain hands-on experience and training that may not currently be available on the job.

Requirements for Certification

The certification process requires the following steps:

1. Complete the four core courses listed in Table 7.10, and pass the test given at the end of each course.

2. Complete one of the elective courses from Table 7.11, and pass the test given at the end of the course.

TABLE 7.10: Required Courses/Tests for Visual Basic Enterprise Development Certified Professional

Course/Test	Course/ Test ID	Course Length
Visual Basic and ActiveX for Enterprise Applications: Hands-On	404	5 days
Developing SQL Server Applications with Visual Basic: Hands-On	227	4 days
Enterprise Web Development with Active Server Pages: Hands-On	409	4 days
Microsoft Transaction Server: Hands-On	413	4 days

TABLE 7.11: Elective Courses/Tests for Visual Basic Enterprise Development Certified Professional

Course/Test	Course/ Test ID	Course Length
Hands-On Visual Basic	304	4 days
Microsoft SQL Server 6.5: A Comprehensive Hands-On Introduction	225	4 days
Win32 GUI Programming: Hands-On	300	4 days
Win 32 Systems and Network Programming: Hands-On	302	4 days
Hands-On Visual InterDev	408	4 days
Hands-On Microsoft Access: Developing Enterprise Applications	407	4 days
Programming Office 97 Applications: Hands-On	308	
Windows Programming with Visual C++ and MFC for C++ Programmers: Hands-On	403	4 days

TABLE 7.11: Elective Courses/Tests for Visual Basic Enterprise Development Certified Professional *(continued)*

Course/Test	Course/Test ID	Course Length
COM and ActiveX Programming with C++: Hands-On	406	4 days
Programming ActiveX with Microsoft Foundation Classes: Hands-On	398	4 days

Administrator

Courses and tests are administered by Learning Tree International (call (800) THE-TREE).

Fee

At this writing, the prices for Learning Tree International courses are $1,295 for a two-day course, $1,745 for a three-day course, $2,195 for a four-day course, and $2,495 for a five-day course. Learning Tree offers some significant discounts for those taking more than one course and for government employees. There is no additional charge for the tests.

Format

Each exam consists of 40 to 60 questions based on the course material. If you fail to pass on the first try, Learning Tree International will arrange for you to take a proctored exam at your place of work.

Windows Programming Certified Professional

This certification program focuses on the skills and knowledge needed in the development of sophisticated Windows applications. A candidate must take four core courses and one elective course, and pass the tests given at the end of each course. The courses and exams are designed to teach and test the candidate's ability to write portable 32-bit Windows programs; create and use graphics resources, dialogues and menus; create multi-threaded applications that use IPC and shared memory; use Visual C++ to develop 32-bit Windows applications; use the Microsoft Foundation Class (MFC) library;

access databases with ODBC; build and deploy reusable software components: ActiveX controls; and "bulletproof" software components using testing and debugging techniques.

Who Needs It

The Learning Tree International Windows Programming Certified Professional certification is a respected, vendor-independent credential that documents an individuals ability to build robust, user-friendly Windows-based applications.

Since the certification program requires comprehensive training classes, Learning Tree International certifications offer a means for those just beginning their programming careers to gain hands-on experience and training that may not currently be available on the job.

Requirements for Certification

The certification process requires the following steps:

1. Complete the four core courses listed in Table 7.12, and pass the test given at the end of each course.

2. Complete one of the elective courses from Table 7.13, and pass the test given at the end of the course.

T A B L E 7.12: Required Courses/Tests for Windows Programming Certified Professional

Course/Test	Course/ Test ID	Course Length
Win32 GUI Programming: Hands-On	300	4 days
Win 32 Systems and Network Programming: Hands-On	302	4 days
Hands-On Visual C++: Windows Programming with MFC for C Programmers	301	5 days
Programming ActiveX with Microsoft Foundation Classes: Hands-On	398	4 days

T A B L E 7.13: Elective Courses/Tests for Windows Programming Certified Professional

Course/Test	Course/ Test ID	Course Length
Exploiting the Advanced Features of MFC: Hands-On	414	4 days
Windows Programming with Visual C++ and MFC for C++ Programmers: Hands-On	403	4 days
COM and ActiveX Programming with C++: Hands-On	406	4 days
C++ for C Programmers: Hands-On	337	4 days
Porting Applications from UNIX to Windows NT: Hands-On	399	4 days
Hands-On TCP/IP Programming	363	4 days
Visual Basic and ActiveX for Enterprise Applications: Hands-On	404	5 days
Hands-On Visual InterDev	408	4 days
Enterprise Web Development with Active Server Pages: Hands-On	409	4 days
Microsoft Transaction Server: Hands-On	413	4 days

Administrator

Courses and tests are administered by Learning Tree International (call (800) THE-TREE).

Fee

At this writing, the prices for Learning Tree International courses are $1,295 for a two-day course, $1,745 for a three-day course, $2,195 for a four-day course, and $2,495 for a five-day course. Learning Tree offers some significant discounts for those taking more than one course and for government employees. There is no additional charge for the tests.

Format

Each exam consists of 40 to 60 questions based on the course material. If you fail to pass on the first try, Learning Tree International will arrange for you to take a proctored exam at your place of work.

UNIX Programming Certified Professional

This certification program focuses on the knowledge and skills involved in developing and writing UNIX applications. A candidate must take four core courses and one elective course, and pass the tests given at the end of each course. The courses and exams are designed to teach and test the candidate's ability to use the features of the UNIX programming interface effectively; initiate, control, and communicate between UNIX processes; use UNIX utilities and tools to increase productivity; build scripts to automate routine tasks; write KornShell scripts to customize and extend the user environment; design scripts to automate complex system administration tasks; develop client/server applications that interoperate across heterogeneous platforms; and access the TCP/IP transport services using UNIX sockets.

Who Needs It

The Learning Tree International UNIX Programming Certified Professional certification is a respected, vendor-independent credential that documents an individual's ability to develop and maintain programs for UNIX-based systems.

Since the certification program requires comprehensive training classes, Learning Tree International certifications offer a means for those just beginning their programming careers to gain hands-on experience and training that may not currently be available on the job.

Requirements for Certification

The certification process requires the following steps:

1. Complete the four core courses listed in Table 7.14, and pass the test given at the end of each course.

2. Complete one of the elective courses from Table 7.15, and pass the test given at the end of the course.

TABLE 7.14: Required Courses/Tests for UNIX Programming Certified Professional

Course/Test	Course/Test ID	Course Length
Hands-On UNIX Programming	333	4 days
Hands-On UNIX Tools and Utilities	396	4 days
KornShell Programming: Hands-On	434	4 days
Hands-On TCP/IP Programming	363	4 days

TABLE 7.15: Elective Courses/Tests for UNIX Programming Certified Professional

Course/Test	Course/Test ID	Course Length
Introduction to Programming: Hands-On	325	4 days
UNIX: A Hands-On Introduction	336	4 days
Perl Programming: Hands-On	431	4 days
Hands-On Java Programming	471	4 days
Hands-On C Programming	338	4 days
Hands-On C Advanced Programming: Techniques and Data Structures	339	4 days
Porting Applications from UNIX to Windows NT: Hands-On	399	4 days
UNIX Workstation Administration: Hands-On	435	4 days
UNIX Server Administration: Hands-On	436	4 days
UNIX System and Network Security: Hands-On	433	4 days

Administrator

Courses and tests are administered by Learning Tree International (call (800) THE-TREE).

Fee

At this writing, the prices for Learning Tree International courses are $1,295 for a two-day course, $1,745 for a three-day course, $2,195 for a four-day course, and $2,495 for a five-day course. Learning Tree offers some significant discounts for those taking more than one course and for government employees. There is no additional charge for the tests.

Format

Each exam consists of 40 to 60 questions based on the course material. If you fail to pass on the first try, Learning Tree International will arrange for you to take a proctored exam at your place of work.

Learning Tree International Resources

For more information this organization's courses and certification programs, contact Learning Tree at:

Web	http://www.learningtree.com/
E-mail	uscourses@learningtree.com
Mail	Learning Tree International
	1805 Library Street
	Reston, VA 20190-5630
Phone	(800) THE-TREE
Fax	(800) 709-6405

Microsoft Certification

- Microsoft Certified Solution Developer (MCSD)

The Microsoft Certified Solution Developer (MCSD) certification is one of Microsoft's premium credentials. This certification program is designed for computer professionals who want to document their ability to develop custom business applications using Microsoft development tools, technologies, and platforms. There are more than 10,000 MCSDs in the world today, and that number is climbing steadily.

The MCSD program has been updated since last year. It includes certification exams that test users' ability to build Web-based, distributed, and commerce applications using Microsoft products, such as SQL Server and Visual Studio.

Recertification or Maintenance Requirements

MCSDs must take action to maintain their certifications. As Microsoft introduces new products and new versions of its operating systems, it retires the tests for previous versions. If you hold a certification that is based on a test that Microsoft is retiring, you will need to take a current test to maintain your certification. You will have at least six months to complete this new test. If you don't take the new test within the allotted time period, your status as an MCSD will no longer be valid.

Benefits of Certification

Microsoft Certified Solution Developers receive the following benefits:

- MCSD logo, certificate, wallet card, and lapel pin
- Access to technical information through a secure MCSD-only Web site
- Use of MCSD logos on stationery and business cards
- Invitations to Microsoft-sponsored conferences and technical briefings
- A free subscription to *Microsoft Certified Professional* magazine
- A one-year subscription to the Microsoft Developer Network Library, which provides an informative CD each quarter
- A one-year subscription to Microsoft TechNet Plus, allowing you to test and evaluate beta products. You will receive all evaluation beta products on CD along with 12 monthly TechNet issues.

- MSDN Online Certified Membership, a new benefit for all MCPs, which gives you access to a number of resources and services (see `http://msdn.microsoft.com/community/mcp` for details).

Microsoft Certified Solution Developer (MCSD)

To attain certification as an MCSD, a candidate must pass three core exams and one elective exam. The core exams cover solution architecture, desktop applications development, and distributed applications development. The elective exams test candidates' expertise with Microsoft development tools. Microsoft's Web site provides exam guidelines, sample tests, lists of suggested courses, and links to authorized training providers (see the "Microsoft Resources" section below).

Who Needs It

The MCSD certification is an excellent way to prove that you can build Web-based, distributed, and commerce applications with Microsoft products. It can also be an excellent designation for independent consultants who want to validate their abilities for potential clients.

Requirements for Certification

The certification process requires the following steps:

1. Pass one of the Desktop Applications Development exams listed in Table 7.16.

2. Pass one of the Distributed Applications Development exams listed in Table 7.17.

3. Pass the solution architecture exam: "Analyzing Requirements and Defining Solution Architectures" (Test ID: 070-100).

4. Pass one elective exam, selected from those listed in Table 7.18. Tests that are listed as both core exams and elective exams can only be counted once toward the MCSD certification.

T A B L E 7.16: MCSD Desktop Applications Development Exams

Test Name	Test ID
Designing and Implementing Desktop Applications with Microsoft Visual C++ 6	070-016
Designing and Implementing Desktop Applications with Microsoft Visual Basic 6	070-176
Designing and Implementing Desktop Applications with Microsoft Visual FoxPro	070-156
Designing and Implementing Desktop Applications with Microsoft Visual J++	*

*For the ID number of this new exam see the MCP Web site (http://www.microsoft.com/mcp/certstep/mcsd.htm).

T A B L E 7.17: MCSD Distributed Applications Development Exams

Test Name	Test ID
Designing and Implementing Distributed Applications with Microsoft Visual C++ 6	070-015
Designing and Implementing Distributed Applications with Microsoft Visual Basic 6	070-175
Designing and Implementing Distributed Applications with Microsoft Visual FoxPro	070-155
Designing and Implementing Distributed Applications with Microsoft Visual J++	*

*For the ID number of this new exam see the MCP Web site (http://www.microsoft.com/mcp/certstep/mcsd.htm).

T A B L E 7.18: MCSD Elective Exams

Test	Test ID
Designing and Implementing Distributed Applications with Microsoft Visual C++ 6	070-015
Designing and Implementing Desktop Applications with Microsoft Visual C++ 6	070-016
Designing and Implementing Data Warehouses with Microsoft SQL Server 7	070-019
Implementing a Database Design on Microsoft SQL Server 6.5	070-027
Designing and Implementing Databases with Microsoft SQL Server 7	070-029
Developing Applications with C++ Using the Microsoft Foundation Class Library	070-024
Implementing OLE in Microsoft Foundation Class Applications	070-025
Designing and Implementing Web Sites with Microsoft FrontPage 98	070-055
Designing and Implementing Commerce Solutions with Microsoft Site Server 3, Commerce Edition	070-057
Developing Applications with Microsoft Visual Basic 5	070-165
Designing and Implementing Distributed Applications with Microsoft Visual Basic 6	070-175
Designing and Implementing Desktop Applications with Microsoft Visual Basic 6	070-176
Application Development with Microsoft Access for Windows 95 and the Microsoft Access Developer's Toolkit	070-069
Designing and Implementing Solutions with Microsoft Office 2000 and Microsoft Visual Basic for Applications	070-091

T A B L E 7.18: MCSD Elective Exams *(continued)*

Test	Test ID
Database Applications with Microsoft Access 2000	070-097
Designing and Implementing Web Solutions with Microsoft Visual InterDev 6	070-152

Administrator

Microsoft tests are administered by Sylvan Prometric and Virtual University Enterprises (VUE). To register for a test with VUE visit the VUE Web site (http://www.vue.com/student-services/). Call Sylvan at (800) 755-3926 to register for Microsoft tests; if outside the U.S., use the online Sylvan Test Center Locator at http://www.sylvanprometric.com to find the nearest testing center. Chapter 3 contains detailed information on taking tests from Sylvan or VUE.

Fee

The fee is $100 per test.

Format

Multiple-choice, closed-book tests. The number of questions and time limit depend on the test selected.

Microsoft Resources

The Microsoft Web site offers practice tests as well as exam preparation guides that detail the objectives of each exam. Microsoft's Web site also offers a listing of Microsoft Certified Technical Education Centers. For more information on this organization's certification programs, contact Microsoft at:

Web	http://www.microsoft.com/mcp/
E-mail	mcp@msprograms.com
Mail	Microsoft Corporation
	One Microsoft Way
	Redmond, WA 98052-6399
Phone	(800) 636-7544
Fax	(425) 936-7329

Quality Assurance Institute (QAI) Certification

- Certified Software Test Engineer

The Quality Assurance Institute (QAI) is an international organization of companies that are interested in effective methods for software quality control and assurance. QAI provides consulting and education services to its member companies. QAI also offers a number of certification programs, including the Certified Quality Analyst and the Certified Software Test Engineer (CSTE). The CSTE Credential, which we cover in this chapter, was developed in 1996. Consult QAI's Web site for information about the Certified Quality Analyst and other certifications (see the "QAI Resources" section below).

Recertification or Maintenance Requirements

The CSTE credential is valid for one year. All CSTEs must obtain at least 40 continuing education credits annually and pay a $20 annual administrative fee to maintain their CSTE status.

Benefits of Certification

CSTEs receive the following benefits:

- Use of the CSTE logo for stationery and business cards
- Certificate
- Lapel pin

Certified Software Test Engineer (CSTE)

The CSTE credential is earned through a combination of education, work experience, and testing. The CSTE candidate first submits an application, which lists education and work experience, and then takes a test. The criteria against which the candidate is judged are based on the CSTE "Body of Knowledge," which includes the following topics related to software quality control:

- Communication
- Professional development

- Quality principles and concepts
- Methods for software development and maintenance
- Test principles and concepts
- Verification and validation methods
- Test management, standards, and environment
- Risk analysis
- Test tactics (approaches, tools, and environment)
- Planning process
- Test design
- Performing tests
- Defect tracking and management
- Quantitative measurement
- Improving the testing process

Who Needs It

The CSTE certification can help you advance to a management or supervisor position in a software development group or company. This credential can also be of value to independent consultants who do contract work for software development companies.

Requirements for Certification

The certification process requires the following steps:

1. Submit an application to the QAI, along with the $250 test fee.

2. Pass the CSTE exam.

Administrator

The CSTE exam is administered by QAI throughout the U.S. Contact QAI to arrange for your exam.

Fee

Contact QAI for current information on test fees.

Format

The CSTE exam consists of four parts, based on the 16 topics listed in the CSTE Body of Knowledge listed above. A score of 75 percent or better on each part is required to pass.

Quality Assurance Institute Resources

For more information on this organization's certification program and courses, contact the Quality Assurance Institute at:

Web	http://www.qaiusa.com
E-mail	certify@qaiusa.com
Mail	Quality Assurance Institute
	7575 Dr. Phillips Blvd., Suite 350
	Orlando, FL 32819
Phone	(407) 363-1111
Fax	(407) 363-1112

Software Publishers Association (SPA) Certification

- Certified Software Manager

The Software Publishers Association (SPA) merged with the Information Industry Association (IIA) on January 1, 1999 to form the Software Information Industry Association (SIIA). This new trade association represents 1,500 software and information companies. SPA Anti-Piracy, now a division of SIIA, enforces copyright law on behalf of about 1,000 member companies.

The Certified Software Manager (CSM) certification program, which was developed by the Software Publishers Association (SPA) prior to the merger, is still offered under the auspices of the SPA at this time.

The CSM Program was designed to address the needs of software managers, technical support specialists, purchasing agents, and resellers who need to protect their own software and ensure that their organizations are software compliant.

Recertification or Maintenance Requirements

There are currently no recertification requirements for Certified Software Managers.

Benefits of Certification

Certified Software Managers receive the following benefits:

- Certificate

Certified Software Manager (CSM)

Attaining SPA's Certified Software Manager (CSM) credential involves passing one exam. Candidates for the CSM attend a six-hour Certified Software Manager Seminar ($395) and study the CSM Student Manual. The CSM Seminar covers the diagnosis and management of software licensing issues, and covers copyright infringement, software piracy, and related issues. Those who attend the seminar receive a copy of the student manual, an anti-piracy video, and SPAudit software. If you do not attend a seminar, you can order the CSM Student Manual from SPA for $195 (see the Publications section of the SPA Web site at http://www.siia.net).

Who Needs It

The Certified Software Manager credential indicates that you know how to protect your organization's software from piracy and ensure that your organization complies with software license agreements.

Requirements for Certification

The certification process requires the following step:

1. Pass the CSM exam. The exam is not taken on the same day as the seminar.

Administrator

The exam is administered by the organization (see the SPA Web site for more information).

Fee

The seminar costs $395 and there is a separate $100 fee for the exam.

Format

The online exam has multiple-choice and true/false questions.

Software Publishers Association (SPA) Resources

For more information on this organization's certification program
and courses, contact SPA at:

Web	http://www.siia.net
E-mail	csminfo@spa.org
Mail	Software & Information Industry Association
	1730 M St. NW, Suite 700
	Washington, DC 20036-4510
Phone	(202) 452-1600
Fax	(202) 223-8756

Sun Certifications

- Sun Certified Programmer

- Sun Certified Developer

- Sun Certified Architect

Sun Microsystems, Inc., is the originator of the Java programming language, and is also well known for its high-performance
computer systems. Sun now offers its Sun Certified Programmer certification on three versions of Java: Java Development Kit (JDK)
1.0.2, JDK 1.1, and Java 2. The Certified Java Developer credential,
which builds on the programmer-level certification, is available for
JDK 1.0.2 and JDK 1.1. A new certification, the Sun Certified Architect for Java Technologies (Java 2) is now available.

Java's certification exams have earned a reputation as being quite
challenging. Four months after the October 1996 introduction of
Java's certification program, it was reported that 55 to 60 percent of
the approximately 100 persons who had attempted the exam up to

that time had failed to pass ("Tough Test Reveals Java Pros," Julia King, *Computer World*, February 3, 1997).

NOTE Sun also offers the Sun Certified Solaris System Administrator and Network Administrator certification programs. These programs are covered in Chapter 5, "Operating Systems Certifications."

Recertification or Maintenance Requirements

Java certifications apply to specific version numbers, so there is no requirement for recertification on a particular version. Since your certification is tied to a certain version of a product, however, you will want become certified on the newest versions, when they become available, if you want to continue to have the most current credential in this area.

Benefits of Certification

Sun Certified Java Programmers, Developers, and Architects receive the following benefits:

- Logo for use on business cards and materials
- Certificate

Sun Certified Programmer

The Sun Certified Java Programmer certification program involves passing a single examination. This exam tests the breadth of the candidate's knowledge of the Java language, and is based on a particular version of Java. The Certified Java Programmer credential can be earned for the following versions:

- JDK 1.0.2
- JDK 1.1
- Java 2

Sun recommends taking one of these two instructor-led, five-day courses as preparation for the Sun Certified Java Programmer exam: Course

SL-275: Java Programming UNIX ($1,995) or Course SL-276: Java Programming Windows 95 ($1,995). Another option in preparing for the exam is to take the self-paced course entitled JavaTutor: Java Programming Library (JTL-SL275; cost is $995).

Who Needs It

The Sun Certified Java Programmer certification is an excellent credential for Java programmers. This certification is also valuable to Web designers and administrators. It can help you advance your career with an organization, or help you get jobs on a freelance basis.

Requirements for Certification

The certification process requires only one step:

1. Pass one of the exams listed in Table 7.19.

TABLE 7.19: Sun Certified Programmer Exams

Test	Test ID
Sun Certified Programmer for JDK 1.0.2	310-020
Sun Certified Programmer for JDK 1.1 OR	310-022
Sun Certified Programmer for JDK 1.1 (IBM candidates only)	310-023
Sun Certified Programmer for Java 2	310-025

Administrator

Call Sun Educational Services at (800) 422-8020 to purchase an exam voucher. You will receive the voucher by mail, as well as information on how and when to take the exam. The exams are taken through Sylvan Prometric. (See Chapter 3 for more information on Sylvan Prometric.)

Fee

Each exam costs $150.

Format

All of these exams contain multiple-choice and short-answer questions. The Sun Certified Programmer for JDK 1.0.2 exam has 77 questions and must be completed in 135 minutes; the passing score is 70 percent. The Sun Certified Programmer for JDK 1.0.2 exam has 60 questions and must be completed in 120 minutes; the passing score is 70 percent. The Sun Certified Programmer for Java 2 exam has 59 questions and must be completed in 120 minutes; passing score is 71 percent. These exams are available in both English and Japanese.

Sun Certified Developer

The Sun Certified Developer certification program builds on the Certified Java Programmer certification. The Developer credential is available at this time for these Java versions:

- JDK 1.0.2

- JDK 1.1

The process of obtaining the Sun Certified Developer credential has two parts. The first part is the programming assignment, which is the performance-based portion of the Developer program. The candidate accesses the Sun Educational Services Certification Database and downloads a Java program and a set of instructions. There is no time limit for completion of this assignment. Once the assignment is completed, the candidate uploads the assignment. Then the candidate is ready for the second part of the certification program: the Sun Certified Java Developer examination. The Developer exam is an essay examination. The programming assignment and essay exam are graded together, and both must be received before assessment can begin.

Sun recommends this instructor-led, five-day course as preparation for the Sun Certified Developer programming assignment and written exam: Course SL-300: Java Programming Language Workshop ($1,995).

Who Needs It

The Sun Certified Java Developer certification is the most advanced and respected credential for Java programmers. This certification is also valuable to Web designers and administrators. It can help you advance your career in an organization, or help you get jobs on a freelance basis.

Requirements for Certification

The certification process requires the following steps:

1. Obtain certification as a Sun Certified Programmer.

2. Complete the Developer programming assignment (see above for details).

3. Take either the Sun Certified Developer exam for JDK 1.0.2 (Test ID: 310-021) or the Sun Certified Developer exam for JDK 1.1 (Test ID: 310-024).

Once the exam is completed, the candidate's programming assignment and examination are assessed together by an independent, third-party assessor within four weeks.

Administrator

The programming assignment component of the certification exam is administered directly by Sun Educational Services. The procedure for the assignment is described above.

To take the written exam, call Sun Educational Services at (800) 422-8020 to purchase an exam voucher. You will receive the voucher by mail, as well as information on how and when to take the exam. The essay exams are taken through Sylvan Prometric. (See Chapter 3 for more information on Sylvan Prometric.)

Fee

The U.S. cost is $250 for the programming assignment, and $150 for the Sun Certified Developer essay exam.

Format

The programming assignment, which is described above, has a passing score of 80 percent.

The Sun Certified Developer written exams comprise 5 to 10 short essay questions that must be completed in 90 minutes. Passing score is 70 percent.

Sun Certified Architect

A candidate who completes the new Sun Certified Architect program will receive the title: Sun Certified Architect for Java Technologies (Java 2). This credential is intended for individuals who design distributed object architectures, incorporate appropriate security measures in Java applications, and provide advice on all aspects of Java use and deployment. The examination for this credential tests the knowledge of candidates on multi-tiered architecture; Web concepts; service-based, object-oriented architecture; client/server design, and migration of legacy systems.

Sun recommends that candidates for this certification take the instructor-led, four-day course entitled Java Technology Architecture Planning and Design (SL-410; cost is $1,995).

Who Needs It

The Sun Certified Architect certification is an appropriate credential for those who make decisions and recommendations on how an organization deploys Java applications. This certification is also valuable to Web designers and administrators.

Requirements for Certification

The certification process requires only one step:

1. Pass the Sun Certified Architect for Java Technologies (Java 2) exam (Test ID: 310-050).

Administrator

Call Sun Educational Services at (800) 422-8020 to purchase an exam voucher. You will receive the voucher by mail, as well as information on how and when to take the exam. The exams are taken through Sylvan Prometric. (See Chapter 3 for more information on Sylvan Prometric.)

Fee

This exam costs $150.

Format

This exam has approximately 60 multiple-choice and short-answer questions. The time limit is two hours, and passing score is 75 percent.

Sun Resources

The Sun Web site offers an exam bulletin for each exam, which details the test's objectives. Sun's Web site also offers a listing of authorized courses. For more information on this organization's certifications and courses, contact Sun at:

Web	http://suned.sun.com/
E-mail	who2contact@chocolate.ebay.sun.com
Mail	Sun Educational Services
	UBRM11-175
	500 Eldorado Blvd
	Broomfield, CO 80021
Phone	(800) 422-8020 or (303) 464-4097
Faxback	(303) 464-4490

CHAPTER

8

Networking Hardware
Certifications

FEATURING

- 3Com Certifications

- Ascend Certification

- Cisco Certifications

- FORE Systems, Inc., Certifications

- IBM Networking Hardware Certification

- Learning Tree International Certifications

- Newbridge Technical Certifications

- Nortel Networks Certifications

- Xylan Certifications

In today's world, if a computer is not networked or capable of connecting to a network in some way, it is like a castaway on a desert island—information exchange with the outside world is limited to the occasional floppy in a bottle. Networks have changed many aspects of our daily lives. The Internet, e-mail, and the World Wide Web are what pop into most people's minds when they think of networking, but networks also control electronic credit card transactions, ATMs, electronic card catalogs at the local library, flight control information, medical records and billing, and the telephone system that allows us to talk to each other across the world instantaneously.

Just as networks have become vital to business, government, and education, so have the networking professionals who can set up, maintain, and secure networks. Having a good knowledge about networks—and the certification to prove it—is an excellent way to get and keep a good job. Any one of the certifications in this chapter is a valuable credential in the networking field because much of the knowledge gained in working with a particular product is applicable to products from other vendors.

NOTE   If you are considering a network-related certification, be sure to also check out Chapter 17, "Organization-Based Certifications," for some very important vendor-independent organization-based networking certifications.

Chapter 8 is the first of six chapters that deal with networking. This chapter concentrates on the physical aspects of the network, i.e., the hardware that connects networks together. The following five chapters deal with the operating systems and protocols that run on those networks (Chapter 9), network management (Chapter 10), telecommunications (Chapter 11), client-server applications and databases (Chapter 12), and, of course, the Internet (Chapter 13).

This chapter covers certifications from the major manufacturers of networking equipment. 3Com's Master of Network Science (MNS) program certifies the skills and knowledge of professionals who use 3Com products. Ascend offers a certification for its product line, which includes remote access and switching equipment. Nortel Networks and Cisco are both well-known for their routers, but are also big players in remote access and switching technology. Nortel Networks offers two levels of certification on a number of different types of technology. Cisco's Certified Internetworking Expert (CCIE) program offers three specializations. In addition, Cisco offers a set of "career certifications," introduced in 1998, with credentials in network support and design at associate and professional levels.

Fore Systems, Inc., a well-known producer of ATM switches, provides the FORE Systems WAN Certified Engineer and the FORE Systems LAN Certified Engineer credentials. Learning Tree International offers vendor-independent certification programs in local area networking, wide area networking, and internetworking. Newbridge Networks offers five certification "streams" related to wide area network technology. Finally, Xylan offers two certifications for its switching technology product line: the Xylan Certified Switch Specialist (XCSS), and the Xylan Certified Switch Expert (XCSE).

Networking certifications are in high demand today because of the recent explosive growth of the telecommunications and networking industries. Those who complete networking certification programs will learn how to improve network functionality, maximize network capacity, and promote network stability. Jobs as network designers, network administrators, and a variety of other titles are open to those who obtain these certifications. Persons who might want to pursue certifications described in this chapter include:

- Network administrators
- Internetworking engineers
- Telecommunications consultants
- Local area networking specialists
- Wide area networking designers
- Wide area switching experts

Use Table 8.1 to compare the number of required tests, the test format, the approximate cost of taking the test(s), the number of required courses, the cost of any required courses, and the relative difficulty of the certification programs in this chapter. The cost information is a general guideline; since things change rapidly in the world of certification programs, once you have selected a specific course of action you may want to double-check the costs.

We classified the difficulty of these certifications into three categories—Moderate, Challenging, and Very Challenging—based on the number of required tests and courses, and the relative difficulty of those tests or lab exams. These ratings are approximate and are offered simply as a general guide to help the reader distinguish between entry-level programs and those that require more advanced skill and knowledge. (This rating scale assumes that one has experience with the product or technology and has studied the appropriate subject content before attempting the exams.)

TABLE 8.1: Networking Hardware Certifications

Certification	# of Required Tests	Test Format(s)	Total Cost of Required Tests	# of Required Courses	Total Cost of Required Courses	Difficulty	Notes
3Com Certification							
Master of Network Science	5 or 6	MC(5) PR(1)	$895 or $995	—	—	◓	Five areas of specialization: LAN Solutions, LAN Solutions Plus, WAN Solutions, Remote Access Solutions, Network Management Solutions
Ascend Certification							
Certified Technical Expert	3	MC, PR	$1,250	—	—	●	
Cisco Certifications							
Certified Cisco Networking Associate (CCNA)	1	MC	VF ($100– $200)	—	—	◓	Specializations include Routing & Switching; and WAN Switching

TABLE 8.1: Networking Hardware Certifications *(continued)*

Certification	# of Required Tests	Test Format(s)	Total Cost of Required Tests	# of Required Courses	Total Cost of Required Courses	Difficulty	Notes
Cisco Certifications *(continued)*							
Certified Cisco Design Associate (CCDA)	1	MC	VF ($100–$200)	—	—	◖	
Certified Cisco Network Professional (CCNP)	2-4	MC	VF	—	—	●	Specializations: Routing & Switching, or WAN Switching. Must first be a CCNA.
Cisco Certified Design Professional (CCDP)	1-4	MC	VF	—	—	●	Specializations: Routing & Switching or WAN Switching. Must first be a CCDA.
Cisco Certified Internetworking Expert (CCIE)	2	MC, PR	$1,200	—	—	●	Specializations include: Routing & Switching, WAN Switching, and Internet Service Provider Dial.
FORE Systems, Inc., Certifications							
FORE Systems LAN Certified Engineer	2	MC, PR	CV	2	$6,000	●	
FORE Systems WAN Certified Engineer	2	MC, PR	CV	2	$6,000	●	
IBM Networking Hardware Certification							
IBM Certified Specialist	1	MC	VF	—	—	○	Areas include: ATM Installation, Workgroup Switches, 8260 Hubs, 2210/2216 Routers, and Route Switches.
Learning Tree International Certifications							
Local Area Networks Certified Professional	5	MC	CV	5	$12,000–$14,000	◖	Discount pricing available; contact Learning Tree

T A B L E 8.1: Networking Hardware Certifications *(continued)*

Certification	# of Required Tests	Test Format(s)	Total Cost of Required Tests	# of Required Courses	Total Cost of Required Courses	Difficulty	Notes
Learning Tree International Certifications *(continued)*							
Internetworking Certified Professional	5	MC	CV	5	$12,000–$14,000	◑	Discount pricing available; contact Learning Tree.
Newbridge Network Certifications							
Newbridge Wise for WANs	6	MC, PR	VF	—	—	●	
Newbridge Wise for ATM	4	MC, PR	VF	—	—	●	
Newbridge Network Certifications							
Newbridge Wise for Switched Routing	3	MC, PR	VF	—	—	●	
Newbridge Wise for WAN Network Administrators	4	MC, PR	VF	—	—	●	
Newbridge Wise for ATM Network Administrators	3	MC, PR	VF	—	—	●	
Nortel Certifications							
Nortel Networks Certified Support Specialist	1	MC	$125	—	—	○	Specializations include Hubs and Shared Media Core Technology, Routing Core Technology, and Switching Core Technology.
Nortel Networks Certified Support Expert	4	MC	$475	—	—	◑	

TABLE 8.1: Networking Hardware Certifications *(continued)*

Certification	# of Required Tests	Test Format(s)	Total Cost of Required Tests	# of Required Courses	Total Cost of Required Courses	Difficulty	Notes
Nortel Certifications *(continued)*							
Nortel Networks Certified Network Architect	—	—	—	—	—	●	Requires a two-part portfolio assessment, including a network case study
Xylan Certifications							
Xylan Certified Switching Specialist (XCSS)	1	MC	$100	—	—	○	
Xylan Certified Switching Expert (XCSE)	1	MC	$300	—	—	◒	You must first be an XCSS

Certification Difficulty: ○ Moderate ◒ Challenging ● Very Challenging

Test Format:: **MC:** Multiple Choice **AT:** Adaptive Testing **LA:** Live Application
PR: Hands-on Lab **NA:** Not Applicable

Test Fee: **VF:** Test Fees can vary; consult testing center. **CV:** Voucher for taking the exam is included in the fee for the required course(s); additional attempts cost extra.

3Com Certifications

- Master of Network Science (MNS)—LAN Solutions

- Master of Network Science (MNS)—LAN Solutions Plus

- Master of Network Science (MNS)—WAN Solutions

- Master of Network Science (MNS)—Remote Access Solutions

- Master of Network Science (MNS)—Network Management Solutions

3Com makes a number of networking products, from network interface cards to enterprise-sized routers and switches. The Master of Network Science (MNS) certification program supports and recognizes the skills and knowledge of professionals who use 3Com products. The MNS program replaces the retired 3Wizard program. Compared to the 3Wizard certification program, the MNS program requires greater knowledge and experience with 3Com products and offers a number of different certification tracks.

Each of the five MNS designations require that the candidate pass a number of online tests and then complete a hands-on lab exam. Once you begin, you have up to two years to complete the certification process.

NOTE 3Com is currently developing another MNS credential in Network Architecture, which should be complete later this year. Candidates for the Network Architecture credential must be knowledgeable in all technologies. If you choose this track, you will have to know more about the products, but less about troubleshooting. Check http://www.certification-update.com/ for updates.

Recertification or Maintenance Requirements

3Com requires all MNS participants to pass a Web-based test on new products every two years. In addition, an MNS must pass a hands-on practical exam every four years.

Benefits of Certification

Those who achieve MNS certification receive the following benefits:

- Priority access to 3Com's senior technical troubleshooters

- Membership in the 3Com Masters' Forum, with opportunities to participate in conferences, seminars, and special events

- Invitation to selected 3Com internal technical training programs

- Free annual subscription to 3Manuals (3Com's technical manual CD-ROM)

Master of Network Science (MNS)—LAN Solutions

The MNS in LAN Solutions is designed for those who implement and maintain Ethernet, fast Ethernet, and gigabit-level Ethernet with 3Com's SuperStack and CoreBuilder hubs and switches.

Who Needs It

This certification is especially useful in demonstrating your ability to design, build, and support a 3Com LAN. It can be a great way to advance your career in an organization that uses 3Com products.

Requirements for Certification

The certification process requires the following steps:

1. You must pass at least five of the six qualifying tests listed below in order to qualify to take the LAN Solutions MNS Lab practical exam. The qualifying tests include:

   - Ethernet Campus Solutions

   - SuperStack II Ethernet and Fast Ethernet Workgroup Solutions

- Gigabit Ethernet Switching with the SuperStack II Switch 3900 and 9300

- Implementing the CoreBuilder 3500 System in a Layer 3 Switched Network

- CoreBuilder 5000 Ethernet and Fast Ethernet Switching Products

- CoreBuilder 2500/6000 High-Function Switches Operation and Configuration

2. Pass the LAN Solutions MNS practical exam.

Administrator

The qualifying tests are Web-based assessments that can be taken after registering at the MNS Web site (http://www.3com.com/). The hands-on practical exam is also scheduled directly with 3Com. The exam is offered a number of times throughout the year at 3Com's testing labs in Hemel Hempstead, UK; Marlborough, Massachusetts; and Singapore.

Fee

The qualifying tests cost $100 each and the practical test costs $495. Fees may vary with geographic location.

Format

The qualifying tests are online multiple-choice assessments. The number of questions varies; each test must be passed with a minimum score of 70 percent.

Master of Network Science (MNS)— LAN Solutions Plus

The MNS in LAN Solutions Plus builds on the MNS—LAN Solutions credential described above. This certification is designed for those who implement and maintain ATM networks that are used as a backbone to connect LANs using ATM-based CoreBuilder, NETBuilder, and SuperStack products.

Who Needs It

This certification is especially useful in demonstrating your ability to design, build, and support a 3Com ATM network. It can be a great way to advance your career in an organization that uses 3Com products.

Requirements for Certification

The certification process requires the following steps:

1. Obtain the MNS—LAN Solutions credential.

2. Pass at least five of the six qualifying tests listed below in order to qualify to take the LAN Solutions Plus MNS Lab practical exam. The qualifying tests include:

   - ATM Campus Solutions

   - Implementing ATM with the SuperStack II Switch 2700, 1000/3000, and 2000 TR

   - Implementing ATM with the CoreBuilder 5000

   - Implementing ATM with the NETBuilder II Router and Core-Builder 2500 High-Function Switch

   - CoreBuilder 7000/7000HD ATM Switching Solutions

   - ATM and VLAN Manager Workshop

3. Pass the LAN Solutions—Plus MNS practical exam.

Administrator

The qualifying tests are Web-based assessments that can be taken after registering at the MNS Web site (`http://www.3com.com/`). The hands-on practical exam is also scheduled directly with 3Com. The exam is offered a number of times throughout the year at 3Com's testing labs in Hemel Hempstead, UK; Marlborough, Massachusetts; and Singapore.

Fee

The qualifying tests cost $100 each and the practical exam costs $495. Fees may vary with geographic location.

Format

The qualifying tests are online multiple-choice assessments. The number of questions varies. Each test must be passed with a minimum score of 70 percent.

Master of Network Science—WAN Solutions

The MNS in WAN Solutions is designed for those who implement and maintain wide area networks using the NETBuilder and Path-Builder series of products.

Who Needs It

This certification is especially useful in demonstrating your ability to design, build, and support a 3Com WAN for your clients. It can be a great way to advance your career in an organization that uses 3Com products.

Requirements for Certification

The certification process requires the following steps:

1. Pass at least five of the six qualifying tests listed below in order to qualify to take the WAN Solutions MNS Lab practical exam. The qualifying tests include:

   - Wide Area Intranet Solutions
   - NETBuilder II Series Configuration and Operation
   - NETBuilder II Series IP Routing
   - NETBuilder II Series Advanced IP Routing
   - NETBuilder II Series Configuration for WAN
   - PathBuilder WAN Switching Configuration and Operation

2. Pass the WAN Solutions MNS practical exam.

Administrator

The qualifying tests are Web-based assessments that can be taken after registering at the MNS Web site (`http://www.3com.com/`). The hands-on practical exam is also scheduled directly with 3Com. The exam is offered a number of times throughout the year at 3Com's testing labs in Hemel Hempstead, UK; Marlborough, Massachusetts; and Singapore.

Fee

The qualifying tests cost $100 each and the practical exam costs $495. Fees may vary with geographic location.

Format

The qualifying tests are online multiple-choice assessments. The number of questions varies and each test must be passed with a minimum score of 70 percent.

Master of Network Science—Remote Access Solutions

The MNS in Remote Access Solutions is designed for those who implement and maintain remote access solutions using 3Com's Total Control and SuperStack remote access products.

Who Needs It

This certification is especially useful in demonstrating your ability to design and build a 3Com remote access solution for your clients. It can be a great way to advance your career in an organization that uses 3Com products.

Requirements for Certification

The certification process requires the following steps:

1. Pass at least five of the six qualifying tests listed below in order to qualify to take the Remote Access Solutions MNS Lab practical exam. The qualifying tests include:

   - Remote Access Solutions

   - Total Control: Installation and Management

   - Total Control: NETServer

   - Total Control: HiPer ARC

   - Total Control: EdgeServer Pro

   - SuperStack II Remote Access 3000 Configuration and Management

2. Pass the Remote Access Solutions MNS practical exam.

Administrator

The qualifying tests are Web-based assessments that can be taken after registering at the MNS Web site (http://www.3com.com/). The hands-on practical exam is also scheduled directly with 3Com. The exam is offered a number of times throughout the year at 3Com's testing labs in Hemel Hempstead, UK; Marlborough, Massachusetts; and Singapore.

Fee

The qualifying tests cost $100 each and the practical exam costs $495. Fees may vary with geographic location.

Format

The qualifying tests are online multiple-choice assessments. The number of questions varies. Each test must be passed with a minimum score of 70 percent.

Master of Network Science—Network Management

The MNS in Network Management is designed for those who manage and maintain 3Com networks using the Transcend network management system.

Who Needs It

This certification is especially useful in demonstrating your ability to manage and maintain a 3Com network for your clients. It can be a great way to advance your career in a organization that uses 3Com products.

Requirements for Certification

The certification process requires the following steps:

1. Pass at least four of the five qualifying tests listed below in order to qualify to take the Network Management MNS Lab practical exam. The qualifying tests include:

   - Transcend Network Management Solutions

   - Transcend Enterprise Manager '97 for NT
     OR
     Managing your Network with Transcend Network Control Services 5.0 for UNIX

- ATM and VLAN Manager Workshop
- Transcend Traffix Manager 2.0 for NT II Series Configuration and Operation

2. Pass the Network Management MNS practical exam.

Administrator

The qualifying tests are Web-based assessments that can be taken after registering at the MNS Web site (`http://www.3com.com/`). The hands-on practical exam is also scheduled directly with 3Com. The exam is offered a number of times throughout the year at 3Com's testing labs in Hemel Hempstead, UK; Marlborough, Massachusetts; and Singapore.

Fee

The qualifying exams cost $100 each and the practical exam costs $495. Fees may vary with geographic location.

Format

The qualifying tests are online multiple-choice assessments. The number of questions varies. Each test must be passed with a minimum score of 70 percent.

3Com Resources

3Com offers courses on each of the test topics listed above. Some of the courses are in self-study format and are available free over the Web. Others are offered in a traditional classroom setting and cost between $800 and $1,600. For more information on this organization's certification program and courses, contact 3Com at:

Web	`Http://www.3com.com/mns`
E-mail	`MNS_Administrator@3Com.com`
Mail	3Com Education Services
	Program Headquarters
	P.O. Box 16100
	Minneapolis, MN 55440
Phone	(800) NET-3COM (638-3266)
	(press option 5, option 2)

Ascend Certification

- Ascend Certified Technical Expert (ACTE)—
  Remote Access

Ascend, founded in 1989, provides technology and equipment solutions for telecommunications carriers, Internet service providers, and corporate customers, worldwide. The company makes devices for remote access, for wide area networking, and for linking telephone switches, network connections, and videoconferencing facilities to phone company networks.

Today, the majority of the leading international telephone companies, global carriers, and network service providers offer Internet access using Ascend equipment. Ascend has installed more than 3,500,000 access concentrator ports (network access points) throughout the world.

The Ascend Certified Technical Expert program was developed in 1997 as a way to certify those who have expertise in installing, configuring, and troubleshooting the Ascend remote-access product line. This certification is valuable to technical professionals working with Ascend products. For example, certification would offer a competitive advantage to Ascend partners who provide remote-access solutions and to technical support staff of Internet service providers using Ascend products.

NOTE Ascend is planning to introduce three additional tracks for the Ascend Certified Technical Expert program, reflecting the specialized roles that technical professionals perform. These will be ACTE—Virtual Private Remote Networking, ACTE—Frame Relay, and ACTE—ATM. Check `http://www.certification-update.com/` for updates.

Recertification or Maintenance Requirements

Ascend's program is new and there is currently no announced policy for maintaining certification. However, Ascend is exploring multiple recertification options for Ascend Certified Technical Experts.

Benefits of Certification

Ascend Certified Technical Experts receive the following benefits:

- A plaque, lapel pin, and Ascend Certified Technical Expert logos for use on business cards and stationery

- High-level technical service from Ascend

- Access to restricted areas of Ascend's Web site

- Inclusion of your company's name and contact information in a directory of Ascend Certified Technical Experts

Designing the Ascend Certified Technical Expert Certification Program

A company may have a variety of reasons to design a certification program: increased visibility for the company, generation of revenue, or the certification of staff in other companies that represent their products. For Ascend, one of the main reasons for designing the Ascend Certified Technical Expert program was to increase the number of skilled Ascend field personnel (both internal and external). When the skill level of their field personnel is increased, calls to Ascend are less frequent and those calls are usually made by someone who has already done some extensive testing.

Ascend's decision to include a lab exam was quite deliberate. "We are really looking for the experts, and not just someone who is competent, or at a journeyman level," said Leslie Owens, Ascend's certification program manager, when interviewed by phone in 1998. "The lab helps us differentiate the borderline person from the real expert. With the written test it is often hard to assess for some issues such as troubleshooting. We really wanted to test real-world expertise. So we felt it was critical to have the lab."

Continued

Ascend's biggest challenge in designing this program was to bring together a variety of talented subject-matter experts, both internal and external, to help design the tests and the practical exam. "We relied on subject-matter experts at every step of the way," says Leslie. "Pulling all of this 'people resource' together was the biggest challenge... and a lot of fun."

Ascend Certified Technical Expert (ACTE) — Remote Access

Becoming an Ascend Certified Technical Expert in Remote Access requires a candidate to pass three tests, the last of which is a hands-on lab test administered at Ascend's headquarters in Alameda, California. The Networking and Telecommunications exam covers advanced networking and telecommunications and explores the technologies on which Ascend products are based. The Remote Access exam covers Ascend's Pipeline, MAX, and Secure Access products. The Technical Expert Troubleshooting lab exam is a two-day test that requires the candidate to configure the Ascend products and third-party management tools, troubleshoot protocol incompatibilities, use debugging and authentication tools, and select and configure bandwidth requirements.

Ascend recommends that candidates have two years of industry experience and three to six months of Ascend product experience prior to attempting certification. Ascend offers several training courses that can help you get started in preparing for the Ascend Certified Technical Expert exams. The courses Ascend recommends as a first step in preparing for the Remote Access exam are:

- The MAX/Pipeline Course—an instructor-led, three-day course that costs $1,200

- The Radius Course—an instructor-led, two-day course that costs $1,000

- The Secure Access Course—a $300 CD-ROM–based self-study course

The course recommended as background for the Ascend Certified Technical Expert Troubleshooting lab test is the Advanced Troubleshooting Course, which is an instructor-led, two-day course that costs $1,000.

Who Needs It

An Ascend certification is a great credential to get if you are in the field of wide area networking and switching and have experience with Ascend products. It can help you establish yourself within your organization or get your foot in the door for a new position.

Requirements for Certification

The certification process requires the following steps:

1. Pass the Ascend Networking and Telecommunications test (Test ID: 101).

2. Pass the Ascend Remote Access Exam test (Test ID: 102).

3. Pass the Ascend Certified Technical Expert Troubleshooting lab test.

Administrator

The Networking and Telecommunications (101) and Remote Access (102) tests are administered by Sylvan Prometric. Call (888) 322-ACTE (press option 1), to register for these tests; if outside the U.S., use the online Sylvan Test Center Locator at http://www.sylvanprometric .com to find the nearest testing center. Chapter 3 contains detailed information on taking tests from Sylvan. The Certified Technical Expert Troubleshooting lab test is administered at Ascend's company facilities in Alameda, California, and can be scheduled by calling (888) 322-ACTE (press option 2).

Fee

The first two tests cost $125 each. The two-day lab exam costs $1,000.

Format

The networking and telecommunications exam has 75 questions, and must be completed in 90 minutes. The remote access exam has 100 questions, and must be completed in 120 minutes. Both are closed-book, computerized tests. The lab test is a two-day, hands-on practical exam that requires the candidate to configure and trouble-shoot Ascend products and third-party management tools.

Ascend Resources

Ascend's preparation courses, which the company recommends, but doesn't require, are offered at Ascend's training centers. Call (888) 322-ACTE (press option 3) to order a self-study course or to register for an instructor-led course. Ascend's Web site offers a list of test objectives for each exam. For more information on this organization's certification program and courses, contact Ascend at:

Web	http://www.ascend.com/
E-mail	acte@ascend.com
Mail	Ascend Communications, Inc.
	One Ascend Plaza
	1701 Harbor Bay Parkway
	Alameda, CA 94502
Phone	(888) 322-ACTE (2283)
International	(510) 747-4300

Cisco Certifications

- Cisco Certified Network Associate (CCNA)

- Cisco Certified Design Associate (CCDA)

- Cisco Certified Network Professional (CCNP)

- Cisco Certified Design Professional (CCDP)

- Cisco Certified Internetworking Expert (CCIE)

Cisco is the world's leading manufacturer of routers and internetworking products; over 70 percent of the routers in use today are Cisco products. Cisco was started in 1984 by Stanford professors Leonard Bosack and Sandy Lerner, a husband and wife team, who designed and built their own router. Since then, Cisco has grown into a company that sells over $6 billion in networking equipment per year.

The Cisco Certified Internetworking Expert (CCIE) has become one of the most coveted vendor-based certifications in the networking field. There are currently fewer than 5,000 CCIEs. While there are many benefits to becoming a CCIE, it is not an easy task; 70 percent of those who take the CCIE practical exam fail on their first attempt. The CCIE designation offers three areas of specialization.

In order to accommodate those networking professionals who wanted Cisco certification but were not ready to take the CCIE test yet, Cisco introduced its series of "Career Certifications" in 1998. These certifications are credentials in their own right, and also serve as stepping stones on the way to CCIE status. The Career Certification program has two basic tracks. The Network Support track includes the Cisco Certified Network Associate (CCNA) and Cisco Certified Network Professional (CCNP) credentials. The Network Design track includes the Cisco Certified Design Associate (CCDA) and Cisco Certified Design Professional (CCDP) credentials.

Recertification or Maintenance Requirements

The recertification policy for the Career Certifications (CCNA, CCNP, CCDA, CCDP) has not been finalized; check http://www .cisco.com/certifications for updates. CCIEs are required to maintain their certifications by passing a recertification test and attending a CCIE technical update conference once every 24 months.

Benefits of Certification

CCNAs, CCNPs, CCDAs, and CCDPs receive the following benefits:

- Graduation letter
- Certificate

- Wallet card
- T-shirt
- Logo for use on business cards and stationery

Cisco Certified Internetworking Experts receive the following benefits:

- Technical support from senior support engineers in Cisco's Technical Assistance Centers
- Access to CCIE chat forums
- Framed CCIE medallion
- Certificate
- Graduation letter
- Logo for use on business cards and stationery
- Invitations to special technical training for CCIEs

Certified Cisco Network Associate (CCNA)

The Certified Cisco Network Associate (CCNA) is Cisco's entry-level certification in the Network Support Track. This program has been very popular—there are already over 4,000 CCNAs. There are two specializations for this certification:

- Routing and Switching
- WAN Switching

The Routing and Switching specialization is the "traditional" certification. The exam for this specialization tests your ability to install, configure, and operate simple routed LAN, routed WAN, and switched LAN networks. The WAN Switching certification tests your ability to install various WAN switches and modems

Who Needs It

The CCNA certification is an excellent way to show current or potential employers that you know how to set up and administer Cisco routers and switches. It can be a great way to launch your career in the lucrative internetworking industry.

Requirements for Certification

The certification process requires the following step:

1. Pass the required test for the specialization you seek (see Table 8.2).

T A B L E 8.2: Required Tests for CCNA Specializations

Specialization	Test	Test ID
Routing and Switching	CCNA 1.0 exam	640-407
WAN Switching	CCNA WAN Switching	640-410

Administrator

The CCNA exams are administered by Sylvan Prometric. Call (800) 829-NETS (6387), choose option 3, and then option 2 to contact Sylvan to register for a Cisco exam; if outside the U.S., use the online Sylvan Test Center Locator at `http://www.sylvanprometric .com/` to find the nearest testing center. (See Chapter 3, "Taking Your Test," for detailed information on taking tests from Sylvan.)

Fee

The test fees range from $100 to $200 (contact Sylvan Prometric for current pricing).

Format

Multiple-choice exams (contact Sylvan Prometric for current information on exam length and passing score).

Certified Cisco Design Associate (CCDA)

The Certified Cisco Design Associate (CCDA) is Cisco's entry-level certification in the Network Design Track. This program has been very popular—there are already over 4,000 CCDAs. There are no specializations for this credential. The CCDA exam tests your ability to design simple routed LAN, routed WAN, and switched LAN networks.

Who Needs It

The CCDA certification is an excellent way to show current or potential employers your ability to design networks using Cisco routers and switches. It can be a great way to launch a career in the lucrative internetworking industry.

Requirements for Certification

The certification process requires the following step:

1. Pass the Designing Cisco Networks exam (Test ID: 640-441)

Administrator

The CCNA exams are administered by Sylvan Prometric. Call (800) 829-NETS (6387), choose option 3, and then option 2 to contact Sylvan to register for a Cisco exam; if outside the U.S., use the online Sylvan Test Center Locator at http://www.sylvanprometric .com/ to find the nearest testing center. (See Chapter 3, "Taking Your Test," for detailed information on taking tests from Sylvan.)

Fee

The test fees range from $100 to $200 (contact Sylvan Prometric for current pricing).

Format

Multiple-choice exams. Contact Sylvan Prometric for current information on exam length and passing score.

Certified Cisco Network Professional (CCNP)

The Certified Cisco Network Professional (CCNP) credential is the expert level certification in the network support track of Cisco's Career Certification program. The next level of certification after the CCNP is the CCIE (described later in this chapter). The specializations available in the CCNP certification are as follows:

- Routing and Switching

- WAN Switching

The exams in the Routing and Switching specialization test your ability to install, configure, operate, and troubleshoot complex routed LAN, routed WAN, and switched LAN networks, and Dial Access Services. The exams in the WAN Switching specialization test your ability to install, configure, troubleshoot, and manage WAN switched networks.

Who Needs It

The CCNP certification is an excellent way to show current or potential employers that you have an advanced level of ability in administering and troubleshooting networks that use Cisco routers and switches. This credential can also be of value to network professionals who do independent consulting and want to validate their expertise for clients.

Requirements for Certification

The certification process requires the following steps:

1. Obtain certification as a CCNA in the specialization of your choosing (CCNA—Routing and Switching or CCNA—WAN Switching).

2. Pass the required tests for your desired specialization (see Table 8.3). Note that Routing and Switching requires either two or four exams, while WAN Switching requires a total of four exams.

T A B L E 8.3: Required Tests for CCNP Specializations

Specialization	Test	Test ID
Routing and Switching	1. Cisco Internetwork Troubleshooting Exam	640-406
	2. EITHER the Foundations of Routing and Switching Exam OR ALL of the following three exams:	640-409
	Advanced Cisco Router Configuration	640-403
	Cisco LAN Switch Configuration	640-404
	Configuring, Monitoring, and Troubleshooting Dialup Services	640-405

TABLE 8.3: Required Tests for CCNP Specializations *(continued)*

Specialization	Test	Test ID
WAN Switching	1. Multiband Switch and Service Configuration	640-419
	2. BPX Switch and Service Configuration	640-425
	3. MGX ATM Concentrator Configuration	640-411
	4. The SVIO exam OR	640-451
	Cisco Strata View Plus	640-422

Administrator

The CCNA exams are administered by Sylvan Prometric. Call (800) 829-NETS (6387), choose option 3, and then option 2 to contact Sylvan to register for a Cisco exam; if outside the U.S., use the online Sylvan Test Center Locator at http://www.sylvanprometric .com/ to find the nearest testing center. (See Chapter 3, "Taking Your Test," for detailed information on taking tests from Sylvan.)

Fee

The test fees range from $100 to $200 (contact Sylvan Prometric for current pricing).

Format

Multiple-choice exams. Contact Sylvan Prometric for current information on exam length and passing score.

Certified Cisco Design Professional (CCDP)

The Certified Cisco Design Professional (CCNP) is the expert level certification in the Network Design track of Cisco's Career Certification program. The next level of certification after the CCNP is the CCIE (described later in this chapter). The specializations available in the CCDP certification are as follows:

- Routing and Switching
- WAN Switching

The exams for the Routing and Switching specialization test your ability to design complex routed LAN, routed WAN, and switched LAN networks. The exams for the WAN Switching specialization test your ability to design and implement an ATM network, design and implement a Frame Relay network, troubleshoot an existing WAN switched network, and manage traffic and voice technologies.

Who Needs It

The CCDP certification is an excellent way to show current or potential employers that you have an advanced level of ability in designing and troubleshooting networks that use Cisco routers and switches. This credential can also be of value to network professionals who do independent consulting and want to validate their expertise for clients.

Requirements for Certification

The certification process requires the following steps:

1. Obtain certification as a CCDA.

2. Pass the required tests for your specialization (see Table 8.4). Note that Routing and Switching requires either two or four exams, while WAN Switching requires one exam.

T A B L E 8.4: Required Tests for CCDP Specializations

Specialization	Test	Test ID
Routing and Switching	1. Cisco Internetwork Design Exam	640-025
	2. EITHER the Foundations of Routing and Switching Exam OR ALL of the following three exams:	640-409
	Advanced Cisco Router Configuration	640-403
	Cisco LAN Switch Configuration	640-404
	Configuring, Monitoring and Troubleshooting Dialup Services	640-405
WAN Switching	Designing Switched WAN Voice Solutions Exam	640-413

Administrator

The CCDP exams are administered by Sylvan Prometric. Call (800) 829-NETS (6387), choose option 3, and then option 2 to contact Sylvan to register for a Cisco exam; if outside the U.S., use the online Sylvan Test Center Locator at http://www.sylvanprometric.com/ to find the nearest testing center. (See Chapter 3, "Taking Your Test," for detailed information on taking tests from Sylvan.)

Fee

The test fees range from $100 to $200 (contact Sylvan Prometric for current pricing).

Format

Multiple-choice exams. Contact Sylvan Prometric for current information on exam length and passing score.

Cisco Certified Internetworking Expert (CCIE)

The CCIE credential is extremely valuable to anyone in the networking field. For some, perhaps the strongest motivation for attempting this certification is that it can be an excellent way to get a job at Cisco or with a Cisco reseller. To attain this certification, the candidate must first pass a qualification test and then a lab exam.

Before attempting this certification, Cisco recommends the following preparation: two or more years of internetwork administration, experience with internetwork installation and troubleshooting, extensive experience with Cisco products in a production environment, and familiarity with all Cisco product and service documentation. Cisco offers several training courses for CCIE candidates, and its Web site provides sample tests and detailed information on the test objectives (see the Resources section for more information).

There are three CCIE specializations:

- Routing and Switching
- WAN Switching
- ISP Dial

The CCIE: Routing and Switching Expert qualifying exam covers general LAN/WAN knowledge; knowledge of the functionalities and protocols of desktop, WAN, and Internet technologies; and knowledge of Cisco-specific technologies, capabilities, and applications. The lab exam requires the candidate to build, configure, and test complex internetworks to provided specifications; diagnose and resolve network faults; and use Cisco debugging tools.

The CCIE: WAN Switching Expert qualifying exam covers general WAN knowledge; time division multiplexing (TDM); knowledge of corporate technologies and applications, including Integrated Services Digital Network (ISDN), Frame Relay, X.25, and Asynchronous Transfer Mode (ATM); knowledge of Cisco-specific technologies; and knowledge of service provider technology. The lab exam requires the candidate to design and implement an ATM network and a frame relay network, troubleshoot an existing WAN switched network, interconnect network nodes, and manage traffic and voice technologies.

The CCIE: Internet Service Provider Expert qualifying exam covers general ISP dial access knowledge; encryption and authentication technologies; subnetting, static/dynamic, and classless interdomain routing (CIDR) addressing; corporate technologies and services such as Integrated Services Digital Network (ISDN), Multichassis Multilink Point-to-Point Protocol (MMP), virtual private dial network (VPDN); and Cisco-specific dial technologies. The lab exam requires the candidate to implement dial firewall and security, implement all forms of dial-on-demand routing, configure router/access servers, and implement transmission protocols.

If a candidate fails a lab exam on the first try, he or she must wait at least 30 days before attempting it again.

Who Needs It

A CCIE certification is one of the most coveted networking certifications. CCIEs are widely recognized as internetworking experts. Some technical professionals undertake CCIE certification in order to gain employment with Cisco or one of their partners.

Requirements for Certification

The certification process requires the following steps:

1. Pass the qualifying exam for the specialization you seek (see Table 8.5).

2. Pass the lab exam for the specialization you seek (see Table 8.5).

T A B L E 8.5: Required Qualifying Exams and Lab Exams for CCIE Specializations

Specialization	Test	Test ID
Routing and Switching	Routing and Switching Expert qualification exam	350-001
	Routing and Switching Expert lab test	

TABLE 8.5: Required Qualifying Exams and Lab Exams for
CCIE Specializations *(continued)*

Specialization	Test	Test ID
WAN Switching	WAN Switching Expert qualification exam	350-007
	WAN Switching Expert lab test	
ISP Dial	ISP Dial Expert qualification exam	350-004
	ISP Dial Expert lab test	

Administrator

The CCIE exams are administered by Sylvan Prometric. Call (800) 204-3926 to contact Sylvan to register for a Cisco exam; if outside the U.S., use the online Sylvan Test Center Locator at `http:// www.sylvanprometric .com/` to find the nearest testing center. (See Chapter 3 for detailed information on taking tests from Sylvan.)

The CCIE lab exams are given by Cisco in various locations throughout the world. Check the Cisco Web site for the location nearest you (see `http://www.cisco.com/certification/`).

Fee

The qualification exam costs $200. The lab exam costs $1,000.

Format

The two-hour, closed-book, computer-based qualification exam has 100 multiple-choice questions; the passing score is 65 percent.

The lab exam is a two-day, hands-on practical exam, evaluated by a senior CCIE internetworking engineer. Point values are given for each configuration scenario and problem; an aggregate score of 80 percent is needed to pass.

Practice Laboratory for Cisco Lab Test

Because the CCIE lab test is known to be a real killer (over half of the candidates fail on their first attempt), Cisco has teamed up with several universities to offer practice laboratories for CCIE candidates. Practice labs are currently available at these U.S. locations:

- University of Colorado at Boulder, Colorado
- Wichita State University, Wichita, Kansas
- University of California Extension, Santa Cruz, Santa Clara, California

Practice laboratories have the following equipment:

- Five 2500 series Cisco Routers (2501, 2511, 2524 (2), 2515)
- Two 4000M Cisco Routers
- Three Ethernet Hubs
- Three Token Ring MAUs
- One Ethernet Patch Panel
- One Serial Patch Panel
- Two ISDN Lines
- Two Modem Lines
- One Server for router configuration and TFTP

It is recommended that participants pass the CCIE qualification exam before attending the practice laboratory. The practice laboratory offers a self-study environment. You can complete a series of lab exercises written by Cisco that are similar to what you will encounter on the actual lab exam. The preparation lab fee is currently $500 per day.

To register, or for additional information, see `http://www.cisco.com/warp/public/625/ccie/practice_labs.html`.

Cisco Resources

Cisco offers several training courses for certification candidates through its Certified Training Partners located throughout the world (see the Cisco Web site for a complete listing). The courses Cisco recommends as preparation for certification include: Introduction to Cisco Router Configuration, Installation and Maintenance of Cisco Routers, Advanced Cisco Router Configuration, Cisco Internetwork Design, and Cisco Internetwork Troubleshooting.

In addition, the Cisco Web site provides sample tests, recommended reading lists, and detailed information on the test objectives. For more information on this organization's certification program and courses, contact Cisco at:

Web `http://www.cisco.com/certifications`
E-mail `ciscotraining@cisco.com`
Mail Cisco Systems, Inc.
170 West Tasman Drive
San Jose, CA 95134-1706
Phone (800) 829-NETS

FORE Systems, Inc., Certifications

- FORE Systems LAN Certified Engineer

- FORE Systems WAN Certified Engineer

FORE Systems is a leading manufacturer of ATM switches and other high-bandwidth products. The company, which recently acquired Berkeley Networks, has a long record of success in developing ATM products. FORE currently offers two certification programs: the FORE Systems WAN Certified Engineer and the FORE Systems LAN Certified Engineer.

Recertification or Maintenance Requirements

FORE requires all FORE Systems Certified Engineers to take a recertification/update course and exam each year.

Benefits of Certification

FORE Certified Engineers receive the following benefit:

- Logo for use on stationery and business cards

FORE Systems LAN Certified Engineer

Attaining this certification involves taking two courses and passing the exams given at the end of each course. The candidate must successfully complete the CORE Products course and the Enterprise EDGE Products course. At the end of each course, written and practical exams are administered. These exams test the candidate's ability to install, configure, and maintain the FORE products covered during the course.

The CORE Products course covers the installation, operation, and maintenance of FORE ATM switches, UNIX and PC ATM adapter cards, and basic ATM theory. The Enterprise EDGE Products course covers the PowerHub and ES line of FORE Products.

Who Needs It

FORE certifications are an excellent way to demonstrate your expertise in ATM switching technology and the use of FORE products. Companies who want to obtain Premier Partner status from FORE are required to employ certified employees.

Requirements for Certification

The certification process requires the following steps:

1. Attend the CORE Products course and pass the written and practical exams at the end of the course.

2. Attend the Enterprise EDGE Products course and pass the written and practical exams at the end of the course.

Administrator

The courses and tests are offered at FORE Systems facilities in the U.S. and throughout the world.

Fee

Each course costs $3,000.

Format

Each course lasts five days, with tests administered on the final day of class.

FORE Systems WAN Certified Engineer

Attaining this certification involves taking two courses and passing the exams given at the end of each course. The candidate must successfully complete the CORE Products course and the Service Provider EDGE Products course. At the end of each course, written and practical exams are administered. These exams test the candidate's ability to install, configure, and maintain the FORE products covered during the course.

The CORE Products course covers the installation, operation, and maintenance of FORE ATM switches; UNIX and PC ATM adapter cards; and basic ATM theory. The Service Provider EDGE Products course covers FORE ATM switching WAN interfaces, as well as CELLPATH 90 and CELLPATH 300 ATM multiplexer products.

Who Needs It

FORE certifications are an excellent way demonstrate your expertise in ATM switching technology and the use of FORE products. Companies who want to obtain Premier Partner status from FORE are required to employ certified employees.

Requirements for Certification

The certification process requires the following steps:

1. Attend the CORE Products course and pass the written and practical exams at the end of the course.

2. Attend the Service Provider EDGE Products course and pass the written and practical exams at the end of the course.

Administrator

The courses and tests are offered at FORE Systems facilities in the U.S. and throughout the world.

Fee

Each course costs $3,000.

Format

Each course lasts five days, with tests administered on the final day of class.

FORE Systems, Inc., Resources

FORE offers a number of Computer Based Training (CBT) modules to help those just starting to work with ATM get up to speed. For more information on this organization's certification program and courses, contact FORE Systems, Inc., at:

Web	http://www.fore.com/
Mail	FORE Systems, Inc.
	1000 FORE Drive
	Warrendale, PA 15086-7502
Phone	(724) 742-4444
Fax	(724) 742-7700

IBM Networking Hardware Certification

- IBM Certified Specialist

IBM makes a number of networking hardware products for local area networks and wide area networks. IBM's certification titles are currently being revised to reflect IBM's current networking hardware product list and to conform to the standard titles of the IBM

Professional Certification program. Currently there is only one level of certification available related to networking hardware: the IBM Certified Specialist.

Recertification or Maintenance Requirements

Courses and tests are updated to reflect new product versions. While recertification is not required, you will want to keep your credential updated by taking the new exams when they become available. Check the Certification Update Web site or the IBM professional certification site for information on the latest courses and tests (see http://www.ibm.com/education/certify).

Benefits of Certification

IBM Certified Specialists receive the following benefits:

- Certificate
- Wallet-size certificate
- Lapel pin
- Use of certification logo

IBM Certified Specialist

To attain certification as an IBM Certified Specialist in one of the IBM networking products, a candidate must pass one exam. IBM recommends that the certification candidate have hands-on experience with IBM networking products before taking the test(s). The IBM Certified Specialist title is currently available in these areas:

- IBM Certified Specialist—ATM Installation
- IBM Certified Specialist—Workgroup Switches
- IBM Certified Specialist—8260 Hubs
- IBM Certified Specialist—2210/2216 Routers
- IBM Certified Specialist—Route Switches

Who Needs It

This certification is especially useful in demonstrating your ability to implement and maintain an IBM network. It can also be a great way to advance your career in an organization that uses IBM networking hardware products.

Requirements for Certification

The certification process requires the following step:

1. Pass the required test for the specialization you seek (see Table 8.6).

T A B L E 8.6:   IBM Certified Specialist Exams

Area of Specialization	Test	Test ID
ATM Installation	ATM Installation	602
Workgroup Switches	Workgroup Switches	603
8260 Hubs	8260 Hubs	604
2210/2216 Routers	2210/2216 Routers	605
Route Switches	Route Switches	608

Administrator

Tests are administered by Sylvan Prometric; call (800) 959-3926 to register for IBM tests; if outside the U.S., use the online Sylvan Test Center Locator at `http://www.sylvanprometric.com/` to find the nearest testing center. (See Chapter 3, "Taking Your Test," for additional information on Sylvan Prometric.)

Fee

Fees for IBM tests vary based on test length and format; call Sylvan Prometric at (800) 959-3926 for pricing.

Format

Computer-based, multiple-choice tests. Call Sylvan Prometric at (800) 959-3926 for current information on the number of questions, time limit, and passing score.

IBM Resources

For more information on this organization's certifications and courses, contact IBM at:

Web	`http://www.ibm.com/certify`
E-mail	`certify@us.ibm.com`
Mail	The Professional Certification Program from IBM
	Mail Drop 3013
	11400 Burnet Road
	Austin, TX 78758
Phone	(800) IBM-TEACH ((800) 426-8322)
Fax	(512) 838-7961

Learning Tree International Certifications

- Local Area Network Certified Professional

- Internetworking Certified Professional

Learning Tree International offers over 150 computer and networking courses throughout the United States, Europe, and Asia. As part of their curriculum in information technology, Learning Tree International offers 27 different professional certification programs, two of which are vendor-independent certifications oriented toward networking hardware. These are the Local Area Network (LAN) Certified Professional and the Internetworking Certified Professional. (See Chapters 4, 5, 7, 13, and 14 for other Learning Tree International certification programs.)

The Learning Tree International Certified Professional credentials may be useful to PC support staff, service technicians, engineers, system and network administrators, and anyone else involved with the maintenance and support of network hardware. This type of certification, which involves taking training courses followed immediately by exams that are based on the objectives of those courses, is especially useful for someone who is just beginning in the field of networking.

Recertification or Maintenance Requirements

There is no maintenance requirement for any of Learning Tree International's certification programs.

Benefits of Certification

Learning Tree International Certified Professionals receive these benefits:

- Framed diploma of Professional Certification
- An official record of the courses that you have completed
- Option of obtaining college credit

NOTE It is possible to obtain college credit for earning your certification or for taking Learning Tree International courses. The American Council of Education (ACE) in Washington DC has worked in cooperation with Learning Tree International to determine college course equivalencies for these courses and certifications. Approximately 1,500 colleges and universities in the United States will accept ACE recommendations for college credit. ACE typically will recommend two college credit hours for each four-day course. Learning Tree International will pay to have your Learning Tree International credentials registered with ACE and you can then request that your transcript be sent from ACE to any college or university. (Check with your college or university registrar to make sure that your institution accepts ACE recommendations for credit.)

Local Area Networks Certified Professional

This certification program involves taking five courses and passing the associated examinations. Four of the courses are required core courses, while the fifth course is selected from a list of options. The test for each course is given on site at the end of the course.

The courses and examinations in this certification program are designed to teach and test the candidate's ability to design, implement, configure, and interconnect local area networks; install and configure the latest Ethernet technologies; analyze the Ethernet protocol and its impact on network performance; troubleshoot multivendor, multiple-protocol LAN environments; develop strategies for LAN monitoring and management; and evaluate and select fast LAN technologies, including FDDI, Fast Ethernet, Gigabit Ethernet, ATM, and 100VG-AnyLan.

Who Needs It

This Learning Tree International certification is an excellent choice for network administrators and engineers who need general education in LAN technologies.

Requirements for Certification

The certification process requires the following steps:

1. Complete four core course and pass the tests given at the end of each course (see Table 8.7).

2. Complete one elective course and pass the test given at the end of the course (see Table 8.8).

T A B L E 8.7: Core Courses for Local Area Network Certified Professional

Course	Course Number	Course Length
Local Area Networks: Implementation and Configuration	352	4 days
Implementing Switched and Fast Ethernet LANs: Hands-On	452	4 days

T A B L E 8.7: Core Courses for Local Area Network Certified Professional *(continued)*

Course	Course Number	Course Length
Hands-On LAN Troubleshooting	254	4 days
Migrating to High Performance LANs	259	4 days

T A B L E 8.8: Elective Courses for Local Area Network Certified Professional

Course	Course Number	Course Length
Introduction to Datacomm and Networks	350	4 days
Hands-On PC Networking	253	4 days
Implementing ATM	279	4 days
Windows 95 Support and Networking: Hands-On	153	5 days
Hands-On Introduction to TCP/IP	367	4 days
Hands-On Internetworking with TCP/IP	467	4 days
Introduction to Internetworking: Bridges, Switches and Routers	364	4 days
Hands-On IntraNetWare: NetWare 4.x Administration	264	5 days
Hands-On SNMP: From Workgroup to Enterprise Networks	464	4 days
Cisco Routers: A Comprehensive Hands-On Introduction	466	4 days

Administrator

Learning Tree International (call (800) THE-TREE).

Fee

At this writing, the prices for Learning Tree International courses are $1,295 for a two-day course, $1,745 for a three-day course, $2,195 for a four-day course, and $2,495 for a five-day course. Learning Tree International offers some significant discounts for those taking more than one course and for government employees.

Format

Each exam consists of 40 to 60 questions. If you fail to pass on the first try, Learning Tree International will arrange for you to take a proctored exam at your place of work.

Internetworking Certified Professional

This certification program involves taking five courses and passing the associated examinations. Four of the courses are required core courses, while the fifth course is selected from a list of options. The test for each course is given on site at the end of the course.

The courses and examinations in this certification program are designed to teach and test the candidate's ability to implement internetworking technologies; segment LANs with bridges and switches; deploy routers to connect LANs into the wide area network; design, implement, and optimize TCP/IP-based Internetworks; add TCP/IP applications and protocols to existing networks; configure detailed router parameters; select appropriate internetworking technologies for your organization; and design scalable networks based on bandwidth, delay, and growth criteria.

Who Needs It

This Learning Tree International certification is an excellent path for network administrators and engineers who need a broad education in LAN and WAN integration and internetworking technologies.

Requirements for Certification

The certification process requires the following steps:

1. Complete four core courses and pass the tests given at the end of each course (see Table 8.9).

2. Complete one elective course and pass the test given at the end of the course (see Table 8.10).

T A B L E 8.9: Core courses for Internetworking Certified Professional

Course	Course Number	Course Length
Introduction to Internetworking: Bridges, Switches and Routers	364	4 days
Hands-On Internetworking with TCP/IP	467	4 days
Hands-On SNMP: From Workgroup to Enterprise Networks	464	4 days
Data Network Design and Performance Optimization	453	4 days

T A B L E 8.10: Elective Courses for Internetworking Certified Professional

Course	Course Number	Course Length
Migrating to High-Performance LANs	259	4 days
Implementing Switched and Fast Ethernet LANs: Hands-On	452	4 days
Deploying Internet and Intranet Firewalls: Hands-On	488	4 days

T A B L E 8.10:   Elective Courses for Internetworking Certified
Professional   *(continued)*

Course	Course Number	Course Length
Implementing ATM	279	4 days
Cisco Routers: A Comprehensive Hands-On Introduction	466	4 days
Configuring Cisco Routers: Advanced Hands-On Workshop	481	4 days
Troubleshooting Cisco Router Internetworks: Hands-On	484	4 days
Implementing OSPF and BGP with Cisco Routers: Hands-On	465	4 days
High-Speed Wide Area Networks	379	4 days
Hands-On TCP/IP Internetworking on Windows NT	154	5 days

Administrator

Learning Tree International (call (800) THE-TREE).

Fee

At this writing, the prices for Learning Tree International courses are $1,295 for a two-day course, $1,745 for a three-day course, $2,195 for a four-day course, and $2,495 for a five-day course. Learning Tree International offers some significant discounts for those taking more than one course and for government employees.

Format

Each exam consists of 40 to 60 questions. If you fail to pass on the first try, Learning Tree International will arrange for you to take a proctored exam at your place of work.

Learning Tree International Resources

For more information on this organization's courses and certification programs, contact Learning Tree International at:

Web	http://www.learningtree.com
E-mail	uscourses@learningtree.com
Mail	Learning Tree International
	1805 Library Street
	Reston, VA 20190-5630
Phone	(800) THE-TREE
Fax	(800) 709-6405

Newbridge Technical Certifications

- Newbridge Wise for WANs

- Newbridge Wise for ATM

- Newbridge Wise for Switched Routing

- Newbridge Wise for WAN Network Administrators

- Newbridge Wise for ATM Network Administrators

Newbridge Networks Corporation designs and manufactures a comprehensive family of networking products and systems—primarily wide area networks (WANs)—used for corporate customers and carrier customers. Newbridge provides fully managed networks for transmitting voice, data, and video traffic that incorporate both new and widely adopted technologies, including asynchronous transfer mode (ATM), frame relay, time-division multiplexing (TDM), and X.25.

Newbridge's customers include the world's 200 largest telecommunications service providers and more than 10,000 public and private enterprises, government organizations, and other institutions. Newbridge is divided into three regions: Europe, Middle East, and Asia (EMA region); North and South America (NSA region); and Asia-Pacific (AP region). Newbridge Networks has its headquarters in Kanata, Canada. Newbridge offers the Newbridge Technical Certification program, previously known as the Newbridge Wise certification program, to support and recognize the skills and knowledge of those who work with its communication technology products. This certification program, initiated in 1996 in Europe, Asia, and the Middle East, is moving to global availability this year.

The Newbridge Technical Certification program is designed to be flexible, allowing technical professionals to tailor their certification programs to specific job needs. It offers discrete certification "streams" in five areas: WANs, ATM, Switched Routing, WAN Network Administrator, and ATM Network Administrator. Each of the streams has three distinct stages: Mandatory, Specialist, and Wise Certification.

Within each stream, mandatory exams cover the basic knowledge of the given technology. To attain a certification, candidates must proceed to the Specialist or Wise level. The successful completion of each specialist exam carries with it the title of Specialist in a particular area. Certification candidates may stop out after becoming a Specialist in one or more areas, or may continue their certification program by completing all Specialist exams in a stream, as well as a practical exam, to achieve Wise certification status. Note that some Specialist exams are common to more than one stream and will allow candidates to progress toward multiple Wise certifications.

NOTE   An additional Wise "stream" of certification will be made available this year: Newbridge Technical Certification for Remote Access. Check the Newbridge Web site or our Certification Update Web site for updates on this (see `http://www.certification-update.com/`).

Recertification or Maintenance Requirements

Newbridge Technical certifications are based on specific products and technologies. As new products and versions become available, certification should be updated accordingly.

Benefits of Certification

Newbridge Specialist and Wise certified individuals receive the following benefit:

- Certificate for each Specialist and Wise exam passed

Newbridge Wise for WANS

Attaining this certification involves passing two mandatory exams, three specialist exams, and a Wise practical exam. The successful completion of each of the three specialist exams carries with it the title of Specialist in a particular area. Certification candidates may stop out after becoming a Specialist in one or more areas, or may continue their certification program by completing all three Specialist exams and the Wise practical exam.

One additional optional Specialist exam is also available in the WAN certification "stream." Candidates who have passed the two mandatory exams may opt to take the 3600 MainStreet ISDN exam (Test ID: 9K0-003), becoming a Specialist in this area. Those who intend to attain Wise certification cannot substitute this optional exam for any of the required Specialist exams, however.

Newbridge offers instructor-led courses that prepare candidates for its exams. These courses are recommended, but not required. Newbridge also provides online study guides for its exams (see the "Newbridge Networks Resources" section for the Web address).

Who Needs It

The Newbridge Wise for WANS certification is an excellent way to build and document your configuration, operation, and support skills for Newbridge products. It can be an excellent way to advance your career in an organization that uses Newbridge networks.

Requirements for Certification

The Wise certification process requires the following steps:

1. Pass a mandatory computer-based 3600 voice and data commissioning exam. Select one of these two exams:

   - 3600 MainStreet Voice and Data Commissioning (Test ID: 9K0-001)
   - 3600 Voice and Data Commissioning Release 7 (Test ID: 9K0-021)

2. Pass a mandatory computer-based 3600 voice and data configuration exam. Select one of these two exams:

   - 3600 MainStreet Voice and Data Configuration (Test ID: 9K0-002)
   - 3600 Voice and Data Configuration Release 7 (Test ID: 9K0-022)

3. Pass a computer-based specialist exam on MainStreet Small Muxes. Select one of these two exams:

   - MainStreet Small Muxes (Test ID: 9K0-015)
   - MainStreet Small Muxes (U.S.) (Test ID: 9K0-215)

4. Pass the specialist MainStreetXpress 46020 WAN Network Management exam (Test ID: NW-009). This is a half-day practical exam.

5. Pass the computer-based specialist MainStreet Frame Relay exam (Test ID: 9K0-027).

6. When all Specialist exams have been completed, pass the Newbridge Wise for WANs exam (Test ID: NW-100). This is a full-day practical exam.

Administrator

Newbridge computer-based tests can be taken from Sylvan Prometric. Call (800) 745-6887 to register for a Sylvan exam; if outside the U.S., use the online Sylvan Test Center Locator at http://www.sylvanprometric.com to find the nearest testing center. Chapter 3, "Taking Your Test," contains detailed information on taking tests from Sylvan.

Newbridge practical exams must be booked directly with Newbridge Networks. Detailed information on how to book these exams, whether in the U.S. or internationally, is provided on the Newbridge Web site (see the "Newbridge Resources" section).

Fee

Exam fees may vary. Contact Sylvan Prometric for computer-based exam fees (see Chapter 3, "Taking Your Test," for more information about Sylvan). Contact Newbridge Networks for practical exam fee information (see the "Newbridge Resources" section).

Format

Computer-based exams range from 60 to 120 minutes in length. Practical exams are half-day or full-day hands-on exams that simulate job situations. "Half-day" exams range in length from thirty minutes to two hours, depending on the specialization, while the full-day Wise practical exams last approximately six hours.

Newbridge Wise for ATM

Attaining this certification involves passing one mandatory exam, two Specialist exams, and a Wise practical exam. The successful completion of each of the two Specialist exams carries with it the title of Specialist in a particular area. Certification candidates may stop out after becoming a Specialist in one or both areas, or may continue their certification program by completing both Specialist exams and the Wise practical exam.

One additional optional Specialist exam is also available in the ATM certification "stream." Candidates who have passed the one mandatory exam may opt to take the MainStreetXpress 36150 Commissioning and Configuration exam (Test ID: 9K0-011), becoming a Specialist in this area. Those who intend to attain Wise certification cannot substitute this optional exam for one of the required Specialist exams, however.

Newbridge offers instructor-led courses that prepare candidates for its exams. These courses are recommended, but not required. Newbridge also provides online study guides for its exams (see the "Newbridge Networks Resources" section for the Web address).

Who Needs It

The Newbridge Wise for ATM certification is an excellent way to build and document your configuration, operation, and support skills for Newbridge products. It can be an excellent way to advance your career in an organization that uses Newbridge networks.

Requirements for Certification

The Wise certification process requires the following steps:

1. Pass the mandatory computer-based ATM Technology exam (Test ID: 9K0-017).

2. Pass the computer-based specialist MainStreetXpress 36170 Commissioning and Configuration specialist exam (Test ID: 9K0-013).

3. Pass the specialist 46020 ATM Network Management exam (Test ID: NW-010). This is a half-day practical exam.

4. When both specialist exams have been completed, pass the Newbridge Wise for ATM exam (Test ID: NW-101). This is a full-day practical exam.

Administrator

Newbridge computer-based tests can be taken from Sylvan Prometric. Call (800) 745-6887 to register for a Sylvan exam; if outside the U.S., use the online Sylvan Test Center Locator at http://www .sylvanprometric.com to find the nearest testing center. Chapter 3, "Taking Your Test," contains detailed information on taking tests from Sylvan.

Newbridge practical exams must be booked directly with Newbridge Networks. Detailed information on how to book these exams, whether in the U.S. or internationally, is provided on the Newbridge Web site (see the "Newbridge Networks Resources" section).

Fee

Exam fees may vary. Contact Sylvan Prometric for computer-based exam fees (see Chapter 3, "Taking Your Test," for more information about Sylvan). Contact Newbridge Networks for practical exam fee information (see the "Newbridge Resources" section).

Format

Computer-based exams range from 60 to 120 minutes in length. Practical exams are half-day or full-day hands-on exams that simulate job situations. "Half-day" exams range in length from thirty minutes to two hours, depending on the specialization, while the full-day Wise practical exams last approximately six hours.

Newbridge Wise for Switched Routing

Attaining this certification involves passing one mandatory exam, one Specialist exam, and a Wise practical exam. The successful completion of the Specialist exam carries with it the title of VIVID Specialist. Certification candidates may stop out after becoming a Specialist, or may continue their certification program by completing the Wise practical exam.

Newbridge offers instructor-led courses that prepare candidates for its exams. These courses are recommended, but not required. Newbridge also provides online study guides for its exams (see the "Newbridge Networks Resources" section for the Web address).

Who Needs It

The Newbridge Wise for Switched Routing certification is an excellent way to build and document your configuration, operation, and support skills for Newbridge products. It can be an excellent way to advance your career in an organization that uses Newbridge networks.

Requirements for Certification

The Wise certification process requires the following steps:

1. Pass the mandatory computer-based ATM Technology exam (Test ID: 9K0-017).

2. Pass the computer-based VIVID (Release 2.1) Product Specialist exam (Test ID: 9K0-019).

3. Pass the Newbridge Wise for Switched Routing exam (Test ID: NW-102). This is a full-day practical exam.

Administrator

Newbridge computer-based tests can be taken from Sylvan Prometric. Call (800) 745-6887 to register for a Sylvan exam; if outside the U.S., use the online Sylvan Test Center Locator at http:// www.sylvanprometric.com to find the nearest testing center. Chapter 3, "Taking Your Test," contains detailed information on taking tests from Sylvan.

Newbridge practical exams must be booked directly with Newbridge Networks. Detailed information on how to book these exams, whether in the U.S. or internationally, is provided on the the Newbridge Web site (see the "Newbridge Networks Resources" section).

Fee

Exam fees may vary. Contact Sylvan Prometric for computer-based exam fees (see Chapter 3 for more information about Sylvan). Contact Newbridge Networks for practical exam fee information (see the "Newbridge Networks Resources" section).

Format

Computer-based exams range from 60 to 120 minutes in length. The practical exam is a full-day hands-on exam that simulates job situations. The full-day Wise practical exam lasts approximately six hours.

Newbridge Wise for WAN Network Administrators

Attaining this certification involves passing two mandatory exams, one Specialist exam, and a Wise practical exam. The successful completion of the Specialist exam carries with it the title of 46020 WAN Network Management Specialist. Certification candidates may stop out after becoming a Specialist, or may continue their certification program by completing the Wise practical exam.

Newbridge offers instructor-led courses that prepare candidates for its exams. These courses are recommended, but not required. Newbridge also provides online study guides for its exams (see the "Newbridge Networks Resources" section for Web address).

Who Needs It

The Newbridge Wise for WAN Network Administrators certification is an excellent way to build and document your configuration, operation, and support skills for Newbridge products. It can be an excellent way to advance your career in an organization that uses Newbridge networks.

Requirements for Certification

The Wise certification process requires the following steps:

1. Pass a mandatory computer-based 3600 voice and data commissioning exam. Select one of these two exams:

   - 3600 MainStreet Voice and Data Commissioning (Test ID: 9K0-001)

   - 3600 Voice and Data Commissioning Release 7 (Test ID: 9K0-021)

2. Pass a mandatory computer-based 3600 voice and data configuration exam. Select one of these two exams:

   - 3600 MainStreet Voice and Data Configuration (Test ID: 9K0-002)

   - 3600 Voice and Data Configuration Release 7 (Test ID: 9K0-022)

3. Pass the 46020 WAN Network Management exam (Test ID: NW-009). This is a half-day practical exam.

4. Pass the Newbridge Wise for WAN Network Administrators exam (Test ID: NW-103). This is a full-day practical exam.

Administrator

Newbridge computer-based tests can be taken from Sylvan Prometric. Call (800) 745-6887 to register for a Sylvan exam; if outside the U.S., use the online Sylvan Test Center Locator at http://www.sylvanprometric.com to find the nearest testing center. Chapter 3, "Taking Your Test," contains detailed information on taking tests from Sylvan.

Newbridge practical exams must be booked directly with Newbridge Networks. Detailed information on how to book these exams, whether in the U.S. or internationally, is provided on the Newbridge Web site (see the "Newbridge Networks Resources" section).

Fee

Exam fees may vary. Contact Sylvan Prometric for computer-based exam fees (see Chapter 3 for more information about Sylvan). Contact Newbridge Networks for practical exam fee information (see the "Newbridge Networks Resources" section).

Format

The computer-based exams for this "stream" range from 90 to 120 minutes in length. Practical exams are half-day or full-day hands-on exams that simulate job situations. "Half-day" exams range in length from thirty minutes to two hours, depending on the specialization, while the full-day Wise practical exams last approximately six hours.

Newbridge Wise for ATM Network Administrators

Attaining this certification involves passing one mandatory exam, one specialist exam, and a Wise practical exam. The successful completion of the specialist exam carries with it the title of 46020 ATM Network Management Specialist. Certification candidates may stop out after becoming a Specialist, or may continue their certification program by completing the Wise practical exam.

Newbridge offers instructor-led courses that prepare candidates for its exams. These courses are recommended, but not required. Newbridge also provides online study guides for its exams (see the "Newbridge Networks Resources" section for the Web address).

Who Needs It

The Newbridge Wise for ATM Network Administrators certification is an excellent way to build and document your configuration, operation, and support skills for Newbridge products. It can be an excellent way to advance your career in an organization that uses Newbridge networks.

Requirements for Certification

The Wise certification process requires the following steps:

1. Pass the mandatory computer-based ATM Technology exam (Test ID: 9K0-017).

2. Pass the 46020 ATM Network Management exam (Test ID: NW-010). This is a half-day practical exam.

3. Pass the Newbridge Wise for ATM Network Administrators exam (Test ID: NW-103). This is a full-day practical exam.

Administrator

Newbridge computer-based tests can be taken from Sylvan Prometric. Call (800) 745-6887 to register for a Sylvan exam; if outside the U.S., use the online Sylvan Test Center Locator at http://www.sylvanprometric.com to find the nearest testing center. Chapter 3, "Taking Your Test," contains detailed information on taking tests from Sylvan.

Newbridge practical exams must be booked directly with Newbridge Networks. Detailed information on how to book these exams, whether in the U.S. or internationally, is provided on the Newbridge Web site (see the "Newbridge Networks Resources" section).

Fee

Exam fees may vary. Contact Sylvan Prometric for computer-based exam fees (see Chapter 3 for more information about Sylvan). Contact Newbridge Networks for practical exam fee information (see the "Newbridge Resources" section).

Format

The computer-based exam for this certification is 60 minutes in length. Practical exams are half-day or full-day hands-on exams that simulate job situations. "Half-day" exams range in length from thirty minutes to two hours, depending on the specialization, while the full-day Wise practical exams last approximately six hours.

Newbridge Networks Resources

The Newbridge Web site provides a comprehensive downloadable information guide about its certification programs. The 40-page guide includes study guides for the exams. International contact information is available online. For more information on this organization's certification program and instructor-led courses in North and South America, contact Newbridge at:

Web	http://www.newbridge.com/
E-mail	jswierk@us.newbridge.com
Mail	Corporate Headquarters
	Newbridge Networks Corporation
	600 March Road, P.O. Box 13600
	Kanata, Ontario K2K 2E6
	Canada
	Or
	North and South America Office
	Newbridge Networks, Inc.
	Customer Training Department
	593 Herndon Parkway
	Herndon, VA 20170-5241
Phone	(800) 343-3600 or (603) 422-0419

Nortel Networks Certifications

- Nortel Networks Certified Support Specialist

- Nortel Networks Certified Support Expert

- Nortel Networks Certified Network Architect

Nortel Networks produces a number of networking products, from routers and hubs to central office switches for telephone companies. Nortel recently acquired Bay Networks, and the companies' two certification programs are currently being revised to create a unified certification framework for all Nortel data and voice product lines. This will allow candidates to pursue certification on data networks, voice networks, or a combination of both.

All candidates currently pursuing a previous Nortel or Bay Networks certification will be allowed to complete their certification with the new framework; they will receive credit for the tests they have already passed. The old tests will fit into the new certification titles in a way that maps well to the certification title the candidates originally sought.

This new common certification framework uses a tiered model that allows for a number of specializations in each certification level. The rollout of this new certification framework is expected to be completed by the end of 1999.

NOTE   In addition to the certification titles we cover here, three other new certifications will be available this year: Certified Design Specialist, Certified Design Expert, and Certified Account Specialist. If you are interested in product sales, be sure to check out these certifications. Visit Nortel Networks' Web site or the Certification Update Web site for more information (see `http://www.certification-update.com/`).

Recertification or Maintenance Requirements

Expert level certifications must be renewed every two years, while Specialist level certifications must be renewed every year. Certified Experts and Specialists wishing to recertify must take the current test for their certification. Certified individuals will be notified of the need for recertification 30 days prior to the expiration of their current certification.

The Nortel Networks Certified Network Architect certification is valid for two years. Candidates who wish to recertify may do so by providing evidence of continued participation in the field of network architecture and design, and submitting a new case study.

Benefits of Certification

All Nortel Certifications provide the following benefits:

- Certification certificate/plaque
- Use of logo
- Automatic distribution of updated Nortel Networks CBTs for new technology/product training (Expert/Architect only)

Nortel Networks Certified Support Specialist

This is Nortel's entry-level certification. This credential documents one's ability to deploy, operate, and troubleshoot Nortel-based networks. This certification is designed for persons who are involved in the day-to-day operational support of Nortel-based networks.

Skills and knowledge covered on the one required test for each specialization include node and network installation, network configuration using default parameters, maintaining network operations, and performing basic problem identification and troubleshooting. Currently five specializations are available for this certification:

- Hubs and Shared Media Core Technology
- Router Core Technology
- Switching Core Technology
- Multi-Service Access Core Technology
- Passport 6000/7000

Who Needs It

The Nortel Certified Support Specialist certification is an excellent way to show current or potential employers your fundamental skills and knowledge of Nortel networking. This credential can be of value to help-desk personnel and others who want to validate their expertise in order to advance their careers.

Requirements for Certification

The certification process requires the following step:

1. Pass the Core Technology exam for the specialization you seek (See Table 8.11).

TABLE 8.11: Core Technology Exams

Specialization	Test	Test ID
Hubs and Shared Media Core Technology	Hubs and Shared Media Core Technology	920-013
Routing Core Technology	Routing Core Technology	920-014
Switching Core Technology	Switching Core Technology	920-016
Multi-Service Access Core Technology	Multi-Service Access Core Technology	920-020
Passport 6000/7000	Passport 6000/7000	920-100

Administrator

Call Sylvan Prometric at (800) 791-EXAM to register for a Nortel exam; if outside the U.S., use the online Sylvan Test Center Locator at `http://www.sylvanprometric.com/` to find the nearest testing center. (See Chapter 3, "Taking Your Test," for detailed information on taking tests from Sylvan.)

Fee

Each test costs $125 to $150.

Format

Computer-based, multiple-choice tests. Call Sylvan Prometric at (800) 791-EXAM for current information on the number of questions, time limit, and passing score.

Nortel Networks Certified Support Expert

A Nortel Networks Certified Support Expert knows how to effectively implement, configure, support, troubleshoot, and optimize Nortel-based networks. Nortel recommends that candidates for this certification have advanced network experience. Skills and knowledge tested include setting up complex networks, sustaining a network throughout the lifecycle of the network, advanced troubleshooting, and problem resolution.

Who Needs It

The Nortel Certified Support Specialist certification is an excellent way to demonstrate that you have an advanced level of knowledge about Nortel networking, and can configure, support, and troubleshoot Nortel-based networks. This credential can help you advance your career in an organization that uses Nortel products.

Requirements for Certification

There are two routes to this certification. In the first route, the certification process requires the following steps:

1. Pass two Core Technology exams (see Table 8.7 in the previous Nortel Certified Support Specialist section).

2. Pass three of the four Advanced Product Exams listed below:

   - WAN/Advanced IP Advanced Product Exam (Test ID: 920-015)

   - Centillion 3.X Advanced Product Exam (Test ID: 920-017)

   - Accelar 1xxx (1.3) Advanced Product Exam (Test ID: 920-018)

   - Network Management with Optivity (Test ID: 920-019)

The alternate route to this certification involves the following steps:

1. Pass the Passport 6000/7000 exam (Test ID: 920-100) (see Table 8.11 above).

2. Pass one of the following exams, which are one-day lab-based practical exams:

   - Passport ATM

- Passport Frame Relay
- Passport ILS
- Passport Voice

Administrator

Call Sylvan Prometric at (800) 791-EXAM to register for a Nortel exam; if outside the U.S., use the online Sylvan Test Center Locator at http://www.sylvanprometric.com/ to find the nearest testing center. (See Chapter 3, "Taking Your Test," for detailed information on taking tests from Sylvan.)

To register for one of the practical exams, contact Nortel Networks Test Center, Merivale Road, Nepean, Ontario, Canada (telephone (613) 768-4110). These exams are offered at Nortel Networks testing facilities.

Fee

The Core Technology exams cost $125. The Advanced Product Exams cost $150. The Passport practical exams cost $1,500 each.

Format

The Core Technology and Advanced Product exams are computer-based, multiple-choice tests. Call Sylvan Prometric at (800) 791-EXAM for current information on the number of questions, time limit, and passing score. The Passport practical exams are full-day, proctored, lab-based exams.

Nortel Certified Network Architect

This designation was created to certify a highly advanced knowledge of Nortel-based networks. Individuals earning this certification know how to develop network solutions and detailed network designs based on a client's requirements. To attain this certification you need to know how to optimize network performance based on end-user applications, how to design detailed network topologies, and you need to have an advanced knowledge of network protocols and architectures. To obtain this certification, you must complete a two-part portfolio assessment.

Who Needs It

The Certified Network Architect certification is an excellent way to show current or potential employers that you have a high level of networking ability. This credential can also be of value to network professionals who do independent consulting and want to validate their expertise for clients.

Requirements for Certification

The certification process requires the following steps:

1. Submit an application with documentation indicating that you have completed a minimum of the following:

   - Five years of networking experience; two years must clearly demonstrate network design experience

   - Five major networking consulting projects; describe the projects and the scope of your involvement

   - Formal education, industry-recognized certifications, and additional work experience should be documented using Nortel's point system. (500 points is required; 150 points minimum must be earned via prior Nortel Networks Certifications.) Contact Nortel for information on the point system.

2. Upon successful completion of the Part 1 application, two (2) case studies will be sent to you; you select one and submit a formal response to Nortel. The case study requirement is explained further in the Format section below.

Administrator

Nortel administers both steps of the Certified Network Architect program; contact the company at (800) 2LANWAN ((800) 252-6926).

Fee

The fee for the case study is $1,000.

Format

The case study is based on actual Nortel Network customer scenarios and usually involves multiple vendor situations. The response must meet specific format requirements related to business needs, network diagrams, technical accuracy, and clarity. The candidate has six weeks to complete their proposed solution, and is limited to 35 pages. Nortel estimates that average time for completion is 40 hours.

Nortel Networks Resources

Nortel offers a number of courses and self-study documents for certification candidates. For more information on this organization's certification program and courses, contact Nortel Networks at:

Web	`http://www.nortelnetworks.com/servsup/certification`
E-mail	`certprog@nortelnetworks.com`
Mail	Nortel Networks Test Center
	1547 Merivale Road
	Nepean, Ontario K2G 3J4
	Canada
Phone	(800) 2LANWAN ((800) 252-6926)

Xylan Certifications

- Xylan Certified Switch Specialist (XCSS)

- Xylan Certified Switch Expert (XCSE)

Xylan is best known for their ATM and LAN switching equipment. They started with one product in 1993, and have grown rapidly since. Xylan currently offers two professional certification programs: the Xylan Certified Switch Specialist (XCSS) and the Xylan Certified Switch Expert (XCSE).

Recertification or Maintenance Requirements

Xylan's certification program has now implemented a recertification requirement. Their new recertification exam will be available this year (check the Xylan Web site for details).

Benefits of Certification

Xylan Certified SwitchExperts receive these benefits:

- Certificate of achievement

- Logo for use on business cards and stationery

- Exclusive technical support access

Xylan Certified Switch Specialist (XCSS)

This certification provides systems engineers with the skills necessary to develop solutions for switched networks. The test for this certification covers the basic concepts of frame and cell switching, the architecture and functionality of Xylan's switching products, and improving network performance and scalability using switching and policy-based subnetworks. This year the exam has been revised to include more questions on ATM. A sample version of the exam is available on the Xylan Web page.

Xylan recommends that candidates have substantive hands-on experience with Xylan switching technologies before attempting certification. In addition, Xylan recommends—but does not require—that those who seek this certification take four preparation courses. Each course involves both classroom instruction and lab work. The courses are offered at Xylan training centers (see the Xylan Resources section for more information). The courses recommended as preparation for the Xylan Certified Switch Specialist (XCSS) exam are as follows:

- Course 201: Product Features and Technical Specifications ($400)

- Course 301: Design and Implementation ($400)

- Course 401: Installation and Support ($400)

- Course 701: ATM with X-Cell ($600)

Who Needs It

The Xylan Certified Switch Specialist credential is a good way to demonstrate your skills with managing switched networks. Right now is an excellent time to have a credential of this type—there are many high paying jobs available for network professionals with experience and credentials in switching technologies.

Requirements for Certification

The certification process requires only one step:

1. Pass the Xylan Certified Switch Specialist exam (Test ID: XY-001). Register online at least three weeks before you plan on taking your test.

Administrator

Xylan exams are administered by Sylvan Prometric. Call (800) 610-3926 to register for an Xylan test; if outside the U.S., use the online Sylvan Test Center Locator at www.sylvanprometric.com to find the nearest testing center. Chapter 3, "Taking Your Test," contains detailed information on taking tests from Sylvan.

Fee

The exam costs $100 ($150 outside the U.S. and Canada).

Format

The exam alsts 75 minutes and has 58 multiple-choice questions. Call Sylvan Prometric at (800) 610-3926 for current test information.

Xylan Certified Switch Expert (XCSE)

This certification builds on the XCSS certification described previously, and involves a hands-on laboratory-based exam. This is Xylan's certification for technical professionals who want to demonstrate their skills in designing, maintaining, and troubleshooting switched networks. Candidates will need to be able to install, configure, and support the OmniSwitch and OmniSwitch/Router.

Hands-on experience with Xylan switching technologies is essential prior to taking the XCSE practical exam. In addition, Xylan recommends—but does not require—that those who are preparing to take the Xylan Certified Switch Expert (XCSE) exam take the four courses listed previously for the XCSS.

Who Needs It

Switching technology is a rapidly growing segment of the networking field. Obtaining a Xylan Certified Switch Expert certification is a great way for those already working in the networking field to move into this high-paying specialty This is also a good credential if you want to document your skills in designing and supporting switched networks.

Requirements for Certification

The certification process requires the following steps:

1. Attain certification as a Xylan Certified Switch Specialist.

2. Pass the Xylan Certified Switch Expert practical exam.

Administrator

Xylan Corporation administers the XCSE practical exam. Call (800) 999-9526 ext. 4768 to get a test date and location. Outside the U.S., call (818) 878-4768.

Fee

The practical exam costs $300 ($500 outside the U.S. and Canada).

Format

This hands-on practical exam takes seven hours and is a two-part exam. In the first part, the candidate builds a complex, predefined multi-protocol, multi-switch network. If the candidate passes part one, "bugs" are then inserted into the network and the candidate has the remaining time to troubleshoot and repair the network.

Xylan Resources

Xylan offers courses for those who are preparing for Xylan certification tests. Each course involves both classroom instruction and lab work. The courses are offered at Xylan training centers located in Calabasas, California; Dover, New Hampshire; Rockville, MD; Singapore; and Hoofddorp, Netherlands. Register for tests online at least three weeks before you plan on taking your test. A sample version of the XCSS exam is available on Xylan's Web page. For more information on this organization's certification program and courses, contact Xylan at:

Web	`http://www.xylan.com/`
E-mail	`training@xylan.com`
Mail	Xylan SwitchExpert Training Program
	26801 West Agoura Road
	Calabasas, CA 91301
Phone	(800) 999-9526 ext. 4768
Outside U.S.	(818) 878-4768

CHAPTER

9

Network Operating Systems
Certifications

FEATURING

- Banyan Certifications

- IBM OS/2 Warp Server Certifications

- Microsoft Certification

- Novell Certifications

Network operating systems—such as Novell's NetWare and Microsoft's Windows NT—have rapidly replaced mainframe computers and mini-computers as the primary medium for sharing files and printers. These systems allow companies to use inexpensive PCs and workstations to provide shared resources to all of their employees—whether in one location or many locations—simultaneously.

There are currently four certification programs related to network operating systems. Banyan's certification program concentrates on the VINES network operating system, which is used primarily to link UNIX servers with a variety of clients. IBM offers several certifications on its PC-based server products—OS/2 Warp Server and OS/2 LAN Server. It was Novell's certification program, initiated in 1989, that really launched the recent explosion of computer and network certification. The Novell certification program, with over 400,000 networking professionals certified, has been wildly successful. Microsoft's program, begun in 1992, also has certified about 400,000 individuals (including Microsoft Certified Professionals, Microsoft Certified Systems Engineers, Microsoft Certified Solutions Developers, and Microsoft Certified Trainers). But there is still plenty of demand for these certifications.

Even though the average MCSE (Microsoft Certified Systems Engineer) has only 1.7 years of networking experience, the average MCSE salary, as of February 1998, was $67,600. (For the latest data on Microsoft certified professionals, go to `http://www.mcpmag.com/` for *Microsoft Certified Professional* magazine's annual salary survey.) Many networking professionals wrestle with the decision about whether to seek certification with Novell or Microsoft. The best option right now may be to do a little of both.

Professionals seeking these certifications include:

- Network administrators
- System administrators

- Field engineers

- Help desk personnel

NOTE UNIX is both a computer operating system and a network operating system. UNIX certifications—including the Sun Certified (Solaris) Network Administrator, the SCO Certified UNIX System Administrator (CUSA) and Advanced Certified Engineer (ACE) certifications, and the Silicon Graphics IRIX System Administrator and Network Administrator certifications—are covered in Chapter 5.

Use Table 9.1 to compare the number of required tests, the test format, the approximate cost of taking the test(s), number of required courses, cost of any required courses, and the relative difficulty of the certification programs in this chapter. The cost information is a general guideline; since things change rapidly in the world of certification programs, once you have selected a specific course of action you may want to double-check the costs.

We classified the difficulty of these certifications into three categories—Moderate, Challenging, and Very Challenging—based on the number of required tests and courses, and the relative difficulty of those tests or lab exams. These ratings are approximate and are offered simply as a general guide to help the reader distinguish between entry-level programs and those that require more advanced skill and knowledge. (This rating scale assumes that one has experience with the product or technology and has studied the appropriate subject content before attempting the exams.)

TABLE 9.1: Network Operating Systems Certifications

Certification	# of Required Tests	Test Format(s)	Total Cost of Required Tests	# of Required Courses	Total Cost of Required Courses	Difficulty	Notes
Banyan Certifications							
Certified Banyan Specialist	3	MC	$375	1	$1,800	◑	
Certified Banyan Specialist: Windows NT	3	MC	$350	2	$3,300	◑	
Certified Banyan Engineer	2	MC	$240	2	$4,500	●	You must first be a Certified Banyan Specialist.
IBM Certifications							
Certified Specialist	1	MC	VF	—	—	○	Specializations: OS/2 Warp Server Administration, OS/2 LAN Server 4.0 Administration.
Certified Systems Expert	3–6	MC	VF	—	—	◑	Specializations: OS/2 Warp Server, OS/2 LAN Server 4.0.
Microsoft Certification							
Microsoft Certified Systems Engineer (MCSE)	6	MC	$600	—	—	●	Pick your elective test carefully and you can get an MCP + Internet at the same time.
Novell Certifications							
Certified Novell Administrator (CNA)	1	AT or MC	$85	—	—	○	Specialize in NetWare 5, intraNetWare, NetWare 3, GroupWise 5, or GroupWise 4.
Certified Novell Engineer (CNE)	7	AT, MC	VF	—	—	●	Specialize in NetWare 5, intraNetWare, NetWare 3, GroupWise 5, or GroupWise 4.

TABLE 9.1: Network Operating Systems Certifications *(continued)*

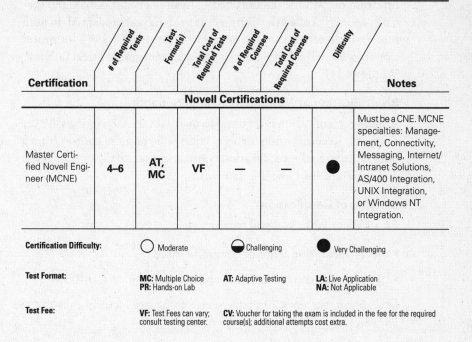

Certification	# of Required Tests	Test Format(s)	Total Cost of Required Tests	# of Required Courses	Total Cost of Required Courses	Difficulty	Notes
Novell Certifications							
Master Certified Novell Engineer (MCNE)	4–6	AT, MC	VF	–	–	●	Must be a CNE. MCNE specialties: Management, Connectivity, Messaging, Internet/Intranet Solutions, AS/400 Integration, UNIX Integration, or Windows NT Integration.

Certification Difficulty: ◯ Moderate ◖ Challenging ● Very Challenging

Test Format: **MC:** Multiple Choice   **AT:** Adaptive Testing   **LA:** Live Application
PR: Hands-on Lab   **NA:** Not Applicable

Test Fee: **VF:** Test Fees can vary; consult testing center.   **CV:** Voucher for taking the exam is included in the fee for the required course(s); additional attempts cost extra.

Banyan Certifications

- Certified Banyan Specialist (CBS)

- Certified Banyan Specialist (CBS): Windows NT

- CBE, formerly Certified Banyan Engineer

Banyan VINES is a networking operating system designed for use in large corporate networks, typically operating on UNIX-based servers. The current version—VINES 8.0—incorporates NT, Novell, and mainframe-based resources into directory services through Banyan's proprietary protocol, StreetTalk.

The Banyan Technical Certification Program offers two levels of certification on VINES: the Certified Banyan Specialist (CBS), and the CBE, formerly called the Certified Banyan Expert credential. In addition, Banyan offers a special designation entitled CBS/NT for professionals who will be implementing and administering StreetTalk for Windows NT.

Recertification or Maintenance Requirements

Annual recertification is required to maintain the CBS or the CBE certification. Recertification involves taking one or more courses from a pool of approved recertification courses; contact Banyan for details and a current list of eligible courses.

Benefits of Certification

As a CBS or CBE, you will receive:

- A certificate and letter of congratulations
- The current copy of the Banyan Knowledge Base CD-ROM

In addition, current CBEs will receive three free incident calls to the Banyan Response Center (in the Americas only)

Certified Banyan Specialist (CBS)

While the Certified Banyan Specialist is the first level of certification with the Banyan VINES network operating system, it is a significant certification on its own. The three required tests and one required five-day course focus on administering and maintaining VINES-based networks. This certification is a prerequisite for the Certified Banyan Engineer (CBE) program described below as well as the Certified Banyan Instructor (CBI) program (see Chapter 15).

Who Needs It

If your company uses a Banyan network, this certification is an excellent way for systems and network administrators and support staff to move up in responsibility or pay; it can also help you to get a new position at a company that uses a Banyan operating system.

Requirements for Certification

The certification process requires the following steps:

1. Pass the Banyan Network Administration test (Test ID: 020-120).

2. Pass the Advanced VINES Administration test (Test ID: 020-210).

3. Attend and complete the Problem Solving for VINES Networks course (Course ID: EDU 310).

4. Pass the Problem Solving for VINES Networks test (Test ID: 020-310)

Administrator

Banyan exams are administered by Sylvan Prometric. Call (800) 736-3926 to register for IBM tests; if outside the U.S., use the online Sylvan Test Center Locator at `http://www.sylvanprometric.com` to find the nearest testing center. (See Chapter 3 for detailed information on taking tests from Sylvan.).

Required courses are offered through Banyan Certified Education Centers (see the "Banyan Resources" section that follows for more information).

Fee

$125 per test. The required problem-solving course costs $1,800.

Format

These computer-generated, multiple-choice tests have 30–60 questions and last 45 to 120 minutes; the time and number of questions depend on the test. Passing score is 65 percent.

Certified Banyan Specialist (CBS): Windows NT

The CBS Windows NT certification concentrates on the integration of Banyan's proprietary protocol, StreetTalk, into NT-based servers. The candidate must take two required courses and pass two Banyan tests. In addition, as part of this certification, the candidate must demonstrate the ability to administer NT servers by becoming a Microsoft Certified Professional.

Who Needs It

This certification is an excellent way for network administrators to demonstrate to current or potential employers their knowledge and ability related to the successful integration and management of VINES and NT hybrid networks. It can also be of value to network planners and designers who must accommodate a variety of network operating systems in their organization.

Requirements for Certification

The certification process requires the following steps:

1. Pass one of the four Microsoft tests listed in Table 9.2 below. Meeting this requirement will also qualify you as a Microsoft Certified Professional (see Chapter 5 for more information on the MCP certification program).

T A B L E 9.2: Microsoft Exam Options for CBS Certification with Specialization in Windows NT

Exam	Test ID
Implementing and Supporting Microsoft Windows NT Workstation 4.0	70-73
Implementing and Supporting Microsoft Windows NT Workstation 3.51	70-42
Implementing and Supporting Microsoft Windows NT Server 4.0	70-67
Implementing and Supporting Microsoft Windows NT Server 3.5	70-43

2. Attend and complete the five-day Banyan Network Administration course (Course ID: EDU 120). If you are already a CBE or CBE, you can take EDU 1230 (StreetTalk for Windows NT Administration—Administrator's Update) instead.

3. Pass the StreetTalk for Windows NT Administration test (Test ID: 020-123).

4. Attend and complete the three-day StreetTalk for Windows NT Internals and Performance Analysis course (Course ID: EDU 1250).

5. Pass the StreetTalk for Windows NT Internals and Performance Analysis test (Test ID: 020-125).

Administrator

Banyan exams are administered by Sylvan Prometric. Call (800) 736-3926 to register for IBM tests; if outside the U.S., use the online Sylvan Test Center Locator at `http://www.sylvanprometric.com` to find the nearest testing center. (See Chapter 3 for detailed information on taking tests from Sylvan.)

Required courses are offered through Banyan Certified Education Centers (see the Banyan Resources section that follows for more information).

Fee

The cost per test is $125. The StreetTalk for Windows NT Administration course costs $1,800 and the StreetTalk for Windows NT Internals and Performance Analysis course costs $1,500.

Format

These computer-generated, multiple-choice tests have 30–60 questions and last 45 to 120 minutes; the time and number of questions depend on the test. Passing score is 65 percent.

CBE

The CBE certification, formerly known as the Certified Banyan Engineer credential, is the premium Banyan certification. It builds on the Certified Banyan Specialist (CBS) title and requires extensive training and testing on VINES networking and troubleshooting. The candidate must complete two required courses and pass two exams.

Who Needs It

Becoming a CBE is an excellent way to achieve a high level of responsibility for network administration in a company that uses a Banyan network operating system. This certification lets others know that you can provide an advanced level of support for Banyan networks, including network design and performance tuning.

Requirements for Certification

The certification process requires the following steps:

1. Attain one of the Banyan CBS certifications described above.

2. Attend and complete the five-day Supporting Network Services course (Course ID: EDU 620).

3. Pass the Supporting Network Services test (Test ID: 020-620).

4. Attend and complete the five-day Network Communications course (Course ID: EDU 630).

5. Pass the Network Communications test (Test ID: 020-630).

Administrator

Banyan exams are administered by Sylvan Prometric. Call (800) 736-3926 to register for IBM tests; if outside the U.S., use the online Sylvan Test Center Locator at http://www.sylvanprometric.com to find the nearest testing center. (See Chapter 3 for detailed information on taking tests from Sylvan.)

Required courses are offered through Banyan Certified Education Centers (see the "Banyan Resources" section that follows for more information).

Fee

$125 per test. Each of the two required courses costs $2,250.

Format

These multiple-choice tests last 60 to 120 minutes; the time and number of questions depend on the test. Passing score is 65 percent.

Banyan Resources

The Banyan Web site offers study guides that detail the objectives of each exam. Banyan's Web site also offers a listing of Certified Education Centers and Banyan Certified Instructors. For more information on this organization's certifications and courses, contact Banyan at:

Web	http://www.banyan.com/support/techcert.htm
E-mail	jbernstein@banyan.com
Mail	Banyan Systems Incorporated
	Educational Services Department
	120 Flanders Road
	Westboro, MA 01581
Phone	(508) 898-1795
Fax	(508) 836-0225

IBM OS/2 Warp Server Certifications

- IBM Certified Specialist—OS/2 Warp Server Administration

- IBM Certified Systems Expert—OS/2 Warp Server

During the 1980s, IBM and Microsoft worked together to develop the OS/2 operating system as a graphical interface for the PC. After a much-publicized breakup of the partnership, IBM continued to develop OS/2 while Microsoft took off in its own direction with Windows.

IBM also developed a PC-based server system, called OS/2 Warp Server, for its OS/2 product line. IBM offers two certifications on its OS/2 Warp Server network operating system: the IBM Certified Specialist—OS/2 Warp Server Administration and the IBM Certified Systems Expert—OS/2 Warp Server.

Recertification or Maintenance Requirements

The IBM OS/2 certifications apply to specific versions of this operating system, so there is no requirement for recertification on a particular version. Since your certification is tied to a certain version of a product, however, you will want become certified on the newest versions when they become available if you want to continue to have the most current credential in this area.

Benefits of Certification

IBM Certified Specialists and Systems Experts receive these benefits:

- Certification logo for use on business cards or stationery
- Certificate
- Wallet-size certificate
- Lapel pin

NOTE For information on other IBM certification programs, see Chapters 4, 5, 8, 13, and 14.

IBM Certified Specialist—OS/2 Warp Server Administration

Attaining certification as an IBM Certified Specialist in OS/2 Warp Server Administration involves passing one required test. This exam covers day-to-day network operation administration tasks including: managing server users, groups, and shared resources; performing server backup/recovery; and other related tasks. IBM recommends that those who seek this certification have basic knowledge of DOS and OS/2 Warp, as well as hands-on experience with OS/2 Warp Server before attempting the exam.

Who Needs It

The IBM Certified Specialist—OS/2 Warp Server Administration certification is a great credential for getting your first position in OS/2 Server administration.

Requirements for Certification

The certification process requires only one step:

1. Pass the IBM OS/2 Warp Server Administration exam (test ID:000-134).

Administrator

IBM tests are administered by Sylvan Prometric. Call (800) 959-3926 to register for IBM tests; if outside the U.S., use the online Sylvan Test Center Locator at http://www.sylvanprometric.com/ to find the nearest testing center. (See Chapter 3 for detailed information on taking tests from Sylvan.)

Fee

Fees for IBM tests vary based on test length and format; call Sylvan Prometric at (800) 959-3926 for pricing.

Format

Computer-based, multiple-choice test. Call Sylvan Prometric at (800) 959-3926 for current information on the number of questions, time limit, and passing score.

IBM Certified Systems Expert—OS/2 Warp Server

Attaining the IBM Certified Systems Expert—OS/2 Warp Server certification involves passing three exams—a platform test, a connectivity/administration test, and an OS/2 Warp Server technical test. For the platform test, the candidate has the option of taking either the OS/2 Warp or the OS/2 Warp 4 Fundamentals test; both cover the fundamentals of the OS/2 Warp operating system. The Warp Server Administration test covers basic OS/2 Warp Server operation, including handling file systems, installation, running applications, and printing. The Warp Server technical test covers basic concepts of planning, installation, customization, usage, and problem resolution with the OS/2 Warp Server platform.

NOTE If you hold an MCSE, CNE, or one of several IBM certifications, you may be able to become an OS/2 Warp Server Certified Systems Expert by taking only one or two tests (see the OS/2 Warp Server certification update information at http://www.ibm.com/education/certify/certs).

Who Needs It

Completing this challenging IBM Certified Systems Expert certification makes you stand out as an expert in OS/2 Warp Server planning and administration. Whether you want to advance in your current company, or obtain a higher paying position elsewhere, this credential can help you meet your goals.

Requirements for Certification

The certification process requires the following steps:

1. Pass one of the following tests:

   - IBM OS/2 Warp (Test ID: 000-133)

   - IBM OS/2 Warp 4 Fundamentals (Test ID: 000-200)

2. Pass the IBM OS/2 Warp Server Administration test (Test ID: 000-134).

3. Pass the IBM OS/2 Warp Server test (Test ID: 000-132).

It is recommended—but not required—that the tests be taken in the order listed.

Administrator

IBM tests are administered by Sylvan Prometric. Call (800) 959-3926 to register for IBM tests; if outside the U.S., use the online Sylvan Test Center Locator at http://www.sylvanprometric.com/ to find the nearest testing center. (See Chapter 3 for detailed information on taking tests from Sylvan.)

Fee

Fees for IBM tests vary based on test length and format; call Sylvan Prometric at (800) 959-3926 for pricing.

Format

Computer-based, multiple-choice test. Call Sylvan Prometric at (800) 959-3926 for current information on the number of questions, time limit, and passing score.

IBM Resources

IBM's Web site offers a number of excellent resources for certification candidates, including test objectives, study guides, and sample tests. Several computer-based training courses and instructor-led training courses are also offered. Another excellent resource, the *OS/2 Warp 4 Server Certification Handbook*, is available for $60 from the IBM Direct publications catalog Web site (`http://www.elink.ibmlink .ibm.com/pbl/pbl`). Request publication number "SG23-7887-00." For more information on these courses and certification programs, contact IBM at:

Web	`http://www.ibm.com/certify`
E-mail	`certify@us.ibm.com`
Mail	Professional Certification Program from IBM
	IBM Corporation, Int. Zip 3013
	11400 Burnet Road
	Austin, TX 78758
Phone	(800) 426-8322
Fax	(512) 838-7961

Microsoft Certification

- Microsoft Certified Systems Engineer (MCSE)

The Microsoft Certified Systems Engineer (MCSE) is one of Microsoft's premium credentials. Attaining this certification requires passing six exams. The exams focus on using Microsoft Windows NT Server and related products.

MCSEs are in high demand. There are over 100,000 MCSEs in the world today, and that number is climbing steadily.

NOTE   We list the exams for the Windows NT 4.0 track, but be sure to check the Certification Update Web site to see if the new exams for Windows 2000 have become available. Appendix B explains how to access the site.

Contributing to Microsoft Certified Professional Exams

Microsoft relies heavily on input from current MCSEs and other Microsoft Certified Professionals to develop and maintain their certification exams. To get this valuable input from practicing professionals, Microsoft invites interested individuals to become technical contributors or contract writers for their exams.

Being a technical contributor involves offering your technical expertise to the exam-development process. A contract writer is a person who concentrates on the writing of exam questions.

If you are interested in contributing to the exams for Microsoft's certification program, see `http://www.microsoft.com/mcp/ examinfo/ certsd.htm` for more information.

Recertification or Maintenance Requirements

MCSEs must take action to maintain their certifications. As Microsoft introduces new products and new versions of its operating systems, it retires the tests for previous versions. If you hold a certification that is based on a test that Microsoft is retiring, you will be informed by certified mail of the need to take a current test to maintain your certification. You will have at least six months to complete this new test; if you fail to do so, your status as an MCSE will no longer be valid.

Benefits of Certification

Microsoft Certified Systems Engineers receive the following benefits:

- An MCSE certificate

- Access to technical information through a secure Web site

- Use of MCSE logos on stationery and business cards

- Invitations to Microsoft-sponsored conferences and technical training sessions

- A free subscription to *Microsoft Certified Professional* magazine

- A one-year subscription to Microsoft TechNet Plus, a new level to the TechNet CD-ROM subscription. Microsoft will send you all evaluation beta products on CD, along with 12 monthly TechNet issues.

Microsoft Certified Systems Engineer (MCSE)

Attaining the Microsoft Certified Engineer certification requires passing four core exams and two elective exams. The operating system exams require candidates to prove their expertise with desktop, server, and networking components. The elective exams require proof of expertise with Microsoft BackOffice products. Microsoft's Web site provides exam guidelines and information about instructor-led training, self-paced training, and online training (see the "Microsoft Resources" section for more information).

NOTE   The only core exams we list here are those for Windows NT 4.0. While it may still be possible to do an MCSE on the Windows NT 3.51 track, we don't advise doing this, and have not listed the exams for that track. The NT 3.51 exams will be retired shortly when the Windows 2000 exams become available.

Who Needs It

The MCSE certification is one of the most widely recognized networking credentials, and has become a standard credential for those involved in network and system administration of Microsoft operating systems. The MCSE is valuable for practicing networking professionals who want to advance their careers.

Requirements for Certification

The certification process requires the following steps:

1. Pass the four core exams listed in Table 9.3 below.

2. Pass two elective exams (see Table 9.4), selecting exams from two different categories listed below. If you pass two exams within the same category, only one will qualify as an MCSE elective.

T A B L E 9.3: Core Exams for MCSE Certification

Exam Name	Test ID
Implementing and Supporting Microsoft Windows NT Server 4.0	70-067
Implementing and Supporting Microsoft Windows NT Server 4.0 in the Enterprise	70-068
EITHER Implementing and Supporting Microsoft Windows NT Workstation 4.0 OR	70-073
Implementing and Supporting Microsoft Windows 95 OR	70-064
Implementing and Supporting Microsoft Windows 98	70-098
Networking Essentials	70-058

TIP If you are already certified as a Novell CNE, Master CNE, or CNI, a Sun Certified Network Administrator for Solaris 2.5 or 2.5, or a Banyan CBS or CBE, Microsoft will waive the requirement for the Networking Essentials exam.

T A B L E 9.4: Elective Exam Options for MCSE NT 4 Track

Category	Exam Name	Test ID
SNA Server	Implementing and Supporting Microsoft SNA Server 4.0	70-085
SMS Server	Implementing and Supporting Microsoft Systems Management Server 1.2 OR	70-018
	Implementing and Supporting Microsoft Systems Management Server 2.0	70-086
Data Warehousing	Designing and Implementing Data Warehouses with Microsoft SQL Server 7.0	70-019
SQL Databases	Implementing a Database Design on Microsoft SQL Server 6.5 OR	70-027
	Designing and Implementing Databases with Microsoft SQL Server 7.0	70-029
Site Server	Implementing and Supporting Web Sites Using Microsoft Site Server 3.0	70-056
TCP/IP	Internetworking Microsoft TCP/IP on Microsoft® Windows NT (3.5-3.51) OR	70-053
	Internetworking with Microsoft TCP/IP on Microsoft Windows NT 4.0	70-059

TABLE 9.4: Elective Exam Options for MCSE NT 4 Track *(continued)*

Category	Exam Name	Test ID
Exchange Server	Implementing and Supporting Microsoft Exchange Server 5 OR	70-076
	Implementing and Supporting Microsoft Exchange Server 5.5	70-081
Internet Information Server	Implementing and Supporting Microsoft Internet Information Server 3.0 and Microsoft Index Server 1.1 OR	70-077
	Implementing and Supporting Microsoft Internet Information Server 4.0	70-087
Proxy Server	Implementing and Supporting Microsoft Proxy Server 1.0 OR	70-078
	Implementing and Supporting Microsoft Proxy Server 2.0	70-088
Internet Explorer	Implementing and Supporting Microsoft Internet Explorer 4.0 by Using the Internet Explorer Administration Kit	70-079

Administrator

Microsoft tests are administered by Sylvan Prometric and Virtual University Enterprises (VUE). To register for a test with VUE visit the VUE Web site (http://www.vue.com/student-services/). Call Sylvan at (800) 755-3926 to register for Microsoft tests; if outside the

U.S., use the online Sylvan Test Center Locator at `http://www.syl-vanprometric.com` to find the nearest testing center. Chapter 3 contains detailed information on taking tests from Sylvan or VUE.

Fee

The fee per test is $100.

Format

Multiple-choice, closed-book tests. The number of questions and time limit depend on the test selected.

TIP Microsoft recently created an extension to the MCSE credential—the MCSE + Internet certification. This credential is valuable for the numerous Microsoft professionals who use their expertise to maintain their company's Internet connectivity and presence. (See Chapter 13 for more information on the MSCE + Internet certification.)

Microsoft Resources

The Microsoft Web site offers practice tests as well as exam preparation guides that detail the objectives of each exam. Microsoft's Web site also offers a listing of Microsoft Certified Technical Education Centers. For more information on this organization's certification programs, contact Microsoft at:

Web	`http://www.microsoft.com/mcp/`
E-mail	`mcp@msprograms.com`
Mail	Microsoft Corporation
	One Microsoft Way
	Redmond, WA 98052-6399
Phone	(800) 636-7544
Fax	(425) 936-7329

Novell Certifications

- Certified Novell Administrator (CNA)

- Certified Novell Engineer (CNE)

- Master Certified Novell Engineer (MCNE)

In 1983, Novell began producing one of the first network operating systems using PC-based servers. At the time, many people were skeptical that PC-based servers could perform well enough to handle business applications. But as Novell kept improving their product—and as PCs became more powerful—people began to see the benefits of this cost-effective solution to file and printer sharing. While the popularity of Windows NT is growing, the majority of networks currently in place use Novell products. Novell has also developed a number of other applications and programs—such as the GroupWise product for e-mail and collaboration, and the ManageWise product for network management—that are very popular.

In 1989, Novell was the first company to offer a certification—the Certified Novell Engineer (CNE)—that validated individuals' expertise in using the Novell network operating system. Novell has since worked hard to develop and promote this certification. As a result, there are currently over 500,000 certified Novell professionals, including over 150,000 CNEs. Novell's certification program is one of the most diverse available today; it allows the candidate to specialize in a wide range of products at each level of certification. Some of Novell's tests are adaptive exams. See Chapter 3 for a discussion of adaptive testing.

Novell offers three basic levels of certification: Certified Novell Administrator (CNA), Certified Novell Engineer (CNE), and Master Certified Novell Engineer (Master CNE). Within each of these levels, a candidate can specialize in one or more Novell products, such as NetWare or GroupWise. In the case of the Master

CNE, specialization can be obtained in one of four general categories (Management, Connectivity, Messaging, or Internet/Intranet Solutions) or one of three client categories (AS/400 Integration, UNIX Integration, or Windows NT Integration).

NOTE Novell also offers a number of Internet certification tracks (see Chapter 13 for details).

Every professional certified by Novell must submit a signed Novell Certification Agreement, which states the conditions for use of the Novell name.

Recertification or Maintenance Requirements

Both CNEs and Master CNEs are required to meet continuing certification requirements as specified by Novell. Because these requirements vary, contact Novell for current details (see the "Novell Resources" section that follows for contact information).

Benefits of Certification

As a Certified Novell Administrator (CNA), you will receive these benefits:

- Access to the password-protected CNA Web site

- Use of CNA logos

- Up-to-date Novell product information

- Online access to key publications and programs

As a Certified Novell Engineer (CNE) or Master CNE, you will receive these benefits:

- Access to the password-protected CNE Net Web site, which offers exclusive benefits for CNEs and Master CNEs

- Logos

- Beta products and early releases

- Quick access to patches and fixes

- Discount on Novell Technical Support incidents

- Free subscription to the *NetWare Connection* magazine

- Discounts on advanced technical training

- Discount on the Novell Support Connection CD subscription

- Novell publications and tools

- CNE Product Link discounts

Certified Novell Administrator (CNA)

NetWare is one of Novell's PC-based server products that allow users to share files and printers on a local area network. NetWare 5 is Novell's latest release of their PC-based server product for local area networks. GroupWise is Novell's group collaboration and mail system.

Becoming a CNA involves passing one exam in the candidate's preferred area of specialization. These exams test a candidate's knowledge of basic administrative tasks such as adding users and groups, managing printers, and monitoring network performance. Novell offers a preparatory course for each of these exams, and also provides a wide choice of self-study options (see the "Novell Resources" section for more information). CNA candidates can select from the following specializations:

- NetWare 5

- intraNetWare

- NetWare 3

- GroupWise 5

- GroupWise 4

Who Needs It

The CNA designation is a great credential for getting your first job in the field of computer networking. Employers know that CNAs have the ability to perform a wide variety of basic administrative tasks.

Requirements for Certification

The certification process requires the following steps:

1. Pass the Novell exam for the specialization you desire (see Table 9.5)

2. Sign and submit the Novell Certification Agreement (available at http://education.novell.com/certinfo/certagrm.htm)..

T A B L E 9.5: CNA Specializations and Required Exams

Specialization	Required Exam	Test ID
NetWare 5	NetWare 5 Administration	050-639
intraNetWare	intraNetWare: NetWare 4.11 Administration exam	050-613
NetWare 3	NetWare 3.1x Administration exam	050-130
GroupWise 5	GroupWise 5 System Administration exam	050-633
GroupWise 4	GroupWise 4 Administration exam	050-154

Administrator

Novell tests are administered by Sylvan Prometric and Virtual University Enterprises (VUE). To register for a test with VUE visit the VUE Web site (http://www.vue.com/student-services/). Call Sylvan at (800) 733-3926 to register for Novell tests; if outside the U.S., use the online Sylvan Test Center Locator at http://www.sylvanprometric.com to find the nearest testing center. Chapter 3 contains detailed information on taking tests from Sylvan or VUE.

Fee

The fee is $95 per test.

Format

Novell tests include both adaptive and traditional format exams. They vary from 30 to 120 minutes in length. For detailed information on the number of questions, length, and format of each test, see Novell's education Web site (`http://education.novell.com/testinfo/testdata.htm`). See Chapter 3 for information on adaptive testing.

Certified Novell Engineer (CNE)

The Certified Novell Engineer (CNE) program builds on the CNA program described above. Attaining the CNE requires the candidate to pass two core CNE exams, three or four exams specific to the desired specialization, and one elective exam—as described in the following sections. These CNE exams test the candidate's ability to provide high-end, solutions-based technical support for Novell networks using the product selected for specialization. Novell offers a preparatory course for each of these exams (see the "Novell Resources "section that follows for more information).

Novell recommends that a candidate complete all exams for the certification within a one-year period to ensure that all exams are still current when the last one is completed. Check the Novell Web site frequently to see which exams are current and which are scheduled for retirement. CNE candidates can select from the following specializations:

- NetWare 5

- intraNetWare

- NetWare 3

- GroupWise 5

- GroupWise 4

NOTE CNEs can become cross-certified in multiple specializations. The guidelines for cross-certification, which are somewhat complex, can be found on the Novell Web site (see the "Novell Resources" section for information).

Who Needs It

The CNE designation—one of the most widely recognized networking credentials—is an excellent way to prove your expertise with Novell networking. Whether you want to advance in your current company, or obtain a higher paying position elsewhere, the CNE can help you meet your goals.

Requirements for Certification

The certification process requires the following steps:

1. Pass the Networking Technologies exam (Test ID: 050-632).

2. Pass the Service & Support exam (Test ID: 050-635).

3. Pass the required tests for the desired specialization, as listed in Table 9.6. Note: the NetWare 5 specialization has three required exams, while the other options each involve four required exams.

4. Pass one of the CNE elective tests listed in Table 9.7.

5. Sign and submit the Novell Certification Agreement (available at `http://education.novell.com/certinfo/certagrm.htm`).

T A B L E 9.6: CNE Specializations and Required Exams

Specialization	Required Tests	Test ID #
NetWare 5	NetWare 5 Administration	050-639
	NetWare 5 Advanced Administration	050-640
	NDS Design and Implementation OR	050-634
	intraNetWare: NetWare 4.11 Design and Implementation	050-601

T A B L E 9.6: CNE Specializations and Required Exams *(continued)*

Specialization	Required Tests	Test ID #
intraNetWare	intraNetWare: NetWare 4.11 Administration	050-613
	intraNetWare: NetWare 4.11 Advanced Administration	050-614
	intraNetWare: NetWare 4.11 Installation and Configuration	050-617
	intraNetWare: NetWare 4.11 Design and Implementation OR	050-601
	NDS Design and Implementation	050-634
NetWare 3	NetWare 3.1x Administration	050-130
	NetWare 3.1x Advanced Administration	050-131
	NetWare 3 Installation and Configuration	050-132
	intraNetWare: NetWare to NetWare 4.11 Update	050-615
GroupWise 5	intraNetWare: NetWare 4.11 Administration	050-613
	GroupWise 5.5 System Administration	050-633
	GroupWise 5.5 Advanced Administration	050-643
	GroupWise Net Access and Connectivity	050-620
GroupWise 4	intraNetWare: NetWare 4.11 Administration	050-613
	GroupWise 4 Administration	050-154
	GroupWise 4 Async Gateway & GroupWise Remote	050-612
	GroupWise 4 Advanced Administration	050-604

T A B L E 9.7: CNE Elective Exam Options

Elective Exam	Test ID	Comment
Securing Intranets with Border Manager	050-629	OK for any of the specializations
Network Management Using ManageWise 2.6	050-641	OK for any of the specializations
Integrating NetWare and Windows NT	050-644	OK for any of the specializations
GroupWise 5.5 System Administration	050-633	Not acceptable for the GroupWise 5 specialization
Building Intranets with intraNetWare	050-627	Only acceptable for the intraNetWare specialization

Administrator

Novell tests are administered by Sylvan Prometric and Virtual University Enterprises (VUE). To register for a test with VUE visit the VUE Web site (http://www.vue.com/student-services/). Call Sylvan at (800) 733-3926 to register for Novell tests; if outside the U.S., use the online Sylvan Test Center Locator at www.sylvanprometric.com to find the nearest testing center. Chapter 3 contains detailed information on taking tests from Sylvan or VUE.

Fee

Each test costs $95.

Format

CNE tests include both adaptive and traditional format exams. They vary from 30 to 120 minutes in length. For detailed information on the number of questions, length, and format of each test, see Novell's education Web site (http://education.novell.com/testinfo/testdata.htm). See Chapter 3 for information on adaptive testing.

Master Certified Novell Engineer (Master CNE)

The Master CNE, Novell's top-of-the-line certification, designates an individual as an expert in network integration. This certification builds on the Certified Novell Engineer (CNE) program described previously. Attaining the Master CNE requires completion of a CNE certification plus the completion of an additional set of required Master CNE core exams, "target" exams, and elective exams—as described below. Novell offers a preparatory course for each of these exams (see the "Novell Resources" section that follows for more information).

Novell recommends that a candidate complete all exams for the certification within a one-year period to ensure that all exams are still current when the last one is completed. Check the Novell Web site frequently to see which exams are current and which are scheduled for retirement. Master CNE candidates can select from the following specializations:

- Management
- Connectivity
- Messaging
- Internet/Intranet Solutions
- AS/400 Integration
- UNIX Integration
- Windows NT Integration

NOTE Master CNEs can become cross-certified in multiple specializations. The guidelines for cross-certification, which are somewhat complex, can be found on the Novell Web site (see the "Novell Resources" section for information).

Who Needs It

Completing this highly challenging Master CNE program makes you stand out as an expert in managing multiple Novell servers and networks.

It can be the ticket to job offers, promotions, and salary increases in companies and government agencies that use Novell.

Requirements for Certification

The certification process requires the following steps:

1. Obtain certification as a Certified Novell Engineer in any specialization (see CNE sections above).

2. Pass the Master CNE core test on Fundamentals of Internetworking (Test ID: 050-611).

3. Pass one of these two core Master CNE exams:

   - NDS Design and Implementation (Test ID: 050-634)

   - intraNetWare: Design and Implementation (Test ID: 050-601)

4. For some of the specializations, one additional Master CNE core exam is required (see Table 9.8).

5. Pass the Target test(s) required for your specialization (see Table 9.9).

6. Some of the Master CNE specializations require that the candidate take one or two elective exams. The number of required exams for each specialization is listed in Table 9.10. A listing of the available Master CNE elective exams is provided in Table 9.11.

NOTE Any test that has been used as a core or target requirement may not be used as an elective in the same track.

TABLE 9.8: Required Additional Core Exams for Some Master CNE Specializations

Specialization	Additional Required Core Exam	Test ID
Management	No additional core exam required	
Connectivity	No additional core exam required	

T A B L E 9.8: Required Additional Core Exams for Some Master CNE Specializations *(continued)*

Specialization	Additional Required Core Exam	Test ID
Messaging	No additional core exam required	
Internet/Intranet Solutions	NetWare TCP/IP Transport	050-145
AS/400 Integration	NetWare for SAA	050-605
UNIX Integration	NetWare TCP/IP OR	050-145
	SCO TCP/IP (SCO exam) OR	090-004
	SCO Open Server Network Administration (SCO exam)	090-054
Windows NT Integration	NetWare TCP/IP	050-145

T A B L E 9.9: Required Target Exams for Master CNE Specializations

Specialization	Required Target Exam(s)	Test ID
Management	Network Management Using ManageWise	050-641
Connectivity	Securing Internets with BorderManager	050-629
Messaging	GroupWise 5.5 Advanced Administration OR	050-643
	GroupWise 4.1 to 5 Differences	050-623

T A B L E 9.9: Required Target Exams for Master CNE Specializations

Specialization	Required Target Exam(s)	Test ID
Internet/Intranet Solutions	Web Server Management AND	050-710
	Managing Netscape Enterprise Server for NetWare	050-712
AS/400 Integration	intraNetWare and AS/400 Integration (IBM exam)	000-051
UNIX Integration	SCO Open Server Release 5 ACE for Master CNE (SCO exam) OR	095-153
	SCO UnixWare 2.1 ACE for Master CNE (SCO exam)	095-154
Windows NT Integration	Integrating NetWare and Windows NT	050-644

T A B L E 9.10: Number of Required Elective Exams for Master CNE Specializations

Specialization	Number of Elective Exams Required
Management	2
Connectivity	2
Messaging	2
Internet/Intranet Solutions	1
AS/400 Integration	0
UNIX Integration	0
Windows NT Integration	1

TABLE 9.11: Available Master CNE Elective Exams

Exam	Test ID
Fundamentals of Network Management	050-606
Printing in an Integrated NetWare Environment	050-622
Securing Intranets with BorderManager	050-629
NetWare for SAA: Installation and Troubleshooting	050-605
NetWare TCP/IP Transport	050-145
NetWare NFS Services: Management, File Sharing, and Printing	050-160
Network Management Using ManageWise 2.6	050-641

Administrator

Novell tests are administered by Sylvan Prometric and Virtual University Enterprises (VUE). To register for a test with VUE visit the VUE Web site (`http://www.vue.com/student-services/`). Call Sylvan at (800) 733-3926 to register for Novell tests; if outside the U.S., use the online Sylvan Test Center Locator at `http://www.sylvanprometric.com` to find the nearest testing center. Chapter 3 contains detailed information on taking tests from Sylvan or VUE.

IBM or SCO exams are administered by Sylvan Prometric. Call (800) 959-3926 to register for IBM tests. Call (800) 775-3926 to register for SCO exams. If outside the U.S., use the online Sylvan Test Center Locator at `http://www.sylvanprometric.com` to find the nearest testing center.

Fee

Novell exams cost $95 each.

Format

Novell tests include both adaptive and traditional format exams. They vary from 30 to 120 minutes in length. For detailed information on the number of questions, length, and format of each test, see Novell's education Web site (`http://education.novell.com/testinfo/testdata.htm`). See Chapter 3 for information on adaptive testing.

Novell Resources

Novell offers an extensive set of classes for CNA, CNE, and Master CNE candidates. A Novell course is offered for each of the Novell exams listed above. Instructor-led courses are offered by Novell Authorized Education Centers (NAECs) and Novell Education Academic Partners (NEAPs). A variety of self-study options are also available.

The Novell Web site offers exam bulletins that detail each test's objectives. Novell's Web site also offers a listing of NAECs and NEAPs. For more information on this organization's certifications and courses, contact Novell at:

Web	`http://education.novell.com/`
E-mail	`edcustomer@novell.com`
Mail	Novell, Inc.
	1555 N. Technology Way, MS Q35
	Orem, UT 84097
Phone	(800) 233-EDUC
Fax	(801) 222-7875
Faxback	(800) 233-EDUC

CHAPTER

10

Network Management
Certifications

FEATURING

- Computer Associates Certifications

- Hewlett-Packard Certifications

- Mercury Interactive Certification

- Pine Mountain Group Certification

- Tivoli Certifications

The certification programs covered in this chapter focus on network management. Network management software is used for large-scale monitoring and troubleshooting of networks that are comprised of equipment and software from multiple vendors. The certifications included here are offered by individual vendors or by consortiums of industry and business interests.

Computer Associates offers the Certified Unicenter Administrator and Certified Unicenter engineer certifications related to Unicenter TNG, its popular enterprise management program. Hewlett-Packard offers a number of specialization options through its HP OpenView Certified Consultant program. Mercury Interactive's Certified Product Specialist (CPS) program documents the skills of technical professionals on its TestSuite and LoadRunner products, which are interactive testing tools. Pine Mountain Group's Certified Net Analyst program offers three specializations related to network monitoring and troubleshooting: Internet, Cross-Technology, and Architect. Tivoli's certification program is based on the Tivoli Enterprise information technology management package and has three levels: Certified Consultant, Certified Enterprise Consultant, and Certified Solutions Expert.

Professionals seeking these certifications might include:

- Help-desk personnel
- Programmers
- Security specialists
- Consultants
- Network administrators

While the focus of this chapter is on certification programs related to network management, training is also available to improve the effectiveness of help-desk operations. One of the best-known organizations in this area is Help Desk 2000. For information about this organization, see the Note below.

NOTE   Help Desk 2000 is a certification and membership organization focused on setting standards and providing education and support for professionals, managers, and directors in the help-desk industry. Help Desk 2000 offers a set of related education and certification programs. The Certified Help Desk Professional (CHDP) credential supports and documents the skills of front-line support personnel. The Certified Help Desk Manager (CHDM) credential helps managers learn to develop and maintain effective and efficient help desks. The Certified Help Desk Director (CHDD) program builds and documents the business and management skills of help-desk directors. Finally, Help Desk 2000 also offers CORE 2000 certification for entire Help Desk operations; this onsite certification process focuses on best practices in these areas: business alignment, business and service culture, and process methodologies. For more information about Help Desk 2000 and its programs, visit the company's Web site (`http:// www.helpdesk2000.org`) or call (800) 350-5781.

Use Table 10.1 to compare the number of required tests, the test format, the approximate cost of taking the test(s), number of required courses, cost of any required courses, and the relative difficulty of the certification programs in this chapter. The cost information is a general guideline; since things change rapidly in the world of certification programs, once you have selected a specific course of action you may want to double-check the costs.

We classified the difficulty of these certifications into three categories—Moderate, Challenging, and Very Challenging—based on the those tests or lab exams. These ratings are approximate and are offered simply as a general guide to help the reader distinguish between entry-level programs and those that require more advanced skill and knowledge. (This rating scale assumes that one has experience with the product or technology and has studied the appropriate subject content before attempting the exams.)

T A B L E 10.1: Network Management Certifications

Certification	# of Required Tests	Test Format(s)	Total Cost of Required Tests	# of Required Courses	Total Cost of Required Courses	Difficulty	Notes
Computer Associates Certifications							
Certified Unicenter Administrator	1	MC	$100	—	—	◑	
Certified Unicenter Engineer	2	MC	$250	—	—	●	
Hewlett-Packard Certification							
HP OpenView Certified Consultant	1–2	MC	VF	—	—	◑	Specializations include: Network Management, Desktop Management, Windows NT Server and Applications Management, UNIX Server and Applications Management, IT Service Manager, and Storage Management.
Mercury Interactive Certification							
Certified Product Specialist (CPS)	—	—	—	1	$1,500–$2,500	◑	Specializations include: TestSuite and LoadRunner. You must also complete a certification project and submit it with a $500 evaluation fee.
Pine Mountain Group Certification							
Certified NetAnalyst	1	MC	CV	1	$1,400–$2,750	◑	Specializations include: Internet, Cross-Technology, and Architect.

T A B L E 10.1:   Network Management Certifications   *(continued)*

Certification	# of Required Tests	Test Format(s)	Total Cost of Required Tests	# of Required Courses	Total Cost of Required Courses	Difficulty	Notes
Tivoli Certifications							
Tivoli Certified Consultant	1–2	MC	VF	—	—	◯	
Tivoli Certified Enterprise Consultant	5	MC	VF	—	—	◑	
Tivoli Certified Solutions Expert	1	MC	VF	—	—	●	

Certification Difficulty: ◯ Moderate   ◑ Challenging   ● Very Challenging

Test Format: **MC:** Multiple Choice   **AT:** Adaptive Testing   **LA:** Live Application
PR: Hands-on Lab   **NA:** Not Applicable

Test Fee: **VF:** Test Fees can vary; consult testing center.   **CV:** Voucher for taking the exam is included in the fee for the required course(s); additional attempts cost extra.

Computer Associates Certifications

- Certified Unicenter Administrator

- Certified Unicenter Engineer

Computer Associates' Unicenter TNG system is an open, cross-platform enterprise management system for the control of heterogeneous networks, i.e., networks that are comprised of equipment and software from multiple vendors. Unicenter TNG is one of the most popular enterprise management software programs.

The Unicenter TNG Certification Program provides training and certification for engineers involved in the deployment and administration of Unicenter TNG.

Recertification or Maintenance Requirements

Computer Associates did not have formal recertification requirements at the time of this writing. Contact Computer Associates for updates (see the "Computer Associates Resources" section for contact information).

Benefits of Certification

In addition to industry recognition of their technical achievements, Certified Unicenter Administrators and Engineers receive the following benefit:

- Use of CUA or CUE logo in advertisements or business literature

Certified Unicenter Administrator

This certification program involves passing one exam. Hands-on experience with the product is considered essential to success in passing the exam.

Who Needs It

The Certified Unicenter Administrator is an excellent credential for entry-level network management professionals. This certification is also valuable to support and help-desk personnel.

Requirements for Certification

The certification process requires the following step:

1. Pass the Unicenter Basics Administration exam (Test ID: 270-201).

Administrator

Computer Associates exams are administered by Sylvan Prometric. Call (800) 859-3926 to register for a Computer Associates test; if outside the U.S., use the online Sylvan Test Center Locator at http://www.sylvanprometric.com to find the nearest testing center. (See Chapter 3, "Taking Your Test," for additional information on Sylvan Prometric.)

Fee

The test costs $100.

Format

The test consists of 100 multiple-choice questions and must be completed in 60 minutes. Passing score is 80 percent.

Certified Unicenter Engineer

This certification program involves passing two exams. Topics covered on the first exam include Unicenter TNG overview and architecture, installing Unicenter TNG, Unicenter TNG agent technology, and Unicenter TNG options. The second test covers advanced Unicenter TNG topics, including integrating WorldView, event management, and Distributed State Machines (DSM); how to customize the WorldView GUI; and how to effectively implement management policies through manager/agent technology. Hands-on experience with the product is considered essential to success in passing the exams.

Who Needs It

The Certified Unicenter Engineer is an excellent credential for network management professionals. This certification is also valuable to support and help-desk personnel.

Requirements for Certification

The certification process requires the following steps:

1. Pass the Unicenter TNG Basics examination (Test ID: 270-112).

2. Pass the Unicenter TNG Advanced examination (Test ID: 270-113).

Administrator

Computer Associates exams are administered by Sylvan Prometric. Call (800) 859-3926 to register for a Computer Associates test; if outside the U.S., use the online Sylvan Test Center Locator at http://www.sylvanprometric.com to find the nearest testing center. (See Chapter 3 for additional information on Sylvan Prometric.)

Fee

Each test costs $125.

Format

Each test consists of 100 multiple-choice questions and must be completed in 60 minutes. Passing score is 80 percent.

Computer Associates Resources

Computer Associates offers courses for preparing for each of the tests mentioned above. For more information on this organization's certifications and courses, contact Computer Associates at:

Web	http://www.cai.com/
Mail	Computer Associates International, Inc.
	Rt. 206 & Orchard Road
	Princeton, NJ 08543
Phone	(800) 237-9273
Fax	(908) 874-7417

Hewlett-Packard Certification

- HP OpenView Certified Consultant

Hewlett-Packard (HP) makes a wide variety of products, from computers and laser printers to specialized medical instruments. In addition, HP makes OpenView, which is one of the most popular network management products. OpenView is a network management system for monitoring and managing networks that are comprised of equipment and software from multiple vendors.

HP's OpenView Certified Consultant program was expanded in 1999 to include a number of specializations that recognize technical competence in selling and supporting HP OpenView. In addition, the Network Management specialization has been modified to allow the candidate to further specialize in either UNIX, Windows NT, or a combination of UNIX and Windows NT specializations.

Recertification or Maintenance Requirements

To maintain their certifications, OpenView Certified Consultants are required to take a recertification exam when a new version of Open-View is released Certified Consultants are given three months after the release of the new certification exam to update their certification status.

Benefits of Certification

HP OpenView Certified Consultants receive this benefit:

- Use of the HP OpenView Certified Consultant logo

HP OpenView Certified Consultant

Attaining this certification involves passing a basic test and one or more specialty tests. The basic exam covers the basic operation of HP OpenView, including configuration of the computer system and the networking environment; basic knowledge of network management; configuration and installation of NNM as a stand-alone management system (non-distributed); and setting up management consoles. The specialization exams focus on a particular implementation or feature of HP OpenView. The available specializations include:

- Network management
- Desktop management
- Windows NT server and applications management
- UNIX server and applications management
- IT service manager
- Storage management

Who Needs It

The HP OpenView Certified Consultant certification is an excellent credential for network management professionals. This certification is also valuable to support and help-desk personnel.

Requirements for Certification

The certification process requires the following steps:

1. Pass the Introduction to HP OpenView exam (Test ID: 490-001).

2. Pass the required test(s) for the specialization you seek (see Table 10.2).

T A B L E 10.2: HP OpenView Certified Consultant Specializations and Required Tests

Specialization	Test	Test ID
Network Management	Network Node Manager for UNIX OR	490-011
	Network Node Manager for Windows NT OR	490-021
	Network Node Manager for UNIX and Windows NT	490-031
Desktop Management	Desktop Administrator	490-040
Windows NT Server and Applications Management	HP OpenView ManageX Fundamentals	491-050
UNIX Server and Applications Management	HP OpenView IT/Operations AND	491-070
	HP OpenView Resource and Performance Management	491-080
IT Service Manager	HP OpenView IT Service Manager	491-060
Storage Management	HP OpenView OmniBack II	491-090

Administrator

HP exams are administered by Sylvan Prometric. Call (800) 549-3926 to register for an HP test; if outside the U.S., use the online Sylvan Test Center Locator at http://www.sylvanprometric.com to find the nearest testing center. (See Chapter 3 for additional information on Sylvan Prometric.)

Fee

The HP OpenView exam costs $70. The Network Node Manager Fundamentals for UNIX exam costs $130. For information on other HP OpenView exams, contact HP.

Format

The HP OpenView exam consists of 27 questions and must be completed in 60 minutes. The passing score is 80 percent. The Network Node Manager Fundamentals for UNIX exam consists of two sections. It has 108 questions and must be completed in 165 minutes. To pass, the candidate must score 70 percent or higher in each of the two sections of the test. For information on other HP OpenView exams, contact HP.

Hewlett-Packard Resources

The HP Web site offers self-assessment practice exams. HP's Web site also offers a listing of preparation courses. For more information on this organization's certifications and courses, contact HP at:

Web	http://www.openview.hp.com
E-mail	ovtraining@fc.hp.com
Phone	(800) 225-1451
Fax	(970) 898-3647

Mercury Interactive Certification

- Certified Product Specialist (CPS)

Mercury Interactive produces automated testing solutions for software. Their product line includes TestSuite, which is an integrated solution for testing Windows-based client/server applications, and LoadRunner, an enterprise load testing tool.

Mercury Interactive Educational Services in North America offers a two-level certification program based on the TestSuite and LoadRunner products for Windows NT. The entry-level certification, described below, is the Certified Product Specialist designation. The second level in Mercury Interactive's certification program is the Certified Product Instructor (CPI). For information about the CPI program, see the company's Web page (http://www.merc-int.com/services/certprog/).

Recertification or Maintenance Requirements

Certified Product Specialists must pay an annual renewal fee of $100.

Benefits of Certification

Mercury Interactive did not have a formal listing of benefits at the time of this writing. Check the company's Web site for possible updates.

Certified Product Specialist (CPS)

The Mercury Interactive CPS credential documents a candidate's ability to use Mercury interactive testing tools and provide user support on these products. Attaining this certification involves attending a required three to five day training class and completing an independent certification project. The CPS certification is available on the following Mercury Interactive products:

- TestSuite
- LoadRunner

Who Needs It

This certification may be valuable for system engineers or support personnel who use Mercury Interactive products or support other users.

Requirements for Certification

The certification process requires the following steps:

1. Attend a public training class on either TestSuite or LoadRunner (3–5 day course).

2. Contact Mercury Interactive Educational Services to get a CPS certification package.

3. Complete the CPS certification project and submit it for evaluation.

Administrator

The certification project requirement is administered by Mercury Interactive (see "Mercury Interactive Resources" section for contact information).

Fee

The CPS project and evaluation costs $500. There is an additional cost of $1,500 to $2,500 for the required course. Annual renewal of certification costs $100.

Format

This certification is based on attending a required public training course and completing a hands-on project. Passing score on the project is 75 percent.

Mercury Interactive Resources

Mercury Interactive's Web site provides details on the available public training courses and training locations. For more information on this organization's certification program and training courses, contact Mercury Interactive at:

Web	http://www.merc-int.com/services/certprog/
E-mail	info@merc-int.com
Mail	Educational Services
	Mercury Interactive Corporation
	1325 Borregas Avenue
	Sunnyvale, CA 94089
Phone	(800) 759-3302 or (408) 822-5200
Fax	(408) 822-5300

Pine Mountain Group Certification

- Certified NetAnalyst

The Pine Mountain Group, founded in 1989, is a consulting and training company that specializes in advanced network monitoring and troubleshooting. The company doesn't make a network analyzer, but rather focuses on how such tools can be put to their best use in the field. Pine Mountain Group offers the Certified NetAnalyst credential, which was designed as a way to help net technologists get up to speed quickly.

Recertification or Maintenance Requirements

The Pine Mountain Group currently has no policy regarding recertification.

Benefits of Certification

Certified NetAnalysts receive the following benefits:

- Certificate

- Use of the Certified NetAnalyst logo for stationery and business cards

Certified NetAnalyst

Obtaining the Certified NetAnalyst credential involves attending one of three courses and taking a test at the end of that course. The courses are not required, but PMG strongly encourages attendance. The Certified NetAnalyst programs offers three specialties:

- Certified NetAnalyst—Internet

- Certified NetAnalyst—Cross-Technology

- Certified NetAnalyst—Architect

The Certified NetAnalyst—Internet program is designed for Internet and ISP support personnel. The course is two days long and includes training on TCP/IP, analysis tools, DNS, firewalls, proxy server, Web servers, and client browsers.

The Certified NetAnalyst—Cross-Technology certifies those with a general understanding of essential and selected topics in network analysis, including the OSI model, LAN technologies, network analysis tools, 10BaseT, Fast Ethernet, Token Ring, IP, ICMP, IPX/SPX, throughput, latency, and Microsoft networking.

The Certified NetAnalyst—Architect tests the candidate's advanced understanding of a variety of network analysis concepts, including internetworking, routers, bridges, RMON, DNS, NetBIOS, HDLC, Frame Relay, WAN Technologies, IP Troubleshooting, TCP, Client-Server Analysis, and ATM.NetAnalyst—Internet.

NOTE A Certified NetAnalyst—Security program is also under development. This program will help analysts understand how hackers break into networks, how data is invaded, and how to prevent attacks. Check Pine Mountain Group's Web site to learn about the course content, course length, and fees related to this new specialization.

Who Needs It

This certification is great for those wanting to advance their careers in network design and analysis. This credential can also be a value to independent consultants who want to validate their expertise to clients.

Requirements for Certification

The certification process requires the following step:

1. Attend the course, and pass the test at the end of the course, for the Certified NetAnalyst designation you seek:

   - Certified NetAnalyst—Internet
   - Certified NetAnalyst—Cross-Technology
   - Certified NetAnalyst—Architect

While Pine Mountain Group recommends candidates take the course for their desired specialization, the tests can also be taken by persons who have not attended the courses.

Administrator

The Pine Mountain Group administers the courses and tests. Candidates can take the test at any sites where Pine Mountain Group training is offered in the U.S. or Europe. Tests can also be taken at NetWorld + Interop. Contact Pine Mountain Group to register for a course.

Fee

The Certified NetAnalyst—Internet cost $1,400. Since this specialization is new, there is an introductory price of $995.50 in effect at the time of this writing (contact Pine Mountain Group for current pricing). Both the Cross-Technology and Architect specialty courses cost $2,750. The test fee is included in the cost of the course.

If you choose to take a test without taking a course, the test fee is $400. There is no charge to retake any test.

Format

The Certified NetAnalyst—Internet is a two-day course. Both the Cross-Technology and Architect specialty courses last five days.

Pine Mountain Group Resources

Pine Mountain Group offers a number of introductory courses, as well as the ones lists above. In addition, parts of courses, or modules, can be taken individually. For more information on this organization's certification program and courses, contact Pine Mountain Group at:

Web	http://www.pmg.com/
Mail	Pine Mountain Group
	Box 849
	20950 Ferretti Road
	Groveland, CA 95321
Phone	(800) 645-8486
Fax	(209) 962-5914

Tivoli Certifications

- Tivoli Certified Consultant

- Tivoli Certified Enterprise Consultant

- Tivoli Certified Solutions Expert

Tivoli, now a division of IBM, makes Tivoli Enterprise, a leading information technology management package that allows information technology staff to automate and manage their computers, networks, and programs.

Tivoli's certification program currently includes three levels of certification. The Tivoli Certified Consultant is the entry-level certification related to Tivoli's Enterprise software. The Certified Enterprise Consultant is the next level of certification and reflects a more advanced knowledge of Tivoli software overall. The Tivoli Certified Solutions Expert is Tivoli's highest certification level and requires specialized product knowledge.

Recertification or Maintenance Requirements

Tivoli currently has no policy regarding recertification, but is exploring recertification options.

Benefits of Certification

Tivoli certified professionals receive the following benefits:

- Certificate

- Use of the Tivoli certified logo for stationery and business cards

Tivoli Certified Consultant

Obtaining the Tivoli Certified Consultant credential involves passing the Tivoli Framework V3.6 Implementation test, as well as one test on an application area within Tivoli Enterprise software. (The exception is in the areas of network management and security, which do not require the Tivoli Framework V3.6 Implementation test.) Specializations for Tivoli Certified Consultants include:

- Network Management
- Distributed Monitoring V3.6
- Deployment V3.6
- User Administration V3.6
- Enterprise Console V3.6
- Security Management
- Problem Management

Who Needs It

The Tivoli Certified Consultant credential is an excellent way to move up from an entry-level help-desk or support position to one of higher responsibility in an organization that utilizes Tivoli.

Requirements for Certification

The certification process requires the following step:

1. Pass the required test(s) for the specialization you seek (see Table 10.3).

T A B L E 10.3: Tivoli Certified Consultant Specializations and Required Tests

Specialization	Test	Test ID
Tivoli Network Management	TME 10 Network Management	000-582
Tivoli Distributed Monitoring	Tivoli Framework V3.6 Implementation Tivoli Distributed Monitoring V3.6 Implementation	000-681 000-683
Tivoli Deployment V3.6	Tivoli Framework V3.6 Implementation Tivoli Deployment V3.6 Implementation	000-681 000-684

TABLE 10.3: Tivoli Certified Consultant Specializations and Required Tests *(continued)*

Specialization	Test	Test ID
Tivoli User Administration V3.6	Tivoli Framework V3.6 Implementation Tivoli User Administration V3.6	000-681 000-685
Tivoli Enterprise Console V3.6	Tivoli Framework V3.6 Implementation Tivoli Enterprise Console V3.6	000-681 000-686
Tivoli Security Management	Tivoli Framework V3.6 Implementation Tivoli Security Management Implementation	000-681 000-587
Tivoli Problem Management	Tivoli Problem Management Implementation	000-590

Administrator

Tivoli exams are administered by Sylvan Prometric. Call (800) 959-3926 to register for an Tivoli test; if outside the U.S., use the online Sylvan Test Center Locator at http://www.sylvanprometric.com to find the nearest testing center. (See Chapter 3 for additional information on Sylvan Prometric.)

Fee

Contact Sylvan Prometric for current pricing for Tivoli exams.

Format

Tivoli exams typically consist of 70–85 questions that must be completed within 90 minutes. A score of 65 percent or better is usually considered the passing score. Contact Tivoli for details on the test you are preparing to take.

Tivoli Certified Enterprise Consultant

Obtaining the Tivoli Certified Enterprise Consultant credential involves passing the Tivoli Framework Implementation test, as well as four additional tests on a special aspect of Tivoli Enterprise. There is currently only one available specialization for the Tivoli Certified Enterprise consultant: Tivoli Implementation.

Who Needs It

The Tivoli Certified Enterprise credential is an excellent way to enter or advance your career in an organization that utilizes Tivoli.

Requirements for Certification

The certification process requires the following steps:

1. Pass the Tivoli Framework V3.6 Implementation test (Test ID: 000-681)

2. Pass four of the elective tests listed in Table 10.4.

T A B L E 10.4: Tivoli Certified Enterprise Consultant Elective Tests

Test	Test ID
TME 10 Network Management	000-582
Tivoli Distributed Monitoring V3.6 Implementation	000-683
Tivoli Deployment V3.6 Implementation	000-684
Tivoli User Administration V3.6	000-685
Tivoli Enterprise Console V3.6	000-686
Tivoli Security Management Implementation	000-587
IBM ADSM Solution Development and Implementation OR	000-240
IBM ADSM V2 and V3 Solution Development and Implementation	000-241

Administrator

Tivoli exams are administered by Sylvan Prometric. Call (800) 959-3926 to register for an Tivoli test; if outside the U.S., use the online Sylvan Test Center Locator at http://www.sylvanprometric.com to find the nearest testing center. (See Chapter 3 for additional information on Sylvan Prometric.)

Fee

Contact Sylvan Prometric for current pricing on Tivoli exams.

Format

Tivoli exams typically consist of 70–85 questions that must be completed within 90 minutes. A score of 65 percent or better is usually considered the passing score. Contact Tivoli for details on the test you are preparing to take.

Tivoli Certified Solutions Expert

Obtaining the Tivoli Certified Solutions Expert credential involves passing one exam. Currently there is only one specialization in this program: Tivoli IT Director. (Check the Tivoli Web site for additional specialties that may be added this certification.) Tivoli IT Director is another network management program in Tivoli's line. The following prerequisites are recommended by Tivoli for anyone attempting the Tivoli IT Director certification exam:

- Knowledge and skill equivalent to the level of a Microsoft Certified Professional for Windows NT Server 4 (Microsoft certification is *not* required)

- Experience with Windows 3.1 and 95, OS/2, and/or NetWare clients

- Usage and configuration experience with supported databases, Internet servers, and hardware

- Java experience

- Understanding of networking and systems management concepts

Who Needs It

The Tivoli Certified Solutions Expert credential is an excellent way to advance your career in an organization that utilizes Tivoli products, including Tivoli IT Director.

Requirements for Certification

The certification process requires the following steps:

1. Pass the Tivoli IT Director Implementation exam
(Test ID: 000-588).

Administrator

Tivoli exams are administered by Sylvan Prometric. Call (800) 959-3926 to register for an Tivoli test; if outside the U.S., use the online Sylvan Test Center Locator at http://www.sylvanprometric.com to find the nearest testing center. (See Chapter 3 for additional information on Sylvan Prometric.)

Fee

Contact Sylvan Prometric for current pricing for Tivoli exams.

Format

The Tivoli IT Director exam consists of 74 questions that must be completed within 90 minutes. A score of 65 percent or better is considered passing.

Tivoli Resources

For more information on this organization's certification program and courses, contact Tivoli at:

Web	http://www.tivoli.com
E-mail	partners@tivoli.com
Mail	Tivoli Systems, Inc.
	9442 Capital of Texas Hwy
	North Austin, TX 78759
Phone	(888) 910-7587

CHAPTER

11

Telecommunications
Certifications

FEATURING

- Callware Technologies Certification

- Computer Telephony Institute Certification

- Dialogic Certification

- PictureTel Certification

Computer telephony is a general term for the integration of computers and telephone technology. To some, it means software that allows you to receive voice mail, e-mail, and faxes all in one convenient system, such as Microsoft's Outlook. To others, it means technology systems that support call centers, where callers are identified for order processing, etc., as their calls come in. Whatever its form, computer telephony is a rapidly growing industry that involves the effective marriage of computer and telephone technologies.

Computer Telephony (CT) applications for mainframes have existed for many years. However, the advent of PC-based CT systems has increased the affordability of these systems for small and medium-sized businesses.

Callware Technologies offers the Certified Network Telephony Engineer certification program, which is based on Callware's Callegra CT integration product. The Computer Telephony Institute offers the Computer Telephony Engineer certification in cooperation with CyberState University, an online training provider. Dialogic offers the Computer Telephony Professional certification for those responsible for implementing CT systems using Dialogic hardware and software. PictureTel offers the Certified Videoconferencing Engineer certification for those responsible for installing and supporting videoconferencing systems.

Those who may be interested in pursuing these certifications include:

- Telephone technicians
- Network administrators
- Traditional PBX and Key system administrators
- Computer programmers

Use Table 11.1 below to compare the number of required tests, the test format, the approximate cost of taking the test(s), number of required courses, cost of any required courses, and the relative difficulty of the certification programs in this chapter. The cost information is a general guideline; since things change rapidly in the world of certification programs, once you have selected a specific course of action you may want to double-check the costs.

We classified the difficulty of these certifications into three categories—Moderate, Challenging, and Very Challenging—based on the number of required tests and courses, and the relative difficulty of those tests or lab exams. These ratings are approximate and are offered simply as a general guide to help the reader distinguish between entry-level programs and those that require more advanced skill and knowledge. (This rating scale assumes that one has experience with the product or technology and has studied the appropriate subject content before attempting the exams.)

T A B L E 11.1: Telecommunications Certifications

Certification	# of Required Tests	Test Format(s)	Total Cost of Required Tests	# of Required Courses	Total Cost of Required Courses	Difficulty	Notes
Callware Technologies Certification							
Certified Network Telephony Engineer (CNTE)	1	MC	Course fee covers exam	1	$2,000–$2,500	◐	Specializations: Windows NT or Novell NetWare.
Computer Telephony Institute Certification							
Computer Telephony Engineer (CTE)	5	MC	$500	5	$2,995	◐	
Dialogic Certification							
Computer Telephony Professional (CTP)	1	MC	$95	—	—	◐	
PictureTel Certification							
Certified Videoconferencing Engineer	1	MC	$175	—	—	●	

Certification Difficulty: ○ Moderate ◐ Challenging ● Very Challenging

Test Format: **MC:** Multiple Choice **AT:** Adaptive Testing **LA:** Live Application
PR: Hands-on Lab **NA:** Not Applicable

Test Fee: **VF:** Test Fees can vary; consult testing center. **CV:** Voucher for taking the exam is included in the fee for the required course(s); additional attempts cost extra.

Callware Technologies Certification

- Certified Network Telephony Engineer

Callware Technologies provides products that integrate a company's voice mail, fax, and e-mail systems into one manageable system. The main Callware product, Callegra, is available for both Microsoft Windows NT and Novell NetWare network operating systems and is used by companies worldwide.

Recertification or Maintenance Requirements

The CNTE program did not have announced recertification requirements at the time of this writing. Contact Callware for updates (see the "Callware Resources" section for contact information).

Benefits of Certification

The CNTE program did not have a formal listing of certification benefits at the time of this writing. Contact Callware for updates (see the "Callware Resources" section for contact information).

Certified Network Telephony Engineer

The Certified Network Telephony Engineer (CNTE) certification demonstrates competency with the Callware suite of products and with computer telephony integration in general. The CNTE credential was introduced in 1994, and was the first certification offered in the computer telephony industry. Callware has certified over 2,700 technicians worldwide.

The CNTE program involves taking a course and passing the exam administered at the end of the course. You must also be either a Microsoft Certified Professional (MCP) or Certified Novell Administrator (CNA), depending on your desired specialization. The CNTE program offers two areas of specialization:

- CNTE: Windows NT
- CNTE: Novell NetWare

Who Needs It

The CNTE certification is an excellent way to document your advanced skills in the implementation and support of Callware products. This credential can also be of value to independent consultants and dealers who install Callware systems and want to validate their expertise for clients.

Requirements for Certification

The certification process requires the following steps:

1. Meet the prerequisite network operating system certification requirement by becoming either a Microsoft Certified Professional (MCP) or Certified Novell Administrator (CNA), depending on your desired specialization. (Alternatively, technicians who have not obtained the MCP or CNA designations can take an equivalency exam from Callware.)

2. Attend the training for the specialization you seek and pass the test at the end of the course (see Table 11.2).

TABLE 11.2: CNTE Courses and Tests

Specialization	Course/Test	Test ID
CNTE: Windows NT	Core Technology, Callegra for Windows NT	551
CNTE: NetWare	Core Technology, Callegra for NetWare	540

Administrator

Callware administers both the courses and the tests. Registration is available through the Web site for Callware dealers (http://www.callware.com/). You need not be a Callware dealer to obtain this certification.

Fee

The course and test for the CNTE: Windows NT specialization cost a total of $2,500. The course and test for the CNTE: Novell NetWare specialization cost a total of $2,000.

Format

Each test consists of 50 questions and must be completed within 120 minutes.

Callware Resources

For more information on this organization's certification program and courses, contact Callware at:

Web `http://www.callware.com/`
Mail Callware Technologies
    8911 South Sandy Parkway
    Sandy, UT 84070
Phone (801) 984-1100

Computer Telephony Institute Certification

- Computer Telephony Engineer (CTE)

The Computer Telephony Institute was founded in 1997 to provide certification for computer telephony professionals. The institute offers the Computer Telephony Engineer (CTE) certification, which involves taking five courses and passing five tests. The courses are offered online through a partnership with CyberState University (See `http://www.cyberstateu.com/`).

The Computer Telephony Institute also sponsors "BootCamps" for those considering the CTE certification. These BootCamps provide a one-day overview of the material contained in the full CTE program. This format is ideal for managers, executives, or others who need an overview of computer telephony technology.

Recertification or Maintenance Requirements

The CTE program did not have announced recertification requirements at the time of this writing. Contact the Computer Telephony Institute for updates (see the "Computer Telephony Institute Resources" section for contact information).

Benefits of Certification

The CTE program did not have a formal listing of certification benefits at the time of this writing. Contact Computer Telephony Institute for updates (see the "Computer Telephony Institute Resources" section for contact information).

Certified Telephony Engineer

To achieve CTE certification, a candidate must complete three core courses and two elective courses, and pass the associated exams. The required core courses include Data Networking, Telephony Fundamentals, and Computer Telephony Integration. The Computer Telephony Institute estimates that those who are new to the field will need about 130 hours to complete this course of study. Those with experience in the field should be able to complete the process more rapidly.

Who Needs It

The CTE certification is an excellent way to demonstrate your skills in computer and telephony integration. It is a great way to establish your credentials in this growing field.

Requirements for Certification

The certification process requires the following steps:

1. Complete the three required core courses:

   - CT-10: Data Networking

   - CT-20: Telephony and Telecommunications

   - CT-30: Computer Telephony Integration

2. Complete two of the following elective courses (additional elective courses are under development, check http://www.ctinstitute.com/ for updates):

   - CS-10: Interactive Voice Response

   - CS-20: Internet Telephony

3. Complete the tests for each of the courses you have taken.

Administrator

The courses and exams are administered by the Computer Telephony Institute in conjunction with CyberState University.

Fee

The total cost for all five courses is $2,995. The tests cost $100 each.

Format

The exams are multiple-choice. Contact the Computer Telephony Institute for additional current test information.

Computer Telephony Institute Resources

For more information on this organization's certification program and courses, contact the Computer Telephony Institute at:

Web	http://www.ctinstitute.com/
E-mail	Dvanoverbeek@ctinstitute.com
Mail	Computer Telephony Institute
	2000 Crow Canyon Place, Suite 185
	San Ramon, CA 94583
Phone	(925) 737-0800
	(877) 284-6784

Dialogic Certification

- Computer Telephony Professional

Dialogic makes products for computer telephony and develops solutions for converging voice and data networks. Dialogic products are used in voice, fax, data call center management, and Internet Protocol telephony applications. The products are used in both customer premise equipment and public network environments. Dialogic offers the Computer Telephony Professional certification program as a way to train and credential those who use and support its products.

Recertification or Maintenance Requirements

The CT Professional program did not have announced recertification requirements at the time of this writing. Contact Dialogic for updates (see the Dialogic Resources section for contact information).

Benefits of Certification

Contact Dialogic for information about certification benefits (see the "Dialogic Resources" section for contact information).

Computer Telephony (CT) Professional

The one exam required for the Computer Telephony (CT) Professional credential tests a candidate's understanding of the CT industry, PC architectures, memory management, peripheral/controller installation, and configuration skills. The exam also tests the candidate's knowledge of telephone networks and protocols, ability to install and configure software in a network environment, and ability to implement CT solutions using Dialogic hardware and software. The CT Professional credential is a required step in becoming a Dialogic Platinum Reseller.

Who Needs It

The CT Professional certification is an excellent way to document your ability to implement CT systems using Dialogic hardware and software. This credential can also be of value to independent consultants who want to validate their expertise for clients.

Requirements for Certification

The certification process requires one step:

1. Pass the CT Professional test.

Administrator

The CT Professional exam is an online test administered by Dialogic. You can both register and take the exam at Dialogic's Web site (http://www.dialogic.com/).

Fee

The test fee is $95.

Format

The exams are multiple-choice. Contact Dialogic for additional current test information.

Dialogic Resources

Dialogic offers a number of courses that are recommended for the CT Professional candidate. For more information on this organization's certification program and courses, contact Dialogic at:

Web	http://www.dialogic.com
Mail	Dialogic World Headquarters
	1515 Route Ten
	Parsippany, NJ 07054
Phone	(800) 755-4444
Fax	(973) 993-9884

PictureTel Certification

PictureTel is one of the world's leading manufacturers of video-conferencing equipment. PictureTel offers the Certified Videoconferencing Engineer (CVE) designation as a way to validate the skills of those responsible for designing, installing, and troubleshooting video-conferencing systems.

Recertification or Maintenance Requirements

CVEs are required to take a test each year to maintain their certification.

Benefits of Certification

Certified Videoconferencing Engineers receive the following benefits:

- CVE Certificate of Accomplishment
- Listing in PictureTel's CVE database

Certified Videoconferencing Engineer

Attaining this certification involves passing one exam. This test assesses the candidate's knowledge of the technical aspects of a videoconferencing system in four core areas: audio, video, telecommunications network, and international standards.

Who Needs It

This certification is valuable to those involved in designing and installing videoconferencing systems. It can also be valuable to independent consultants who want to validate their knowledge of videoconferencing technology for potential clients.

Requirements for Certification

The certification process requires only one step:

1. Pass the Certified Videoconferencing Engineer test (Test ID: 1K1-001).

Administrator

Call Sylvan Prometric at (888) 283-5452 to register for the Certified Videoconferencing Engineer exam; if outside the U.S., use the online Sylvan Test Center Locator at http://www.sylvanprometric.com/ to find the nearest testing center. (See Chapter 3, "Taking Your Test," for detailed information on taking tests from Sylvan.)

Fee

The test fee is $175.

Format

The test is multiple-choice and must be completed in 75 minutes.

PictureTel Resources

The PictureTel Web site offers more information on the certification program and the required exam. PictureTel's Web site also offers a listing of preparatory courses. For more information on this organization's certifications and courses, contact PictureTel at:

Web	http://www.picturetel.com
Mail	PictureTel Corporation
	100 Minuteman Road
	Andover, MA 01810
Phone	(978) 292-5000

12

Client/Server and Database
System Certifications

FEATURING

- Centura Certifications

- Informix Certifications

- Microsoft Certification

- Oracle Certifications

- Sybase Certifications

This chapter covers several highly specialized certification programs designed by vendors that make database and client/server products. Centura, Informix, Microsoft, Oracle, and Sybase all offer certifications on their database products. These certifications focus on the tasks involved in administering and managing large databases for a variety of purposes.

Professionals seeking these certifications might include:

- Database administrators

- Database programmers

- Network administrators

- Information systems managers

Inprise Certification

A few months after it acquired Visigenic Software, Borland changed its name to Inprise Corporation, Inc. While Inprise is the new name of the company, you will find that many Inprise products are still offered under the recognized trade name of borland.com: for example, Borland C++. Another of borland.com's best-known products, Delphi, is one of the most popular client/server development systems.

Currently, all of the Borland and Inprise certifications are being revised and are not available. For information about when new certifications programs will be released, check the Insprise Web site (http://www.inprsie.com/) or the Certification-Update Web site (http://www.certification-update.com/).

Use Table 12.1 presented below to compare the number of required tests, the test format, the approximate cost of taking the test(s), number of required courses, cost of any required courses, and the relative difficulty of the certification programs in this chapter. The cost information is a general guideline; since things change rapidly in the world of certification programs, once you have selected a specific course of action you may want to double-check the costs.

We classified the difficulty of these certifications into three categories—
Moderate, Challenging, and Very Challenging—based on the number of
required tests and courses, and the relative difficulty of those tests or lab
exams. These ratings are approximate and are offered simply as a general
guide to help the reader distinguish between entry-level programs and
those that require more advanced skill and knowledge. (This rating scale
assumes that one has experience with the product or technology and has
studied the appropriate subject content before attempting the exams.)

T A B L E 12.1: Client/Server Certifications

Certification	# of Required Tests	Test Format(s)	Total Cost of Required Tests	# of Required Courses	Total Cost of Required Courses	Difficulty	Notes
Centura Certifications							
Centura Certified Developer	1	MC	$120	—	—	○	
Centura Certified Database Administrator	1	MC	$120	—	—	○	
Informix Certifications							
Informix Certified Database Specialist	2	MC	$300	—	—	◐	
Informix Certified System Administration	2	MC	$300	—	—	◐	
Informix Certified Dynamic 4GL Professional	2	MC	$300	—	—	◐	
Microsoft Certification							
Microsoft Certified Database Administrator	5	MC, AT	$500	—	—	◐	
Oracle Certifications							
Certified Database Administrator	4–5	MC	$500–$625	—	—	●	Specializations: Oracle 7.3 and Oracle 8.

TABLE 12.1: Client/Server Certifications *(continued)*

Certification	# of Required Tests	Test Format(s)	Total Cost of Required Tests	# of Required Courses	Total Cost of Required Courses	Difficulty	Notes
Oracle Certifications							
Certified Application Developer	5	MC	$625	—	—	●	Specializations: Developer/2000 Release 1 and Developer/2000 Release 2.
Sybase Certifications							
Sybase Certified Associate	1	MC	VF	—	—	○	Specializations: PowerBuilder Developer, Adaptive Server Administrator, SQL Developer.
Sybase Certified Professional	1	MC	VF	—	—	●	Specializations: PowerBuilder Developer, Adaptive Server Administrator.

Certification Difficulty: ○ Moderate ◑ Challenging ● Very Challenging

Test Format:
MC: Multiple Choice **AT:** Adaptive Testing **LA:** Live Application
PR: Hands-on Lab **NA:** Not Applicable

Test Fee:
VF: Test Fees can vary; consult testing center. **CV:** Voucher for taking the exam is included in the fee for the required course(s); additional attempts cost extra.

Centura Certifications

- Centura Certified Developer

- Centura Certified Database Administrator

Centura Software makes a number of database products, but their core product line is the SQLBase 7 database product. Centura offers two certifications on SQLBase 7, and related products: the

Centura Certified Developer and the Centura Certified Database Administrator (DBA). The Developer certification is based on in-depth knowledge of client technology, object-oriented programming, and application design. The DBA certification is based on in-depth knowledge of server technology, including SQLBase advanced features, performance tuning, and database design.

Recertification or Maintenance Requirements

The SQLBase certifications apply to specific version numbers of the database product, so there is no requirement for recertification on a particular version. Since your certification is tied to a certain version of a product, however, you will want to become certified on the newest versions when they become available, if you want to continue to have the most current credential.

Benefits of Certification

Centura Database Developers and Administrators receive these benefits:

- A listing in Centura's Web-based referral service
- Logo for use on business cards and stationery
- Access to Centura technical e-mail lists and newsgroups

Centura Certified Developer

Attaining this certification involves passing one exam. The Centura Certified Developer test focuses on the use of Centura's development tools, SQLWindows16, SQLWindows32, and the Centura Team Developer. The topics covered on the exam include Centura Team Developer and SQL fundamentals, object-oriented programming, MDI Windows, building a database application, table windows, and generating reports. Centura recommends that certification candidates either have at least one year of hands-on experience with the products or have six months' experience and take the course entitled "Developing Applications with Centura Team Developer." Information about this course can be found on Centura's Web site (see "Centura Resources" below).

Who Needs It

Certification as a Centura Certified Developer can be very valuable to independent consultants and contractors who want to document their abilities to develop client/server applications for potential clients. This certification can also be helpful to an individual seeking a full-time job as a developer of client/server applications.

Requirements for Certification

The certification process requires only one step:

1. Pass the Centura Client/Server Developer exam.

Administrator

Centura exams are administered by Sylvan Prometric. Call (800) 387-3926 to register for Centura tests; if outside the U.S., use the online Sylvan Test Center Locator at http://www.sylvanprometric.com to find the nearest testing center. (See Chapter 3, "Taking Your Test," for detailed information on taking tests from Sylvan.)

Fee

The fee is $120.

Format

This test is a multiple-choice exam consisting of approximately 82 questions. Call Sylvan Prometric at (800) 387-3926 for current information on exam length and passing score.

Centura Certified Database Administrator (DBA)

Attaining certification as a Centura Certified Database Administrator involves passing one exam. The DBA certification exam tests the candidate's in-depth knowledge of relational databases, normalization, transaction management, lock administration, and performance management. Centura recommends that the certification candidate have two years' experience with administrating an SQLBase environment, or have one year of experience and take the "Managing SQLBase Databases" course. Information about this course can be found on Centura's Web site (see "Centura Resources" below).

Who Needs It

Certification as a Centura Database Developer can be very valuable to independent consultants and contractors who want to document their abilities to manage Centura database systems for potential clients. This certification can also be helpful to individuals seeking a full-time job developing client/server applications.

Requirements for Certification

The certification process requires only one step:

1. Pass the Centura Client/Server Database Administrator exam.

Administrator

Centura exams are administered by Sylvan Prometric. Call (800) 387-3926 to register for Centura tests; if outside the U.S., use the online Sylvan Test Center Locator at http://www.sylvanprometric.com to find the nearest testing center. (See Chapter 3, "Taking Your Test," for detailed information on taking tests from Sylvan.)

Fee

The fee is $120.

Format

The test is a multiple-choice exam consisting of approximately 42 questions. Call Sylvan Prometric at (800) 387-3926 for current information on the exam length and passing score.

Centura Resources

The Centura Web site offers a listing of exam objectives and sample questions for each exam. In addition, Centura can provide you with a listing of Centura Certified Training Partners—organizations that offer training courses on Centura products. For more information on this organization's certifications and courses, contact Centura at:

Web   http://www.centurasoft.com/training/
        certification/
E-mail centuraps@centurasoft.com

Mail   Centura Software
              975 Island Drive
              Redwood Shores, CA 94065
Phone   (650) 596-3400 or (800) 444-8782

Informix Certifications

- Informix Certified Database Specialist

- Informix Certified Systems Administrator

- Informix Certified 4GL Developer

- Informix Certified Dynamic 4GL Professional

Informix produces a popular database program (also called Informix) for UNIX-based computers. Informix offers several certifications related to its products, including the Informix Certified Database Specialist, the Informix Certified Systems Administrator, the Informix Certified Dynamic 4GL Developer, and the Informix Certified Dynamic 4GL Professional.

Recertification or Maintenance Requirements

All certifications offered in the Informix Certified Professional Program (ICPP) are based on specific versions of Informix products. As products and respective certifications become available, certifications should be updated accordingly. Certified Professionals may represent themselves as being certified for only the specific version of the product that is listed on their certificate.

Benefits of Certification

Informix Certified Professionals receive:

- Certificate of achievement
- Use of the Informix Certified Professional logo

- Access to the TechInfo Center and "Club ICP" for Informix certified professionals

- Subscriptions to *TechNotes*, a quarterly Technical Support journal; *CS Times*, a quarterly Customer Services newsletter; and *Informix* magazine

- Lapel pin, polo shirt, and desk clock

- Special sponsored events for Informix certified professionals

Informix Certified Database Specialist

The Database Specialist certification is designed for individuals who implement and manage Informix Dynamic Server databases. To attain this certification you must pass two exams, which will test your proficiency in the areas of database and data models, entity relationships, SQL constructs, data integrity, Informix data types, creating Informix databases, and the commands needed to maintain and manage Informix databases.

Informix recommends that candidates take the following courses as preparation for the required tests:

- Relational Database Design

- Structured Query Language

- Advanced Structured Query Language

- Managing and Optimizing Informix Dynamic Server Databases

Informix's Web site provides descriptions of the recommended courses, as well as detailed descriptions of test content and sample test questions. For more information see the "Informix Resources" section below.

Who Needs It

Informix Database Specialist certification is valuable if you want to get a job as a database operator/administrator, database analyst, or database technical support professional at a company that uses Informix. It can also be a valuable title for independent consultants and contractors who want to document their abilities for potential clients.

Requirements for Certification

The certification process requires the following steps:

1. Pass the Database Fundamentals exam (Test ID: 660-111).

2. Pass the Managing and Optimizing Informix Dynamic Server Databases exam (Test ID: 660-112).

Administrator

Informix exams are administered by Sylvan Prometric. Call (800) 977-3926 to register for Informix tests; if outside the U.S., use the online Sylvan Test Center Locator at http://www.sylvanprometric.com to find the nearest testing center. (See Chapter 3, "Taking Your Test," for detailed information on taking tests from Sylvan.)

Fee

The fee is $150 per exam.

Format

The Database Fundamentals multiple-choice exam consists of 68 questions that must be completed in 90 minutes. A score of 82 percent is required to pass. The Managing and Optimizing Informix Dynamic Server Databases multiple-choice exam consists of 70 questions that must be completed in 90 minutes. A score of 80 percent is required to pass.

Informix Certified System Administrator

The System Administrator certification is designed for individuals who configure, maintain, and tune Informix Dynamic Server databases. Attaining this certification involves passing two exams, which test your database proficiency regarding knowledge of the components of a Dynamic Server system, configuring and monitoring Dynamic Server, UNIX utilities for Dynamic Server processing, managing logs and archives of databases, and performance management of the Dynamic Server system. The candidate should understand multi-threaded architecture, client/server connectability issues, and how to set up a multiple residency environment.

Informix recommends that candidates take the following courses to prepare for the required tests:

- System Administration: Informix Dynamic Server
- Performance Tuning: Informix Dynamic Server (UNIX)

Informix's Web site provides descriptions of the recommended courses, as well as detailed descriptions of test content and sample test questions.

Who Needs It

The System Administrator Informix Dynamic Server certification is valuable if you are looking for a job administrating mission-critical client/server applications at a company that uses Informix. It can also be a valuable title for independent consultants and contractors who want to document their abilities for potential clients.

Requirements for Certification

The certification process requires the following steps:

1. Pass the Informix Dynamic Server System Administration exam (Test ID: 660-211).

2. Pass Informix Dynamic Server Performance Tuning exam (Test ID: 660-212).

Administrator

Informix exams are administered by Sylvan Prometric. Call (800) 977-3926 to register for Informix tests; if outside the U.S., use the online Sylvan Test Center Locator at http://www.sylvanprometric.com to find the nearest testing center. (See Chapter 3, "Taking Your Test," for detailed information on taking tests from Sylvan.)

Fee

The fee is $150 per exam.

Format

The Informix Dynamic Server System Administration exam consists of 71 multiple-choice questions that must be completed in 90 minutes. A score of 74 percent is required to pass. The Informix Dynamic

Server Performance Tuning exam consists of 44 multiple-choice questions that must be answered in 60 minutes. A score of 84 percent is required to pass.

Informix Certified 4GL Developer

To become an Informix Certified 4GL Developer you must be proficient in using Informix 4GL to create custom database applications. Two exams are required for the Informix Certified 4GL Developer certification.

The required exams for this certification cover the following topics: databases and data models; entity relationships; SQL constructs; data integrity; Informix data types; creating menus; handling concurrent users; managing screen interaction; managing forms and windows; using program variables; selecting, inserting, updating, and deleting data; managing cursors; handling program and user errors; managing transactions; handling query-by-example logic; and writing reports.

Informix recommends that candidates take the following courses to prepare for the required tests:

- Relational Database Design
- Structured Query Language
- Advanced Structured Query Language

Informix's Web site provides descriptions of the recommended courses, as well as detailed descriptions of test content and sample test questions.

Who Needs It

These credentials are valuable if you are looking for a job creating custom database applications at a company that uses Informix. These can also be valuable titles for independent consultants and contractors who want to document their abilities for potential clients.

Requirements for Certification

The certification process requires the following steps:

1. Pass the Database Fundamentals exam (Test ID: 660-111).

2. Pass the Informix 4GL Development exam (Test ID: 660-301).

Administrator

Informix exams are administered by Prometric. Call (800) 977-3926 to register for Informix tests; if outside the U.S., use the online Sylvan Test Center Locator at http://www.sylvanprometric.com to find the nearest testing center. (See Chapter 3, "Taking Your Test," for detailed information on taking tests from Sylvan.)

Fee

The fee is $150 per exam.

Format

The Database Fundamentals multiple-choice exam consists of 68 questions that must be completed in 90 minutes. A score of 82 percent is required to pass. The Informix 4GL Development multiple-choice exam consists of 90 questions that must be completed in 90 minutes. A score of 78 percent is required to pass.

Informix Certified Dynamic 4GL Professional

To become an Informix Dynamic 4GL Professional, you must be proficient in using Informix 4GL to create custom database applications. The Informix Dynamic 4GL Professional builds on the Informix Certified 4GL Developer certification. The exam required for the Informix Certified Dynamic 4GL Professional credential covers the new GUI-enhanced Dynamic 4GL.

Informix recommends that candidates take the following course to prepare for the required test:

- Developing Applications Using Informix 4GL

Informix's Web site provides descriptions of the recommended courses, as well as detailed descriptions of test content and sample test questions.

Who Needs It

These credentials are valuable if you are looking for a job creating custom database applications at a company that uses Informix. These can also be valuable titles for independent consultants and contractors who want to document their abilities for potential clients.

Requirements for Certification

The certification process requires the following steps:

1. Obtain Certified 4GL Developer status as described above.

2. Pass the Informix Dynamic 4GL Development exam (Test ID: 660-302).

Administrator

Informix exams are administered by Sylvan Prometric. Call (800) 977-3926 to register for Informix tests; if outside the U.S., use the online Sylvan Test Center Locator at http://www.sylvanprometric.com to find the nearest testing center. (See Chapter 3, "Taking Your Test," for detailed information on taking tests from Sylvan.)

Fee

The fee is $150.

Format

This is a multiple-choice test. Contact Sylvan for current information on number of questions and passing score.

Informix Resources

The Informix Web site offers additional information and sample tests for each exam, as well as information on taking the recommended courses. For more information on this organization's certifications and courses, contact Informix at:

Web   http://www.informix.com/certification

E-mail	certification@informix.com
Mail	Informix Software
	4100 Bohannon Drive
	Menlo Park, CA 94025
Phone	(650) 926-6300
Fax	(650) 926-6872

Microsoft Certification

- Microsoft Certified Database Administrator (MCDBA)

The Microsoft Certified Database Administrator is Microsoft's premier designation for professionals responsible for installing and administering Microsoft SQL Server. The MCDBA credential denotes a high level of expertise with the Microsoft SQL Server product.

Recertification or Maintenance Requirements

As Microsoft introduces new products and new versions of its operating systems, it retires the tests for previous versions. If your certification is based on a test that Microsoft is retiring, you will be informed by certified mail of the need to take a current test to maintain your certification. You will have at least six months to complete this new test; if you do not pass the test your status as a MCDBA will no longer be valid.

Benefits of Certification

Microsoft Certified Database Administrators receive the following benefits:

- An MCDBA certificate

- A one-year subscription to TechNet Plus, a new level to the TechNet CD-ROM subscription, which allows professionals to test and evaluate beta products. Subscribers to TechNet Plus will receive all evaluation beta products on CD along with 12 monthly TechNet issues.

- Access to technical information through a secured Web site

- Use of MCDBA logos on stationery and business cards

- Invitations to Microsoft-sponsored conferences and technical briefings

- A free one-year subscription to *SQL Server Magazine*

- A free subscription to *Microsoft Certified Professional* magazine

Microsoft Certified Database Administrator (MCDBA)

Attaining this certification requires passing five exams. Candidates must pass all four core exams and one of five available electives. The core exams cover both Microsoft SQL Server and the operating system on which it runs—Windows NT Server.

The candidate is expected to have hands-on experience with SQL Server and Windows NT Server prior to attempting the exam. Microsoft's Web site provides exam guidelines, sample tests, and links to authorized training providers (see the "Microsoft Resources" section that follows).

Who Needs It

The MCDBA certification is an excellent way to demonstrate your proficiency with SQL server and Windows NT Server for potential clients or employers. This certification can also be valuable to support and help-desk personnel.

Requirements for Certification

The certification process requires the following steps:

1. Pass all four core exams listed in Table 12.2.

2. Pass one of the elective exams listed in Table 12.3.

T A B L E 12.2: MCDBA Core Exams

Exam	Test ID
Administering Microsoft SQL Server 7.0	70-028
Designing and Implementing Databases with Microsoft SQL Server 7.0	70-029
Implementing and Supporting Microsoft Windows NT Server 4.0	70-067
Implementing and Supporting Microsoft Windows NT Server 4.0 in the Enterprise	70-068

T A B L E 12.3: MCDBA Elective Exams

Exam	Test ID
Designing and Implementing Distributed Applications with Microsoft Visual C++ 6	70-015
Designing and Implementing Data Warehouses with Microsoft SQL Server 7.0	70-019
Internetworking with Microsoft TCP/IP on Microsoft Windows NT 4.0	70-059
Implementing and Supporting Microsoft Internet Information Server 4.0	70-087
Designing and Implementing Distributed Applications with Microsoft Visual Basic 6	70-175

Administrator

Microsoft tests are administered by Sylvan Prometric and Virtual University Enterprises (VUE). To register for a test with VUE visit the

VUE Web site (http://www.vue.com/student-services/). Call Sylvan at (800) 755-3926 to register for Microsoft tests; if outside the U.S., use the online Sylvan Test Center Locator at http://www.sylvanpro-metric.com to find the nearest testing center. Chapter 3, "Taking Your Test," contains detailed information on taking tests from Sylvan or VUE.

Fee

Test fee is $100.

Format

These are multiple-choice, closed-book tests. The number of questions and time limit depend on the test selected.

Microsoft Resources

For more information on this certification program, contact Microsoft at:

Web	http://www.microsoft.com/mcp/
E-mail	mcp@msprograms.com
Mail	Microsoft Corporation
	One Microsoft Way
	Redmond, WA 98052-6399
Phone	(800) 636-7544
Fax	(425) 936-7329

Oracle Certifications

- Certified Database Administrator

- Certified Application Developer

Oracle produces a number of different software programs, but the company is best known for its Oracle database system. The

Oracle Certified Professional program offers two certification paths: the Certified Database Administrator and the Certified Application Developer.

Recertification or Maintenance Requirements

Oracle announces requirements for recertification based on the release of new products and upgrades. Previously obtained certifications are valid for six months following an announcement of recertification requirements.

Benefits of Certification

Oracle Certified Professionals receive:

- Use of Oracle Certified Professional logo
- Certificate

Certified Database Administrator

To become an Oracle Certified Database Administrator, you must pass either four or five tests, depending on the version of Oracle you select as your specialization. These exams cover knowledge of the essential aspects of the SQL language, Oracle administration, backup and recovery, networking, and performance tuning of the system. Candidates can specialize in either Oracle 7.3 or Oracle 8.

Who Needs It

The Certified Database Administrator credential demonstrates your skill and expertise in administering Oracle database systems. If your company is already using Oracle, this certification may be a great way to advance your career.

Requirements for Certification

The certification process requires the following steps:

1. Pass the Introduction to Oracle: SQL and PL/SQL exam.

2. Pass the required exams for your specialization (see Table 12.4).

3. Sign the certification agreement and submit it to Oracle.

T A B L E 12.4: Oracle Certified Database Administrator Exams

Specialization	Required Exams
Oracle 7.3	Oracle 7.3 Database Administration
	Oracle 7.3 Backup and Recovery
	Oracle 7.3 Performance and Tuning
Oracle 8	Oracle 8 Database Administration
	Oracle 8 Backup and Recovery
	Oracle 8 Performance and Tuning
	Oracle 8 Network Administration

NOTE If you fail a test, you must wait at least 30 days before you retake that exam. You may attempt a particular test up to three times in a twelve-month period. Requests for exemption from this requirement must be made in writing to Robert Pedigo, Manager, Oracle Certified Professional Program, Oracle Corporation, 500 Oracle Parkway-M/S SB-4, Redwood Shores, CA 94065.

Administrator

Oracle exams are administered by Sylvan Prometric. Call (800) 891-3926 to register for Oracle tests; if outside the U.S., use the online Sylvan Test Center Locator at http://www.sylvanprometric.com to find the nearest testing center. (See Chapter 3, "Taking Your Test," for detailed information on taking tests from Sylvan.)

Fee

The fee is $125 per exam.

Format

The exams are multiple-choice tests consisting of 60 to 70 questions that must be completed in 90 minutes.

Certified Application Developer

To become an Oracle Certified Application Developer for Developer/2000, you must pass five tests. These exams cover knowledge of the essential aspects of the SQL language, creating procedures using Oracle Procedure Builder, using Developer/2000, and managing the user interface. Candidates can specialize in Developer/2000 Release 1 or Developer/2000 Release 2.

Who Needs It

The Certified Application Developer credential demonstrates your skill and expertise in developing Oracle database systems. If your company is already using Oracle, this certification can be a great way to advance your career.

Requirements for Certification

The certification process requires the following steps:

1. Pass the Introduction to Oracle: SQL and PL/SQL exam.

2. Pass the Developer PL/SQL Program Units exam.

3. Pass the required exams for your specialization (see Table 12.5).

4. Sign the certification agreement and send it to Oracle.

TABLE 12.5: Oracle Certified Application Developer Exams

Specialization	Required Exams
Developer/2000 Release 1	Developer/2000 Forms 4.5 I Developer/2000 Forms 4.5 II Developer/2000 Reports 2.5
Developer/2000 Release 2	Developer/2000 Build Forms I Developer/2000 Build Forms II Developer/2000 Build Reports

NOTE If you fail a test, you must wait at least 30 days before you retake that exam. You may attempt a particular test up to three times in a twelve-month period. Requests for exemption from this requirement must be made in writing to Robert Pedigo, Manager, Oracle Certified Professional Program, Oracle Corporation, 500 Oracle Parkway-M/S SB-4, Redwood Shores, CA 94065.

Administrator

Oracle exams are administered by Sylvan Prometric. Call (800) 891-3926 to register for Oracle tests; if outside the U.S., use the online Sylvan Test Center Locator at http://www.sylvanprometric.com to find the nearest testing center. (See Chapter 3, "Taking Your Test," for detailed information on taking tests from Sylvan.)

Fee

The fee is $125 for each exam.

Format

The exams are multiple-choice tests consisting of 60 to 70 questions that must be completed in 90 minutes.

Oracle Resources

The Oracle Web site offers a program guide that details the objectives for each exam. For more information on this organization's certifications and courses, contact Oracle at:

Web	http://www.oracle.com/
Mail	Oracle Corporation
	500 Oracle Parkway
	Redwood Shores, CA 94065
Phone	(650) 506-7000
Fax	(650) 506-7200

Sybase Certifications

- Sybase Certified Associate
- Sybase Certified Professional

Sybase produces the PowerBuilder database application development tool, as well as Adaptive Server Enterprise 11.5, and the Sybase SQL server database system. The Sybase Certified Associate program offers three specializations: PowerBuilder Developer, Adaptive Server Administrator, and SQL Developer. The Sybase Certified Professional program, which builds on the Associate-level program, offers specializations in PowerBuilder Developer and Adaptive Server Administrator.

At this time, Sybase is still offering certification programs on its SQL Server 11 and PowerBuilder 5 products. For information on these programs check the Sybase Web site (see the "Sybase Resources" section below for information on how to access this site).

Recertification or Maintenance Requirements

To ensure that skills are kept current, all Sybase-certified professionals are encouraged to take a migration test with each major new release of PowerBuilder. Certifications offered in the Sybase program are based on specific product versions. Certified professionals may represent themselves as certified for only the specific product and product version listed on their certificate.

Benefits of Certification

Sybase Certified Associates and Professionals receive the following benefits:

- Certificate and ID card
- Logo

- Name included in the Adaptive Server Administrator Directory (a listing of database administrators), or the PowerBuilder Developer Directory (a listing of client/server developers). These are lists that employers can consult to locate qualified technical professionals.

Sybase Certified Associate

The Sybase Certified Associate certification is the first level of certification offered by Sybase, and offers specializations in three products. It is a prerequisite to obtaining certification as a Sybase Certified Professional. Sybase offers instructor-led and self-study courses for each specialization. One exam is required for each of the following specializations:

- PowerBuilder Developer

- Adaptive Server Administrator

- SQL Developer

Those who want to specialize in PowerBuilder Developer need to have proficiency in fundamental and advanced PowerBuilder 6. Sybase recommends that candidates have six months' PowerBuilder experience and take these four courses: Fast Track to PowerBuilder, Mastering Data Windows, Advanced PowerBuilder Controls, and Building Object-Oriented Applications with PowerBuilder.

Those who want to specialize in Adaptive Server Administrator need to have skill in designing, administering, and supporting Sybase Adaptive Server Enterprise 11.5. Sybase recommends that candidates have three months' experience with the product and take these three courses: Fast Track to Adaptive Server Enterprise 11.5, System & Database Administration for ASE 11.5, and Powering UP with ASE 11.5.

Those who want to specialize in SQL Developer need to have skill in designing applications and writing effective SQL code. Sybase recommends that candidates have three months of database development experience with the product and take these four courses: Fast Track to Adaptive Server Enterprise 11.5, Advanced Transact SQL, Logical Database Design, and Physical Database Design.

Who Needs It

The Sybase Certified Associate credential is valuable if you want to get a job creating client-server applications or administering Sybase databases. It can also be a valuable title for independent consultants and contractors who want to document their abilities for potential clients.

Requirements for Certification

The certification process requires only one step:

1. Pass the exam required for the desired specialization, as listed below in Table 12.6.

T A B L E 12.6: Sybase Certified Associate Exams

Specialization	Required Exam	Test ID
PowerBuilder Developer	Certified PowerBuilder 6 Associate	510-301
Adaptive Server Administrator	ASE 11.5 Server Administration (Associate-level) OR	510-011
	ASE 11.5 Migration	510-010
SQL Developer	SQL Developer	510-013

Administrator

Sybase tests are administered by Sylvan Prometric and Virtual University Enterprises (VUE). To register for a test with VUE call (800) 243-7184 or visit the VUE Web site (http://www.vue.com/student-services/). Call Sylvan at (800) 407-3926 to register for Sybase tests; if outside the U.S., use the online Sylvan Test Center Locator at http://www.sylvanprometric.com to find the nearest testing center. (Chapter 3, "Taking Your Test," contains more information on taking tests from Sylvan or VUE.)

Fee

Fees for Sybase tests can vary; call Sylvan Prometric at (800) 407-3926 or VUE at (800) 243-7184 for pricing.

Format

Each test has approximately 60 multiple-choice questions. Contact Sylvan at (800) 407-3926 or VUE at (800) 243-7184 for the latest information on the number of questions and passing score.

Sybase Certified Professional

The Sybase Certified Professional certification is Sybase's advanced-level certification program. It builds on the Sybase Certified Associate credential. Sybase offers instructor-led and self-study courses for each specialization. One exam is required for each of the following specializations:

- PowerBuilder Developer

- Adaptive Server Administrator

Candidates for the specialization in PowerBuilder Developer need to have an in-depth understanding of PowerBuilder and experience in building real-world applications. Sybase recommends that candidates have at least twelve months' experience with PowerBuilder and take these two courses: Building PowerBuilder Distributed Applications and Building PowerBuilder Internet Applications.

Candidates for the specialization in Adaptive Server Administrator need to have proficiency in database administration and advanced performance, design, optimization, disaster management, and tuning concepts. Sybase recommends that candidates have at least three to six months' experience with Adaptive Server Enterprise and take the Sybase course entitled Performance and Tuning for DBAs: ASE 11.5.

Who Needs It

The Sybase Certified Professional credential is valuable if you want to get a high-level job creating client/server applications and/or administering Sybase servers. It can also be a valuable title for independent consultants and contractors who want to document their abilities for potential clients.

Requirements for Certification

The certification process requires the following steps:

1. Achieve Sybase Certified Associate certification. The Associate-level certification should be in the same specialization as the desired Professional-level certification.

2. Pass the exam for the desired specialization (see Table 12.7).

T A B L E 12.7: Sybase Certified Professional Exams

Specialization	Required Exam	Test ID
PowerBuilder	Certified PowerBuilder 6 Professional Migration	510-303
Adaptive Server Administrator	ASE 11.5 Server Administration (Professional)	510-012

Administrator

Sybase tests are administered by Sylvan Prometric and Virtual University Enterprises (VUE). To register for a test with VUE call (800) 243-7184 or visit the VUE Web site (http://www.vue.com/student-services/). Call Sylvan at (800) 407-3926 to register for Sybase tests; if outside the U.S., use the online Sylvan Test Center Locator at http://www.sylvanprometric.com to find the nearest testing center. (Chapter 3, "Taking Your Test," contains more information on taking tests from Sylvan or VUE.)

Fee

Fees for Sybase tests can vary; call Sylvan Prometric at (800) 407-3926 or VUE at (800) 243-7184 for pricing.

Format

Each test has 60 multiple-choice questions. Contact Sylvan at (800) 407-3926 or VUE at (800) 243-7184 for the latest information on the number of questions and passing score.

Sybase Resources

The Sybase Web site offers study guides that detail the objectives of each exam. Sybase also offers a number of self-study and instructor-led courses through Sybase Authorized Education Partners. For more information on this organization's certifications and courses, contact Sybase at:

Web	http://slc.sybase.com/
Mail	SYBASE, Inc.
	Corporate Headquarters
	6475 Christie Avenue
	Emeryville, CA 94608-1050
Phone	(800) 8-SYBASE
Faxback	(888) 792-7329

CHAPTER

13

Internet Certifications

- HyCurve Certifications

- IBM Certification

- Learning Tree International Certifications

- Microsoft Certifications

- Novell Certifications

- Open Market Certification

- ProsoftTraining.com Certifications

T he list of certification programs related to the Internet is growing and changing rapidly. Within the past year, almost every Internet certification program has been redesigned. New vendor-based certification programs have emerged almost every month. As yet, however, no single Internet certification has become known as the one best certification to get. We have tried to include in this chapter the most interesting and reputable offerings that were available at the time we went to press. Be sure to check the Certification Update Web site for the latest information; several new Internet certification programs are currently under development (see Appendix B for details on how to access the Web site). Certification programs related to Internet security are now covered in a separate chapter (see Chapter 14, "Computer and Network Security Certifications," for descriptions of computer and network security certification programs).

Most of the growth and change in Internet certifications has paralleled the burgeoning growth in the use of the Internet by business and industry. Many companies desperately want to hire professionals who can design, implement, and maintain an Internet presence for their organizations. As a result, many individuals have found that it was worthwhile to spend $5,000 to $10,000 on training and certification in order to snag a high-paying job with such a company.

Professionals seeking an Internet certification might include:

- Webmasters
- Web page designers
- Internet service provider staff
- Java, Perl, or ActiveX programmers
- Internet and intranet managers
- Network administrators

To promote quality in existing and emerging Internet certification programs, the Association of Internet Professionals has developed standards—in the form of a "common core" of skills—to provide benchmarks that all Internet certifications should test. They would like to see this "core" applied to all academic, organization-based, and vendor-based Internet certification programs. This will help certification candidates to distinguish which programs meet basic quality standards by looking for the Association of Internet Professionals endorsement (see http://www.association.org/ for more information on this topic).

This chapter covers both vendor-specific and vendor-independent certification programs that address Internet strategies, procedures, and protocols. HyCurve, formerly named USWeb Learning, is an Internet training company that offers certification programs in Web design, Web administration, and Web application development. IBM offers the IBM Certified Solutions Expert certification in Net.Commerce, which addresses security for financial transactions on the Internet. The Learning Tree International certification program now offers three vendor-independent Internet credentials. Microsoft now offers the new Microsoft Certified Professional (MCP) + Site Building credential, which focuses on skills related to the design, implementation and maintenance of interactive Web sites. Microsoft also offers the Microsoft Certified Professional (MCP) + Internet and Microsoft Certified Systems Engineer (MCSE) + Internet certifications, which document skills related to the implementation of intranet and Internet solutions using Microsoft products. Novell offers the Certified Internet Professional program, which provides four certifications for Internet professionals. Open Market's Certified Internet Engineer (CIE) program certifies those who use Folio products for Internet commerce. ProsoftTraining.com, previously known as Prosoft/Net Guru Technologies, offers certification programs in all aspects of the Internet, from Web site design and business strategies to server administration.

Alternatives in Internet Training and Certification

If you aren't currently interested in completing a vendor-based certification program, there are other ways to document your knowledge in specific areas. There are a growing number of companies that offer certifications

Continued

on a per-course basis. That is, after completing one of their courses you can take a certification exam and become "certified" for that particular course from that company.

Some people may find this type of documentation useful in their jobs. It can impress the supervisor who has paid to send you to training— not only did you attend and complete the course, but you also passed the certification exam! One of the most widely-known companies that offer such per-course certifications is CyberTech. CyberTech has taken this approach online with a series of self-study courses and certification tests.

CyberTech

CyberTech Certification involves a process of online self-study in conjunction with an online or CyberTech Testing Center administered test. CyberTech offers most of these certification tests for under $100. The fee covers:

- The actual CyberTech Certification exam at a Registered Testing Center

- Online, printable textbooks/courseware

- Online pretests with links to correct answers in textbooks

- One free preview test to give you an idea of what to expect on the certification exam

- Upon successful completion of the test, a listing in CyberTech GOLD (Graduate On-Line Database), a job placement database, and a CyberTech Certification Certificate

CyberTech currently offers certification tests on over 100 courses. For a complete listing and more detailed information contact CyberTech at:

Web: `http://www.getcertified.com/`
E-mail: `info@cy-tech.com`
Mail: CyberTech Institute, Inc.
          6029 Memorial Hwy.
          Tampa, FL 33615
Phone: (888) 467-1500
Fax: (813) 882-9237

Use Table 13.1 below to compare the number of required tests, the test format, the approximate costs of taking the test(s), number of required courses, costs of any required courses, and the relative difficulty of the certification programs in this chapter. The cost information is a general guideline; since things change rapidly in the world of certification programs, once you have selected a specific course of action you may want to double-check the costs.

We classified the difficulty of these certifications into three categories—Moderate, Challenging, and Very Challenging—based on the number of required tests and courses, and the relative difficulty of those tests or lab exams. These ratings are approximate and are offered simply as a general guide to help the reader distinguish between entry-level programs and those that require more advanced skill and knowledge. (This rating scale assumes that one has experience with the product or technology and has studied the appropriate subject content before attempting the exams.)

T A B L E 13.1: Internet Certification Programs

Certification	# of Required Tests	Test Format(s)	Total Cost of Required Tests	# of Required Courses	Total Cost of Required Courses	Difficulty	Notes
HyCurve Certifications							
HyCurve Web Design Specialist	3	MC	$325	—	—	◖	Additional vendor exams are also required.
HyCurve Administration Specialist	3	MC	$325	—	—	◖	Additional vendor exams are also required.
HyCurve Applications Specialist	3	MC	$325	—	—	◖	Additional vendor exams are also required.

T A B L E 13.1: Internet Certification Programs *(continued)*

Certification	# of Required Tests	Test Format(s)	Total Cost of Required Tests	# of Required Courses	Total Cost of Required Courses	Difficulty	Notes
IBM Certification							
Certified Solutions Expert: Net.Commerce	1	MC	VF	—	—	○	
Learning Tree Certifications							
Internet/Intranet Certified Professional Certified Professional	5	MC	CV	5	$12,000–$14,000	◑	Discount pricing available; contact Learning Tree.
Web Administration and Development Certified Professional	5	MC	CV	5	$12,000–$14,000	◑	Discount pricing available; contact Learning Tree.
Notes/Domino Certified Professional	5	MC	CV	5	$12,000–$14,000	◑	Discount pricing available; contact Learning Tree.
Microsoft Certifications							
Microsoft Certified Professional (MCP) + Internet	3	MC	$300	—	—	◑	
Microsoft Certified Professional (MCP) + Site Building	2	MC	$200	—	—	○	
Microsoft Certified Systems Engineer (MCSE) + Internet	9	MC	$900	—	—	●	

T A B L E 13.1: Internet Certification Programs *(continued)*

Certification	# of Required Tests	Test Format(s)	Total Cost of Required Tests	# of Required Courses	Total Cost of Required Courses	Difficulty	Notes
Novell Certifications							
Certified Internet Business Strategist	1	MC	VF	—	—	◯	
Certified Web Designer	4	MC	VF	—	—	◑	
Certified Intranet Manager	5	MC	VF	—	—	◑	
Certified Internet Architect	5	MC	VF	—	—	◑	
Open Market Certification							
Folio 4 Certified Infobase Engineer	2	MC	$190	—	—	◑	
ProsoftTraining.com Certifications							
Certified Internet Webmaster (CIW) Level 1	1	MC	CV	—	—	◯	
Certified Internet Webmaster (CIW) Level 2	2–3	MC	$300–$450	—	—	◑	Specializations include Site Designer, Application Developer, Enterprise Developer, Server Administrator, Internetworking Professional, Security Professional, and E-Commerce Professional.

Certification Difficulty: ◯ Moderate   ◑ Challenging   ● Very Challenging

Test Format:
MC: Multiple Choice   **AT:** Adaptive Testing   **LA:** Live Application
PR: Hands-on Lab   **NA:** Not Applicable

Test Fee:
VF: Test Fees can vary; consult testing center.   **CV:** Voucher for taking the exam is included in the fee for the required course(s); additional attempts cost extra.

HyCurve Certifications

- HyCurve Web Design Specialist

- HyCurve Administration Specialist

- HyCurve Applications Specialist

HyCurve, formerly known as USWeb Learning, is a training company that offers several new certifications for the Internet professional. While HyCurve maintains close ties with the USWeb organization, it is a separate company headquartered in San Francisco, CA. HyCurve certifications include both vendor-neutral and vendor-specific portions. Three certification programs are currently available, and several more will be offered soon.

Recertification or Maintenance Requirements

There are currently no recertification or maintenance requirements for HyCurve certifications.

Benefits of Certification

Certified HyCurve Specialists receive the following benefit:

- Certificate

NOTE HyCurve is currently developing several additional certifications, such as the HyCurve Security Specialist. Check the Certification Update Web site periodically to get the latest information.

HyCurve Web Design Specialist

This certification targets the skills needed by graphic designers and multimedia producers. Attaining this certification involves passing three HyCurve exams plus a vendor-based Web design exam. The candidate has a choice of Corel or Adobe specialization.

Certification candidates are expected to have experience with HTML design and programs such as Adobe Photoshop. HyCurve Web Design Specialists must be able to do the following:

- Design effective user interfaces and navigation for a Web site.

- Identify the appropriate level of interactivity for target audiences.

- Apply effective design principles, such as storyboarding, page layout, font usage, color, and interactivity, to Web site design.

- Optimize graphical and multimedia elements to address bandwidth, cross-platform, and cross-browser issues.

- Create and incorporate multimedia elements, such as animations, audio, and streaming video, for Web sites.

HyCurve offers optional exam preparation courses that cover the above topics.

Who Needs It

This certification is an excellent way to show current or potential employers that you know how to design an interactive and graphically sound Web site. This credential can also be of value to consultants who do independent Web design work and want to validate their expertise for clients.

Requirements for Certification

The certification process requires the following steps:

1. Pass the Building Web Documents with HTML exam (VUE ID: 1210s; Sylvan ID: HC0-121).

2. Pass the Planning Web Site Requirements exam (VUE ID: 1250s; Sylvan ID: HC0-125).

3. Pass the Information & Media Design for the Web exam (VUE ID: 4510s; Sylvan ID: HC0-451).

4. Pass the required test for the vendor specialization you seek. See Table 13.2 for a listing of approved vendor exams.

T A B L E 13.2: Vendor Specialization Exams for the HyCurve Web Design Specialist Certification

Vendor Specialization	Test	Test ID
Adobe	Photoshop 5	9A0-006
	OR	
	Illustrator 7	9A0-005
Corel	CorelDraw 5	CorelDraw 5

Administrator

HyCurve tests are administered by Sylvan Prometric and Virtual University Enterprises (VUE). To register for a test with VUE visit the VUE Web site (http://www.vue.com/student-services/) or call (877) 411-4141. Call Sylvan at (800) 631-3926 to register for HyCurve tests; if outside the U.S., use the online Sylvan Test Center Locator at http://www.sylvanprometric.com to find the nearest testing center. Chapter 3, "Taking Your Test," contains detailed information on taking tests from Sylvan or VUE.

Fee

The Building Web Documents with HTML and Planning Web Site Requirements exams cost $100 each. The Information & Media Design for the Web exam costs $125. See Chapter 6, "Software Certifications," for pricing on Adobe and Corel exams.

Format

HyCurve exams consist of 45 to 50 multiple-choice questions and must be completed in one hour.

HyCurve Administration Specialist

This certification track is for system administrators and Webmasters who have experience supporting network services in a UNIX or Windows NT environment. The HyCurve Administration Specialist provides the day-to-day management of Internet services, including: determining technical requirements, installing and configuring Web servers, administering security procedures, and performing post-installation testing.

The HyCurve Administration Specialist candidate must be able to do the following:

- Plan Web server system requirements and provide capacity planning procedures.

- Install and configure a Web server, e-mail server, news server, telnet server, and supporting software-search engines, SSL encryption, anonymous FTP, push technologies, streaming technologies, and collaborative technologies.

- Provide security and authentication management services.

- Administer Web server applications, including custom applications, client server requests, and executable programs.

- Provide strategies to improve Web server performance and troubleshoot problems.

HyCurve offers optional exam preparation courses that cover the above topics.

Who Needs It

This certification is an excellent way to show current or potential employers that you know how to deploy and maintain a Web server. This credential can also be of value to consultants who do independent Web server administration work and want to validate their expertise for clients.

Requirements for Certification

The certification process requires the following steps:

1. Pass the Building Web Documents with HTML exam (VUE ID: 1210s; Sylvan ID: HC0-121).

2. Pass the Planning Web Site Requirements exam (VUE ID: 1250s; Sylvan ID: HC0-125).

3. Pass the Performing Effective Internet Administration exam (VUE ID: 3510s; Sylvan ID: HC0-351).

4. Pass the required test for the vendor specialization you seek. See Table 13.3 for a listing of approved vendor exams.

TABLE 13.3: Vendor specialization exams for the HyCurve Administration Specialist certification

Vendor Specialization	Test	Test ID
Microsoft	Implementing and Supporting Miscrosoft IIS Server 4 OR	70-087
	Designing and Implementing Commerce Solutions with Microsoft Site Server 3	70-057
Santa Cruz Operation	SCO UNIX System OR	090-001
	SCO OpenServer Release 5	090-052
Novell	Web Server Management	050-710
Lotus	Domino Web Development	190-281

Administrator

HyCurve tests are administered by Sylvan Prometric and Virtual University Enterprises (VUE). To register for a test with VUE visit the VUE Web site (http://www.vue.com/student-services/) or call (877) 411-4141. Call Sylvan at (800) 631-3926 to register for HyCurve tests; if outside the U.S., use the online Sylvan Test Center Locator at www.sylvanprometric.com to find the nearest testing center. Chapter 3 contains detailed information on taking tests from Sylvan or VUE.

Fee

The Building Web Documents with HTML and Planning Web Site Requirements exams cost $100 each. The Performing Effective Internet Administration exam costs $125. See Chapter 9, "Network Operating Systems Certifications," for pricing information on Microsoft and Novel exams. See Chapter 6, "Software Certifications," for pricing information on Lotus exams. See Chapter 5, "Operating Systems Certifications," for pricing information on Santa Cruz Operation exams.

Format

HyCurve exams consist of 45 to 50 multiple-choice questions and must be completed in one hour.

HyCurve Applications Specialist

This certification track is for programmers and database developers who are responsible for planning and deploying database-powered Web applications. It requires familiarity with object-oriented programming concepts, rudimentary Java, and one dialect of SQL.

The HyCurve Applications Specialist candidate must be able to do the following:

- Evaluate a requirements document and recommend the appropriate database and middleware applications.

- Understand how Internet, intranet, and extranet applications may affect the use of indexes, normalization, and other features of the data model.

- Determine effective security measures to protect sensitive data.

- Write server-side functions and client-side applications.

- Create and implement testing and deployment plans.

HyCurve offers optional exam preparation courses that cover the above topics.

Who Needs It

This certification is an excellent way to show current or potential employers that you know how to develop Web-based applications. This credential can also be of value to consultants who do independent Web development work and want to validate their expertise for clients.

Requirements for Certification

The certification process requires the following steps:

1. Pass the Building Web Documents with HTML exam (VUE ID: 1210s; Sylvan ID: HC0-121).

2. Pass the Planning Web Site Requirements exam (VUE ID: 1250s; Sylvan ID: HC0-125).

3. Pass the Planning and Deploying Web Applications exam (VUE ID: 6510s; Sylvan ID: HC0-651).

4. Pass the required test for the vendor specialization you seek. See Table 13.4 for a listing of approved vendor exams.

T A B L E 13.4: Vendor Specialization Exams for the HyCurve Applications Specialist Certification

Vendor Specialization	Test	Test ID
Oracle	Introduction to Oracle: SQL and PL/SQL	1
Microsoft	Implementing a Database Design on Microsoft SQL Server OR	70-027
	Designing and Implementing Web Solutions with Microsoft Visual InterDev 6 OR	70-152
	Designing and Implementing Distributed Applications with Microsoft Visual Basic	70-175
Lotus	Notes Application Development	*190-271 or **190-171
Sun	Sun Certified Java Programmer	310-020
Sybase	Certified PowerBuilder 6.0 Associate	360-301
IBM	VisualAge for Java Enterprise Edition	084

*multiple choice
**live application

Administrator

HyCurve tests are administered by Sylvan Prometric and Virtual University Enterprises (VUE). To register for a test with VUE visit the VUE Web site (http://www.vue.com/student-services/) or call (877) 411-4141. Call Sylvan at (800) 631-3926 to register for HyCurve tests; if outside the U.S., use the online Sylvan Test Center Locator at http://www.sylvanprometric.com to find the nearest testing center. Chapter 3 contains detailed information on taking tests from Sylvan or VUE.

Fee

The Building Web Documents with HTML and Planning Web Site Requirements exams cost $100 each. The Planning and Deploying Web Applications exam costs $125. See Chapter 12, "Client/Server and Database System Certifications," for pricing on Oracle, Microsoft, and Sybase exams. See Chapter 6, "Software Certifications," for information on the Lotus exam and Chapter 7, "Programming Certifications," for information on the Sun exam.

Format

HyCurve exams consist of 45 to 50 multiple-choice questions and must be completed in one hour.

HyCurve Resources

HyCurve offers courses that map directly to the tests listed in Table 13.4. For more information on this organization's certification program and courses, contact HyCurve at:

Web	http://www.HyCurve.com/
E-mail	info@hycurve.com
Mail	185 Berry Street, Suite 3500
	San Francisco, CA 94107
Phone	(415) 371-5300
FAX	(415) 371-7971

IBM Certification

- IBM Certified Solutions Expert—Net Commerce

IBM offers the IBM Certified Solutions Expert—Net.Commerce credential based on its Net.Commerce product. The Net.Commerce product facilitates secure financial transactions on the Internet.

NOTE IBM offers another Internet-related certification: the IBM Certified Solutions Expert—Firewall. This certification is based on the Firewall product, which facilitates security for links between the Internet and private company intranets. For information on this certification, see Chapter 14, "Computer and Network Security Certifications."

Recertification or Maintenance Requirements

IBM Internet certifications apply to specific version numbers of the Net.Commerce product, so there is no requirement for recertification on a particular version. Since your certification is tied to a specific version of a product, however, you will want to become certified on the newest versions, when they become available, if you want to continue to have the most current credential in this area.

Benefits of Certification

IBM Certified Solutions Experts receive these benefits:

- Certificate
- Wallet-size certificate
- Lapel pin
- Use of certification logo

Certified Solutions Expert—Net.Commerce

To attain certification as an IBM Certified Solutions Expert in Net.Commerce, a candidate must pass one exam. The exam for this certification covers planning, configuring, and implementing Net.Commerce to meet customer needs for secure financial transactions over the Internet. IBM recommends that the candidate have hands-on experience with the Net.Commerce System, and Windows NT and/or AIX (IBM's version of UNIX) prior to taking the exam. In addition, IBM recommends that candidates have working knowledge of TCP/IP, Secure Sockets Layer (SSL), Hyper-Text Transfer Protocol (HTTP), and HyperText Transfer Protocol Secured (HTTPS).

Who Needs It

This certification is an excellent credential for those responsible for Internet "store fronts" and other financial transactions over the Internet. It can also be valuable to consultants who design and implement Internet stores for clients.

Requirements for Certification

The certification process requires only one step:

1. Pass the Planning, Implementing, and Supporting IBM Net.Commerce Version 3 Product exam (Test ID: 000-451).

Administrator

Tests are administered by Sylvan Prometric; call (800) 959-3926 to register for IBM tests; if outside the U.S., use the online Sylvan Test Center Locator at http://www.sylvanprometric.com/ to find the nearest testing center. (See Chapter 3 for additional information on Sylvan Prometric.)

Fee

Fees for IBM tests vary based on test length and format; call Sylvan Prometric at (800) 959-3926 for pricing.

Format

The exam is a computer-based, multiple-choice test. Call Sylvan Prometric at (800) 959-3926 for current information on the number of questions, time limit, and passing score.

IBM Resources

IBM's Web site offers a number of excellent resources for certification candidates, including test objectives, study guides, and a sample test. For more information on this organization's certifications and courses, contact IBM at:

Web	`http://www.ibm.com/certify`
E-mail	`certify@us.ibm.com`
Mail	The Professional Certification Program from IBM
	Mail Drop 3013
	11400 Burnet Road
	Austin, TX 78758
Phone	(800) IBM-TEACH ((800) 426-8322)
Fax	(512) 838-7961

Learning Tree International Certifications

- Internet/Intranet Certified Professional

- Web Administration and Development Certified Professional

- Notes/Domino Certified Professional

Learning Tree International is a worldwide training organization that currently offers over 150 computer and networking courses in the United States, Europe, and Asia. As part of their curriculum in information technology, Learning Tree International offers 27 different vendor-independent professional certification programs, three of which are Internet-related. (For information on additional Learning Tree International certification programs, see Chapters 4, 5, 7, and 8.)

The Learning Tree International Internet/Intranet Certified Professional certification is based on the mastery of a comprehensive set of internetworking service and support courses. This credential may be useful to Webmasters, network support staff, Internet service providers, network engineers, and anyone else involved with the maintenance and support of intranets and Internet connections.

The Learning Tree International Web Administration and Development Certified Professional certification is based on the mastery of a comprehensive set of Web design and development courses. This credential may be useful to administrators, developers, Webmasters, intranet/Internet specialists, and others responsible for developing and maintaining Web sites.

The Learning Tree International Notes/Domino Certified Professional certification is based on the mastery of a set of courses on Notes and Domino development and administration. This credential may be useful to applications developers, network support specialists, programmers, and others who implement, administer, and support Notes applications and Domino Web sites.

Recertification or Maintenance Requirements

There is no recertification requirement for any of Learning Tree International's certification programs.

NOTE   It is possible to obtain college credit for Learning Tree International certifications or courses. The American Council of Education (ACE) in Washington, D.C., has worked in cooperation with Learning Tree International to determine college course equivalencies for these courses and certifications. Approximately 1,500 colleges and universities in the United States will accept ACE recommendations for college credit. As a general rule, ACE will recommend two college credit hours for each four-day course. Learning Tree International will pay to have your Learning Tree International credentials registered with ACE and you can then request that your transcript be sent from ACE to any college or university. (Check with your college or university registrar to make sure that your institution accepts ACE recommendations for credit.)

Benefits of Certification

Learning Tree International PC Service and Support Certified Professionals receive the following benefits:

- A framed diploma of Professional Certification
- An official record of the courses that you have completed
- The option to obtain college credit

Internet/Intranet Certified Professional

This certification program consists of taking four core courses and one elective course, and passing the tests given at the end of each course. The courses and exams are designed to teach and test the candidate's ability to choose and implement various Internet connection options; install, configure, and maintain an Internet or intranet server; develop a Web site using HTML and CGI; use all major TCP/IP application services including FTP, Gopher, and Web browsers; analyze security threats from the Internet; and develop a comprehensive security policy to protect an organization's systems and data.

Who Needs It

The Learning Tree International Internet/Intranet Certified Professional credential is a respected vendor-independent certification for those who want to develop Web site strategies for businesses, design and implement intranets, or connect internal networks to the Internet. Since the certification program requires comprehensive training classes, Learning Tree International certifications offer a means for those just beginning their networking careers to gain hands-on experience and training that may not currently be available on the job.

Requirements for Certification

The certification process requires the following steps:

1. Complete the four core courses listed in Table 13.5, and pass the test given at the end of each course.

2. Complete ONE of the elective courses from Table 13.6 and pass the test given at the end of the course.

T A B L E 13.5: Required Courses/Tests for Internet/Intranet Certified Professional

Course Name	Course/ Test ID	Course Length
Introduction to the Internet and Intranets for Business: Hands-On	469	4 days
Developing a Web Site: Hands-On	470	4 days
Intranet Technologies: A Comprehensive Hands-On Introduction	475	4 days
Implementing Web Security: Hands-On	486	4 days

T A B L E 13.6: Elective Courses/Tests for Internet/Intranet Certified Professional

Course Name	Course/ Test ID	Course Length
Hands-On Java Programming	471	4 days
Hands-On Microsoft Internet Information Server 4	163	4 days
Netscape Servers for Intranet Development: Hands-On	485	5 days
Oracle Web Application Server: A Comprehensive Hands-On Introduction	238	4 days
Perl Programming: Hands-On	431	4 days
Hands-On Introduction to TCP/IP	367	4 days
Hands-On Microsoft Internet Information Server 4	163	4 days
Domino Web Site Development: Hands-On	182	4 days

TABLE 13.6: Elective Courses/Tests for Internet/Intranet Certified Professional *(continued)*

Course Name	Course/ Test ID	Course Length
Hands-On JavaScript: Building Interactive Web Sites	489	4 days
Internet and Intranet Security: A Comprehensive Introduction	468	4 days
Hands-On Visual InterDev	408	4 days

Administrator

Tests are administered by Learning Tree International (call (800) THE-TREE).

Fee

At this writing, the prices for Learning Tree International courses are $1,295 for a two-day course, $1,745 for a three-day course, $2,195 for a four-day course, and $2,495 for a five-day course. Learning Tree offers some significant discounts for those taking more than one course and for government employees. There is no additional charge for the tests.

Format

Each exam consists of 40 to 60 questions based on the course material. If you fail to pass on the first try, Learning Tree International will arrange for you to take a proctored exam at your place of work.

Web Administration and Development Certified Professional

This certification program consists of taking four core courses and one elective course, and passing the tests given at the end of each course. The courses and exams are designed to teach and test the candidate's ability to install, configure, and secure a Web server for your corporate intranet or Internet Web site; configure database interfaces for your intranet or Internet site; secure Web communications, sites, and electronic commerce applications; exploit the features of your Web server and operating system to tighten security; build powerful Web content using the latest tools and techniques; enhance Web pages using Dynamic HTML, JavaScript, and Java applets; and administer and maintain an intranet or Internet Web site.

Who Needs It

The Learning Tree International Web Administration and Development Certified Professional credential is a respected vendor-independent certification for those who want to establish and maintain an effective presence on the Web. A person with this credential knows how to install and configure a Web server; design attractive, meaningful Web content; carry out secure electronic commerce; and secure Web communications and Web sites. Since the certification program requires comprehensive training classes, Learning Tree International certifications offer a means for those just beginning their networking careers to gain hands-on experience and training that may not currently be available on the job.

Requirements for Certification

The certification process requires the following steps:

1. Complete the three core courses listed in Table 13.7, and pass the test given at the end of each course.

2. Complete the requirement for a fourth core course by taking ONE of the four courses listed in Table 13.8, and passing the test given at the end the course.

3. Complete one of the elective courses from the list in Table 13.9 and pass the test given at the end of the course.

T A B L E 13.7: Required Courses/Tests for Web Administration and Development Certified Professional

Course/Test	Course/ Test ID	Course Length
Developing a Web Site: Hands-On	470	4 days
Implementing Web Security: Hands-On	486	4 days
Designing and Building Great Web Pages: Hands-On	487	4 days

T A B L E 13.8: Options for Required Fourth Course/Test for Web Administration and Development Certified Professional

Course/Test	Course/ Test ID	Course Length
Hands-On Microsoft Internet Information Server 4	163	4 days
Domino Web Site Development: Hands-On	182	4 days
Oracle Web Application Server: A Comprehensive Hands-On Introduction	238	4 days
Netscape Servers for Intranet Development: Hands-On	485	5 days

T A B L E 13.9: Elective Courses/Tests for Web Administration and Development Certified Professional

Course/Test	Course/ Test ID	Course Length
Hands-On Java Programming	471	4 days
Introduction to the Internet and Intranets for Business: Hands-On	469	4 days
Perl Programming: Hands-On	431	4 days

TABLE 13.9: Elective Courses/Tests for Web Administration and Development Certified Professional *(continued)*

Course/Test	Course/Test ID	Course Length
Hands-On Introduction to TCP/IP	367	4 days
Hands-On JavaScript: Building Interactive Web Sites	489	4 days
Internet and Intranet Security: A Comprehensive Introduction	468	4 days
Hands-On Visual InterDev	408	4 days
Windows NT 4 Workstation and Server: Hands-On	455	5 days

Administrator

Courses/tests are administered by Learning Tree International (Call (800) THE-TREE).

Fee

At this writing, the prices for Learning Tree International courses are $1,295 for a two-day course, $1,745 for a three-day course, $2,195 for a four-day course, and $2,495 for a five-day course. Learning Tree offers some significant discounts for those taking more than one course and for government employees. There is no additional charge for the tests.

Format

Each exam consists of 40 to 60 questions based on the course material. If you fail to pass on the first try, Learning Tree International will arrange for you to take a proctored exam at your place of work.

Notes/Domino Certified Professional

This certification program consists of taking four core courses and one elective course, and passing the tests given at the end of each course. The courses and exams are designed to teach and test the candidate's ability to deploy Notes in an organization; build robust client/server applications; migrate existing Notes applications to the Web; install, configure, and manage Lotus Notes networks; support an enterprise-wide workgroup infrastructure; design and develop a Domino Web site; and enhance a Web site with Domino add-ins.

Who Needs It

The Learning Tree International Internet/Intranet Certified Professional credential is a respected vendor-independent certification for those who develop Notes applications and administer Domino Web sites. Since the certification program requires comprehensive training classes, Learning Tree International certifications offer a means for those just beginning their networking careers to gain hands-on experience and training that may not currently be available on the job.

Requirements for Certification

The certification process requires the following steps:

1. Complete the four core courses listed in Table 13.10, and pass the test given at the end of each course.

2. Complete ONE of the elective courses from the list in Table 13.11 and pass the test given at the end of the course.

T A B L E 13.10:   Required Courses/Tests for Notes/Domino Certified Professional

Course/Test	Course/Test ID
Notes and Domino: A Comprehensive Hands-On Introduction	179
Notes Application Development: Hands-On	180
Notes and Domino System Administration: Hands-On	181
Domino Web Site Development: Hands-On	182

TABLE 13.11: Elective Courses/Tests for Notes/Domino Certified Professional

Course/Test	Course/Test ID
Developing a Web Site: Hands-On	470
Internet and Intranet Security: A Comprehensive Introduction	468
Hands-On JavaScript: Building Interactive Web Sites	489
Hands-On Java Programming	471
Java for Enterprise Systems Development: Hands-On	472
Windows NT 4 Workstation and Server: Hands-On	455
Designing and Building Great Web Pages: Hands-On	487
Hands-On Internetworking with TCP/IP	467
Introduction to Client/Server Computing	369
Local Area Networks: Implementation and Configuration	352

Administrator

Course/test administrator is Learning Tree International (call (800) THE-TREE).

Fee

At this writing, the prices for Learning Tree International courses are $1,295 for a two-day course, $1,745 for a three-day course, $2,195 for a four-day course, and $2,495 for a five-day course. Learning Tree offers some significant discounts for those taking more than one course and for government employees. There is no additional charge for the tests.

Format

Each exam consists of 40 to 60 questions based on the course material. If you fail to pass on the first try, Learning Tree International will arrange for you to take a proctored exam at your place of work.

Learning Tree International Resources

For more information about this organization's courses and certification programs, contact Learning Tree at:

Web	http://www.learningtree.com/
E-mail	uscourses@learningtree.com
Mail	Learning Tree International
	1805 Library Street
	Reston, VA 20190-5630
Phone	(800) THE-TREE
Fax	(800) 709-6405

Microsoft Certifications

- Microsoft Certified Professional (MCP) + Internet

- Microsoft Certified Professional (MCP) + Site Building

- Microsoft Certified Systems Engineer (MCSE) + Internet

In 1997, Microsoft created its first two Internet-specific certifications as extensions to their well-known Microsoft Certified Professional (MCP) and Microsoft Certified Systems Engineer (MCSE) programs (see Chapters 2 and 6, respectively, for more information on the MCP and MCSE certification programs). These certifications are titled the Microsoft Certified Professional (MCP) + Internet and Microsoft Certified Systems Engineer (MCSE) + Internet. In 1998, Microsoft added the MCP + Site Building credential to its set of Internet-related certifications.

The MCP + Internet credential affirms an individual's ability to install, maintain, enhance, and troubleshoot an Internet server using Microsoft products. The MSCE + Internet credential, in addition to certifying the basic MCSE competencies, indicates an individual's ability to customize, deploy, and support Microsoft Internet Explorer 4.0; host a

Web server; implement, administer, and troubleshoot systems that use Microsoft's implementation of TCP/IP; develop and publish Web sites; and set up facilities for online commerce while maintaining a high degree of security. The MCP + Site Building certification documents a technical professional's ability to design and maintain complex, interactive Web sites.

Recertification or Maintenance Requirements

As Microsoft introduces new products and new versions of its operating systems, it retires the tests for previous versions. If you hold a certification that is based on a test that Microsoft is retiring, you will be informed by certified mail of the need to take a current test to maintain your certification. You will have at least six months to complete this new test.

Benefits of Certification

As an MCP + Internet, MCP + Site Builder, or MCSE + Internet, you will receive the following benefits:

- A certificate, wallet card and lapel pin

- Access to technical information through a secured Web site

- Logo for use on stationery and business cards

- Invitations to Microsoft-sponsored conferences and technical briefings

- A free subscription to *Microsoft Certified Professional* magazine

- MSDN Online Certified membership, which gives you access to technical resources and services, and connects you to the MCP community. Some benefits are available only in English, or only in certain countries (for more information see http://msdn.microsoft .com/community/mcp).

As an MCSE + Internet, you will also become eligible for MCSE benefits if you have not already received them (see Chapter 9, "Network Operating Systems Certification," for more on the MCSE certification program).

Microsoft Certified Professional (MCP) + Internet

To attain the Microsoft Certified Professional + Internet certification, a candidate must pass three exams. These exams will test your knowledge on the following topics: security planning, installation and configuration of server products, managing server resources, extending servers to run CGI scripts or ISAPI scripts, monitoring and analyzing server performance, and troubleshooting problems.

If you are not already an MCP, passing the first test toward this certification will make you a Microsoft Certified Professional (see Chapter 2 for more information on this certification). The two additional required exams for this certification can also be applied toward achieving higher-level Microsoft certifications. The MCP + Internet is a good stepping-stone on the path to one of Microsoft's premium certifications, such as the Microsoft Certified Systems Engineer (MCSE) or the MCSE + Internet. (See Chapter 6, "Software Certifications," for more information on the MCSE certification; the MCSE + Internet is described in this chapter.)

Who Needs It

The MCP + Internet certification is a good entry point for technical professionals interested in network and system administration of Internet Web sites using Microsoft products. This certification can also be valuable to support and help-desk personnel.

Requirements for Certification

The certification process requires that the candidate pass three required exams (see Table 13.12).

T A B L E 13.12:   Required Tests for MCP + Internet

Test	Test ID
Internetworking Microsoft TCP/IP on Microsoft Windows NT 4.0	070-059
Implementing and Supporting Microsoft Windows NT Server 4.0	070-067

T A B L E 13.12:   Required Tests for MCP + Internet   *(continued)*

Test	Test ID
Implementing and Supporting Internet Information Server 3.0 and Microsoft Index Server 1.1 OR	070-077
Implementing and Supporting Microsoft Internet Information Server 4.0	070-087

Administrator

Microsoft tests are administered by Sylvan Prometric and Virtual University Enterprises (VUE). To register for a test with VUE visit the VUE Web site (http://www.vue.com/student-services/). Call Sylvan at (800) 755-3926 to register for Microsoft tests; if outside the U.S., use the online Sylvan Test Center Locator at http://www.sylvanprometric .com to find the nearest testing center. Chapter 3 contains detailed information on taking tests from Sylvan or VUE.

Fee

The fee is $100 per test.

Format

Multiple-choice, closed-book tests. The number of questions and time limit depend on the test selected.

Microsoft Certified Professional (MCP) + Site Building

To attain the Microsoft Certified Professional + Site Building certification, a candidate must pass two exams. If you are not already an MCP, passing the first test toward this certification will make you a Microsoft Certified Professional (see Chapter 5, "Operating System Certifications," for more information on the MCP certification).

The exams for this certification will test your knowledge about planning, building, maintaining, and managing Web sites using Microsoft technologies.

Who Needs It

The MCP + Site Building certification is a great credential for professionals who manage interactive Web sites that incorporate database connectivity, multimedia, and searchable content, using Microsoft products.

Requirements for Certification

The certification process requires the following step:

1. Pass two of the three exams listed in Table 13.13.

T A B L E 13.13: MCP + Site Building Tests

Test	Test ID
Designing and Implementing Web Sites with Microsoft FrontPage 98	070-055
Designing and Implementing Commerce Solutions with Microsoft Site Server 3.0, Commerce Edition	070-057
Designing and Implementing Web Solutions with Microsoft Visual InterDev 6.0	070-152

Administrator

Microsoft tests are administered by Sylvan Prometric and Virtual University Enterprises (VUE). To register for a test with VUE visit the VUE Web site (`http://www.vue.com/student-services/`). Call Sylvan at (800) 755-3926 to register for Microsoft tests; if outside the U.S., use the online Sylvan Test Center Locator at `http://www.sylvanprometric.com` to find the nearest testing center. Chapter 3, "Taking Your Test," contains detailed information on taking tests from Sylvan or VUE.

Fee

The fee is $100 per test.

Format

The exams are multiple-choice, closed-book tests. The number of questions and time limit depend on the test selected.

Microsoft Certified Systems Engineer + Internet

Attaining this certification requires passing seven core operating system exams and two elective exams. Many of these exams, however, are the same tests required for other Microsoft certifications. If one attains the MCP + Internet certification discussed previously, all three of those exams will apply toward this certification. Likewise, if one has already attained an MCSE, some of those exams may apply; specifically, the MCSE tests on the Windows NT 4.0 track and the optional exams related to the Internet can be applied toward this certification.

The core exams for this certification cover the basic concepts and skills involved with installing, using, and troubleshooting a Windows NT Server and a client operating system such as Windows NT Workstation, Windows 95, or Windows 98. Also required are the networking essentials exam, which covers basic network technologies and troubleshooting, and the TCP/IP exam, which covers TCP/IP networking and troubleshooting. The other required exams focus on setting up a Web site using Microsoft Internet Information Server and installing client Web software. The two elective exams focus on other Microsoft server topics and advanced networking topics. Microsoft's Web site provides exam guidelines, sample tests, etc., and links to authorized training providers. (See the Microsoft Resources section that follows for more information.)

Who Needs It

The MCSE certification is one of the most widely recognized networking credentials. The MCSE + Internet is ideal for those who want to distinguish themselves as having an expert level of technical knowledge and skills relating to the Internet; it can be a great way to advance your career.

Requirements for Certification

The certification process requires the following steps:

1. Pass the seven core exams listed in Table 13.14.

2. Pass two elective exams, selecting exams from different categories listed in Table 13.15. (If you pass two exams within the same category, only one will qualify as an MCSE + Internet elective.)

T A B L E 13.14: Required Tests for MCSE + Internet

Test	Test ID
Networking Essentials	070-058
Internetworking with Microsoft TCP/IP on Microsoft Windows NT 4.0	070-059
Implementing and Supporting Microsoft Windows 95 OR	070-064
Implementing and Supporting Microsoft Windows NT Workstation 4 OR	070-073
Implementing and Supporting Microsoft Windows 98	070-098
Implementing and Supporting Microsoft Windows NT Server 4	070-067
Implementing and Supporting Microsoft Windows NT Server 4 in the Enterprise	070-068
Implementing and Supporting Microsoft Internet Information Server 3.0 and Microsoft Index Server1.1 OR	070-077
Implementing and Supporting Microsoft Internet Information Server 4	070-087
Implementing and Supporting Microsoft Internet Explorer 4 by Using the Internet Explorer Administration Kit	070-079

TABLE 13.15: Elective Tests for MCSE + Internet

Category	Test	Test ID
SQL Server	Administering Microsoft SQL Server 6.5 OR	070-026
	Administering Microsoft SQL Server 7	070-028
Database Design	Implementing a Database Design on Microsoft SQL Server 6.5 OR	070-027
	Designing and Implementing Databases with Microsoft SQL Server 7	070-029
Exchange Server	Implementing and Supporting Microsoft Exchange Server 5 OR	070-076
	Implementing and Supporting Microsoft Exchange Server 5.5	070-081
SNA Server	Implementing and Supporting Microsoft SNA Server 4.0	070-085
Proxy Server	Implementing and Supporting Microsoft Proxy Server 1.0 OR	070-078
	Implementing and Supporting Microsoft Proxy Server 2	070-088
Site Server	Implementing and Supporting Web Sites Using Microsoft Site Server 3.0	070-056

NOTE If you are already certified as a Novell CNE, Master CNE, or CNI, a Banyan CBS or CBE, or a Sun Certified Network Administrator for Solaris 2.5 or 2.6, Microsoft will waive the requirement for the networking essentials exam (Test ID: 70-058).

Administrator

Microsoft tests are administered by Sylvan Prometric and Virtual University Enterprises (VUE). To register for a test with VUE visit the VUE Web site (http://www.vue.com/student-services/). Call Sylvan at (800) 755-3926 to register for Microsoft tests; if outside the U.S., use the online Sylvan Test Center Locator at www.sylvanprometric.com to find the nearest testing center. Chapter 3 contains detailed information on taking tests from Sylvan or VUE.

Fee

The fee is $100 per test.

Format

Multiple-choice, closed-book tests. The number of questions and time limit depend on the test selected.

Microsoft Resources

The Microsoft Web site offers practice exams as well as exam preparation guides that detail the objectives of each exam. Microsoft's Web site also offers a listing of Microsoft Authorized Technical Education Centers. For more information on this organization's certification programs, contact Microsoft at:

Web	http://www.microsoft.com/mcp/
E-mail	mcp@msprograms.com
Mail	Microsoft Corporation
	One Microsoft Way
	Redmond, WA 98052-6399
Phone	(800) 636-7544
Fax	(425) 936-7329

Novell Certifications

- Certified Internet Business Strategist

- Certified Web Designer

- Certified Intranet Manager

- Certified Internet Architect

The Novell Certified Internet Professional program was developed in 1997 to certify Internet professionals who maintain and support Internet connections and sites. The Certified Internet Professional program emphasizes combining effective business communication with Internet technology skills. The program currently includes four tracks relating to key job categories for Internet professionals: Internet Business Strategist, Web Designer, Intranet Manager, and Internet Architect.

Novell offers recommended courses as preparation for each of the tests. Although these courses are not required, they do cover the material tested on the required exams.

Recertification or Maintenance Requirements

Certified Internet Professionals are required to meet continuing certification requirements as specified by Novell. Because recertification requirements can vary from year to year, contact Novell for current details (see the Novell Resources section that follows for more information).

Benefits of Certification

All Novell Certified Internet Professionals receive the following benefits:

- Use of logos

- Two-user license of intraNetWare 4.11

Certified Internet Business Strategist

The Internet Business Strategist certification is designed for those who plan how a company can best use the Internet to meet its business goals. The certification program includes topics such as how to develop a business plan for the deployment of a Web site, how to contract for and manage Web development, how to design an online marketing strategy, and how to increase company productivity using Internet technology.

Only one test is required for this certification. Novell recommends the following two courses as preparation for this test:

- Novell 600: Internet Business Strategies
- Novell 650: Mastering the Net with Netscape Navigator

Who Needs It

Novell's Internet Business Strategist certification is a great way to demonstrate your expertise in leveraging the Internet to meet your company's goals. It can also be a valuable credential for freelance Internet business consultants who want to validate their skills for potential clients.

Requirements for Certification

The certification process requires two steps:

1. Pass the Internet Business Strategies Test (Test ID: 050-701).

2. Submit a signed Novell Education Certification Agreement.

Administrator

Novell tests are administered by Sylvan Prometric and Virtual University Enterprises (VUE). To register for a test with VUE, call 800-511-8123 or visit the VUE Web site (http://www.vue.com/student-services/). To register for a test with Sylvan, call (800) 733-3926; if outside the U.S., use the online Sylvan Test Center Locator at http://www.sylvanprometric.com to find the nearest testing center. Chapter 3 contains detailed information on taking tests from Sylvan or VUE.

Fee

The test fee is $95 per exam.

Format

Novell tests include both adaptive and traditional format exams. Contact Sylvan Prometric or VUE for current test information.

Certified Web Designer

Novell's Web Designer credential targets computer professionals who design and publish intranet and Internet Web pages. This certification is valuable to graphic artists, writers, editors, and anyone else who is actively involved in the production of Web pages. The certification program covers the following topics: designing effective user interfaces, designing Web pages to be viewed by a variety of Web clients, producing fast-loading Web pages, and effectively using multimedia and animation in Web pages.

The certification process involves passing four tests. Novell recommends taking the following courses as preparation for the tests:

- Novell 600: Internet Business Strategies
- Novell 650: Mastering the Net with Netscape Navigator
- Novell 654: Web Authoring and Publishing
- Novell 655: Advanced Web Authoring
- Novell 660: Designing an Effective Web Site

Who Needs It

Novell's Web Designer certification is a great way to demonstrate your expertise in creating and publishing effective Web sites for your company. It can also be a valuable credential for freelance Web designers who want to validate their skills for potential clients.

Requirements for Certification

The certification process requires the following steps:

1. Pass the Internet Business Strategies exam (Test ID: 050-701).

2. Pass the Web Authoring and Publishing exam (Test ID: 050-704).

3. Pass the Advanced Web Authoring exam (Test ID: 050-706).

4. Pass the Designing an Effective Web Site exam (Test ID: 050-703).

5. Submit a signed Novell Education Certification Agreement.

Administrator

Novell tests are administered by Sylvan Prometric and Virtual University Enterprises (VUE). To register for a test with VUE, call 800-511-8123 or visit the VUE Web site (http://www.vue.com/student-services/). To register for a test with Sylvan, call (800) 733-3926; if outside the U.S., use the online Sylvan Test Center Locator at http://www.sylvanprometric.com to find the nearest testing center. Chapter 3 contains detailed information on taking tests from Sylvan or VUE.

Fee

The test fee is $95 per exam.

Format

Novell tests include both adaptive and traditional format exams. Contact Sylvan Prometric or VUE for current test information.

Certified Intranet Manager

Novell's Intranet Manager program targets already-certified Certified Novell Administrators (CNAs) and Certified Novell Engineers (CNEs) who need to deploy and manage intranets (see Chapter 9 for more information about the CNA and CNE certification programs). CNA or CNE certification is not a prerequisite for this program; if you are not already a CNA, however, you will become one during the completion of the Intranet Manager certification program.

Five tests are required for this certification. These tests cover topics including Web authoring and publishing using HTML, developing CGI and Perl scripts, and managing a Web server. Novell recommends the following courses in preparation for these tests:

- Novell 600: Internet Business Strategies

- Novell 650: Mastering the Net with Netscape Communicator

- Novell 654: Web Authoring and Publishing

- Novell 655: Advanced Web Authoring

- Novell 656: Web Server Management

- Novell 520: intraNetWare: NetWare 4.11 Administration or Novell 526: intraNetWare: NetWare 3 to NetWare 4.11 Update

Who Needs It

Jobs are plentiful for those who can create and manage intranet and Internet Web sites and connections. This certification allows you to demonstrate to potential employers that you have advanced knowledge and skill in this area. The Intranet Manager certification can also be a valuable credential for freelance Internet consultants.

Requirements for Certification

The certification process requires the following steps:

1. Pass the five tests listed in Table 13.16.

2. Submit a signed Novell Education Certification Agreement.

T A B L E 13.16: Required Exams for Certified Intranet Manager

Test	Test ID
Internet Business Strategies	050-701
Web Authoring and Publishing	050-704
Advanced Web Authoring	050-706
Web Server Management	050-710*
IntranetWare: NetWare 4.11 Administration OR	050-613*
IntraNetWare: NetWare 3 to NetWare 4.11 Update	050-615*

* It may be possible to substitute a test from another vendor for this test; contact Novell Education for details.

Administrator

Novell tests are administered by Sylvan Prometric and Virtual University Enterprises (VUE). To register for a test with VUE, call 800-511-8123 or visit the VUE Web site (http://www.vue.com/student-services/). To register for a test with Sylvan, call (800) 733-3926; if outside the U.S., use the online Sylvan Test Center Locator at http://www.sylvanprometric.com to find the nearest testing center. Chapter 3 contains detailed information on taking tests from Sylvan or VUE.

Fee

The test fee is $95 per exam.

Format

Novell tests include both adaptive and traditional format exams. Contact Sylvan Prometric or VUE for current test information.

Certified Internet Architect

Novell's Internet Architect certification is designed for network administrators who are responsible for providing their organization with a secure and efficient connection to the Internet. A candidate must hold an approved network operating system certification and must pass five exams.

The required tests cover the following topics: configuring and installing TCP/IP; planning TCP/IP addressing; installing and configuring DNS and FTP services; installing and configuring a proxy server; planning and configuring an internetwork; and installing and managing a Web server. Novell recommends the following courses as preparation for these tests:

- Novell 216: Fundamentals of Internetworking

- Novell 605: NetWare TCP/IP Transport

- Novell 658: DNS and FTP Server Installation and Configuration

- Novell 770: Securing Intranets with BorderManager

- Novell 656: Web Server Management

Who Needs It

This certification is an excellent way to demonstrate your expertise in TCP/IP networking and Internet services. It can be the ticket to employment with an Internet service provider or Web-hosting service.

Requirements for Certification

The certification process requires the following steps:

1. As a prerequisite, the candidate must hold one of the following network operating systems certifications (see Chapter 5, "Operating Systems Certifications," and Chapter 9, "Network Operating Systems Certifications," for information on these certifications):

   - Certified Novell Engineer (CNE)

   - Microsoft Certified Systems Engineer (MCSE)

   - Santa Cruz Operations, Inc. Advanced Certified Engineer (ACE)

   - Sun Certified Solaris Administrator (CSA)

2. Pass the five required exams listed in Table 13.17.

3. Submit a signed Novell Education Certification Agreement.

T A B L E 13.17: Required Exams for Certified Internet Architect

Test	Test ID
Fundamentals of Internetworking	050-611
NetWare TCP/IP Transport	050-145*
DNS & FTP Server Installation and Configuration	050-712
Web Server Management	050-710*
Securing Intranets with BorderManager	050-629

* It may be possible to substitute a test from another vendor for this test; contact Novell Education for details.

Administrator

Novell tests are administered by Sylvan Prometric and Virtual University Enterprises (VUE). To register for a test with VUE, call 800-511-8123 or visit the VUE Web site (http://www.vue.com/student-services/). To register for a test with Sylvan, call (800) 733-3926; if outside the U.S., use the online Sylvan Test Center Locator at http://www.sylvanprometric.com to find the nearest testing center. Chapter 3 contains detailed information on taking tests from Sylvan or VUE.

Fee

The test fee is $95 per exam.

Format

Novell tests include both adaptive and traditional format exams. Contact Sylvan Prometric or VUE for current test information.

Novell Resources

The Novell Web site offers detailed information about the recommended courses and required exams for the Certified Internet Professional program. It provides practice exams as well as study guides that detail the objectives of each exam. The Novell Web site also provides a listing of Novell Authorized Education Centers. For more information on this organization's certification programs, contact Novell at:

Web	http://education.novell.com/
E-mail	edcustomer@novell.com
Mail	Novell, Inc.
	1555 N. Technology Way, MS Q35
	Orem, UT 84097
Phone	(800) 233-EDUC
Fax	(801) 222-7875
Faxback	(800) 233-EDUC

Open Market Certification

- ▪ Folio 4 Certified Infobase Engineer (CIE)

Open Market offers a comprehensive set of products for Internet commerce: Transact 4 provides online payment processing, order management, and customer service; LiveCommerce allows the creation of Internet catalogs; ShopSite builds Internet storefronts; and Folio 4 facilitates Internet and CD-ROM publishing as well as the management of internal corporate information.

The Certified Infobase Engineer (CIE) program certifies the knowledge and skills of professionals who use Folio products. The Folio 4 CIE program is covered here. Open Market also offers the Folio 3.1 CIE program, which involves taking one exam and completing an Infobase project (see the Open Market Web site for further information on the Folio 3.1 program).

Recertification or Maintenance Requirements

The CIE program did not have announced recertification requirements at the time of this writing. Contact Open Market for updates (see the "Open Market Resources" section for contact information).

Benefits of Certification

The CIE program did not have a formal listing of certification benefits at the time of this writing. Contact Open Market for updates (see the Open Market Resources section for contact information).

Folio 4 Certified Infobase Engineer (CIE)

The Certified Infobase Engineer program is designed to document the skills of technical professionals who use the Folio product line. Attaining this certification involves passing two exams. A candidate is expected to have a wide knowledge of the features of Folio products. The first exam covers the use and support of the Folio Views client, while the second exam covers the design and implementation of Folio 4 Infobases and the support of Folio 4 Workbench. A detailed list of exam topics is provided on Open Market's Web site (see Open Market Resources section for more information).

Who Needs It

The Certified Infobase Engineer (CIE) credential is valuable for professionals who use Open Market Folio products for Internet commerce and electronic publishing. This certification indicates that you know how to implement and support Folio 4 Infobases.

Requirements for Certification

The certification process requires the following steps:

1. Pass the Folio 4 Views Client Skills exam (Test ID: 760-002).

2. Pass the Folio 4 Infobase Building Skills exam (Test ID: 760-003).

Administrator

The Open Market exams are administered by Sylvan Prometric. Call Sylvan at (800) 769-3926 to register; if outside the U.S., use the online Sylvan Test Center Locator at http://www.sylvanprometric.com to find the nearest testing center. (See Chapter 3 for detailed information on taking tests from Sylvan.)

Fee

Each test costs $95 in North America, and $155 internationally.

Format

The exams are closed-book, computer-based tests with multiple-choice, multiple-correct, point and click, and short fill-in questions. The Views Client Skills exam includes 35 questions, lasts 45 minutes, and has a passing score of 83 percent. The 60-minute Infobase Building Skills exam has 43 questions and a passing score of 72 percent.

Open Market Resources

Open Market offers instructor-led courses on Folio 4 products. The Open Market Web site provides information about these course, study guides for the two Folio 4 exams, and information about the

Folio 3.1 CIE program. For more information on this organization's certification program and courses, contact Open Market's Folio Certification program at:

Web	`http://www.openmarket.com/service/edu/`
Mail	Folio Corporation
	5072 N. 300 W.
	Provo, UT 84604
Phone	(800) 228-1084 or (801) 229-6441

ProsoftTraining.com Certifications

- Certified Internet Webmaster (CIW) Level 1

- Certified Internet Webmaster (CIW) Level 2

Through its Certified Internet Webmaster (CIW) program, ProsoftTraining.com certifies the skills of technical professionals in eight areas related to the Internet. This comprehensive set of vendor-neutral certifications can be useful to a broad range of computer and networking professionals, from hard-core TCP/IP and UNIX networkers to Web page designers. The eight available tracks for training include: Foundations, Site Designer, Application Developer, Enterprise Developer, Server Administrator, Internetworking Professional, Security Professional, and E-Commerce Professional.

The CIW program is a four-level program designed for professionals who develop, administer, secure, and support Internet or intranet services. At the time this book went to press, levels 3 and 4 were still under development. The CIW Level 1 certification is the entry point in the CIW program. Only one track, Foundations, is offered at Level 1. At Level 2, candidates choose from seven different tracks. Level 3 will include vendor-specific certifications, while Level 4, intended to denote a high level of mastery, will involve both testing and verification of practical experience. Levels 3 and 4 are scheduled for release in late 1999.

While no courses are required for CIW certification, ProsoftTraining .com offers instructor-led courses to prepare candidates for any CIW certification. Some of the courses are also available in the ProFlex distance learning format.

The CIW certification program is recognized by the Association of Internet Professionals (AIP), the National Association of Webmasters (NAW), the Institute for Certification of Computing Professionals (ICCP), and the Internet Certification Institute International (ICII).

NOTE ProsoftTraining.com also offers a certification program for those who want to be ProsoftTraining.com instructors. For information, see Chapter 15, "Instructor and Trainer Certifications."

Recertification or Maintenance Requirements

CIWs must be recertified when ProsoftTraining.com announces significant changes to the CIW courseware or examination. Such changes occur at least every twelve months, and are announced on the CIW Web site and by e-mail.

Benefits of Certification

All ProsoftTraining.com Certified Internet Webmasters receive the following benefits:

- CIW logos to use on business cards and stationery
- Access to a special CIW Web site
- A personalized certificate

Certified Internet Webmaster (CIW) Level 1

The CIW Level 1 credential is an introductory level certification that indicates that one knows the basics of E-business. It also prepares the successful candidate to move on to the several CIW Level 2 specializations. Attaining this certification involves passing one exam. The exam covers basic information about the Internet and World Wide Web, including the client/server model, the OSI RM, networking, TCP/IP, HTML, search strategies, and Internet applications.

A five-day ProsoftTraining.com training program is recommended, but not required, as preparation for the exam. The program includes the Basic Internet Fundamentals course (one day), the Advanced Internet Business Fundamentals course (one day), the HTML Fundamentals course (one day), and the Networking Fundamentals course (two days). Content descriptions of each of the above recommended courses are available online (see http://www.prosofttraining.com/).

Who Needs It

This certification is a great way to learn the fundamentals of creating and maintaining Web pages. It can help you get your foot in the door with a company that wants to have an Internet presence. It can also be a valuable first credential for becoming a freelance Web site designer.

Requirements for Certification

The certification process requires only one step:

1. Pass the CIW Foundations exam (Test ID: 310).

Administrator

CIW tests are administered by Sylvan Prometric. Call (800) 380-EXAM to register for ProsoftTraining.com tests; if outside the U.S., use the online Sylvan Test Center Locator at http://www.sylvanprometric.com to find the nearest testing center. Chapter 3 contains detailed information on taking tests from Sylvan.

Fee

The test costs $150 in the U.S.

Format

Computer-based, multiple-choice, closed-book test in English. The 100 questions must be answered in a 75-minute time period. To pass, the candidate must attain a minimum score of 75 percent overall and at least 70 percent in each module.

Certified Internet Webmaster (CIW) Level 2

The Certified Internet Webmaster (CIW) Level 2 certification builds on the Level 1 CIW and requires one or two exams, depending on the track selected. Optional preparation courses are offered for each specialization. Level 2 allows CIWs to specialize in one or more of seven tracks:

- CIW Site Designer
- CIW Application Developer
- CIW Enterprise Developer
- CIW Server Administrator
- CIW Internetworking Professional
- CIW Security Professional
- CIW E-Commerce Professional

The CIW Site Designer credential is for professionals who design, implement, and maintain hyperlink-driven Web sites, including Web authors, marketing and communications professionals, graphic designers, and others. The ProsoftTraining.com Design Methodology and Technology course (five days) is recommended as preparation for the Site Designer exam. The course covers authoring and scripting languages, content creation and management tools, and digital media tools.

The CIW Application Developer credential is for professionals who implement data-driven Web sites using scripting and authoring languages, including Webmasters, software developers, desktop publishers, and others. A 10-day ProsoftTraining.com training program is recommended, but not required, as preparation for the Application Developer exam. The program includes the JavaScript Fundamentals course (two days); the Fundamentals of CGI using Perl course (two days); the Server-Side Scripting and Security course (three days); and either the Visual Java using Visual Age course (two days) or the Visual Java using Visual Café course (two days).

The CIW Enterprise Developer credential requires the candidate to pass both the CIW Application Developer exam and one additional exam. This credential is for database architects and other professionals who develop n-tier database and legacy connectivity solutions using Java. A 10-day ProsoftTraining.com training program is recommended, but not required, as preparation for the Enterprise Developer exam. The program includes the Java Programming Fundamentals course (five days); the Enterprise Development with CORBA and Java course (two days); the Enterprise Development with JDBC course (one day); and the Enterprise Development with JFC Swing course (two days).

The CIW Server Administrator credential is for professionals who manage corporate Internet and intranet servers, including LAN/WAN administrators, systems administrators, network engineers, and others. A five-day ProsoftTraining.com training program is recommended, but not required, as preparation for the System Administrator exam. The program includes the Internet System Management course (two days) and the Advanced Internet System Management course (three days).

The CIW Internetworking Professional credential is for professionals who design network architecture and monitor network performance, including network engineers, network and internetworking engineers, LAN/WAN administrators, and others. A seven-day Prosoft-Training.com training program is recommended, but not required, as preparation for the Internetworking Professional exam. The program includes the TCP/IP Internetworking course (two days); Advanced TCP/IP Concepts and Practices course (three days); and the SNMP Network Management course (three days).

The CIW E-Commerce Professional credential requires the candidate to pass both the CIW Internetworking Professional exam and one additional exam. This credential is for professionals who design and deliver E-Commerce sites, including network server administrators, firewall administrators, application developers, Webmasters, and others. A five-day ProsoftTraining.com training program is recommended, but not required, as preparation for the E-Commerce Professional exam. The program includes the E-Commerce Concepts and Practices course (two days) and the E-Commerce Strategy and Solutions course (three days).

Content descriptions of each of the above recommended courses are available online (see http://www.prosofttraining.com/).

Who Needs It

The CIW Level 2 certifications can help you obtain a job or career advancement in a number of Internet-related areas. These certifications can also help consultants and freelance Web developers establish their credibility with clients.

Requirements for Certification

The certification process requires the following steps:

1. Attain CIW Level 1 certification (described previously).

2. Pass the CIW exam(s) required for the desired certification track, as listed in Table 13.18.

T A B L E 13.18: Required Exams for CIW Level 2 Tracks

CIW Level 2 Track	Exam	Test ID
Site Designer	CIW Site Designer	320
Application Developer	CIW Application Developer	330
Enterprise Developer	CIW Application Developer AND	330
	CIW Enterprise Developer	340
System Administrator	CIW System Administrator	350
Internetworking Professional	CIW Internetworking Professional	360
Security Professional	CIW Internetworking Professional AND	360
	CIW Security Professional	370
E-Commerce Professional	CIW Internetworking Professional AND	360
	CIW E-Commerce Professional	380

Administrator

CIW tests are administered by Sylvan Prometric. Call (800) 380-EXAM to register for ProsoftTraining.com tests; if outside the U.S., use the online Sylvan Test Center Locator at http://www.sylvanprometric .com to find the nearest testing center. Chapter 3 contains detailed information on taking tests from Sylvan.

Fee

The test costs $150 in the U.S.

Format

The exams are computer-based, multiple-choice, closed-book tests in English. Each test has 100 questions that must be answered in a 75-minute time period. To pass a test, the candidate must attain a minimum score of 75 percent overall and at least 70 percent in each module.

ProsoftTraining.com Resources

This organization's Web site provides descriptions of the content of each of the instructor-led courses, as well as information about the ProFlex distance learning courses. For more information on this organization's certifications and courses, contact ProsoftTraining.com at:

Web	http://www.prosofttraining.com/
E-mail	ciw@prosofttraining.com
Mail	Certification Services
	ProsoftTraining.com
	3001 Bee Caves Road
	Suite 100
	Austin, TX 78746
Phone	(512) 328-6140
Fax	(512) 328-5239

CHAPTER

14

Computer and Network Security Certifications

FEATURING

- Check Point Certifications

- IBM Certification

- International Information Systems Security Certification Consortium (ISC)^2 Certification

- Information Systems Audit and Control Association (ISACA) Certification

- Learning Tree Certification

Computer and network security is of paramount importance to many corporations and organizations. By connecting their computer systems to the Internet, they have not only opened the door to electronic commerce, but have also opened their systems to outside attack. There are currently five certification programs directly related to computer and network security. The first two programs covered in this chapter, from Check Point and IBM, certify an individual on the use of specific products from those companies. The other three certification programs—the Certified Information Systems Security Professional designation, offered by the International Information Systems Security Certification Consortium, the Certified Information Systems Auditor credential, offered by Information Systems Audit and Control Association, and the System and Network Security Certified Professional, offered by Learning Tree International—emphasize computer security from a vendor-independent perspective. These certifications are highly sought after and recognized in the computer security field.

Professionals seeking these certifications might include:

- Help-desk personnel
- Programmers
- Security specialists
- Consultants
- Network administrators

Use Table 14.1 below to compare the number of required tests, the test format, the approximate cost of taking the test(s), the number of required courses, the cost of any required courses, and the relative difficulty of the certification programs in this chapter. The cost information is a general guideline; since things change rapidly in the world of certification programs. Once you have selected a specific course of action you may want to double-check the costs.

We classified the difficulty of these certifications into three categories—Moderate, Challenging, and Very Challenging—based on the number of required tests and courses, and the relative difficulty of those tests or lab exams. These ratings are approximate and are offered simply as a general guide to help the reader distinguish between entry-level programs and those that require more advanced skill and knowledge. (This rating scale assumes that one has experience with the product or technology and has studied the appropriate subject content before attempting the exams.

T A B L E 14.1: Computer and Network Security Certifications

Certification	# of Required Tests	Test Format(s)	Total Cost of Required Tests	# of Required Courses	Total Cost of Required Courses	Difficulty	Notes
Check Point Certifications							
Check Point Certified Network Traffic Engineer (CNTE)	2	MC	$200	—	—	◗	
Check Point Certified Infrastructure Engineer (CIE)	4	MC	$400	—	—	●	
Check Point Certified Security Engineer (CSE)	6	MC	$600	—	—	●	
IBM Certification							
Certified Solutions Expert—Firewall	1	MC	VF	—	—	○	
International Information Systems Security Certification Consortium (ISC)[2] Certification							
Certified Information Systems Security Professional (CISSP)	1	MC	$395	—	—	◗	Three years of field experience required.

T A B L E 14.1: Computer and Network Security Certifications *(continued)*

Certification	# of Required Tests	Test Format(s)	Total Cost of Required Tests	# of Required Courses	Total Cost of Required Courses	Difficulty	Notes
Information Systems Audit and Control Association (ISACA) Certification							
Certified Information Systems Auditor (CISA)	2	MC	$295–$385	—	—	●	Five years of field experience required. Annual dues are also required.
Learning Tree International Certification							
System and Network Security Certified Professional	5	MC	CV	5	$12,000–$14,000	◑	Discount pricing available; contact Learning Tree.

Certification Difficulty: ○ Moderate   ◑ Challenging   ● Very Challenging

Test Format: MC: Multiple Choice   AT: Adaptive Testing   LA: Live Application
PR: Hands-on Lab   NA: Not Applicable

Test Fee: VF: Test Fees can vary; consult testing center.   CV: Voucher for taking the exam is included in the fee for the required course(s); additional attempts cost extra.

Check Point Certifications

- Certified Network Traffic Engineer (CNTE)

- Certified Infrastructure Engineer (CIE)

- Certified Security Engineer (CSE)

FireWall-1, a security product for defending networks from external and internal attack, is probably Check Point's best-known product, but Check Point actually makes a number of network products for a variety of platforms. Check Point products allow network administrators to implement traditional security measures and also to develop centralized policy-based security management strategies. Check Point's recently revised certification program is aligned with its product line, and focuses on three areas: security, traffic control, and IP address management.

Recertification or Maintenance Requirements

Check Point continuously updates its training and testing to reflect new or changing technology within its products, and does require recertification as new versions of their products are released. Check Point certifications are valid for at least 18 months from the date of completion. Check Point notifies certified professionals of their expiring certifications, and provides a 6-month grace period after the 18-month recertification date.

Benefits of Certification

CSEs, CNTEs, and CIEs receive the following benefits:

- Free access to Check Point Technical Support staff for three support incidents

- One free issue of SecurNet, a technical reference CD containing information on Check Point products, the related knowledge base, and the latest patches and fixes

- Use of the Check Point certified professional logo

Certified Network Traffic Engineer (CNTE)

The CNTE credential documents a network administrator's knowledge of bandwidth management and the issues surrounding network congestion on Internet and intranet links. The CNTE credential is designed for end users and resellers who administrate policy-based, enterprise-wide, bandwidth management solutions using Check Point products. A CNTE candidate must pass two Check Point traffic control exams. Check Point recommends, but does not require, that candidates attend a set of related courses offered at Check Point Authorized Training Centers. Check Point also recommends that candidates for this certification have a good working knowledge of UNIX and Windows network technology, general knowledge of the FireWall-1 product, general knowledge of Internet communications, and detailed knowledge of the FloodGate-1 and Connect Control products.

Who Needs It

The CNTE credential documents a network administrator's knowledge of bandwidth management. This certification can help you advance your networking career at a company that uses Check Point products. Check Point credentials can also be of value to independent consultants who want to validate their expertise for clients.

Requirements for Certification

The certification process requires the following steps:

1. Pass the Check Point Fundamentals of TCP/IP exam.

2. Pass the Check Point Bandwidth Management Using FloodGate-1 exam.

Administrator

Check Point certification exams are offered through a network of testing centers throughout the world. Consult the Check Point Web site for a listing of testing centers. Check Point also plans to offer some Web-based exams in the near future.

Fee

Each exam costs $100.

Format

Each exam has approximately 75 multiple-choice questions and must be completed within 90 minutes.

Certified Infrastructure Engineer (CIE)

The CIE certification is designed for network administrators who control IP address and name spaces using Check Point products. To attain this certification, a candidate must pass four Check Point exams. Check Point recommends that candidates have a working knowledge of Windows network technology and Internet communications, and have general knowledge of DNS, BIND, the MetaIP product, and TCP/IP.

Who Needs It

The CIE credential documents a networking professional's ability to manage enterprise-wide IP network infrastructures. Check Point credentials can also be of value to independent consultants who want to validate their expertise for clients.

Requirements for Certification

The certification process requires the following steps:

1. You must pass the Check Point Fundamentals of TCP/IP exam.

2. You must pass the Check Point Introduction to Bandwidth Management Using MetaIP exam.

3. You must pass the Check Point DNS & Bind exam.

4. You must pass the Check Point Administering MetaIP for the Advanced User exam.

Administrator

Check Point certification exams are offered through of network of testing centers throughout the world. Consult the Check Point Web site for a listing of testing centers. Check Point also plans to offer some Web-based exams in the near future.

Fee

Each exam costs $100.

Format

Each exam has approximately 75 multiple-choice questions and must be completed within 90 minutes.

Certified Security Engineer (CSE)

The CSE credential is designed for end-users and resellers who have a sophisticated level of knowledge about security, enterprise networks, and the management of multiple secure systems using Check Point products. A CSE candidate must successfully pass a set of six Check Point security exams. Check Point recommends, but does not require, that candidates attend a set of related courses offered at Check Point Authorized Training Centers. Check Point also recommends that candidates for this certification have a good working knowledge of UNIX and Windows network technology, Internet communications, and detailed knowledge of the FireWall-1 and VPN-1™ products.

Who Needs It

The CSE credential is a great way to advance your networking security career at a company that uses Check Point products. Because they address both general and advanced security requirements, Check Point credentials can also be of value to independent consultants who want to validate their expertise for clients.

Requirements for Certification

The certification process requires the following steps:

1. Pass the Check Point Fundamentals of TCP/IP exam.

2. Pass the Check Point Firewall Essentials exam.

3. Pass the Check Point Security Essentials exam.

4. Pass the Check Point Introduction to FireWall-1 Management exam.

5. Pass the Check Point Advanced FireWall-1 Management exam.

6. Pass the Check Point VPN-1/Appliance Administration exam.

Administrator

Check Point certification exams are offered through of network of testing centers throughout the world. Consult the Check Point Web site for a listing of testing centers. Check Point also plans to offer some Web-based exams in the near future.

Fee

Each exam costs $100.

Format

Each exam has approximately 75 multiple-choice questions and must be completed within 90 minutes.

Check Point Resources

Check Point offers a number of preparation courses for their certification programs. For more information on these certification programs and courses, contact Check Point at:

Web	http://www.checkpoint.com
E-mail	info@checkpoint.com
Mail	Check Point Software Technologies, Inc.
	Three Lagoon Drive, Suite 400
	Redwood City, CA 94065
Phone	650-628-2000
Fax	650-654-4233

IBM Certification

- IBM Certified Solutions Expert—Firewall

IBM's eNetwork Firewall product runs on AIX and Windows NT. This product traces its history back to IBM's first Firewall products introduced in 1985. It provides corporations with a means of protecting their networks from outside attack by implementing three critical firewall architectures—filtering, proxy, and circuit level gateways.

The IBM Certified Solutions Expert—Firewall certification validates a candidate's ability to use the IBM Firewall product to create secure links between the Internet and private company intranets.

Recertification or Maintenance Requirements

This IBM certification applies to a specific version of the Firewall product, so there is no requirement for recertification on this particular version. Since your certification is tied to a specific version of a product, however, you will want to become certified on the newest versions, when they become available, if you want to continue to have the most current credential in this area.

Benefits of Certification

IBM Certified Solutions Experts receive these benefits:

- Certificate
- Wallet-sized certificate
- Certification logo
- Lapel pin

Certified Solutions Expert—Firewall

To attain certification as an IBM Certified Solutions Expert—Firewall, a candidate must pass one exam. This exam tests the candidate's knowledge about the design and installation of a firewall using IBM's Firewall product. The candidate can select a test on either the AIX or Windows NT operating system. IBM recommends that the certification candidate have hands-on experience with TCP/IP and the Firewall product prior to taking the test. Test objectives, study guides, and sample tests are available on IBM's Web site (see the IBM Resources section that follows for the Web address).

Who Needs It

The IBM Certified Solutions Expert—Firewall certification identifies you as being qualified to hold a high level of responsibility for company Internet and intranet security. IBM specifically recommends this certification to those who are responsible for assessing network security requirements as they relate to a firewall, designing firewall solutions, and installing, customizing, and supporting firewall installations. This certification is also valuable to freelance security consultants.

Requirements for Certification

The certification process requires only one step:

1. You must pass either the eNetwork Firewall for Windows NT exam (Test ID: 000-250) or the Planning, Implementing, and Supporting the Firewall for AIX exam (Test ID: 000-558).

Administrator

Tests are administered by Sylvan Prometric. Call (800) 959-3926 to register for IBM tests; if outside the U.S., use the online Sylvan Test Center Locator at http://www.sylvanprometric.com/ to find the nearest testing center. (See Chapter 3 for additional information on Sylvan Prometric.)

Fee

Fees for IBM tests vary based on test length and format; call Sylvan Prometric at (800) 959-3926 for pricing.

Format

These are computer-based, multiple-choice tests. The eNetwork Firewall for Windows NT exam consists of 58 questions that must be completed in 60 minutes. The Planning, Implementing, and Supporting the IBM Firewall for AIX exam consists of 75 questions that must be completed in 90 minutes. Call Sylvan Prometric at (800) 959-3926 for the latest information on the number of questions, time limit, and passing score.

IBM Resources

IBM's Web site offers a number of excellent resources for certification candidates, including test objectives, study guides, and sample tests. For more information on this certification program, contact IBM at:

Web	http://www.ibm.com/certify
E-mail	certify@us.ibm.com
Mail	The Professional Certification Program from IBM Mail Drop 3013 11400 Burnet Road Austin, TX 78758
Phone	(800) IBM-TEACH ((800) 426-8322)
Fax	(512) 838-7961

International Information Systems Security Certification Consortium (ISC)² Certification

- Certified Information Systems Security Professional

The International Information Systems Security Certification Consortium, known as (ISC)², is a nonprofit alliance composed of several groups, including the SIG-CS of the Data Processing Management Association, the Computer Security Institute, the Information Systems Security Association, the Canadian Information Processing Society, the International Federation for Information Processing, several agencies of the United States and Canadian governments, and Idaho State University. These organizations have cooperated to formulate a standard certification program for computer security professionals—the Certified Information Systems Security Professional (CISSP) program.

There are currently more than 1,500 CISSP-certified professionals. (ISC)² estimates, however, that there may be as many as 20,000 individuals in the computer security field that could benefit from CISSP certification, and that number appears to be growing. According to an industry report, budgets for information security staffing are expected to rise 18 percent annually, and information security employment—as a percentage of total employment—increased by nearly 100 percent between 1990 and 1997 ("1997 Information Security Staffing Levels and the Standard of Due Care," Computer Security Institute and Charles Cresson Wood of Baseline Software; for more information see `http://www.gocsi.com/prelease.htm`).

Recertification or Maintenance Requirements

CISSP certified professionals must maintain their certification by earning 120 Continuing Professional Education (CPE) credits over each three-year recertification period. Two-thirds of the CPE credits must be earned in activities directly related to the information systems security profession, while the other one-third may be earned in educational activities that enhance one's overall professional skills, knowledge, and competency. CISSP certified professionals must also pay an annual $50 recertification fee.

Benefits of Certification

While this certification doesn't offer the incidental benefits provided with some other vendor-based certifications, it is likely to offer benefits with regard to career advancement. As a vendor-independent authentication of an individual's skill in information security, the CISSP certification is now specified as a preferred or required credential for a growing number of security-related positions.

Certified Information Systems Security Professional (CISSP)

(ISC)² requires that candidates for this certification have three years of hands-on experience in the computer security field before attempting the one required exam. The certification exam questions for each candidate are selected from a pool of 1,700 multiple-choice questions. These questions cover the spectrum of the 10 topical areas, referred to as "test domains," that comprise the Common Body of Knowledge (CBK) for the information systems security field: access control systems and methodology; operations security; cryptography; applications and systems development; business continuity and disaster planning; telecommunications and network security; security architecture and models; physical security; security management practices; and law, investigation, and ethics.

It is expected that most candidates will find the exam difficult unless they review the topics listed above. To help candidates prepare, (ISC)² has developed an information system security CBK Review Seminar. This seminar consists of eight days of instruction, presented as two four-day modules.

Who Needs It

The CISSP certification is an excellent way to demonstrate your knowledge as a computer security expert, whether to your current employer or to potential employers. It can also be an excellent certification for independent consultants who want to showcase their computer security skills for potential clients.

Requirements for Certification

The certification process requires the following steps:

1. Acquire the prerequisite three years of direct work experience in information systems security.

2. Agree to the (ISC)² Code of Ethics (contact (ISC)² for a copy).

3. Pass the CISSP exam.

Administrator

The test is administered by (ISC)².

Fee

The fee is $395.

Format

The exam consists of 250 multiple-choice questions and must be completed in 6 hours. A scaled score of 700 out of 1,000 is required for passing.

(ISC)² Resources

A draft study guide containing a description of the CBK test domains, sample test questions, and a list of reference materials is available to candidates at cost upon request. To obtain a copy, send a large, self-addressed shipping label and $10 for Priority Mail handling within the U.S. For airmail delivery outside the U.S., the cost (including postage) in U.S. dollars is: Canada—$10.42; Mexico—$13.46; other countries—$18.80. For more information on this organization's certifications and courses, contact (ISC)² at:

Web	http://www.isc2.org/
E-mail	info@isc2.org
	Or
	isc2office@compuserve.com
Mail	(ISC)²
	415 Boston Turnpike, Suite 105
	Shrewsbury, MA 01545-3469
Phone	(508) 845-9200
Fax	(508) 845-2420

Information Systems Audit and Control Association (ISACA) Certification

- Certified Information Systems Auditor (CISA)

The Information Systems Audit and Control Association (ISACA) is an international nonprofit professional organization of computer security professionals that has more than 19,000 members. ISACA sponsors a number of important conferences in the security field and has offered the well-known certification program—the Certified Information Systems Auditor—since 1979.

Recertification or Maintenance Requirements

To maintain certification, Certified Information Systems Auditors (CISAs) must take a minimum of 120 contact hours of continuing education every three years. ISACA specifies that a minimum of 20 hours of continuing education must be taken annually. Contact hours—which refer to clock hours, not course credits—can be earned by attending conferences, courses, and other professional development opportunities in the field. CISAs must also pay an annual maintenance fee.

Benefits of Certification

Certified Information Systems Auditors receive the following benefits:

- CISA logo for use on business cards and materials
- Wall certificate
- CISA newsletter

Certified Information Systems Auditor (CISA)

Qualifying for the CISA designation requires that the candidate meet an experience prerequisite, adhere to a code of ethics, pass an examination, and maintain certification through substantive continuing education requirements. The exam is offered only once each year. The CISA exam focuses on the following five topics:

- Information systems audit standards and practices and information systems security and control practices (8%)

- Information systems organization and management (15%)

- Information systems process (22%)

- Information systems integrity, confidentiality, and availability (29%)

- Information systems development, acquisition, and maintenance (26%)

Who Needs It

The CISA certification is an excellent way to validate your skills as an information systems control and security expert, whether for a current employer or for potential employers. It can also be an excellent designation for independent consultants who want to show potential clients proof of their abilities.

Requirements for Certification

The certification process requires the following steps:

1. Have a minimum of five years of experience in information systems auditing, control, or security. (Contact ISACA about substitutions and waivers of the experience requirement. Experience is verified independently with employers.)

2. Pass the CISA exam.

3. Agree to abide by the Information Systems Audit and Control Association Code of Professional Ethics.

4. Submit an application for certification.

5. Meet the annual continuing education requirements.

A candidate may choose to take the CISA exam prior to meeting the experience requirement, although the CISA designation will not be awarded until all requirements are met. If this is done, the application for certification must be submitted within five years of passing the CISA exam.

Administrator

ISACA administers all CISA exams.

Fee

The exam is given only once each year, usually in the month of June. Check the ISACA Web site for the test date. Early registration costs $295 for ISACA members and $385 for non-members. Late registration costs $325 for ISACA members and $425 for non-members.

ISACA dues for 1999 are $100, plus a one-time new member fee of $30. A student membership is available for $50 for full-time students or retired persons.

Format

The CISA Examination consists of 200 multiple-choice questions, administered during a four-hour session. Contact ISACA at certification@isaca.org for a registration form, or download it from ISACA's Web site. The exam is offered in the following languages: Dutch, English, French, German, Hebrew, Italian, Japanese, Korean, and Spanish.

Approximately 10 weeks after the test date, candidates will receive score reports. Candidates receiving a scaled score of 75 or better will pass the examination. To ensure the confidentiality of scores, test results will not be reported by telephone, fax, or e-mail.

ISACA Resources

The ISACA Web site offers an exam bulletin that details the test objectives and test registration procedures. In addition, candidates receive a guide to the CISA Examination after ISACA receives the completed registration form and payment. This guide provides a detailed outline of the subject areas covered on the examination, as well as a suggested list of reference materials, glossary of terms, and a sample copy of the answer sheet used for the exam. For more information on this organization's certification program, contact the Information Systems Audit and Control Association at:

Web	`http://www.isaca.org/`
E-mail	`certification@isaca.org`
Mail	Information Systems Audit and Control Association
	3701 Algonquin Road, Suite 1010
	Rolling Meadows, Illinois 60008
Phone	(847) 253-1545
Fax	(847) 253-1443

Learning Tree International Certification

- System and Network Security Certified Professional

Learning Tree International is a worldwide training organization that currently offers over 150 computer and networking courses in the United States, Europe, and Asia. As part of their curriculum in information technology, Learning Tree International offers 27 different vendor-independent professional certification programs, four of which are Internet-related. (For information on additional Learning Tree International certification programs, see Chapters 4, 5, 7, and 8.)

The Learning Tree International System and Network Security Certified Professional certification is based on the mastery of a comprehensive set of Web security courses. This credential may be useful to managers, network and system administrators, technical staff, support personnel, users, and others responsible for system security.

Recertification or Maintenance Requirements

There is no recertification requirement for Learning Tree International's certification programs.

NOTE   It is possible to obtain college credit for Learning Tree International certifications or courses. The American Council of Education (ACE) in Washington, D.C. has worked in cooperation with Learning Tree International to determine college course equivalencies for these courses and certifications. Approximately 1,500 colleges and universities in the United States will accept ACE recommendations for college credit. As a general rule, ACE will recommend two college credit hours for each four-day course. Learning Tree International will pay to have your Learning Tree International credentials registered with ACE and you can then request that your transcript be sent from ACE to any college or university. (Check with your college or university registrar to make sure that your institution accepts ACE recommendations for credit.)

Benefits of Certification

Learning Tree International Certified Professionals receive the following benefits:

- Framed diploma of Professional Certification

- An official record of the courses that you have completed

- Option of obtaining college credit

System and Network Security Certified Professional

This certification program consists of taking four core courses and one elective course, and passing the tests given at the end of each course. The courses and exams are designed to teach and test the candidate's ability to deploy firewalls, data encryption and decryption, and other countermeasures to reduce system susceptibility; implement and maintain data and systems security for Windows NT or UNIX; build a firewall to defend your network from external attack; secure NT or UNIX systems from internal and external threats; secure Web communications, servers, and sites; "harden" Windows NT or UNIX for use as part of a firewalled system; and develop an intranet/Internet security policy to protect your systems and data.

Who Needs It

The Learning Tree International System and Network Security Certified Professional credential is a respected vendor-independent certification for those who want to maintain the security of mission-critical data, and design and implement an organization's security strategy. Since the certification program requires comprehensive training classes, Learning Tree International certifications offer a means for those just beginning their networking careers to gain hands-on experience and training that may not currently be available on the job.

Requirements for Certification

The certification process requires the following steps:

1. Complete four core courses as listed in Table 14.2 and pass the test given at the end of each course (note that for the fourth core course, you have two options).

2. Complete one of the elective courses from the list in Table 14.3 and pass the test given at the end of the course.

TABLE 14.2: Required Courses/Tests for Learning Tree System and Network Security Certified Professional

Course/Test	Course/Test ID	Course Length
Internet and Intranet Security: A Comprehensive Introduction	468	4 days
Implementing Web Security: Hands-On	486	4 days
Deploying Internet and Intranet Firewalls: Hands-On	488	4 days
Windows NT Security OR	162	5 days
UNIX System and Network Security	433	4 days

T A B L E 14.3: Elective Courses/Tests for System and Learning Tree Network Security Certified Professional

Course/Test	Course/Test ID	Course Length
Windows 95 Support and Networking: Hands-On	153	5 days
Windows NT Optimization and Troubleshooting: Hands-On	160	5 days
Notes and Domino System Administration: Hands-On	181	5 days
Hands-On Microsoft Systems Management Server	156	4 days
Hands-On intraNetWare: NetWare 4.x Administration	264	5 days
UNIX: A Hands-On Introduction	336	4 days
UNIX Server Administration: Hands-On	436	4 days
Data Network Design and Performance Optimization	453	4 days
Windows NT 4 Workstation and Server: Hands-On	455	4 days
Developing a Web Site: Hands-On	470	4 days

Administrator

Courses and tests are administered by Learning Tree International (Call (800) THE-TREE).

Fee

At this writing, the prices for Learning Tree International courses are $1,295 for a two-day course, $1,745 for a three-day course, $2,195 for a four-day course, and $2,495 for a five-day course. Learning Tree offers some significant discounts for those taking more than one course and for government employees. There is no additional charge for the tests.

Format

Each exam consists of 40 to 60 questions based on the course material. If you fail to pass on the first try, Learning Tree International will arrange for you to take a proctored exam at your place of work.

Learning Tree International Resources

For more information about this organization's courses and certification programs, contact Learning Tree International at:

Web	http://www.learningtree.com/
E-mail	uscourses@learningtree.com
Mail	Learning Tree International
	1805 Library Street
	Reston, VA 20190-5630
Phone	(800) THE-TREE
Fax	(800) 709-6405

CHAPTER

15

Instructor and Trainer
Certifications

FEATURING

- Adobe Certification

- Banyan Certifications

- Chauncey Group International Certification

- Corel Certification

- Lotus Certifications

- Microsoft Certification

- Novell Certifications

- ProsoftTraining.com Certification

A number of the vendors and organizations that offer the certification programs described in this book also offer related training, either at their own corporate facilities or through authorized training centers. These training programs and courses are taught by instructors that the vendor or the training center recognizes as qualified to teach an "official" course. When courses are offered directly by a vendor, the course instructors are usually selected and qualified through an internal training program. However, many of the vendors that partner with training centers have designed instructor certification programs that are open to anyone who wants to become an instructor or trainer.

Becoming a certified instructor can lead to lots of great career opportunities. Companies and individuals spend millions of dollars each year to take training programs. As a result, trainers are in high demand and are often well paid, with salaries that can range from $50,000 to over $100,000 per year. In fact, in her 1998 salary survey of Microsoft professionals in *Microsoft Certified Professional Magazine*, Linda Briggs indicated that salaries for Microsoft Certified Trainers had increased by $12,000 over a one-year period, to an average of $77,000 nationwide. See the "Microsoft Certification" section that follows for more data on the costs and benefits of being an MCT.

Individuals seeking training certifications include computer and networking professionals who want to be able to deliver training either within their current organization or as an employee or contractor for a training organization. (See Chapter 1, "Instructor-led Training," for information on different types of training organizations.)

Certification programs for instructors or trainers tend to involve three educational components. To become certified as an instructor by a particular company, an individual will typically need to:

- Demonstrate technical competence with one or more of the company's products

- Provide evidence of competence in instructional techniques

- Complete training on the specific course content and sequence associated with the company's education curriculum

This chapter covers certification programs for instructors and trainers who want to provide authorized training for specific vendors, including Adobe, Banyan, Corel, Lotus, Microsoft, Novell, and ProsoftTraining.com. The vendor-independent Certified Technical Trainer (CTT) credential, offered by the Chauncey Group International, is also covered. This widely respected certification program is a required component of several of the vendor-based training certifications.

Use Table 15.1 to compare the number of required tests, the test format, the approximate cost of taking the test(s), number of required courses, cost of any required courses, and the relative difficulty of the certification programs in this chapter. The cost information is a general guideline; since things change rapidly in the world of certification programs, once you have selected a specific course of action you may want to double-check the costs.

TABLE 15.1: Instructor/Trainer Certifications

Certification	# of Required Tests	Test Format(s)	Total Cost of Required Tests	# of Required Courses	Total Cost of Required Courses	Difficulty	Notes
Adobe Certification							
Adobe Certified Training Provider	—	—	—	—	—	◐	You must be an Adobe Certified Expert on the product you will teach and provide verification of your instructor skills.
Banyan Certifications							
Certified Banyan Instructor (CBI)	—	—	—	1	VF	●	Must be a CBS. Must also be a CTT, have vendor instructor certification, or take an approved instructional skills course.
CBI: Problem Solving for VINES	—	—	—	1	VF	●	Must obtain CBI status first.

T A B L E 15.1: Instructor/Trainer Certifications *(continued)*

Certification	# of Required Tests	Test Format(s)	Total Cost of Required Tests	# of Required Courses	Total Cost of Required Courses	Difficulty	Notes
Chauncey Group International Certification							
Certified Technical Trainer (CTT)	1	MC	$150	—	—	◒	Also requires a performance video ($135 fee for processing).
Corel Certification							
Corel Certified Instructor	—	—	—	—	—	◒	You must first be a Corel Certified Expert in the product you want to teach. You must also possess the CTT certification or an industry-recognized equivalent. $200 application fee.
Lotus Certifications							
Certified Lotus End-User Instructor	—	—	—	—	—	○	You must obtain certification as a Certified Lotus Specialist (CLS) in either Lotus Notes R4 or Lotus Notes R5 and provide proof of instructional experience.
Certified Lotus Instructor: Level One	2	MC	VF (~$200)	3	VF ($1,500–2,000)	◒	Must provide proof of instructional experience.
Lotus Certifications *(continued)*							
Certified Lotus Instructor: Level Two	2	MC	VF (~$200)	3	VF ($2,000–2,500)	●	Must also have experience teaching Level One courses.
Microsoft Certification							
Microsoft Certified Trainer	—	—	—	—	—	◒	Must prove instructional skills (CTT, instructional course, or other vendor trainer certification) and pass the test for the course you want to teach.

T A B L E 15.1: Instructor/Trainer Certifications *(continued)*

Certification	# of Required Tests	Test Format(s)	Total Cost of Required Tests	# of Required Courses	Total Cost of Required Courses	Difficulty	Notes
Novell Certifications							
Certified Novell Instructor (CNI)	—	—	—	—	—	●	Obtain CNE, prove instructional skills (CTT or course), take the courses you want to teach, and pass the test for courses you will teach.
Master CNI	—	—	—	—	—	●	Obtain Master CNE, prove instructional skills (CTT or course), take the courses you want to teach, and pass test for courses you will teach.
ProsoftTraining.com Certification							
Prosoft Certified Trainer (PCT)	1	MC	CV	2	VF	◐	You can become a PCT in any of the eight tracks offered in ProsoftTraining.com's Certified Internet Webmaster (CIW) program (see Chapter 10 for more information about the CIW tracks).

Certification Difficulty: ○ Moderate   ◐ Challenging   ● Very Challenging

Test Format:: **MC:** Multiple Choice   **AT:** Adaptive Testing   **LA:** Live Application
PR: Hands-on Lab   **NA:** Not Applicable

Test Fee: **VF:** Test Fees can vary; consult testing center.   **CV:** Voucher for taking the exam is included in the fee for the required course(s); additional attempts cost extra.

We classified the difficulty of these certifications into three categories—Moderate, Challenging, and Very Challenging—based on the number of required tests and courses, and the relative difficulty of those tests or lab exams. These ratings are approximate and are offered simply as a general guide to help the reader distinguish between entry-level programs and those that require more advanced skill and knowledge. (This rating scale assumes that one has experience with the product or technology and has studied the appropriate subject content before attempting the exams.)

Adobe Certification

- Adobe Certified Training Provider (ACTP)

Adobe produces a number of excellent page layout and imaging programs used in desktop publishing and for producing Web pages, and it offers a number of related product-specific certifications through the Adobe Certified Expert program (see Chapter 6, "Software Certifications," for details). Previously, Adobe offered an Adobe Certified Instructor (ACI) program to train instructors to teach at Adobe Authorized Learning Provider (AALP) training centers. As of 1999, the ACI and AALP programs have been combined and converted into the new Adobe Certified Training Program (ACTP).

The ACTP program is for individual instructors, training businesses, and academic institutions that teach Adobe products. Becoming an ACTP allows you to teach the official Adobe curriculum for the product(s) for which you are certified as an Adobe Certified Expert. Candidates can obtain certification to teach one or more of the following products: Illustrator 7.0, Acrobat 3.0, After Effects 3.1, FrameMaker 5.5, PageMaker 6.5, PageMill 2.0, and Photoshop 4.0.

Recertification or Maintenance Requirements

Existing ACIs and AALPs can become ACTPs by completing the ACTP agreement, which is available online at the Adobe Web site. After the new agreement is processed, you will receive an ACTP welcome kit with a certificate and a password that allows you to download your new logo. There is no fee to join the ACTP program.

Benefits of Certification

Adobe Certified Training Providers (ACTPs) receive the following benefits:

- Certificate
- Listing on the Adobe Web site
- Use of the ACTP logo
- Beta software when available

Adobe Certified Training Provider (ACTP)

The ACTP program certifies individual instructors as well as training businesses, and academic institutions that teach Adobe products. Adobe Certified Training Providers are highly qualified technical trainers, proficient both in using Adobe software and in teaching others how to use it. To this end, certification candidates must pass an Adobe Product Proficiency exam to demonstrate skill in using a particular product, and must also verify their instructional skills.

Who Needs It

This certification allows you to train people within your company or at an outside training facility using the official Adobe curriculum. This can be an excellent way to increase your worth to your company or to get started on a lucrative career as a professional trainer.

Requirements for Certification

The certification process for an individual requires the following steps:

1. Submit an ACTP application, agreeing to its terms and conditions (available online at the Adobe Web site).

2. Become an Adobe Certified Expert (see Chapter 6 for details).

3. Verify your skills as an instructor by submitting one of the following:

   - Proof of certification as a Certified Technical Trainer (see the "Chauncey Group Certification" section in this chapter)
   - Valid teaching credential

- Valid Microsoft Certified Trainer (MCT), Certified Lotus Instructor (CLI), or Certified Novell Instructor (CNI) credential (these programs are described elsewhere in this chapter)

Adobe Resources

The Adobe Web site offers a listing of Adobe Certified Training Providers (ACTPs). For self-paced training, Adobe recommends the *Classroom in a Book* series of self-paced workbooks and *DigitalThink* Web-based Training; information about these resources is available on the Web site. For more information on this organization's certifications and courses, contact Adobe at:

Web	`http://www.adobe.com/supportservice training/ctpprogram.html`
E-mail	`certification@adobe.com`
Mail	Certification Coordinator
	Adobe Systems, Inc.
	M/S WT7-120
	345 Park Avenue
	San Jose, CA 95110-2704
Phone	(800) 685-4172
Fax	(408) 537-4033

Banyan Certifications

- Certified Banyan Instructor (CBI)

- Certified Banyan Instructor (CBI): Problem Solving for VINES Networks Authorization

Banyan VINES is a networking operating system designed by Banyan for use in large corporate networks, typically operating on UNIX-based servers. The current version—VINES 8—incorporates NT, Novell, and mainframe-based resources into directory services through Banyan's proprietary protocol, StreetTalk.

The Certified Banyan Instructor (CBI) credential is necessary for professional trainers who want to teach the Banyan education curriculum. The CBI is the most basic credential for teaching Banyan courses and workshops. CBIs are authorized to teach the VINES Administration and Advanced VINES Administration courses.

Additional training can allow CBIs to teach other Banyan courses. CBIs currently can receive an endorsement that allows them to teach the Problem Solving for VINES Networks course. The requirements for teaching other Banyan courses are still under development, but all will require completion of the CBI credential as a prerequisite.

Recertification or Maintenance Requirements

Banyan Certified Instructors are not required to take any action to maintain their instructor credential *per se*, but they must maintain their Certified Banyan Specialist (CBS) status. To maintain CBS certification you may be required to take a class or pass a test in order to teach a new course or to teach courses on newer software versions.

Benefits of Certification

Banyan Certified Instructors will receive these benefits:

- A congratulatory letter and plaque
- A "Certified Banyan Instructor" black briefcase bag
- A copy of the *CBInsider* quarterly newsletter

Certified Banyan Instructor (CBI)

The process of becoming a Certified Banyan Instructor has three steps. The CBI candidate must demonstrate instructional skills, prove technical competence, and attend an authorization session that covers a review of the content and the flow of Banyan courses. The first two steps must be completed prior to attending the CBI Authorization Session at Banyan. On completion of the basic CBI certification program, you will be authorized to teach the Banyan Network Administration (EDU120) and Advanced VINES Administration (EDU210) courses.

Who Needs It

The CBI certification is necessary for those who want to teach any Banyan courses or workshops. This credential can be an excellent way to increase your worth to your company. It can also be a useful credential for acquiring an instructor position with a training organization.

Requirements for Certification

The certification process requires the following steps:

1. Provide proof of instructional skills by one of the following methods:

   - Obtain certification as a Certified Technical Trainer (see "Chauncey Group Certification" below)

   - Become certified as an instructor for another vendor (Lotus, Microsoft, or Novell)

   - Attend one of the following instructional skills courses approved by Banyan:

     A. Instructional Techniques course from Friesen, Kaye and Associates (see www.fka.com or call (800) FKA-5585 for details)

     B. Effective Classroom Instruction from Practical Management, Inc. (call (800) 444-9101 for details)

2. Candidate must be a current CBS certified professional and demonstrate technical competence by scoring a minimum score on (a) either the VINES Administration (EDU110) or the Banyan Network Administration Course (EDU120) and (b) the Advanced VINES Administration (EDU210) tests. To qualify as a candidate for the CBI Authorization course, you must have an overall score of 85% on each test, or no more than one section on each test with a score less than 75%. Banyan recommends that the candidate attend the current courses for these exams.

3. Attend a Banyan Instructor Authorization Session (Course ID: AUT400-7). These sessions are offered only twice each year at Banyan's Westboro Education Center, in Massachusetts. The Banyan Instructor presenting this session evaluates the candidate and makes final recommendations for CBI Authorization.

NOTE CBIs who want to teach the Problem Solving for VINES Networks (EDU310) course must meet additional authorization requirements (see below).

Administrator

The Banyan authorization session is scheduled directly with Banyan (see the "Banyan Resources" section below for information). The CBS exams are scheduled through Sylvan Prometric (see Chapter 9, "Network Operating Systems Certifications," for information on CBS exams).

Fee

The fee for this authorization course is $1,800, but it is subject to change; call Banyan at (508) 898-1795 for current pricing.

Format

The authorization session consists of a three-day course taught by an authorized Banyan instructor.

Certified Banyan Instructor (CBI): Problem Solving for VINES Networks Authorization

CBIs who want to teach the hands-on Problem Solving for VINES Networks (EDU310) course must meet one additional requirement beyond the CBI certification. They will need to participate in an additional Banyan authorization session specific to this course. In this session, candidates will receive the instructor guide for the course and assist a Banyan instructor with the lab setup and classroom activities for a Problem Solving for VINES Networks course.

Who Needs It

This credential is necessary for technical trainers who want to teach the Banyan Problem Solving for VINES Networks course.

Requirements for Certification

The certification process requires the following steps:

1. Obtain certification as a CBI (see "Certified Banyan Instructor (CBI)" above).

2. To qualify as a candidate for the Problem Solving for VINES Networks Authorization (AUT410-7) session, an overall score of 85 percent on the Problem Solving for VINES Networks (EDU310) test is required; in addition, the candidate may not score less than 75 percent on more than one section of the test.

3. Attend the Problem Solving for VINES Networks Authorization session (AUT410-7) at Banyan's Westboro Education Center in Massachusetts. The candidate will assist the Banyan instructor with lab setup and classroom activities during a regularly scheduled Problem Solving for VINES Networks course.

Administrator

The Banyan authorization session is scheduled directly with Banyan (see the Banyan Resources section).

Fee

The fee for this authorization course is $1,200, but it may change; call Banyan at (508) 898-1795 for current pricing.

Format

The authorization session for the problem-solving course consists of co-teaching a three-day course with an authorized instructor.

Banyan Resources

For more information on this organization's certifications and courses, contact Banyan at:

Web	http://www.banyan.com/support/cbi.htm
E-mail	Jbernstein@banyan.com
Mail	Judi Bernstein
	Program Coordinator/Certification Programs
	Banyan Systems Incorporated
	Educational Services Department
	120 Flanders Road
	Westboro, MA 01581
Phone	(508) 898-1795
Fax	(508) 836-0225

Chauncey Group International Certification

- Certified Technical Trainer (CTT)

The Chauncey Group is a subsidiary of the Educational Testing Service (ETS), a private measurement and research organization that develops and administers academic tests, such as the GRE and SAT. The Chauncey Group has developed several certification programs, including the premier vendor-independent certification for technical trainers: the Certified Technical Trainer (CTT) program.

The CTT program, created in 1995, is based on a set of professional standards for instructor knowledge and classroom performance defined by the International Board of Standards for Training, Performance, and Instruction (ibstpi). These widely recognized standards for technical training are described in the book *Instructor Competencies: The Standards, Volume I* (published by The Chauncey Group), and are also referred to as the ibstpi standards.

While the CTT program has been most widely acknowledged and used within the computer industry, the knowledge and skills it provides are also applicable to other types of technical training. The CTT credential will be valuable in a wide variety of settings.

NOTE   Chauncey Group offers a second credential, the Certified Professional Development Trainer (CPDT), which targets the same instructor competencies but focuses more on employee and organizational development—management, leadership, and communication skills (for information on the CPDT program, see http://www.chauncey.com).

Recertification or Maintenance Requirements

The CTT credential is good for five years. When five years have passed, trainers must repeat the certification process to retain their credential.

Benefits of Certification

Certified Technical Trainers receive these benefits:

- A certificate and a CTT lapel pin

- Copies of the CTT logo for use on business cards and stationery

- Listing in the CTT Certification Registry, which is available to employers and industry groups

Certified Technical Trainer (CTT)

The CTT Program was initially created to eliminate redundancies among instructor certification programs in the computer training and education business. The CTT certification process involves a computer-based exam and a videotaped performance assessment. The exam must be taken prior to the performance assessment.

The questions on the computer-based exam are designed to assess the trainer's understanding of the content and application of the ibstpi standards. The book describing the standards, *Instructor Competencies: The Standards, Volume I,* can be ordered from Chauncey Group (see Chauncey Group Resources section for more information).

Bring along a photograph of yourself when you take the test. The Sylvan testing center will mark the photo with a special stamp. When you later submit your performance video, you will also enclose the stamped photo so it can be compared with your likeness in the videotape.

The performance video is used to evaluate the trainer's ability to apply the ibstpi standards in a real training setting. You will need to make a videotape of yourself teaching a training class using a specified set of the competencies from the ibstpi standards. It will be graded and the results reported back within a few weeks. The videotape must be submitted within three months of passing the computer-based exam. Chauncey Group offers a videotape entitled "Creating a Successful Videotape for the CTT Performance Assessment" to help candidates prepare their own videotapes.

For detailed information on getting your CTT, be sure to download the comprehensive CTT bulletin (see http://www.chauncey.com).

Who Needs It

This widely recognized certification can be the first important step toward a career in training in a variety of technical arenas. The CTT is an excellent way for computer professionals to prove their abilities to teach training courses, and is a key component in obtaining additional training certifications with a number of vendors.

Requirements for Certification

The certification process requires the following steps:

1. Pass the computer-based CTT exam. At the same time, get your photograph stamped, as described above.

2. Within three months of passing the test, submit your 20-minute performance assessment videotape. Enclose the submission forms from the online candidate bulletin, your photo, and a copy of your test report.

Administrator

The CTT exam is administered by Sylvan Prometric. Call (800) 727-8490 to register for Chauncey Group tests; if outside the U.S., use the online Sylvan Test Center Locator at www.sylvanprometric.com to find the nearest testing center. (See Chapter 3, "Taking Your Test," for additional information on Sylvan Prometric.)

Fee

The fee is $150 for the computer-based exam, $135 for evaluation of the performance video.

Format

The computer-based exam consists of 105 multiple-choice questions and must be completed in one hour and 45 minutes. Allow an additional 15 minutes for a short pre-test tutorial and an exit evaluation.

Chauncey Group International Resources

The Chauncey Group Web site offers a comprehensive bulletin about the CTT program, including a summary of the ibstpi standards as well as hints on preparing for the written exam and creating your video submission. You can order a copy of the standards book ($15.95) and video ($25.95) previously mentioned by calling 800-258-4914. For more information on this organization's certifications and courses, contact The Chauncey Group at:

Web	http://www.chauncey.com/itt/cttp001.html
E-mail	cttp@chauncey.com
Mail	The Chauncey Group International
	P.O. Box 6541
	Princeton, NJ 08541-6541
Phone	(800) 258-4914
Fax	(609) 720-6550

Corel Certification

- Corel Certified Instructor (CCI)

Corel Corporation, maker of several excellent word processing, spreadsheet, presentation, and drafting programs, offers a certification program for instructors who want to teach courses on these programs. Corel Certified Instructors (CCIs) can teach these courses at numerous training companies that have been authorized as Corel Training Partners. CCIs may become approved to teach one or more of the following applications: WordPerfect, Quattro Pro, Corel Presentations, CorelDRAW, and Corel Photo-Paint.

Recertification or Maintenance Requirements

Corel Certified Instructor certifications are based on specific products and specific versions. As new products and versions become available, certification should be updated accordingly.

Benefits of Certification

Corel Certified Instructors receive these benefits:

- CCI Certificate and approval letter
- Use of CCI program logos
- Direct referrals from Corel, when applicable
- Discounts on single copies of Corel academic products
- Access to a private CCI Web site
- Monthly online newsletter from Corel's education division

Corel Certified Instructor (CCI)

This certification program has two main components. First, the candidate must pass the examination on the selected Corel application at the Corel Certified Expert (CCE) User level (for more information about the Corel software certification exams, see Chapter 6, "Software Certifications"). Second, the candidate must become a Certified Technical Trainer (see "Chauncey Group Certification" above), or attain an industry-recognized equivalent certification as designated in the requirements listed below.

It is expected that a candidate will acquire a minimum of six months of experience working with computer applications—word processors, spreadsheets, and database applications—prior to applying for this certification, as well as a minimum of six months of teaching experience, tutoring, or hands-on consulting work.

CCIs can become approved to teach one or more of the following applications:

- Word Perfect
- QuattroPro
- Corel Presentations
- CorelDRAW
- Corel Photo-Paint

Who Needs It

This certification allows you to teach Corel courses for your company or at an outside training facility. This can be an excellent way to increase your worth to your present employer or to begin a career as a professional trainer.

Requirements for Certification

The certification process requires the following steps:

1. Pass the appropriate exams for the application you want to teach at the Corel Certified Expert (CCE) User level. (See Chapter 6, Software Certifications," for information on these exams.)

2. Submit proof of successful completion of the Certified Technical Trainer program (see "Chauncey Group Certification" described previously in this chapter) or an industry-recognized equivalent (Certified Novell Instructor, WordPerfect Certified Instructor, Lotus Notes Certified Instructor, or Microsoft Certified Trainer).

3. Submit a completed CCI application form, signed CCI agreement, a signed trademark usage agreement, a detailed resume, and an application fee of $200.

Fee

The application fee is $200. This fee may be waived; contact Corel for details.

Corel Resources

The Corel Web site offers exam bulletins that detail the objectives of each exam. For more information on this organization's certifications and courses, contact Corel at:

Web	http://www.corel.com/learning/training/
E-mail	custserv2@corel.com
Mail	Corel Corporation
	1600 Carling Avenue
	Ottawa, Ontario
	K1Z 8R7
	Canada

Phone	(800) 772-6735
Fax	(613) 761-9176
Faxback	(613) 728-0826, ext. 3080

Lotus Certifications

- Certified Lotus End-User Instructor (CLEI)

- Certified Lotus Instructor (CLI): Level One

- Certified Lotus Instructor (CLI): Level Two

Lotus was launched in 1982 with the popular spreadsheet program, Lotus 1-2-3. Since then, Lotus has branched out into several other areas, including business collaboration software (Lotus Notes) and the software for the Internet (Lotus Domino). Lotus offers an instructor certification program for those who want to teach courses on Lotus products. This program is designed for individuals who will be employed by Lotus Authorized Education Centers (LAECs) or Lotus Education Academic Partners (LEAPs), or who plan to become independent certified Lotus instructors.

Lotus offers two types of instructor certification. The entry-level Certified Lotus End-user Instructor (CLEI) is for those who teach Lotus Education end-user training courses. The CLEI builds on the entry-level Certified Lotus Specialist (CLS) designation. Getting your CLEI can be an entry point toward getting a higher-level Lotus instructor certification. (For more information about the CLS designation, see the Lotus Certification section of Chapter 6.)

The Certified Lotus Instructor (CLI) program is open only to persons who are already experienced technical trainers, and requires a high level of Lotus product knowledge and familiarity with the Lotus curriculum. The CLI certification builds on the Certified Lotus Professional (CLP) program. (For more information about the CLP designation, see the Lotus Certification section of Chapter 6.)

Within the CLI program, Lotus offers several levels of instructor certification for those who want to teach courses on Lotus products. Level One Certified Lotus Instructors (CLIs) can teach Level One Lotus classes. Level Two CLIs can teach both Level One and Level Two Lotus classes, as explained in the Level Two CLI section.

In most cases, the teaching of more advanced Lotus classes requires that—after completion of Level Two certification—the trainer attend the additional course he or she wants to teach, purchase the instructor kit for that course, and pass the certification exam for that course. An extensive list of the additional course-specific instructor certification requirements for CLIs is provided online (see http://www.lotus .com/instructor).

NOTE If you want to become an independent Certified Lotus End-User Instructor (CLEI) or Certified Lotus Instructor (CLI) you must complete additional steps, which are outlined on the Lotus Education Web site.

Recertification or Maintenance Requirements

To maintain their certifications, CLIs are required to attend instructor update training classes on the courses they teach when the related Lotus products are upgraded.

Benefits of Certification

Certified Lotus End-User Instructors (CLEIs) receive these benefits:

- Certificate

- Use of CLEI logo

- Benefits of the CLS, including a bimonthly newsletter and logo usage

Certified Lotus Instructors (CLIs) receive these benefits:

- Use of CLI logo

- Updates on product and courseware changes

- Access to an online instructor discussion forum and interactive instructor and courseware databases

- Access to a private CLI Web site that provides instructor news and product updates

- Opportunity to serve on CLI Advisory Council

- Benefits of the CLP, including a bimonthly newsletter and logo usage

Certified Lotus End-User Instructor (CLEI)

As part of their certification process, prospective CLEIs must obtain certification as a Certified Lotus Specialist (CLS) in either Lotus Notes R4 or Lotus Notes R5. The following prerequisites are required for acceptance into the CLI program:

- At least one year of end-user training experience in a networked environment

- At least one year of experience with networks, PC hardware, software installation, and maintenance on any platform

- A minimum of three months of experience with Lotus products

Who Needs It

In North America, the CLEI program is a way for end-user instructors to receive recognition. In other countries, the CLEI certification is necessary as an entry point for individuals who will be employed by Lotus Authorized Education Centers or plan to become independent certified Lotus instructors.

CLEIs who are certified in Lotus Notes R4 can teach these courses: Lotus Notes Basics, Lotus Notes: Beyond Basics, Lotus Notes Power User, Lotus Notes Mobile User, Calendaring & Scheduling, Using Notes Mail, and Moving to Notes Mail. CLEIs who are certified in Lotus Notes R5 can teach these courses: Introducing the Notes Client, Extending the Notes Client, Working in Domino Databases, Using Notes Calendaring & Scheduling, and Moving to Notes Mail.

Requirements for Certification

The certification process requires the following steps:

1. Meet the prerequisites previously described.

2. Submit the following items to the CLEI Program for approval:

   - Completed CLEI application and instructor agreement (available online at http://www.lotus.com/certification)

   - Five to ten sample evaluations from end-user training done within the last year

   - Current resume

3. Attain certification as a CLS in Lotus Notes R4 or Lotus Notes R5. It is strongly recommended that those who get their CLS in Lotus Notes R4 do so by taking the Application Development 1 exam (Test ID: 190-271). It is strongly recommended that those who get their CLS in Lotus Notes R5 do so by taking the Domino R5 Designer Fundamentals exam (Test ID: 191-520). (See Chapter 6 for information on CLS certification.)

NOTE If you have attained R4 CLEI certification, you can become an R5 CLEI by getting your CLS in R5. It is not necessary to reapply into the program.

Administrator

Lotus exams can be taken from Sylvan Prometric or CATGlobal. Call (800) 745-6887 to register for a Lotus exam through Sylvan; if outside the U.S., use the online Sylvan Test Center Locator at www.sylvanprometric.com to find the nearest testing center. To take your test through CATGlobal, see their Web site at http://www.catglobal.com/ for registration information. Chapter 3 contains detailed information on taking tests from Sylvan and CATGlobal.

Fee

The exams for the CLS program are usually $100 each, but cost can vary. Independent CLIs must maintain membership in the Lotus Business Partners Program and pay any associated fees.

Format

The format of the CLS exams is covered in Chapter 6.

Certified Lotus Instructor (CLI): Level One

The CLI certification program requires candidates to have proven technical training skills as well as proficiency with Lotus products and curriculum. Lotus recommends that CLI candidates allow a minimum of three months to achieve Level One certification. The following prerequisites are required for acceptance into the CLI program:

- At least one year of technical training experience in a networked environment

- At least one year of experience with networks, PC hardware, software installation, and maintenance on any platform

- A minimum of three months of experience with Lotus products

Those who seek CLI certification must actually attend each Lotus course they intend to teach. While technical professionals seeking software certifications as Certified Lotus Professionals (see Chapter 6 for more information) may use self-study and computer-based training to prepare for their certification tests, those who seek CLI status must attend the required courses. Each course you attend must be taught by a Certified Lotus Instructor; a copy of your Course Completion Certificate will be required as proof of attendance.

Who Needs It

The CLI certification is necessary for individuals who will be employed by Lotus Authorized Education Centers or plan to become Independent Certified Lotus Instructors. Level One CLI certification allows the teaching of Level One courses.

Requirements for Certification

The certification process requires the following steps:

1. Meet the prerequisites described above.

2. Submit the following items to the CLI Program for approval:

   - Completed CLI application and instructor agreement (available online at Lotus Web site)

- Five to ten sample evaluations from end-user training done within the last year

- Current resume

3. If approved, attend the Level One Lotus classes listed below and pass the corresponding CLP certification exams (see Chapter 6 for more information on these tests):

   - Application Development 1

   - System Administration 1

4. Attain certification as a CLP Application Developer or CLP System Administrator (this requires passing one additional exam; see Chapter 6 for information on these certifications).

5. Pass the Lotus Level I Instructor Certification Evaluation (ICE) class. This is a three-day course that evaluates a candidate's ability to teach Level One Notes courses (i.e., Application Development I and System Administration I). The ICE class must be taken within six months of original application. All required documentation listed above must be submitted at least three weeks prior to taking the ICE class.

Administrator

The ICE course is available at Lotus headquarters and at Lotus Authorized Education Centers (LAECs).

Lotus exams can be taken from Sylvan Prometric or CATGlobal. Call (800) 745-6887 to register for a Lotus exam through Sylvan; if outside the U.S., use the online Sylvan Test Center Locator at www.sylvanprometric.com to find the nearest testing center. To take your test through CATGlobal, see their Web site at http://www.catglobal.com/ for registration information. Chapter 3 contains detailed information on taking tests from Sylvan and CATGlobal.

Fee

The exams for the Level One Lotus classes are usually $100 each, but can vary. The Level One ICE class fee is $1,500, which includes the cost of two instructor guide kits.

Independent CLIs must maintain membership in the Lotus Business Partners Program and pay any associated fees.

Format

The three-day Level One Instructor Certification Evaluation (ICE) class incorporates an in-class performance evaluation. The format of the CLP exams is covered in Chapter 6.

Certified Lotus Instructor (CLI): Level Two

Level Two of the CLI program builds on the Level One CLI certification above. Level Two CLIs specialize in either application development or system administration; they can then teach those Level Two courses in addition to the Level One Lotus courses. The two Level Two CLI specializations are named as follows:

- Application Development Level 2 (AD2) CLI

- System Administration Level 2 (SA2) CLI

Lotus recommends that CLI candidates allow up to a year for completion of the process for Level Two or higher instructor certification, depending upon their level of product knowledge and degree of flexibility when scheduling classes.

Those who seek CLI certification must actually attend each Lotus course they intend to teach. While technical professionals seeking software certifications as Certified Lotus Professionals (see Chapter 6 for more information) may use self-study and computer-based training to prepare for these same certification tests, those who seek CLI status must attend the required courses. Each course you attend must be taught by a Certified Lotus Instructor; a copy of your Course Completion Certificate will be required as proof of attendance.

NOTE Level Two certification doesn't prepare a CLI to teach all Lotus courses. The teaching of more advanced Lotus classes requires that— after completion of Level Two certification—you must attend the additional course you want to teach, purchase the instructor kit for that course, and pass the certification exam for that course. An extensive list of the additional course-specific instructor certification requirements for CLIs is provided online (see http://www.lotus.com/instructor).

Who Needs It

The CLI program is necessary for individuals who want to teach Level Two courses for Lotus Authorized Education Centers or as Independent Certified Lotus Instructors. In addition to Level One courses, a Level 2 AD2 CLI can teach Application Development 2, and a Level 2 SA2 CLI can teach System Administration 2. Level 2 CLI certification is also a necessary step in attaining approval to teach additional advanced courses.

Requirements for Certification

The certification process requires the following steps:

1. Attain Level One CLI certification.

2. Take and successfully complete one of the two courses listed below—select the course appropriate for the title you seek:

   ▪ Application Development 2 course

   ▪ System Administration 2 course

3. Pass one of the two exams listed below—select the exam appropriate for the title you seek:

   ▪ Application Development 2 exam (Test ID190-272)

   ▪ System Administration 2 exam (Test ID190-275)

4. Submit proof of good class evaluations as follows:

   ▪ If you seek AD2 CLI status, teach the AD1 course at least twice and the SA1 course at least once with class evaluation scores averaging 80 percent or higher (submit ALL evaluation scores electronically to Lotus Education).

   ▪ If you seek SA2 CLI status, teach the SA1 course at least twice and the AD1 course at least once with class evaluation scores averaging 80 percent or higher (submit ALL evaluation scores electronically to Lotus Education).

5. Complete a two-day Lotus Instructor Certification Enablement (ICE) class appropriate for the title you seek, either the ICE Level 2 Application Development (AD2) class or the ICE Level 2 System Administration (SA2) class.

Administrator

The ICE courses are scheduled at various locations. Contact the Lotus Education Helpline ((800) 346-6409) for a schedule.

Lotus exams can be taken from Sylvan Prometric or CATGlobal. Call (800) 745-6887 to register for a Lotus exam through Sylvan; if outside the U.S., use the online Sylvan Test Center Locator at http://www.sylvanprometric.com to find the nearest testing center. To take your test through CATGlobal, see their Web site at http://www.cat-global .com/ for registration information. Chapter 3 contains detailed information on taking tests from Sylvan and CATGlobal.

Fee

The exams for the Level Two Lotus classes are $100 each, but can vary. The Level Two ICE classes cost U.S. $1,000 each, which includes the cost of the instructor guide kit.

Independent CLIs must maintain membership in the Lotus Business Partners Program and pay any associated fees.

Format

The two-day Level Two Instructor Certification Enablement (ICE) class incorporates activities that prepare CLIs to teach more effectively. The format of the CLP exams is covered in Chapter 6.

Lotus Resources

For more information on this organization's certifications and courses, contact Lotus at:

Web	http://www.lotus.com/
Mail	CLI Program Coordinator
	Lotus Development
	One Charles Park
	Cambridge, MA 02141-2130
Phone	(617) 693-2615
Fax	(617) 693-2409

Microsoft Certification

- Microsoft Certified Trainer (MCT)

Microsoft courses are designed to educate computer professionals who use, support, and implement solutions that use Microsoft technology. Microsoft Certified Trainers (MCTs) are certified by Microsoft as technically and instructionally qualified to deliver Microsoft Official Curriculum instructor-led courses at Microsoft Authorized Technical Education Centers (ATECs).

In a 1998 survey in *Microsoft Certified Professional Magazine*, Linda Briggs provided survey data indicating a new MCT with less than six months of experience averaged a starting salary of $47,500, while MCTs with over eight years of experience pulled down average salaries of $85,600. Briggs noted that MCTs also tend to spend a lot of time and money on their *own* training in order to stay current, averaging over 200 hours per year at a cost of almost $7,000. She also suggested that the hottest combination of training credentials to hold was the MCT with an MCP + Internet (see Chapter 13 for information on the MCP + Internet certification program); according to Briggs, in 1998, trainers with these two credentials billed their time at an average of $159 per hour.

NOTE Updated salary survey information on MCPs is provided annually in the July issue of the *Microsoft Certified Professional Magazine.*

Recertification or Maintenance Requirements

Maintaining your status as a Microsoft Certified Trainer requires the following:

- Maintain high satisfaction ratings on student course evaluations
- Keep technical skills up-to-date and pass any additional required exams

- Meet any new continuing certification criteria developed by Microsoft

- Take part in activities sponsored by your local Microsoft field office

Benefits of Certification

Microsoft Certified Trainers receive these benefits:

- Certificate

- Transcript that lists courses you are eligible to teach

- Logo for use on stationery and business cards

- Access to private MCT Web site, which provides the latest product and training information, access to newsgroups, and the *Microsoft Education Forum* newsletter

- Free one-year subscription to *Microsoft Certified Professional Magazine*

- Invitation to Microsoft training events

Microsoft Certified Trainer

In order to use the Microsoft Official Curriculum for a training course, an instructor must be a Microsoft Certified Trainer, and must be authorized to teach that particular course.

The process of becoming an MCT requires that you submit for approval an application that substantiates your credentials as a technical trainer. Once your application is approved, you have 90 days to obtain your first course certification. You will go through an MCT course certification approval process for each course you want to teach. You will not be considered an MCT in full standing—eligible for MCT benefits—until you have completed the course certification requirements to teach at least one course. If you don't achieve your first course certification within 90 days, you must reapply.

If you are not already a Microsoft Certified Professional (MCP), you may become one during this process (if the course you want to teach requires an MCP exam). MCP exams (covered in Chapter 7, "Programming Certifications," and in Chapter 10, "Network Management Certifications") certify your ability to use and support Microsoft products.

Who Needs It

This certification allows you to teach courses—within your company or at an outside authorized training facility (ATEC)—using official Microsoft courseware. This can be an excellent way to increase your worth to your present employer or to begin a career as a professional trainer.

Requirements for Certification

The certification process requires the following steps:

1. Submit a completed Microsoft Certified Trainer application, which requires proof of your instructional presentation skills as a technical trainer in one of the following ways:

   - Obtain the Certified Technical Trainer credential (see "Chauncey Group Certification" previously described in this chapter)

   - Attend a Microsoft-approved instructional presentation skills course (see http://www.microsoft.com/train_cert/mct/ for a list of approved courses)

   - Provide proof of certification as a trainer with another vendor—Novell, Lotus, Santa Cruz Operation, Banyan VINES, Cisco Systems, or Sun Microsystems

2. If approved, complete your first course certification within 90 days. To attain MCT course certification approval for the first course you intend to teach, you must:

   - Pass any prerequisite MCP exams

   - Prepare to teach the course by studying the Microsoft trainer kit for that course (obtainable by approved MCT candidates by calling (800) 457-1766)

   - Attend the class at a Microsoft Authorized Technical Education Center—either a publicly taught course or a course designed specifically for trainer preparation (referred to as a T-prep course)

   - Complete a Microsoft course preparation checklist

   - Pass the MCP exam for the course; you also may be required to pass an MCT assessment exam (this information is found on a private Web site that is provided for MCTs)

- Apply for course certification.

3. To attain additional MCT course certifications, follow the steps outlined above, with one exception—you may either physically attend the course or learn the material through self-study.

4. If you are an independent MCT—not sponsored by an ATEC— you must submit an application fee.

Administrator

Tests are administered by Sylvan Prometric. Call (800) 755-3926 to register for Microsoft tests; if outside the U.S., use the online Sylvan Test Center Locator at http://www.sylvanprometric.com to find the nearest testing center. Chapter 3 contains detailed information on taking tests from Sylvan.

Courses are available from Microsoft Authorized Technical Education Centers.

Fee

Most of the exams cost $100 each, but cost may vary. The cost of attending each course will vary with location. For more information see the Microsoft sections of Chapters 9 and 12. Consult Sylvan Prometric for exam information, and Microsoft for course information.

The application fee for independent MCTs is $200.

Microsoft Resources

The Microsoft Web site offers a detailed MCT application packet and other information about the certification program. For more information on this organization's certifications and courses, contact Microsoft at:

Web	http://www.microsoft.com/mcp/
E-mail	mcp@msprograms.com
Mail	Microsoft Corporation
	One Microsoft Way
	Redmond, WA 98052-6399
Phone	(800) 636-7544
Fax	(425) 936-7329

Novell Certifications

- Certified Novell Instructor (CNI)

- Master Certified Novell Instructor (Master CNI)

Novell has offered a network operating systems certification—the Certified Novell Engineer (CNE)—since 1987, and has recently added new levels to this widely recognized technical certification. Novell also offers the respected Certified Novell Instructor (CNI) credential.

Novell courses are taught only by Novell-certified instructors who are employed by or contract their services to Novell Authorized Education Centers (NAECs) or Novell Education Academic Partners (NEAPs). NAECs are training organizations authorized to offer Novell courses, and include Novell distributors, resellers, consultants, retail organizations, and independent training organizations.NEAPs are colleges and universities that teach Novell courses as part of their regular curriculum.

With the recent elimination of the Certified InfiLearning Instructor certification, the CNI program now offers two levels of instructor certification: Certified Novell Instructor (CNI) and Master Certified Novell Instructor (Master CNI). Instructors can teach only those Novell courses that they have acquired specific authorization to teach.

Recertification or Maintenance Requirements

Master CNIs must meet annual Master CNI update requirements. They must also keep their CNE status active and current in order to maintain their CNI status. Certification update requirements are flexible and can be selected from a list of options found on Novell's Education Web site at http://education.novell.com/. CNIs must also pay an annual $200 fee.

Benefits of Certification

Certified Novell Instructors (CNIs) and Master CNIs receive these benefits:

- Certificate

- Access to the Novell Instructor Web site

- E-mail updates on program and course changes via CNI Express

- Quarterly Instructor Guide CDs

- Access to CNI Channel Link, a private instructor forum

- Discounts on Novell software, training videos, and publications

- Name and course authorizations added to private list accessible to education centers

- Invitations to instructor conferences and events, including the BrainShare conference

Certified Novell Instructor (CNI)

The Certified Novell Instructor (CNI) credential is for trainers that want to concentrate on teaching Novell products, including advanced topics. In addition to providing evidence of instructional skills, CNIs must also be certified as Certified Novell Engineers (CNEs).

Novell's requirement for demonstrated instructional skills can be met by providing evidence of Certified Technical Trainer (CTT) status (see "Chauncey Group Certification" explained earlier) or by passing a Novell Instructor Performance Evaluation (IPE). The IPE is a two-day evaluation given at a Novell corporate training facility. The IPE involves an orientation session and then the on-site preparation and delivery of a presentation on a course topic chosen by the evaluator.

Once certified, a CNI can become authorized to teach any instructor-led Novell course—including those in the CNA, CNE, Master CNE, and Certified Internet Professional tracks—by attending the course and passing the course exam at the instructor level (see Chapter 10 for more information on the several Novell networking certifications).

Novell expects that instructors at all levels have in-depth knowledge of microcomputer concepts, including hardware and operating systems, at least one year of hands-on experience in the computing or networking industry, and at least one year of experience teaching adults in a classroom setting.

Who Needs It

This certification allows you to teach Novell courses as a Novell Authorized Education Centers (NAEC) instructor, Novell Education Academic Partners (NEAP) instructor, or contract instructor. This can be an excellent way to increase your worth to your present employer or to boost your career as a professional trainer.

Requirements for Certification

The certification process requires the following steps:

1. Obtain and maintain certification as a Certified Novell Engineer (see Chapter 9 for more information on the CNE).

2. Submit an application and signed agreement. This can be done online at http://education.novell.com/ or when taking any Novell test at an authorized testing center.

3. Pass a Novell Instructor Performance Evaluation (described above) or submit a CTT certificate.

4. Acquire individual course instructor authorizations by attending each course and passing the course exam at the instructor level.

Administrator

Novell tests are administered by Sylvan Prometric and Virtual University Enterprises (VUE). To register for a test with VUE, call (800) 511-8123 or visit the VUE Web site (see http://www.vue.com/student-services/). To register for a test with Sylvan, call (800) 733-3926; if outside the U.S., use the online Sylvan Test Center Locator at www.sylvanprometric.com to find the nearest testing center. Chapter 3 contains detailed information on taking tests from Sylvan or VUE.

Fee

Tests cost $95 each.

Format

All exams are closed-book, computer-based tests. Depending on the course, exams may be in traditional format (60–90 questions, 60–180 minute time limit, graded on a percentage) or adaptive format (30-minute exams that determine your level of proficiency using a minimum number of questions). Both traditional and adaptive exams can contain performance-based questions (problem-solving scenarios and simulations).

Master Certified Novell Instructor (Master CNI)

The Master Certified Novell Instructor (Master CNI) certification, initiated in November 1997, is Novell's most prestigious credential for technical trainers. Master CNIs must have two years of CNI teaching experience and be certified as Master Certified Novell Engineers (Master CNEs). In addition, they must complete an Annual Update Requirement to keep their technical skills up to date.

Master CNIs can expand their course certifications for standard Novell Education courses simply by passing the course exams (regular CNIs must attend the courses). Master CNIs also may apply as speakers for Novell's annual BrainShare technical conference.

Who Needs It

The Master CNI certification offers CNIs a way to further their certification and improve their competitiveness in the job market.

Requirements for Certification

The certification process requires the following steps:

1. Work as a CNI for two years.

2. Earn and maintain certification as a Master CNE (see Chapter 9, "Network Operating Certifications," for more information).

3. Meet an Annual Update Requirement initially and annually thereafter.

4. Obtain individual course instructor authorizations by passing the course exams at the instructor level.

Administrator

Novell tests are administered by Sylvan Prometric and Virtual University Enterprises (VUE). To register for a test with VUE, call (800) 511-8123 or visit the VUE Web site (see http://www.vue.com/student-services/). To register for a test with Sylvan, call (800) 733-3926; if outside the U.S., use the online Sylvan Test Center Locator at http://www.sylvanprometric.com to find the nearest testing center. Chapter 3 contains detailed information on taking tests from Sylvan or VUE.

Fee

Tests cost $95 each.

Format

All exams are closed-book, computer-based tests. Depending on the course, exams may be in traditional format (60–90 questions, 60–180 minute time limit, graded on a percentage), adaptive format (30-minute exams that determine your level of proficiency using a minimum number of questions). Both traditional and adaptive exams can contain performance-based questions (problem-solving scenarios and simulations).

Novell Resources

For more information on this organization's certifications and courses, contact Novell at:

Web	http://education.novell.com/
E-mail	edcustomer@novell.com
Mail	Novell Education Customer Solutions Team
	Novell, Inc.
	Mail Stop Orm-Q354
	1555 North Technology Way
	Orem, UT 84097
Phone	(800) 233-3382, Option 4 or (801) 861-3382
Fax	(801) 222-7875

ProsoftTraining.com Certification

- Prosoft Certified Trainer (PCT)

ProsoftTraining.com certifies the skills of technical professionals in several areas related to the Internet through their Certified Internet Webmaster (CIW) program. The CIW program, which offers eight tracks, including enterprise development, security, and E-Commerce, is described in Chapter 13. ProsoftTraining.com courses can be taught only by Prosoft Certified Trainers (PCTs). The PCT program, which was developed in 1998 to replace the Prosoft/NGt Certified Instructor program, allows instructors to obtain their PCT credential in any of the eight tracks offered in the CIW program.

Recertification or Maintenance Requirements

PCTs must be recertified when ProsoftTraining.com announces significant changes to the CIW courseware or examinations. Such changes occur at least every 12 months, and are announced on the CIW Web site and by e-mail.

PCTs must also adhere to the PCT agreement, submit their student evaluation forms on a monthly basis, and maintain high-quality instruction skills.

Benefits of Certification

As a Prosoft Certified Trainer (PCT), you will receive:

- All benefits accorded to CIWs (see Chapter 13, "Internet Certifications," for more information)

- Use of CIW and PCT certification logo on business cards, etc.

- Online access to content and materials specifically designed for trainers

Prosoft Certified Trainer (PCT)

A candidate can become a PCT in any of the eight tracks offered in ProsoftTraining.com's Certified Internet Webmaster (CIW) program (see Chapter 13 for more information about the CIW tracks). Attaining PCT status requires the candidate to pass the appropriate CIW exams, carry complementary training certification (Chauncey Group's CTT, Microsoft's MCT, or Novell's CNI), and attend a course to learn how ProsoftTraining.com courses are set up and taught.

Who Needs It

This certification is essential if you want to conduct ProsoftTraining.com courses in your area. This can be an excellent way to boost your career as a professional trainer.

Requirements for Certification

The certification process requires the following steps:

1. Pass the CIW exam(s) for the desired track.

2. Attain one of the following training certifications (all options are described elsewhere in this chapter):

   - Chauncey Group's CTT

   - Microsoft Certified Trainer (MCT)

   - Certified Novell Instructor (CNI)

3. Attend a ProsoftTraining.com train-the-trainer course or an instructor-led public CIW course in the track you wish to teach. The train-the-trainer course covers the ProsoftTraining.com course material and provides additional material on classroom setup and technology issues.

4. Submit a PCT application form and exam results to ProsoftTraining.com.

Administrator

CIW tests are administered by Sylvan Prometric. Call (800) 380-EXAM to register for ProsoftTraining.com tests; if outside the U.S., use the online Sylvan Test Center Locator at www.sylvanprometric.com to find the nearest testing center. Chapter 3 contains detailed information on taking tests from Sylvan.

The ProsoftTraining.com train-the-trainer course is available through Prosoft Certified Training Centers (PCTCs). See the ProsoftTraining.com Web site for information on PCTCs.

Fee

The cost of the train-the trainer course can vary. Contact your Prosoft Certified Training Center for details. CIW exams cost $150 each (see Chapter 13 for more information on ProsoftTraining.com's CIW certification program).

ProsoftTraining.com Resources

For more information on this organization's certifications and courses, contact ProsoftTraining.com at:

Web	http://www.prosofttraining.com/
E-mail	pct@prosofttraining.com
Mail	Certification Services
	ProsoftTraining.com.
	3001 Bee Caves Road
	Suite 100
	Austin, TX 78746
Phone	(512) 328-6140
Fax	(512) 328-52371

CHAPTER

16

Other Vendor-Based
Certifications

FEATURING

- Citrix Certification

- PCDOCS/Fulcrum Certification

- Vinca Certification

T he certification programs covered in this chapter focus on aspects of computing and networking that did not fit neatly into the previous chapters, i.e., thin clients, server clustering, etc. The certifications included here are offered by individual vendors.

Citrix is famous for their pioneering work in thin-client technology, and recently licensed their WinFrame code to Microsoft for inclusion in Windows 2000 and Windows NT Terminal Server Edition. The newly revised Citrix certification program, titled the Citrix Certified Administrator program, allows candidates to specialize in one of two tracks: WinFrame 1.8 or MetaFrame 1.8.

PCDOCS/Fulcrum makes several products for document management, and offers the Certified DOCS Professional certification program for those with advanced knowledge of their DOCSOpen product. Finally, Vinca offers the Certified Vinca Engineer (CVE) certification in support of their fault-tolerance programs for Windows NT and Novell NetWare.

Professionals seeking these certifications might include:

- Help-desk personnel
- Document and imaging specialists
- Consultants
- Network administrators

Use Table 16.1 to compare the number of required tests, the test format, the approximate cost of taking the test(s), number of required courses, cost of any required courses, and the relative difficulty of the certification programs in this chapter. The cost information is a general guideline; since things change rapidly in the world of certification programs, once you have selected a specific course of action you may want to double-check the costs.

We classified the difficulty of these certifications into three categories—Moderate, Challenging, and Very Challenging—based on the number of required tests and courses, and the relative difficulty of those tests or lab exams. These ratings are approximate and are offered simply as a general guide to help the reader distinguish between entry-level programs and those that require more advanced skill and knowledge. (This rating scale assumes that one has experience with the product or technology and has studied the appropriate subject content before attempting the exams.)

TABLE 16.1: Other Vender-Based Certifications

Certification	# of Required Tests	Test Format(s)	Total Cost of Required Tests	# of Required Courses	Total Cost of Required Courses	Difficulty	Notes
Citrix Certification							
Citrix Certified Administrator (CCA)	1	MC	VF	—	—	◐	Specializations include: WinFrame 1.8 and MetaFrame 1.8.
PCDOCS/Fulcrum Certification							
Certified PCDOCS Professional	1	MC	VF	—	—	◐	
Vinca Certification							
Vinca Certified Engineer	2	MC, PR	CV	1	$590	◐	

Certification Difficulty: ◯ Moderate   ◐ Challenging   ● Very Challenging

Test Format: **MC:** Multiple Choice   **AT:** Adaptive Testing   **LA:** Live Application
PR: Hands-on Lab   **NA:** Not Applicable

Test Fee: **VF:** Test Fees can vary: consult testing center.   **CV:** Voucher for taking the exam is included in the fee for the required course(s); additional attempts cost extra.

Citrix Certification

- Citrix Certified Administrator (CCA)

Started in 1989, Citrix Systems, Inc., is a pioneer in thin-client computing. Thin-client computing allows a user on any platform (Macintosh, Windows 3.1, UNIX, Windows CE, or Windows 95/98/NT) to connect to a very powerful PC-based server and run applications on the server itself (as opposed to downloading the application to the client and running it there). The client just acts as a display terminal for the session or program that is running on the server.

Recertification or Maintenance Requirements

Citrix designations apply to specific version numbers of MetaFrame and WinFrame, so there is no requirement for recertification on a particular version. Since your certification is tied to a certain version of a product, however, you will want to become certified on the newer versions, when they become available, if you want to continue to have the most current credential in this area.

Benefits of Certification

Citrix Certified Administrators receive the following benefits:

- Use of the CCA logo for stationery and business cards
- Certificate
- CCA lapel pin

Citrix Certified Administrator (CCA)

Since the inception of the Citrix Certified Administrator program only a few years ago, nearly 5,000 people have obtained CCA status. The certification process involves passing one exam that tests your knowledge of either Citrix WinFrame or MetaFrame. CCAs can specialize in one of the following areas:

- WinFrame 1.8
- MetaFrame 1.8

Citrix offers these optional courses as preparation for their certification exams: Course CTX-181 WinFrame Administration and Course CTX-302.2 MetaFrame Administration.

Who Needs It

The CCA certification is an excellent credential for independent consultants who set up thin-client servers and systems and want to validate their expertise for clients. This credential is also useful for system administrators and for technical staff of Citrix resellers.

Requirements for Certification

The certification process requires the following step:

1. Pass the required test for the specialization you seek (See Table 16.2).

T A B L E 16.2:   Citrix Specializations

Specialization	Test	Test ID
WinFrame 1.8	WinFrame Administration	118
MetaFrame 1.8	MetaFrame Administration	218

Administrator

Citrix exams are administered by Sylvan Prometric. Call (800) 481-3926 to register for a Citrix test; if outside the U.S., use the online Sylvan Test Center Locator at http://www.sylvanprometric.com to find the nearest testing center. (See Chapter 3, "Taking Your Test," for additional information on Sylvan Prometric.)

Fee

Contact Sylvan for current pricing.

Format

Each multiple-choice exam lasts one hour.

Citrix Resources

Citrix offers courses to help you prepare for the CCA tests, as well as a number of other courses on WinFrame and MetaFrame. For more information on this organization's certification program and courses, contact Citrix at:

Web	http://www.citrix.com
Mail	Citrix Systems, Inc.
	6400 NW 6th Way
	Fort Lauderdale, FL 33309
Phone	(800) 437-7403
	(954) 267-3000

PCDOCS/Fulcrum Certification

- Certified DOCS Professional

PCDOCS/Fulcrum produces a number of document management systems. One of their most popular products, DOCSOpen, is a client-server product that allows users to store, locate, and manage information across a wide range of platforms and networks. DOCSOpen add-ons include DOCS Imaging, DOCS Routing, CyberDOCS, DOCS Unplugged, DOCS Binder, DOCS Interchange for Microsoft Exchange, DOCS Interchange for Lotus Notes, DOCS Document Sentry Agent (DSA), and DOCS Development Kit (DDK). PCDOCS/Fulcrum offers the Certified DOCS Professional certification program to allow computer professionals to document their ability to use and manage DOCSOpen.

Recertification or Maintenance Requirements

The Certified DOCS Professional program did not have announced recertification requirements at the time of this writing. Contact PCDOCS/Fulcrum for updates (see the "PCDOCS/Fulcrum Resources" section for contact information).

Benefits of Certification

Certified DOCS Professionals (CDP) receive the following benefits:

- Use of the CDP logo for stationery and business cards
- Certificate

Certified DOCS Professional (CDP)

Obtaining the Certified DOCS Professional (CDP) certification involves taking one test. This exam tests your ability to install and administer the DOCSOpen 3.*x* product. During the test, the candidate will be asked which database engine they would prefer to be tested on. The choices are MS SQL, Oracle, and Sybase. You will only be required to answer questions for that particular engine.

Who Needs It

The CDP certification is a good way to demonstrate your skills and knowledge of DOCSOpen. It can help you advance your career in an organization that uses PCDOCS.

Requirements for Certification

The certification process requires one step:

1. Pass the Certified DOCS Professional exam.

Administrator

PCDOCS exams are administered by Sylvan Prometric. Call (800) 925-3926 to register for a PCDOCS test; if outside the U.S., use the online Sylvan Test Center Locator at http://www.sylvanprometric.com to find the nearest testing center. (See Chapter 3 for additional information on Sylvan Prometric.)

Fee

Contact Sylvan Prometric for current pricing information.

Format

The CDP exam consists of 75 multiple-choice questions that must be completed within 120 minutes. The exam is open book. Candidates may bring notes, books, and laptop computers. The only information not allowable is a copy of the test or the test questions/answers in any format. The passing score is 80 percent.

PCDOCS/Fulcrum Resources

PCDOCS/Fulcrum offers a number of courses to help you prepare for the certification test. In addition, sample tests are available on their

Web site. For more information on this organization's certification program and courses, contact PCDOCS/Fulcrum at:

Web	`http://www.pcdocs.com/`
Mail	PC DOCS/Fulcrum
	25 Burlington Mall Road
	Burlington, MA 01803
Phone	(781) 273-3800
Fax	(781) 272-3693

Vinca Certification

- Vinca Certified Engineer

Vinca Corporation offers a number of products designed to increase the fault tolerance of network servers, including Windows NT, Novell NetWare, and OS/2 Warp Server. Vinca's Standby*Server* program allows network administrators to set up a backup server for all critical data and applications. Then, if the main server fails, the backup server will immediately pick up where the main one left off.

Recertification or Maintenance Requirements

The Vinca Certified Engineer program did not have announced recertification requirements at the time of this writing. Contact Vinca for updates (see the "Vinca Resources" section for contact information).

Benefits of Certification

Vinca Certified Engineers receive the following benefits:

- Certificate

Vinca Certified Engineer (VCE)

Obtaining the Vinca Certified Engineer (VCE) certification involves taking a one-day course and passing a test. The test is given at the end of the day. The candidate may select either of two courses. The first course concentrates on Vinca products for NetWare. The second course focuses on products for Windows NT. Either course satisfies the technical requirements for becoming an Authorized Vinca Reseller (AVR).

Who Needs It

The Vinca Certified Engineer credential is an excellent way to show current or potential employers that you have knowledge and experience in designing and implementing high-availability clustering solutions for NetWare and NT. It can be a great way to move up in a company that sells and implements Vinca products.

Requirements for Certification

The certification process requires the following step:

1. Attend the one-day courses and pass the test for either NetWare or Windows NT offered at the end of the day of training.

Administrator

The VCE training and exams are administered by Vinca. The courses are offered at the Vinca Headquarters in Orem, Utah, and at regional locations throughout the U.S. Contact Vinca for information on the current training schedule and registration.

Fee

The two-day training session costs $590.

Format

Contact Vinca for details on the current format of the VCE tests.

Vinca Resources

For more information on this organization's certification program and courses, contact the Vinca Corporation at:

Web	http://www.vinca.com/
E-mail	training@vinca.com
Mail	Vinca Corporation
	1201 North 800 East
	Orem, UT 84097
Phone	(801) 223-3100
Fax	(801) 223-3107

CHAPTER

17

Organization-Based
Certifications

FEATURING

- BICSI Registrations

- CNX Consortium Certification

- CompTIA Certifications

- ICCP Certification

- National Association of Communications Systems Engineers (NACSE) Certifications

- Xplor International Certification

Up to this point, this book has primarily described certification programs offered by vendors—those companies that make and sell the products for which they offer certifications. While these programs are often very rigorous and difficult, some people feel that there are inherent problems with vendor-based certifications. (For the viewpoint of a leader in organization-based certification, see the sidebar by Bob Kile later in this chapter.) The most significant criticism is that when a person becomes certified on a particular product, he or she does not get the full range of experience and knowledge that is required in real-world situations. The desire to address this problem was the primary motivation behind the creation of the organization-based certifications described in this chapter.

Organization-based or "vendor-neutral" certification programs are well respected in the computer and networking fields because they tend to be comprehensive and standards-based. They cover many products and concepts without promoting one vendor's products over another's. Developed by a wide range of experts in a particular field, organization-based certifications also tend to encompass a broader range of skills and abilities than vendor-based certifications. In addition, many of these certifications recognize that the role of a computer or networking professional involves a variety of professional activities and requires a set of non-technical skills, such as interpersonal and communication skills.

An additional benefit of an organization-based certification is that, at least in some cases, you can join the organization and receive member benefits such as group insurance policies, opportunities for professional development, and job referral and placement services. Most organization-based certifications do not provide the same type of benefits as vendor-based ones, such as free CDs or free access to technical support. They do, however, provide this important benefit: a widely recognized, vendor independent validation of your skills and knowledge.

Some of the certifications covered in this chapter are among the most prestigious in the computer and networking fields. Professionals seeking these certifications include a wide range of computer professionals, from those just beginning their careers to experienced network and computer professionals.

BICSI offers the Registered Communications Distribution Designer (RCDD) Program, the RCDD/LAN Specialty Program, and the Cabling Installation Registration Program. These programs document the skills of experts who design and install cabling and networking for new and existing buildings. The Certified Network Expert credential, which certifies vendor-independent networking expertise, is offered by the CNX Consortium, an association of industry representatives. The Computer Technology Industry Association, or CompTIA, offers three important certifications: the A+ certification for computer service technicians, the Network + certification for beginning network troubleshooters, and the Certified Document Architect for imaging specialists. The Institute for Certification of Computing Professionals (ICCP), which was founded all the way back in 1973, offers the Certified Computing Professional credential, which covers many different aspects of computing and networking. The National Association of Communications Systems Engineers offers a variety of certifications for network professionals, ranging from entry level to expert. Finally, Xplor International offers the Electronic Document and Printing Professional (EDPP) certification, which validates the skills of those involved in electronic document and printing management.

Use Table 17.1 below to compare the number of required tests, the test format, the approximate costs of taking the test(s), number of required courses, costs of any required courses, and the relative difficulty of the certification programs in this chapter. The cost information is a general guideline; since things change rapidly in the world of certification programs, once you have selected a specific course of action you may want to double-check the costs.

We classified the difficulty of these certifications into three categories—Moderate, Challenging, and Very Challenging—based on the number of required tests and courses and the relative difficulty of those tests or lab exams. These ratings are approximate and are offered simply as a general guide to help the reader distinguish between entry-level programs and those that require more advanced skill and knowledge. (This rating scale assumes that one has experience with the product or technology and has studied the appropriate subject content before attempting the exams.)

T A B L E 17.1: Organization-Based Certifications

Certification	# of Required Tests	Test Format(s)	Total Cost of Required Tests	# of Required Courses	Total Cost of Required Courses	Difficulty	Notes
BICSI Certifications							
Registered Communications Distribution Designer (RCDD)	1	MC	$200	—	—	◑	Requires annual membership ($100) and two years of experience.
RCDD Local Area Network Specialty	1	MC	$100	—	—	◑	Must be an RCDD.
Cabling Installation Registration Program	1–3	MC	$150–$450	—	—	●	Specializations include: Apprentice, Installer, Technician.
CNX Consortium Certification							
Certified Networking Expert	1	MC	$250	—	—	●	Specializations: Token Ring, Ethernet, FDDI, or LAN Cabling.
CompTIA Certifications							
A+	2	MC	$190–$220	—	—	●	
Network +	1	MC	VF	—	—	◑	
Certified Document Image Architect	1	MC	$150–165	—	—	◑	

T A B L E 17.1: Organization-Based Certifications *(continued)*

Certification	# of Required Tests	Test Format(s)	Total Cost of Required Tests	# of Required Courses	Total Cost of Required Courses	Difficulty	Notes
ICCP Certifications							
Associate Computer Professional	2	MC	$230	—	—	◐	
Certified Computer Professional	3–4	MC	$350–$400	—	—	●	
National Association of Communications Systems Engineers							
NACSE Computer Technician	1	MC	VF	—	—	○	Requires NACSE membership ($75).
NACSE Network Technician	1	MC	VF	—	—	◐	Requires NACSE membership ($75).
NACSE Associate Network Specialist	1	MC	VF	—	—	◐	Requires NACSE membership ($75).
NACSE Senior Network Specialist	1	MC	VF	—	—	●	Requires NACSE membership ($75).
Xplor International Certification							
Electronic Document and Printing Professional (EDPP)	—	—	—	—	—	●	Certification is based on experience and a Certification Portfolio detailing examples of your work.

Certification Difficulty: ○ Moderate   ◐ Challenging   ● Very Challenging

Test Format: **MC:** Multiple Choice   **AT:** Adaptive Testing   **LA:** Live Application
PR: Hands-on Lab   **NA:** Not Applicable

Test Fee: **VF:** Test Fees can vary: consult testing center.   **CV:** Voucher for taking the exam is included in the fee for the required course(s); additional attempts cost extra.

BICSI Registrations

- Registered Communications Distribution Designer (RCDD)

- RCDD/LAN Specialty

- Cabling Installation Registration Program

BICSI, a not-for-profit telecommunications association, was founded in 1974 when employees of several telephone companies got together to offer service and support to the professionals who design and construct telecommunications infrastructures within buildings. At that time, the name BICSI stood for Building Industry Consulting Service International. The name was chosen because each of the Bell companies had a Building Industry Consulting Service department, which concentrated on designing telecommunications wiring systems for new and existing commercial properties. Since divestiture of the Bell companies, however, these departments no longer exist as such. In the 1990s, BICSI decided to drop its full name and instead refer to itself as "BICSI: A Telecommunications Association."

BICSI currently has over 15,000 members in over 70 countries and offers training programs throughout the world. BICSI's programs are called registration programs, rather than certification programs. BICSI has three registration programs—the Registered Communications Distribution Designer (RCDD) Program, the RCDD/LAN Specialty Program, and the Cabling Installation Registration Program. These programs register qualified professionals who design and install cabling and networking for new and existing buildings, including telephone, cable television, and data communications transport systems and related infrastructures. The Cabling Installation Registration Program has three levels: Apprentice, Installer, and Technician.

Recertification or Maintenance Requirements

The RCDD registration is valid for three years. Renewing your RCDD designation for each three-year period involves taking the following actions:

- Maintain an uninterrupted BICSI membership

- Complete a minimum of 45 credit hours of training related to distribution design during each three-year period, including one BICSI-sponsored three-day conference (contact BICSI for details and a list of approved courses)

- Submit a renewal application and $100 renewal fee

The Cabling Installation Registration Program has different renewal requirements for the three levels. Apprentice-level registrations are valid for two years and are not renewable—you must move on to either the Installer or Technician level. Installer and Technician registrations are good for two years and are renewable by doing the following:

- Complete the On-the-Job Training requirements (described below)

- Provide proof of current installation activity

- Complete a minimum of 12 credit hours of continuing education

Benefits of Certification

Registered Communications Distribution Designers and Cabling Installation participants receive this benefit:

- Use of the RCDD or Cabling Installation logo on letterheads, business cards, etc.

Registered Communications Distribution Designer (RCDD)

Two prerequisites must be met prior to attempting the required exam for the RCDD designation. First, you must be a member of BICSI (annual membership fee is $100). Second, you must have at least two years of experience in cabling distribution design in commercial, campus, and multifamily buildings.

In addition, you must submit an application form detailing your experience and three letters of reference. One letter must be from your current employer; if you are self-employed, you must provide a letter explaining your involvement in the design of low-voltage distribution systems. Another letter should be from a client for whom you have done design work, and one should be a personal reference. This application package must also be accompanied by a $100 nonrefundable application fee.

The exam for this registration covers information on appropriate national codes as well as policies and methods of telecommunications distribution design. BICSI provides a manual of information that candidates will want to study in preparing for the exam (see the "BICSI" Resources section for more information).

Who Needs It

RCDD certification is an important credential for telecommunications designers, electrical engineers, consultants, systems integrators, telephone company personnel, or anyone who is involved in the design and installation of low-voltage wiring infrastructure in new or existing buildings. It can also be an excellent way for independent contractors to showcase their abilities for potential clients.

Requirements for Certification

The registration process requires the following steps:

1. Meet the prerequisites: BICSI membership and minimum of two years of experience in distribution design.

2. Submit application package for approval (see above for details).

3. If approved, pass the BICSI RCDD exam.

You must pass the exam within one year of application approval. If you do not pass, you can retake it twice within a one-year period ($100 fee per attempt). If you fail three times, you must wait a full year from your last attempt before reapplying.

Administrator

BICSI administers the exam throughout the year at BICSI-sponsored conferences, and at selected sites across the world. See the BICSI Web site for details.

Fee

The exam fee is $100. Additional fees include the $100 BICSI membership fee and the $100 application fee.

Format

This closed-book, multiple-choice exam lasts three and one-half hours. There are 280 questions and a score of 78 percent is required to pass.

RCDD: LAN Specialty

The LAN specialization can be obtained by those who already have acquired the RCDD certification. You must submit an application and three letters of reference regarding your LAN experience. In addition you must pass an additional exam that tests your ability to correctly design local area network cabling systems. BICSI provides a manual of information that candidates will want to study in preparing for the exam (see the "BICSI Resources" section for more information).

Who Needs It

This specialization is an excellent way to demonstrate your ability to design and install LAN cabling systems. It can be a good credential for independent contractors and architects who want to show potential clients clear evidence of their LAN knowledge and skills.

Requirements for Registration

The certification process requires the following steps:

1. Obtain and maintain RCDD certification (follow the steps described above).

2. Submit the LAN application package, with three letters of reference, and the $100 exam fee.

3. Pass the BICSI RCCD/LAN Specialty exam.

Administrator

BICSI administers the exam throughout the year at BICSI-sponsored conferences, and at selected sites around the world. See the BICSI Web site for details.

Fee

The fee for the RCDD/LAN exam is $100.

Format

This closed-book, multiple-choice exam lasts two hours. There are 115 questions and a score of 78 percent is required to pass.

Cabling Installation Registration Program

The BICSI Cabling Installation Registration Program is a three-level registration program for cable installers. The importance of proper cable installation is often overlooked, but it is critical to the reliability of a network. The levels of registration offered in the Cabling Installation program are as follows:

- Apprentice
- Installer
- Technician

The Apprentice level is for people with little or no on-the-job installation experience. The Installer level requires two years of voice, data or video cabling experience. The Technician level is designed for those with over five years of experience.

Training is available through BICSI and other organizations certified by BICSI to teach the curriculum using BICSI's training materials. See BICSI's Web site for a complete list of these organizations. Training is offered at locations in North America and other countries. BICSI provides a manual of information that candidates will want to study in preparing for the exam (see the "BICSI Resources" section for more information).

Who Needs It

These registrations are an excellent way to show current or potential employers your ability to do a quality installation job. It can be very valuable to your employers to have registered installers on staff. This credential can also be of value to those who do independent installations and want to validate their expertise for clients.

Requirements for Registration

The registration process requires the following step:

1. Complete the requirements for the specialization you seek (see Table 17.2).

TABLE 17.2: Requirements of BICSI Cabling Installation Program

Level	Requirements
Apprentice	A. Complete the Apprentice Examination Application and submit it to BICSI at least two weeks before your exam date (contact BICSI for a copy of the application).
	B. Complete the two-part Apprentice Exam.
Installer	A. Submit the Installer Experience form to BICSI.
	B. Complete the Installer Examination Application and submit it to BICSI at least two weeks before your exam date (contact BICSI for a copy of the application).
	C. Complete the two-part Installer Exam.
Technician	A. Submit the Technician Experience form to BICSI.
	B. Complete the Technician Examination Application and submit it to BICSI at least two weeks before your exam date (contact BICSI for a copy of the application).
	C. Complete the two-part Technician Exam.

Administrator

BICSI administers the exam throughout the year. See the BICSI Web site for dates and locations.

Fee

Each of the exams has a $50 application fee, plus a $50 fee for the written exam, and a $50 fee for the hands-on exam. To retake either the written exam or the entire hands-on exam, you must pay an additional fee of $50 per exam.

Format

Each test consists of two parts: a written section and a hands-on test. The written exam must be completed within two hours. The hands-on exam tests your ability to perform tasks appropriate to the level of certification you are pursuing, and takes approximately 40 minutes to one hour.

BICSI Resources

The BICSI Web site offers exam bulletins that detail each test's objectives. BICSI recommends using their *Telecommunications Distribution Methods Manual* in preparing for the RCDD exam. The *LAN and Internetworking Design Manual* is recommended for those who are preparing for the RCDD/LAN exam. For all three levels of the Cabling Installation Program, independent study of BICSI's *Telecommunications Cabling Installation Manual* is recommended. For more information on this organization's registrations and courses, contact BICSI at:

Web	www.bicsi.org
E-mail	bicsi@bicsi.org
Mail	BICSI
	8610 Hidden River Parkway
	Tampa, FL 33637
Phone	(813) 979-1991
Fax	(813) 971-4311
Faxback	(800) 242-7405; ask to be transferred to the voice mail system, then press 9 to access the fax service

CNX Consortium Certification

- Certified Network Expert

The Certified Network Expert (CNX) certification program was developed by a multi-vendor group called the CNX Consortium. The following companies make up the CNX Consortium: GN Nettest,

Nortel Networks, Cisco Systems, Hewlett-Packard, Microtest, Network Associates, Optimized Engineering, The AG Group, TOYO Corporation, and Wavetek, Wandel & Goltermann (WWG).

This certification is designed for network professionals who are responsible for network analysis and troubleshooting. Becoming a CNX involves passing an exam on one of the following technologies: Token Ring, Ethernet, FDDI, or LAN Cabling. The Ethernet and Token Ring exams are published in English, German, and Japanese, while the FDDI and LAN Cabling exams are only available in English. The tests require knowledge of the use of protocol analyzers to diagnose and isolate network problems.

Recertification or Maintenance Requirements

There are currently no recertification requirements for Certified Network Experts.

Benefits of Certification

The main benefit of becoming a CNX is that it demonstrates your high level of networking abilities and knowledge to current and potential employers. Certified Network Experts also receive:

- A CNX certificate and plaque
- Use of the CNX logo on business cards and stationery

Certified Networking Expert

Becoming a CNX involves passing an exam on one type of networking technology. Each certification exam leads to a separate CNX specialization. CNX recommends that candidates have several years of networking experience prior to attempting an exam. Preparatory courses are not required, but they are available. While none of the CNX Consortium companies can call their courses "CNX" courses, some relevant courses are offered by Wavetek, Wandel & Goltermann (WWG); Optimized Engineering; and NAI. The four CNX specializations available are:

- CNX: Token Ring
- CNX: Ethernet

- CNX: FDDI

- CNX: LAN Cabling

The CNX Token Ring specialization requires extensive knowledge of IEEE Token Ring specifications. Topics covered on the exam include use of control bits such as priority, monitor count, ARI/FCI, error-detection, functional address, and source-routing-present, as well as poll/neighbor notification, station insertion and removal, soft error reporting, contention, and beaconing with fault domain isolation.

The CNX Ethernet specialization requires extensive knowledge of IEEE Ethernet specifications. Topics covered on the exam include similarities, differences, and areas of incompatibility between Ethernet implementations using Version 2, 802.3, SNAP, and Novell; bit patterns associated with frame corruption including propagation delay problems, reflection problems, environmental noise, and faulty hardware; and media access technology, such as preamble generation, bit jam, exponential backoff algorithm, SQE heartbeat, and jabbering.

The CNX FDDI specialization requires extensive knowledge of ANSI FDDI specifications. Topics covered on the exam include interoperation and relationships between FDDI state machine functions for PMD, PHY, MAC, and SMT, including the significance of the field in each frame; and details and specifications of ring operation and timers involved with ring-poll, station insertion and removal, and error reporting, including physical configurations for concentrators and stations. The exam also covers TCP/IP and has a new section on real-life FDDI scenarios.

The CNX LAN Cabling specialization requires extensive knowledge of wiring systems. Topics covered include UTP, STP, ScTP, and fiber tests, including attenuation, NEXT, wiremap, length, and impedance, and their acceptable values in typical LAN cabling environments; current EIA/TIA/ISO cabling standards, link/channel models, and appropriate installation practices; and cabling requirements for common LAN networks, such as 10BASE-T, Token Ring, FDDI, TP-PMD, 100BASE-T, 100VGAnyLAN, and ATM.

Who Needs It

The CNX certification is valuable to advanced networking professionals who want to document for current or potential employers their ability to install, maintain, and troubleshoot networks. It can also be an excellent way for independent consultants and trainers to showcase their abilities for potential clients.

Requirements for Certification

The certification process requires the following step:

1. Pass the required tests for the specialization you seek (See Table 17.3).

T A B L E 17.3: Required Tests for CNX Specializations

Specialization	Test
CNX: Token Ring	Token Ring CNX exam
CNX: Ethernet	Ethernet CNX exam
CNX: FDDI	FDDI CNX exam
CNX: LAN Cabling	LAN Cabling CNX exam

Administrator

Call Sylvan Prometric at (800) CNX-EXAM ((800) 269-3926) to register for a CNX exams; if outside the U.S., use the online Sylvan Test Center Locator at http://www.sylvanprometric.com/ to find the nearest testing center. (See Chapter 3, "Taking Your Test," for information on taking tests from Sylvan.)

Fee

The test costs $250; retakes are $100.

Format

Each two-hour test consists of approximately 60 multiple-choice questions. Some questions are multi-answer questions. The exception is the FDDI exam, which consists of 70 single-answer questions. Candidates must score 75 percent to pass. CNX is in the process of republishing several of these exams to add "upper-layer" questioning, introduce real-life scenarios, and replace multi-answer questions with single-answer questions.

CNX Resources

The CNX Web site offers an excellent pre-test guide, sample test questions, and a suggested reading list. For more information on this organization's certifications, contact CNX at:

Web   `http://www.cnx.org/`
E-mail   `Webmaster@cnx.org`

The Web site also provides links to member organizations, some of which, as noted above, offer relevant exam preparation courses. CNX also suggests the persons listed below as relevant contacts for the CNX certification program:

Stan Rosen
Wavetek, Wandel & Goltermann
Research Triangle Park, NC
(919) 941-5730
`stan.rosen@wg.com`

Mahboud Zabetian
AG Group, Inc.
Walnut Creek, CA
(925) 937-7900.

Joe Bardwell
Optimized Engineering Corporation
Mountain View, CA
(650) 934-3949
`joeb@optimized.com`

CompTIA Certifications

- A+

- Network+

- Certified Document Imaging Architect

The Computer Technology Industry Association (CompTIA) is a not-for-profit organization formed in 1982 to foster cooperation in the computer industry. Today over 6,000 computer resellers, computer manufacturers, and computer service companies are members of CompTIA.

CompTIA currently offers three certifications: the A+ certification, the Network+ certification, and the Certified Document Imaging Architect (CDIA). The A+ certification is designed as a benchmark for competence in basic computer repair. CompUSA, Inc., one of the largest computer resellers, requires all their service personnel to obtain A+ certification. The Network+ certification is new for 1999 and certifies basic networking knowledge. The CDIA certification designates an advanced level of skill in working with document imaging technology and techniques.

Recertification or Maintenance Requirements

As of this writing there are no maintenance requirements for these certifications. CompTIA does, however, update the A+ tests periodically to reflect advances in PC hardware and operating systems.

Benefits of Certification

Benefits of A+ and Network+ certification include:

- Use of the A+ or Network+ logo
- Certificate

- If 50 percent or more of a company's computer service technicians are A+ certified, the company can be designated an A+ Authorized Service Center and be listed in CompTIA's directory

Certified Document Imaging Architects receive these benefits:

- Use of the CDIA logo

- Listing in the CDIA central registry—a database of qualified CDIA professionals that companies consult when they are hiring document imaging personnel

A+ Certification

The A+ certification program targets those who want a certification that validates their competence as computer service professionals. There are currently over 100,000 A+ certified professionals. The A+ certification is widely recognized as the standard for measuring a technician's ability to diagnose and repair computer hardware and operating system problems. Certification consists of passing a minimum of two tests: a Core exam that tests general knowledge and abilities, and one Specialty exam that tests knowledge and skills in working with a particular operating system.

The Core exam covers the following topics: microcomputers, displays, storage media, printers, basic operating systems (DOS, Windows), modems, buses, and CD-ROMs. The test is divided into eight sections that reflect a computer repair technician's areas of job responsibility: installation, configuration, and upgrading; diagnosis and troubleshooting; safety and preventative maintenance; motherboard/processors/memory; printers; portable systems; basic networking; and customer satisfaction. The Specialty exam focuses on operating-system environments. The only current Specialty option is DOS/Windows, as the Macintosh Specialty exam is no longer available. Additional specializations may become available soon. Once candidates pass the Core exam and the Specialty exam, they receive a certificate that mentions the Specialty module they passed, for example, "A+ certification with a specialty in DOS/Windows environments."

Who Needs It

The A+ certification is a great way to enter the field of computer repair and installation. This widely recognized credential indicates to a potential employer that you have the skills to diagnose and repair a wide variety of hardware and operating system problems.

Requirements for Certification

The certification process requires the following steps:

1. Pass the A+ Core exam (Test ID: 220-101).

2. Pass the DOS/Windows Specialty exam (Test ID: 220-102).

Candidates must pass both exams within a 90-day period.

Administrator

Call Sylvan Prometric at (800) 776-4276 to register for an A+ exam; if outside the U.S., use the online Sylvan Test Center Locator at http://www.sylvanprometric.com/ to find the nearest testing center. (See Chapter 3 for detailed information on taking tests from Sylvan.)

Fee

Test fees are discounted for candidates employed by organizations that are members of CompTIA. Each test costs $128 for employees of nonmember organizations. The same tests cost $78 each for employees of member organizations. To receive the CompTIA discount price, have your CompTIA membership number handy when registering for the test.

Format

The 60-minute A+ Core exam has 69 questions and a passing score of 65 percent. The 75-minute DOS/Windows exam has 70 questions and a passing score of 66 percent.

Network+ Certification

The Network+ certification is CompTIA's newest credential. It is designed to document the network knowledge of technicians with 18 to 24 months' experience in the IT industry. Earning the Network+ certification requires basic knowledge of network topologies and technologies as well as knowledge of how to configure and install TCP/IP.

Who Needs It

The Network+ certification is a great way to enter the field of networking. This credential indicates to a potential employer that you have the skills to diagnose and repair a broad variety of network problems.

Requirements for Certification

The certification process requires the following step:

1. Pass the Network+ exam.

Administrator

Call Sylvan Prometric at (888) 895-6116 to register for the Network+ exam; if outside the U.S., use the online Sylvan Test Center Locator at http://www.sylvanprometric.com/ to find the nearest testing center. (See Chapter 3 for detailed information on taking tests from Sylvan.)

Fee

The exam fee is $135.

Format

This is a multiple-choice test consisting of 65 questions. A score of 68 percent is required to pass.

Certified Document Imaging Architect (CDIA)

CompTIA's CDIA credential recognizes knowledge and skill in the document imaging industry. Document imaging involves scanning and storing documents in digital form, either as images or text, using optical character recognition software. Candidates are expected to be able to plan, design, and write specifications for an imaging system.

One test is required for this certification. It consists of eight sections designed to cover the key areas of responsibility for an imaging architect: input and capture, display, storage, communications, output, standard computing environment, integration, and management applications.

Who Needs It

This certification is the *de facto* standard for knowledge and skill in document imaging. It can be valuable in obtaining a position in a wide range of companies that rely on document imaging specialists.

Requirements for Certification

The certification process requires only one step:

1. Pass the Certified Document Imaging Architect exam.

Administrator

Call Sylvan Prometric at (800) 909-3926 to register for the CDIA exam; if outside the U.S., use the online Sylvan Test Center Locator at http://www.sylvanprometric.com/ to find the nearest testing center. (See Chapter 3 for detailed information on taking tests from Sylvan.)

Fee

The testing fee is $150 for individuals employed by an organization that is a member of CompTIA, and $165 for nonmembers. To receive the CompTIA discount price, have your CompTIA membership number handy when registering with Sylvan Prometric for the test.

Format

The 60-minute test has 68 multiple-choice questions. A score of 77 percent is required to pass.

CompTIA Resources

The CompTIA Web site offers a list of objectives and sample questions for each exam. The site also provides links to numerous self-study and instructor-led preparation courses. For more information on this organization's certifications and courses, contact CompTIA at:

Web	http://www.comptia.org
E-mail	certification@comptia.org
Mail	CompTIA
	450 East 22nd Street, Suite 230
	Lombard, IL 60148-6158
Phone	(630) 268-1818
Fax	(630) 268-1384

ICCP Certification

- Associate Computing Professional

- Certified Computing Professional

The Institute for Certification of Computing Professionals (ICCP) was founded in 1973 to develop professional standards for the computing industry. ICCP previously offered three certification programs: the Certificate in Data Processing, Certified Computer Programmer, and Certified Systems Professional. These programs have been folded into one: the Certified Computing Professional (CCP) credential. Over 50,000 individuals have obtained ICCP certification.

CCP Candidates are expected to have at least two years of work experience prior to certification. The certification process involves passing a series of tests that cover a wide range of topics. These topics reflect the breadth of job duties that may confront the computing professional. In addition, ICCP has created the Associate Computing Professional (ACP) designation, for those just starting out in the computing industry.

Recertification or Maintenance Requirements

There is no requirement for ACP recertification; it is expected that those with the ACP designation will want to move on to the CCP credential as soon as they have more experience.

The CCP designation is valid for three years. To maintain your CCP credential, you must provide proof of 120 contact hours of professional development activities during each three-year period. These activities may include:

- Taking additional Specialty or Language exams

- Retaking the exams you previously passed

- Participating in educational and other professional activities

Contact ICCP for more details on ways to maintain your certification status.

NOTE ICCP now accepts any courses taken from Learning Tree International for professional development credit.

Benefits of Certification

Associate Computing Professionals and Certified Computing Professionals receive the following benefits:

- A certificate
- Use of the ACP or CCP logo on business cards and stationery

Associate Computing Professional (ACP)

The ACP is designed to certify an individual's general knowledge of the computing industry and at least one programming language. There is no experience requirement for the ACP. Obtaining this designation involves passing the Core exam and one Language exam.

Who Needs It

The ACP designation is best suited for those new to the computing industry, or the recent college graduate who wishes to gain professional credentials. It is an excellent way to show current or potential employers your programming skills.

Requirements for Certification

The certification process requires the following steps:

1. Pass the CCP Core exam with a score of 50 percent or better.

2. Pass one of the Language exams with a score of 50 percent or better (see Table 17.5 in the CCP section that follows for a list of available Language exams).

3. Agree to abide by the ICCP Code of Ethics, Conduct, and Good Practice (available on the ICCP Web site).

Administrator

To take an ICCP test, send your application and test fee to ICCP. After you have been accepted in the testing program, ICCP will give you the phone number for scheduling your test at a Sylvan Prometric center.

Fee

The Core exam costs $149; the Language tests cost $79 each.

Format

The Core exam consists of 110 multiple-choice questions and must be completed in 90 minutes. The Language exams consist of 66 multiple-choice questions and must be completed in 60 minutes. The passing score for ACPs on the Core and Language exams is 50 percent.

Certified Computing Professional (CCP)

The CCP certification program is oriented toward experienced computing professionals. Candidates are expected to have 48 months of full-time experience in computer-based information systems before attempting this certification. Contact ICCP for further information on qualifying experience and academic alternatives to this requirement.

The certification process involves passing a Core exam and meeting an additional exam requirement. The additional exam requirement can be met in several ways: by passing two Specialty exams, by passing one Specialty exam and two Language exams, or by passing one Specialty exam and holding a vendor- or organization-based certification that is on the ICCP-approved list (contact ICCP for the current list). The passing score on the ICCP exam is higher (70%) for CCP candidates than for ACP candidates. The candidate must also agree to abide by a code of ethical conduct. All certification steps must be completed within a three-year period.

Who Needs It

The CCP certification is an excellent general certification for computer professionals who perform a wide variety of tasks. It can be an excellent tool for career advancement, or it can serve as a valuable qualification for freelance consultants.

Requirements for Certification

The certification process requires the following steps:

1. Meet the experience prerequisite (explained above).

2. Pass the CCP Core exam.

3. Meet the additional exam requirements in one of the following ways:

   - Pass two Specialty exams (see Table 17.4).

   - Pass one Specialty exam and two Language exams (see Table 17.5).

   - Pass one Specialty exam and hold a vendor- or organization-based certification that is on the ICCP-approved list (contact ICCP for the current list).

4. Submit a letter from a person who can verify your work experience.

5. Agree to abide by the ICCP Code of Ethics, Conduct, and Good Practice (available on the ICCP Web site).

All the required steps for the CCP certification process must be completed within a 36-month period.

TABLE 17.4: CCP Specialty Exams
(One or more as needed, as explained above.)

Management
System Development
Communications
Systems Programming
Systems Security
Microcomputing and Networks
Procedural Programming
Business Information Systems
Office Information Systems
Software Engineering
Data Resource Management

T A B L E 17.5: CCP Language Exams (as needed, as previously explained)

Pascal
BASIC
RPG/400
COBOL
C (or substitute the Learning Tree International C exam)
C++ (or substitute the Learning Tree International C++ exam)

Administrator

To take an ICCP test, send your application and test fee to ICCP. After you have been accepted in the testing program, ICCP will give you the phone number for scheduling your test at a Sylvan Prometric center.

Fee

The Core and Specialty exams cost $149 each; the Language tests cost $79 each.

Format

The Core and Specialty exams consist of 110 multiple-choice questions and must be completed in 90 minutes. The passing score for CCPs on both Core and Specialty exams is 70 percent.

The Language exams consist of 66 multiple-choice questions and must be completed in 60 minutes. The passing score for a CCP on a Language exam is 70 percent.

ICCP Resources

The ICCP Web site offers sample tests and test objectives for the Core exam. In addition, the ICCP Education Foundation, in cooperation with Bird Professional Publications, offers a number of review courses. Several other organizations provide audiotapes, videotapes, and books to help you prepare for the ICCP exams (see the ICCP Web site for a complete listing). For more information on this organization's certifications and courses, contact ICCP at:

Web	http://www.iccp.org/
E-mail	74040.3722@compuserve.com
Mail	ICCP
	2200 East Devon Avenue, Suite 247
	Des Plaines, IL 60018
Phone	(847) 299-4227
Fax	(847) 299-4280

Why Vendor-Independent Certification?

By Bob Kile, Executive Director

NACSE

NACSE is an international association of information technology professionals who believe that the present process of network communication and Internet credentialing is in a state of crisis. We are dismayed by the lack of professionalism and knowledge standards in the industry.

Is There an Industry Crisis? NACSE Thinks So. Here's Why:

- The explosion of technologies in data, voice, and visual communications has created an enormous unfilled demand for these skills at all levels. Currently, there are upwards of 400,000 open technical jobs in the U.S. market.

- The proliferation of the Internet and intranets has further increased industry needs. The demand is huge and the supply of skilled professionals is almost nonexistent.

- Until recently, colleges and universities in the U.S. didn't offer courses in networking or network communications. Most courses that have been offered are related to programming or engineering. As a result, graduates from these programs are not well qualified to work in networking and related information technology fields.

Continued

- The vendor segment of the industry has one primary objective: to ensure that their products and services are properly sold, installed, and supported by knowledgeable people. However, vendors don't have any motivation or need to ensure that their students have a real understanding of networking in general. To be sure, NACSE is not against vendor training. It is a needed and necessary part of the industry. Many of our members, in fact, hold Novell, Cisco, Microsoft, and other certifications. What NACSE wants to protect against is the assumption that such certifications can be a substitute for an objective, international, standards-based credentialing program.

- The technology keeps advancing at a rapid pace. For example, high-speed needs like GIGA-BIT Ethernet, ATM, Frame Relay, and Category 7 wiring all require that network professionals have ongoing education.

- We need meaningful and applicable standards for those who must design, support, and troubleshoot these new technologies. We want to avoid having the government step in and set these standards for us.

- Résumés and vendor certifications simply cannot tell the whole story for employers. Human resources personnel don't have the knowledge needed to evaluate these applicants' technical skills. At the same time, information technology managers don't have time to establish internal standards, develop evaluation tests, and screen applicants themselves. The cost of this problem to corporate America is enormous. It can easily take a year to take a new hire though the system far enough to determine whether he or she is capable of doing the job—a costly process, at best.

Why are Vendor-Neutral Credentials the Answer?

- Vendor credentials verify one's knowledge of a particular product or family of products. The vendor education, while very valuable, will always be based on a particular company's view of the information technology world. A true professional must have a broader, neutrally-based educational background because the real world is

Continued

broad and neutrally-based. No real-world information technology environment uses just one operating system or just one hardware platform.

The NACSE Model

NACSE stands out as a nonprofit, peer-to-peer, professional credentialing organization that establishes networking and Internet standards through a community of working information technology professionals. Here are the features of our model:

1. We develop standards with the help of a consortium of information technology leaders who meet regularly to review the real-world, day-to-day needs of the information technology community.

2. Those standards have been organized and bundled into a structured curriculum by development professionals.

3. The curriculum is reviewed and delivered by professional educators at accredited colleges and universities. All of our courses must carry some kind of accreditation. The available formats include degree programs, short-term accelerated classes, evenings or weekend courses, and Web-based courses.

4. The entire process is reviewed and certified by a neutral group of professionals. Professionals in the field are best qualified to determine what skills, knowledge, and experience are needed in a particular area. In this way, a high quality of delivery is maintained, and the skills and knowledge earned by the students are readily recognized by the industry at large.

5. We require recertification at every level to ensure that the skills of those we have trained are current.

NACSE Testing and Standards Benefit the Industry in Several Ways:

- Benefits for our members: Through its charter, NACSE is dedicated to maintaining rigorous knowledge and skill standards, assisting in providing the necessary educational channels, and providing appropriate testing programs to fulfill each member's professional objectives.

Continued

- Benefits for industry clients: Without the existence of neutral, professionally-based evaluation standards, a client has no way of evaluating a network professional's knowledge, skill, or abilities. It would be akin to having no professional standards to set requirements for how your physician practices medicine, how your lawyer practices law, or how your accountant takes care of your financial and tax matters. NACSE aids industry clients by providing a comprehensive, tiered set of vendor-neutral networking certifications that can help them detect qualified applicants.

- Benefits for the industry at large: Clearly, the working professionals in this industry must be the ones who provide standards, guidance, and leadership. Yes, the vendors build the technology products for the needs of the industry. But if we are to provide unbiased, effective support of vendors' products for our clients, educational standards should not be set by the vendors themselves.

NACSE Certifications

- NACSE Computer Technician

- NACSE Network Technician

- NACSE Associate Network Specialist

- NACSE Senior Network Specialist

The National Association of Communications Systems Engineers (NACSE) is a nonprofit organization that was formed specifically for certifying network professionals. This organization determined that there was a lack of good vendor-neutral networking certification programs and created an extensive certification program to certify individuals in the following areas: Networking and Data Communications; Network Operations; Network Management Planning, Decisions, and

Analysis; Network Technical Sales; and Power, Cable Testing, and Installation. NACSE has also created a number of Webmaster certifications. We present four of the most important NACSE certifications here; see http://www.nacse.com/ to request information on all of NACSE's certifications.

Recertification or Maintenance Requirements

All NACSE certifications require annual or biannual recertification testing. Contact NACSE for the recertification requirement for your certification title.

Benefits of Certification

All NACSE certified individuals receive the following benefits:

- Certificate and wallet card
- Membership benefits, which include job referral assistance, medical and dental plans, retirement and financial planning, etc. NACSE Computer Technician (NCT)

The NACSE Computer Technician (NCT)

The NACSE Computer Technician (NCT) credential is designed for those with basic computer and application knowledge, including knowledge of MS-DOS, basic UNIX commands, and basic computer construction and design. Recommended experience/education includes an associate degree in a computer-related field or A+ certification (see the CompTIA section in this chapter for information on the A+ certification).

Who Needs It

This credential can be of value to those who do independent consulting and want to validate their expertise for clients. It can also be a good starting point for a career in the computer and networking industry.

Requirements for Certification

The certification process requires the following steps:

1. Join NACSE.

2. Pass the NCT written test.

3. Sign and accept the NACSE Code of Ethics and Professional Conduct.

Administrator

Tests are administered by NACSE; contact them at (303) 690-9808 to arrange a test.

Fee

NACSE membership fee is $75 annually. Fees for the tests can vary; call NACSE at (303) 690-9808 for current pricing.

Format

This is a multiple-choice test. Contact NACSE at (303) 690-9808 for the latest information on the number of questions and passing score.

NACSE Network Technician (NNT)

The NACSE Network Technician (NNT) credential builds on the NCT certification and is designed for those with basic network installation and administration skills. The exam requires knowledge of physical cabling, troubleshooting, cable testing techniques, and an understanding of data communications terminology. Recommended experience/education includes an associate degree in a computer-related field, A+ certification, and experience with networks.

Who Needs It

This certification can get you a job in the networking field. It can also be of value to those who do independent consulting and want to validate their expertise for clients.

Requirements for Certification

The certification process requires the following steps:

1. Join NACSE.

2. Meet the NCT requirements.

3. Pass the NNT written test.

4. Sign and accept the NACSE Code of Ethics and Professional Conduct.

Administrator

Tests are administered by NACSE; contact them at (303) 690-9808 to arrange a test.

Fee

NACSE membership fee is $75 annually. Fees for the tests can vary; call NACSE at (303) 690-9808 for current pricing.

Format

The test format is multiple-choice. Contact NACSE at (303) 690-9808 for the latest information on the number of questions and passing score.

NACSE Associate Network Specialist (NANS)

The NACSE Associate Network Specialist (NANS) credential builds on the NCT and NTT certifications and is designed for those with more advanced network installation and administration skills. Candidates need to have knowledge of network operating systems (Windows NT, Novel NetWare, UNIX), routers, hubs, MAUs, switches, network protocols, and traffic analysis. Recommended experience/education includes an associate degree in a computer-related field, a network operating system certification (MCSE, CNE, etc.), and several years' experience with networks.

Who Needs It

The NANS certification can help you advance in your networking career. This credential also can be of value to those who do independent consulting and want to validate their expertise for clients.

Requirements for Certification

The certification process requires the following steps:

1. Join NACSE.

2. Meet the NCT and NNT requirements, as described previously.

3. Pass the NANS written test.

4. Sign and accept the NACSE Code of Ethics and Professional Conduct.

Administrator

Tests are administered by NACSE; contact them at (303) 690-9808 to arrange a test.

Fee

NACSE membership fee is $75 annually. Fees for the tests can vary; call NACSE at (303) 690-9808 for current pricing.

Format

The test format is multiple-choice. Contact NACSE at (303) 690-9808 for the latest information on the number of questions and passing score.

NACSE Senior Network Specialist (NSNS)

The NACSE Senior Network Specialist (NSNS) credential builds on the NCT, NNT, and NANS certifications and is designed for those with advanced network installation and administration skills. Candidates need to have a detailed knowledge of network protocols, network addressing, routers, and WAN technology (T1, T3, ISDN, Frame Relay, ATM). Recommended experience/education includes a bachelor's degree in a computer-related field, network operating system certification (MCSE, CNE, etc.), and at least 3 years of experience with networks.

Who Needs It

This credential can help you move up in the computer and networking industry. It can also be of value to those who do independent consulting and want to validate their expertise for clients.

Requirements for Certification

The certification process requires the following steps:

1. Join NACSE.

2. Meet the NCT, NNT, and NANS requirements, described previously.

3. Pass the NSNS written test.

4. Sign and accept the NACSE Code of Ethics and Professional Conduct.

Administrator

Tests are administered by NACSE; contact them at (303) 690-9808 to arrange a test.

Fee

NACSE membership fee is $75 annually. Fees for the tests can vary; call NACSE at (303) 690-9808 for current pricing.

Format

This is a multiple-choice test. Contact NACSE at (303) 690-9808 for the latest information on the number of questions and passing score.

NACSE Resources

NACSE offers a number of resources for certification candidates. You can request a listing of NACSE-certified courses available from various colleges and universities. For more information on this organization's certification program and courses, contact NACSE at:

Web	http://www.nacse.com
Email	bkile@nacse.com
Mail	National Association of Communication Systems Engineers
	18029 E. Dorado Ave.
	Aurora, CO 80015
Phone	(303) 690-9808
Fax	(303) 752-9288

Xplor International Certification

- Electronic Document and Printing Professional (EDPP)

Xplor International is a not-for-profit organization based in Torrance, California. Xplor is composed of over 2,700 companies and organizations that are involved in the $124 billion electronic document industry. Since the Xplor certification program began in 1990,

130 individuals have been certified as Electronic Document and Printing Professionals (EDPPs).

Recertification or Maintenance Requirements

The Electronic Document and Printing Professional certification is valid for five years. A $25 certification maintenance fee must be paid each year. To be eligible to have your certification extended for another five years, you must also accumulate 250 certification maintenance points during each five-year period. These points are accumulated through educational and professional activities; contact Xplor for further information.

Benefits of Certification

This certification provides a widely recognized, vendor-independent validation of your skills and knowledge regarding electronic document and printing systems.

Electronic Document and Printing Professional (EDPP)

The Electronic Document and Printing Professional (EDPP) credential is designed for those involved in the use and management of electronic document and printing systems. To attain this certification, the candidate must meet basic requirements in the areas of work experience, contribution to the industry, and educational background. Candidates must also document their experience in the electronic document industry through examples of their work.

The EDPP "Body of Knowledge" developed by Xplor is used for evaluating the candidate. This body of knowledge consists of the following areas related to electronic document and printing systems:

- Communication technologies
- Document architectures
- Document composition
- Document delivery
- Document management

- Intelligent documents and document capture

- Internet, intranet, extranet, and WWW

- Legal issues

- Management

- Marketing and sales

- Printing, hardware, and print-on-demand

- Storage, imaging, and archival and retrieval

Who Needs It

The EDPP certification is an excellent credential for professionals in the electronic document industry.

Requirements for Certification

The certification process requires the following steps.

1. You must first submit an application demonstrating that you have met the following requirements:

   - Employment requirements

     A. Current employment in the field of electronic document systems

     B. A minimum of five years experience in the field of electronic document systems

     C. The majority of this experience was in one or more of the disciplines defined in the EDPP Body of Knowledge (see detailed explanation above)

   - Acceptance of the Electronic Document and Printing Professional Code of Ethics

2. Submit a Certification Portfolio detailing your professional achievements, along with three examples of your work.

Administrator

Xplor evaluates the Certification Portfolios in June and July of every year.

Fee

The application fee is $35. The Portfolio evaluation fee is $200 for members of Xplor and $330 for non-members. The yearly maintenance fee is $25.

Format

The Certification Portfolio is submitted to Xplor. Contact Xplor for more information on submitting your Portfolio.

Xplor International Resources

For more information on this organization's certification program and courses, contact Xplor International at:

Web	http://www.xplor.org
E-mail	stephanie@xplor.org
Mail	Manager, Member Services
	Xplor International
	24238 Hawthorne Blvd.
	Torrance, CA 90505-6505
Phone	(310) 791-9549
Fax	(310) 375-4240

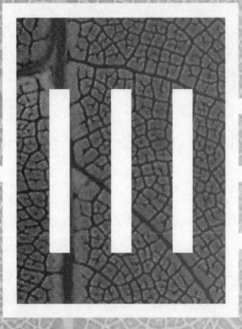

PART

III

Appendices

APPENDIX

A

Retired and Renamed
Certifications

For a variety of reasons, several certification programs have recently been retired. Sometimes this happens when a company is purchased by another company or when a company simply takes a different path in its product development. In other cases, a company may decide that its program is in need of so much revision that it would be easier to scrap it entirely and start all over again.

Other certification programs have been continued under a different name, in one form or another, as the certifying company merged with another company or was acquired by another organization. The following certifications have been renamed, retired, or never really got off of the ground.

3Com 3Wizard

3Com's 3Wizard program was originally designed as a technical training and certification program for the company's resellers. The program had several certification levels that could be achieved by passing product-specific tests in several different technologies. This program was phased out in 1997, but was replaced by the 3Com Master of Network Science (MNS) in late 1998. See Chapter 8, "Networking Hardware Certifications," for details on the MNS program.

A+ Macintosh Certification

CompTia dropped the A+ Macintosh specialization in mid 1998. There are no plans to return this specialization to the A+ program, and all the Macintosh questions have been removed from the Core exam as well. For information on the A+ DOS/Windows specialization, see Chapter 17, "Organization-Based Certifications."

Apple Certified Server Engineer

The Apple Certified Server Engineer (ACSE) certification program involved three exams that were designed to assess an individual's ability to install, maintain, and troubleshoot Apple's Workgroup Server and to manage AppleTalk-based networks. Apple required each Apple Premium Server Reseller to have at least one ACSE on staff. As is widely known, Apple has been in the process of restructuring the company. Apple discontinued its ACSE program in the fall of 1997 and currently has no plan to bring the program back.

Bay Networks

Bay Networks merged with Northern Telecommunications in mid-1998 and is now a division of Nortel Networks. Bay certifications have been grandfathered into the Nortel certification program, which has been revised to include certification on the Bay product line. See Chapter 8, "Networking Hardware Certifications," for information on available Nortel certifications.

Borland

A few months after it acquired Visigenic Software, Borland changed its name to Inprise Corporation, Inc. Inprise is the new name of the company, but you will find that many of the products are still offered under the recognized trade name of Borland, for example Borland C++. Currently all of the Borland and Inprise certifications are being revised and are not available. For information about when new certification programs will be released, check the Inprise Web site (http://www.inprise.com/) or the Certification-Update Web site (http://www.certification-update.com/).

Shiva Remote Access Specialist

The Shiva program was initially announced in March of 1997, but never actually materialized. When we spoke to a Shiva representative, we were told that the decision to not implement the program coincided with a change in management. Shiva currently has no plans for a certification program, but they do offer a number of classes on their remote access products.

U.S. Robotics Certified Support Professional

This certification program was phased out when U.S. Robotics was purchased by 3Com in 1997. Some aspects of this program were incorporated into 3Com's new Master of Network Science certification program.

US Web

USWeb has gone through a lot of changes in the past couple of years. The USWeb training division was spun off as a wholly-owned subsidiary named USWeb Learning in mid-1998. USWeb Learning has since broken off from USWeb as an independent company and has changed its name to HyCurve. For information on HyCurve certifications, see Chapter 13, "Internet Certifications."

APPENDIX

B

Certification Update:
A Web Resource for the Latest
Certification Information

I t can be difficult to keep up with the availability and content of certification programs. Company mergers, changes in product lines and management, and other events, cause some companies to rapidly change, add, or delete specific certifications within their certification programs. For example, during the three months we spent in the final preparation of this edition of this book, one certification program by a major vendor was retired, two new certification programs were launched, and five certification programs underwent major revisions and additions.

To help you keep up with the latest changes to these certification programs, we have set up the Certification Update Web site as a supplement to this book. The address is: `http://www.certification-update.com/`.

This companion Web site provides updates to the certification information and links to online resources that can help you meet your career and certification goals. Several vendors plan to contact us directly prior to the release of new certifications and tests; by accessing the Web site, you will have first access to this information. You will find the following areas on the Certification Update Web site:

News and Announcements   Information on new certifications, and changes to certifications covered in the book.

Certification Programs   Links to vendor certification programs mentioned in these pages.

Job-Hunting Resources for the Computer and Networking Professional   Links to information on constructing an effective resume and conducting a job search. You will also find links to job postings around the world.

Training Resources   Links to providers of computer- and instructor-based training as well as information on self-study guides and books.

Index

Note to the Reader: Page numbers in **bold** indicate the principal discussion of a topic or the definition of a term. Page numbers in *italic* indicate illustrations.